The Good
GARDEN
GUIDE

The Good
GARDEN
GUIDE

ONTARIO'S
OUTSTANDING GARDENS

PATRICIA SINGER

with photographs by
John de Visser, Sidney Feitelberg
& Turid Forsyth

The BOSTON
MILLS PRESS

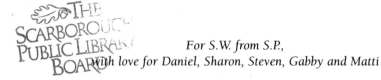

For S.W. from S.P.,
with love for Daniel, Sharon, Steven, Gabby and Matti

"Life, I love you —
the smallest wildflower explodes my senses."
– ANONYMOUS

Canadian Cataloguing in Publication Data

Singer, Patricia, 1936–
The good garden guide: Ontario's outstanding gardens

Includes index.
ISBN 1-55046-169-9

1. Gardens - Ontario - Guidebooks. 2. Ontario -
Description and travel - Guidebooks. I. De Visser, John,
1930– . II. Feitelberg, Sidney. III. Forsyth, Turid.
IV. Title

SB466.C32057 1996   712'.09713   C96-930915-5

Text copyright © Patricia Singer, 1996
Photographs copyright © John de Visser, Sidney Feitelberg, Turid Forsyth, 1996

Design by Gillian Stead
Printed in Canada

First published in 1996 by
THE BOSTON MILLS PRESS
132 Main Street
Erin, Ontario
N0B 1T0
Tel 519-833-2407
Fax 519-833-2195

An affiliate of
Stoddart Publishing Co. Limited
34 Lesmill Road
North York, Ontario, Canada
M3B 2T6

The publisher gratefully acknowledges the support of the Canada Council and
Ontario Arts Council in the development of writing and publishing in Canada.

CONTENTS

PREFACE

I must confess to being a natural nosey parker, especially when it comes to other people's gardens, and what better place than Britain to feed this voyeuristic need.

Every Saturday morning for years, my Mum and I would set out in search of Paradise. She would don an outrageous hat to keep the sun out of her eyes or the rain off her head, and pack a seemingly bottomless bag that held everything from sweets to safety pins, "just in case," and a very battered copy of the National Trusts Guide to Historic Homes and Gardens. Her enthusiasm as well as her inability to resist any driveway or turning, especially those that said No Trespassing, lead us to some of the most unexpected and beautiful places imaginable.

When I came to Canada almost eleven years ago, at what some would argue was the dawning of time as far as Canadian gardening is concerned, I felt bereft. No more little adventures, no delicious tea at the end of a hard day's visiting, and above all I missed the wonderful sense of anticipation of rediscovering Paradise for the umpteenth time.

Four years ago I became acquainted with the Toronto Civic Garden Centre garden tours, which made me realize that a minor revolution was taking place in Canadian gardening. I have been involved with arranging these tours over the past three years and was astounded by how many fellow garden snoops there are, and how many buses we could fill, if only we had the space. One thought led to another, and thanks to the cooperation and generosity of the gardeners involved, the first guide book to Ontario's gardens has been born.

I realize that I have not covered the entire province, but I have tried to give as large a representation as I could, concentrating on locations that, for the most part, have a strong sense of place. In the case of public and historic sites of interest, as well as the nurseries, I have included only those with gardens. If after you have visited the gardens in this book, you think that you or someone you know has a special place that might be suitable for inclusion, Boston Mills Press would love to hear from you.

Almost all gardeners are dreamers, in search of that first and perfect Eden. Grand English manor, whimsical cottage garden, ornamental vegetable gardens, a collection of old roses, a trough full of alpines, or simply the leaf of a lady's-mantle cradling a dewdrop, whatever the vision, the unifying forces among gardeners are their enthusiasm and stoic optimism. I am constantly surprised at how many times I have been told that the garden is a place of relaxation after a hard day's work, despite the fight against critters, blight, plague, invisible thorns, aching backs and the vicissitudes of our Ontario climate. Exciting, elating, soothing, or just plain frustrating, their sometime heaven on earth can also be a hell. Hope certainly springs eternal in the gardener's breast. I would like to thank these intrepid souls for allowing us to take a peek at their very special worlds. Gardeners of Ontario, I salute you!

How To Use This Guide

Addresses are not given unless specified to protect the privacy of the owners, and will be supplied by the owners when you make your appointment.

Location For private gardens, the nearest town is usually noted. Directions will be provided when you book your appointment. Details are given for historic and public gardens and nurseries. You should be able to find your way with any good map of Ontario.

Open days and hours should be confirmed with public and historic gardens, and adhered to please, unless otherwise stated.

Appointments I have tried to arrange the book in such a way that you are able to make up "days out" in almost all areas. About a third of the gardeners have opted to use Woodgreen Community Centre to arrange the bookings for them. This is a charitable organization and a small fee will be charged for the service (see Entrance fees), which includes appointments, and information about addresses and directions. This will be very convenient, particularly where there is more than one garden open on the same day and a single telephone call will take the place of four (see Visiting Arrangements through Woodgreen Community Centre, page 203). If there are other gardens open in the same area "by appointment" with the owner, you could combine the two. Please do not phone the owners after 7:30 p.m.

Cancellations Remember that you are guests of the gardeners. Please treat them as you would like to be treated. If for any reason you cannot keep your appointment, telephone to cancel as soon as possible.

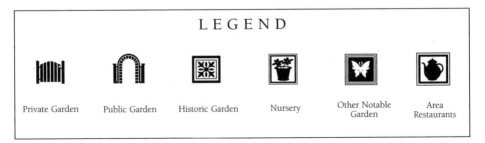

LEGEND					
Private Garden	Public Garden	Historic Garden	Nursery	Other Notable Garden	Area Restaurants

Entrance fees and donations Private gardens that are open "by appointment" with the owner are free unless otherwise indicated. Gardens open through Woodgreen Community Centre are $3 per garden up to three gardens, and $10 for four or more. Children under twelve are free. Information for public and historic gardens is given in the book.

Other Notable Gardens are generally small gardens, best seen with other gardens in the area.

Photography Please ask permission of the gardener before taking photographs, and be careful where you tread when looking through the viewfinder — many a precious plant has been trampled on this way.

Toilet facilities Please do not ask to use the gardener's washrooms except in dire need.

Restaurants are listed at the end of each chapter. I have tried to choose pretty cafés and tea shops for light lunches and teas.

Regret Toddlers, strollers and dogs are not allowed in the private gardens. Please check public and historic gardens and nurseries.

Remember a sun hat, comfortable shoes, insect repellent, sunscreen and a drink of water!

Wheelchair access Check with the private gardeners and nurseries and with Woodgreen Community Centre when booking your appointment. For most public and historic gardens, accessibility has been noted.

Woodgreen Community Centre provides over fifty programs for 21,000 individuals of all ages from all walks of life, with an emphasis on reaching the most vulnerable members of the community. With cutbacks in government funding, non-government assistance is becoming increasingly essential. We are pleased to be working in conjunction with the centre through your support in visiting those gardens that have opted to participate in the scheme.

Aurora / Nobleton / Richmond Hill / Thornhill / Uxbridge

AURORA

▐▓▌ Harry Lumsden
416-469-5211 ext. 199
Conditions   zone 5, clay loam in a valley
Plot size   several acres
Open through Woodgreen Community Centre, May through July, by appointment

❧ **Rare native plants, scree beds, ponds, bog garden**

Retired biologist and keen naturalist Harry Lumsden likes nothing
more than to have his fingers in earth and feathers. As one of the
foremost authorities in Canada on trumpeter swans and an avid plant
collector, he can happily do both. Although emphatic that he is not a
"designer," Harry has formed a harmonious union between natural landscape and cultivated garden. Fascinated by certain genera of plants for their
beauty or interesting biology, he grows more than thirty species of plants
rare in Ontario, and many more from seeds acquired at seed exchanges.

At the entrance to the property, on the east slope, an alkaline scree bed
houses a collection of slowly developing Arctic alpine species. Harry is
experimenting with three acid scree and sand beds by the side of the
house. In the spring an unmown meadow in the lawn becomes a multi-
coloured Persian carpet of *Fritillaria meleagris*, crocus and *Bulbocodium*.
To the south of the house, under a stand of mature spruce and clumps of
European hazel, is a woodland garden and a bed of carefully nurtured
seedling rhododendrons.

Around the marshy shores of the large garden pond, peaty paths
meander through a richly planted bog filled with plants for every season.
Spring heralds the colourful iris parade, which includes the unusual deep
red to purple-black *Iris chrysographes*. At least six species of primulas
bloom in profusion alongside the bold upright heads of *Primula florindae*.
Later in the season, white-flowering crab is decorated with little red flowers of a *Clematis* Graveteye Beauty that scrambles through its branches.
Hostas, skunk cabbage, and the graceful blue camassia grow on the cen-

tre islands surrounded by water lilies. Interesting alliums bloom successively from early spring to late summer, and counted among Harry's
favourites is a large collection of salvias.

Harry Lumsden has created a plant lover's paradise here — heaven for
anyone interested in nature, and for the swans, who are occasionally
allowed in to do the weeding.

David and Dierdre Tomlinson, *Merlin's Hollow*
905-841-7121
Aurora: Highway 404 and the Aurora Sideroad
Conditions　　　heavy duty, northeast slopes
Plot size:　　　just under an acre
*Open second Saturday in May, second Saturday in June, first Saturday in July,
and Sunday of the following weekend, 10 to 5; special perennial garden course
April to October (see below); offered for sale are a wide range of unusual
plants grown, and about 450 kinds of perennial seed from their own garden*

**Large perennial beds; fragrant garden with a thyme lawn; alpine, bog,
pond and shade gardens**

David Tomlinson, landscape designer and consummate plantsman, is
a familiar figure to many Ontario gardeners. He designed his own
well-known garden in 1981 as a series of gardens within a garden. It now
houses over 1,500 different plants, many of them grown from seed; his
helpmate in this great undertaking is his wife Dierdre, otherwise known
as "the gardener's boy."

Enclosed by high cedar hedges and connected by vine-covered archways, each area of their garden has its own character. In a raised bed near
the house, David has planted for winter interest; bleached spears of a
hardy pampas grass and the peeling, rust-coloured bark of *Acer griseum*
show up well against the dark green cedar hedge.

An archway leads to the perennial gardens, where extravagantly scalloped borders are filled with interesting perennials that bloom in
successive waves of colour throughout the seasons. Clematis-covered
arbours divide this area from the back of the house, where an alpine
gravel garden puts on a marvellous display, especially in spring. Around
the new pond that dominates this area, a giant rock garden is in progress.
David, who spends all his autumns digging, has prepared gullies, both

alkaline and acid, to hold a wide selection of plants, including the lovely blue Himalayan poppy, bog plants, and a collection of primulas.

For the Tomlinsons, the more plants they grow, the greater the diversity of wildlife they attract. All sorts are catered to, with bat houses on the chimney, a hibernation pit for snakes, and native fish to feed the growing army of toads.

In 1992 a fragrant garden and pergola were added. Surrounding a spectacular thyme lawn, paths wander between the low stone walls that edge the raised beds overflowing with lavender, buddleia and daphne mingled with herbs and shrub roses and old-fashioned dianthus, some dating back to the 1700s. Even in winter, after a snow melt, the air is filled with perfume. Two pink-berried mountain ash (budded by David onto regular stock) glow in the winter sun. There are plans for a knot garden and fern walk. "And then," says David, "we are finished." Perhaps.

David and Dierdre offer a unique "hands on" gardening course in their garden. It consists of six two-hour sessions, spaced throughout the growing season, from April to October, and is designed to cover all aspects of the cultivation of perennial plants, from the care of old-fashioned favourites such as delphiniums to choosing suitable companion plantings to practical gardening skills.

NOBLETON

IIIIIII Pat and Bill Harris, King Creek Farm
416-469-5211 ext. 199
King Township
Conditions   zone 5a; mostly clay loam, river valley
Plot size   approximately 350 acres
Open through Woodgreen Community Centre, Monday to Thursday, fourth week of July

❦ Formal brick garden, ornamental vegetable garden, perennials, lovely setting

The perennial borders that sweep away from each side of the entrance gate and all around the house are planted with great drifts of Canadian native plants and perennials, setting the scene for the cornucopia that follows. Dorothea Lovatt Dixon of Horteus has designed a garden that marries the bucolic landscape and charming 1830s farmhouse to a series of interesting and beautiful spaces, providing constantly changing pictures throughout the year.

Paths of granite sets and flagstone draw the eye around corners, down the steps beside the artesian-fed rockery pools to the river and ponds. Here, a pair of mute swans, Elizabeth and Philip, glide among the golden-rod and purple eupatorium.

Wander round the back of the house and pause on the lovely terrace with its planting of hazy perovskia, the Fairy rose, and lavender to drink in the glory of the view. The air is filled with the sound of moving water. Follow the path around the west side of the house past drifts of epimedi-ums, mahonia and hostas to where a pair of geometric steel gates guard a peaceful courtyard around a mossy pool. An ornamental vegetable gar-den, bounded by a looped-rope fence swagged with runner beans, grape and sweat peas, is presided over by a large vine statue, baton in hand, conducting the cabbage patch.

A more formal brick garden, radiating from a new conservatory ad-dition to the house, provides spaces that are pleasing to work in. Pat experiments with unusual combinations of beautiful useful plantings that are changed each year. The walled herb garden is being changed into a fruit garden with the introduction of dwarf apple trees, and the herbs have been relocated nearer the conservatory. The maintenance of this garden is an ongoing labour of love.

RICHMOND HILL

Susan Chater
416-469-5211 ext. 199

Conditions   zone 6b; heavy glacial clay, flat
Plot size   100 x 200 feet
Open through Woodgreen Community Centre, third Saturday in June, third Saturday in July

❦ Two ponds, English-style herbaceous borders, peony collection

Having spent eleven itinerant years working around the world, the Chaters felt the need to put down roots when they arrived in Canada fifteen years ago. And what better way than to plant a garden on their half-acre property.

Susan has used only local materials in building her garden, from hardy native plants to boulders salvaged from roadworks on nearby Highway 7. These dramatic glacial granite rocks have been placed under the sumac tree behind the larger of two lily ponds, and a collection of grasses, including the graceful *Miscanthus gracillis* and pretty striped Zebra grass, thrive in the bog garden. Planted along the water's edge are dwarf atilbes, miniature hostas and *Iris kemferi*. Low-growing alpines, saxifragas, penstemons, sedums and the like mingle with heathers and auriculas, filling the bed that borders a paved terrace edged with peonies and softened by hostas and lady's-mantle.

A rose-covered arbour frames an old apple tree, a sheet of blue scillas spread around its gnarled trunk, followed by daffodils and tulips to coincide with the apple blossoms. From the first crocus to the final fall aster, colour is provided with stately verbascums, silvery artemisias, delphiniums, poppies and a large collection of peonies crowding the herbaceous borders that curve in great arcs around the property.

The profusion of blooms, in combinations of vibrant and cool colours, serve as model for Susan's paintings.

In the shade garden an interesting set of decorative structures has been added to give support to various climbers — Dutchman's pipe climbs a tower made from rustic cedar posts, a rose makes its way through a fence of rough-hewn wagon wheels — more evidence of this artist's creative imagination.

THORNHILL

Marion and Alex Jarvie
37 Thornheights Road, Thornhill, ON, L3T 3L9
905-731-1800
Two blocks south of Highway 7, east one block on Kirk Drive; north on Thornheights Road

Conditions   zone 5, clay/loam
Plot size   2/3 acre

Open first weekend in June, Saturday and Sunday, 10 to 4; otherwise by appointment; plants and seedlings always available

❧ **Remarkable plant collection, perennial border, alpine and scree garden, bog garden, woodland beds, fragrant garden, Mediterranean garden**

When Marion Jarvie returned the form I sent her, the words "You're kidding" were written large against the request for the plant list. And no wonder, as this talented gardener is well known across Canada for her prodigious collection of flora, as well as for her considerable knowledge in all things horticultural.

The garden has been evolving since 1965 and has come a very long way from the vegetables, roses and perennials available then. Today, the raised beds and 80-foot border is planted for all seasons, with the focus on summer and fall. Glowing coral-coloured alstromerias light up the bed under the windows of the house, and between the cracks of a flagstone terrace, lime green Irish moss spreads its ferny fingers in all directions.

Across the lawn, a magnificent alpine garden made up of rocks and scree is planted with some of Marjorie's most treasured finds — dwarf conifers, birch, willow, daphnes, and alpines, many of them rather rare.

A large, 19-by-14-foot pond adjacent to the bog garden is filled with pitcher plants, andromeda and *Iris ensatas*. A gorgeous array of primulae brighten the spring garden, with lobelia cultivars carrying on into fall.

In late spring, blossoms shimmer in the woodland beds. The garden is set aglow with a splendid collection of dogwoods such as *Cornus florida*, *Cornus kousa* and *Cornus alternifolia argenta*, voluptuous goblet flowers of magnolia, as well as rhododendrons, azaleas, graceful Stewartia and the yellow-flowered corylopsis. Underplanted to complement it all are many assorted woodland perennials, including orchids, double bloodroot and the dainty corydalis.

The cornucopia of delights continues in the "fragrant garden," filled with bulbs, roses, honeysuckle and magnolia, and in the Mediterranean bed, which plays host to plants for hot, dry climates, including sphaeralcea and yucca. Marjorie is particularly fond of the scarlet-flowered *Zaushneria*, planted in combination with the intense blue flowers of *Cerastostigma plumbagoides*, making a lovely show for the fall.

Marion lectures on a wide variety of topics and she and her husband run inspirational tours to see plants in remote, beautiful places. "The creativity of gardening," says Marion, "has fostered a sense of real accomplishment."

UXBRIDGE

Grace and Rodger Inglis, *Four Winds*
905-529-3457
Scugog district, just east of Uxbridge
Conditions zone 5; steep bank, exposed, woodland
Open by appointment only; group visits preferably for non-profit organizations

❧ Terraced garden, woodland garden

Perched on the top of a valley, this lovely farmhouse with its century-old snake fence and barn has been in the family for many years. Today the potato fields have been transformed into a magical garden where fluttering poppies, giant thistles, veronicas, roses, lilies and fragrant herbs fill the sunbaked terraces of the hillside and rugosa roses line the perimeter of the pretty vegetable garden.

A cedar track gradually leads down into a cool, mysterious wood. Under a magnificent canopy of white pine, cedar, oak and whispering aspen, a carpet of trilliums have seeded themselves by the thousands in a shiny sea of green vinca, planted by Grace's father many years ago. Artfully placed statues peer out from between the trees, and at the top of the slope, Rodger has built a belvedere, from where you can look out over the whole magnificent scene.

Marjorie and Real Hogue, Jeff and Laura Mason,
Mason Hogue Gardens
3520 Durham Road 1, RR 4, Uxbridge, ON, L9P 1R4
905-649-3532
Coppins Corners: junction of Roads 1 and 2
Conditions zone 5a; snow cover; sand/gravel, mead lowland
and slopes
Open May 2 to October 27, Thursday to Sunday and holiday Mondays, 10 to 5; free guided garden walk daily in June, 11 a.m. (allow 45 minutes to an hour); traditional English cream tea in the garden (please bring your own garden chair); Wednesdays only, $7.50 each (register in advance)

❧ Rock garden, scree garden, over seventy varieties of hardy perennial geraniums

Marjorie Mason Hogue is well known as a plantswoman of note and an enthusiastic lecturer, with a particular interest in perennial cranesbills (hardy geraniums) and unusual rock plants. She shares the running of her fascinating nursery with her husband, Real, and son Jeff, who does most of the propogating. As their property is perched on the edge of a gravel pit, where the only water supply is a 13-foot dug well, conservation is essential. They have created a series of extremely interesting demonstration gardens, coaxing bloom out of the most difficult of sites and offering hope to all gardeners with problem areas.

Xerophytic gardening (gardening without water) has been the answer here. Very poor soil is improved with organic and gravel mulches to keep the earth cool, the perfect environment for a large collection of unusual alpines. Penstemons, rock roses, potentillas and soapworts all thrive under a relentless sun on the windswept sandy slope.

Through an arch at the front of the house, very different conditions prevail. Beside a shady pool, complete with waterfall, you will see more than eighty perennial geraniums, as well as a large variety of unusual perennials. The list keeps on growing.

To the right of the house, up a fairly steep slope, the scree garden is laid out on a plateau. Treasures you won't find at your corner garden centre invite you to peer closely into their exquisite faces. *Dianthus cruentus, Anthyllis vulneraria* with its sprawling red and yellow flowers, and blue-purple *Penstemon hirsutis*, are but a few.

When you have toured the gardens, browse awhile in the nursery and shop area where Marjorie and Jeff are always available to answer any questions you may have, however complicated. You will take home a wealth of inspiration and knowledge, and I dare you not to be tempted by the splendid array of out-of-the-ordinary "goodies" that are for sale.

Aurora

The Coffee Bean
114810 Yonge Street
905-713-1305
Daily 7 a.m. to 10 p.m.; tea, coffee, pastries, daily pasta specials.

Tortes and Tarts
14900 Yonge Street
905-727-4662
Daily; serving coffee, salads, sandwiches.

Richmond Hill

The Burr House
528 Carrville Road (between Yonge and Bathurst Streets)
905-884-0327
May through September, volunteers serve coffee, tea and scones, $3 per person, Friday and Sunday 12:30 to 4:30, Saturdays 10 to 4:30; local arts and crafts sold.

Uxbridge

Hobby Horse Arms
37 Main Street North
905-852-6126
Daily, serving pub lunch or full-course meal in dining room.

Barrie / Midland / Muskoka

BARRIE

Jerry and Kathy Wade, *Rose Lea*
205 Cherry Court, Barrie, ON, L4N 4A5
705-722-6163
Barrie: from Highway 401 at Innisfil Beach Road, east to Highway 11 to
Big Bay Point, east on Big Bay Point, west on Cherry Court
Conditions   zone 5; sandy loam, level
Plot size   1/2 acre
Open July 1; also other times, July through mid-September, by appointment

❧ Demonstration rose garden

This garden in the middle of a twenty-five-year-old subdivision is truly
a bed of roses. Grass paths invite you to walk between the lovingly
tended beds filled with over 250 roses of every sort, from mini to climber.
Kathy and Jerry Wade are also developing a large fern and hosta collection along the shady side of the house, and at the back of the property,
behind a cedar hedge, they are recreating a "little piece of Muskoka" with
native plant material and imported rocks. The red-painted Japanese
bridge that crosses the lily pond provides a strong colour contrast to the
evergreens, grasses and variegated water irises below and surrounding it.
This garden is well known in Barrie, and Kathy and Jerry are always
happy to see visitors. ·

Barrie Horticultural Society Arboretum
In Sunnidale Park at Cundles Road and Sunnidale Road (west of
Highway 401)
Open year-round; wheelchair access

The park has an outstanding lilac dell and two rose beds containing
more than 200 roses. Most of the trees and shrubs have been planted
as memorials to loved ones and are labelled with the common and scien-
tific names. This 12-acre arboretum is the main project of the Barrie
Horticultural Society and is maintained by its volunteers.

MIDLAND

Wye Marsh Wildflower Garden
Wye Marsh Wildlife Centre
Box 100, Midland, ON, L4R 4K6
Off Highway 12; near entrance to Wildlife Centre
Open daily 10 to 6; wheelchair access

The garden is divided into five specific areas. One is devoted to the flora of Simcoe County; another, the flora of Ontario; there is a woodland garden with a pond; an arboretum is now being developed; and another garden, Willie's Rock Garden, is named for "Willie," whose love of trilliums is rewarded here.

The ground was broken for the garden by Seniors for Wye Marsh in 1988. Self-supported through the sale of pressed flowers, notepaper and seeds from their gardens, this volunteer group is dedicated to the preservation of the wilderness. A complete catalogue of wildflowers grown here is available.

MUSKOKA

Muskoka Lakes Museum
Box 432, Port Carling, ON, P0B 1J0
705-765-5367, fax 705-765-6271
Island Park in centre of village of Port Carling; park at community centre and take footbridge to island
Open June, September, October 10 to 4; July and August 10 to 5; Sundays 12 to 4; closed Mondays in June; closed Mondays, Tuesdays in September and October; entrance fee charged; no wheelchair access in building

The herb garden here displays many traditional herbs and flowers, including culinary and medicinal herbs as well as those used for dyeing, fragrance and insect control. Perennials share beds with annuals.

Muskoka Pioneer Village
Box 2802, Huntsville, ON, P0A 1K0
705-789-7576
Huntsville: from main street, Muskoka Road 3, east on Burnell Road, past high school
Open Victoria Day to June 30, Saturday and Sunday 11 to 4; July 1 to September 30, daily 11 to 4; October 1 to Thanksgiving, Saturday and Sunday 11 to 4; entrance fee; some wheelchair access

There are three main historically themed gardens: Survival, Innkeeper and Kitchen gardens. An Eco Stroll was developed in the summer of 1995 around the Village's own Lake Cann. A guide sheet is available detailing the flora, trees, fauna and insects in their natural habitat. Wildflowers grow in profusion here.

Bracebridge

The Inn on the Falls
705-645-2245
Daily, 11:30 to 10, luncheon and dinner.

Huntsville

The Inn at Grandview
on Fairy Lake
705-789-4417
Formal dining room at the Inn serves luncheon year-round 11:30 to 2, dinner from 5; Dockside

Restaurant by the lake serves light luncheons and snacks July and August 11:30 to 10.

Port Carling

Tap & Grill
Uptown
705-765-6983
Daily, 8 a.m. to 11 p.m.; outdoor patio seats 65, indoor restaurant seats 60.

Bowmanville / Oshawa / Whitby

BOWMANVILLE

[icon] Sharon and Brian Edey
416-469-5211 ext. 199
Conditions   zone 5b; sand
Plot size   1 1/2 acres
Open through Woodgreen Community Centre, first weekend of July

❧ **Perennials, pond, woodland, dried-flower garden**

It's evident from the moment one enters her front gate that Sharon Edey loves English gardens. Ten years ago all that was here was a gravel pit. However, after many tons of topsoil and a lot of hard work, this picture-perfect garden feels as if it has been here forever.

The beds on each side of the gently curving walkway to the pretty blue-and-white heritage-style house overflow with billowing hedges of spirea goldflame, columbine, straw flowers, peonies, daisies and delphiniums. Wisteria twines round the gingerbread porch surrounded by fat bushes of Persian lilac. Sharon has deliberately overplanted throughout the garden to create this established feeling as well as to keep the weeds at bay. A white picket fence at the side of the house encompasses a rose garden and a new pond where she is talking about planting "things to weep into water, and maybe some grasses."

An arch in the cedar hedge leads to a large cottage garden that backs onto a ravine, carpeted in the spring with daffodils, tulips and iris, while a mass of trilliums covers the ravine. Come summer a very different mood is conveyed with washes of purples and pinks, Sharon's favourite cleomes adding drama to the roses, larkspur and phlox that fill the borders with colour and fragrance. Rustic paths attractively edged with shorn saplings pass through clematis-covered willow arches, made by her husband and sons, to what was the vegetable plot, where flowers grown for drying are taking over. Ferny asparagus, juicy watermelons and tomatoes still flourish along with sunflowers seeded by the birds.

Meals are enjoyed on the patio behind a weathered picket fence covered in morning glories, secluded from the lawn and children's activities. A haze of blue forget-me-nots and miniature bulbs are succeeded by thyme and alyssum that creep through the flagstone, mingling their fragrance with the bergamot and roses blooming in the adjacent bed.

Nearly everything Sharon grows is from seed. At the time of writing there were no plans for any further changes, but when those seedlings begin to make their appearance, I wouldn't want to bet on it.

OSHAWA

Marvin W. Belfour, *Marvin's Garden*
427 Prestwick Court, Oshawa, ON, L1J 7R6
416-469-5211 ext. 199; 905-579-9076
Conditions　　　zone 5b; amended with sandy loam; sloped to creek
Plot size　　　65 x 170 feet
Open through Woodgreen Community Centre, first and second Saturday of July; or by appointment for tour of garden

Over 200 varieties of roses and at least 1,000 different plants

Marvin Belfour's garden is a testament to his love of growing plants and the anticipation of experiencing the excitement of the new. This show-stopping garden, is always expanding and now extends beyond the fence line almost to the creek. Serpentine borders and island beds awash with colour from successive blooms throughout the season interrupt the expanse of lawn. Irises, day lilies, peonies, malva, campanulas, delphiniums, onorpordums, poppies — and roses, of which there are over two hundred species — give pleasure for months on end.

The garden spills onto city property, part of which is beside a public walkway, with Thornton Woods providing an ever-changing backdrop. The most surprising thing to Marvin is the number of people who bring friends and family for a visit by way of the walkway. He cordially invites you to join them.

Lenore and David Derham, *Our Love Garden*
416-469-5211 ext. 199; 905-433-4067
Conditions:　　zone 5a; sandy
Plot size　　　50 x 40 feet
Open through Woodgreen Community Centre, first Saturday of July, 10 to 4; otherwise by appointment with owner

❧ Japanese style, water features, bonsai collection

Lenore and David Derham have created an oasis of peace and serenity in the centre of the city, a private and secluded world away from it all where they can share their mutual love for this unusual garden.

An Oriental theme has been used in this small corner lot, which is divided up by the clever use of different levels, beautifully detailed screens, arbours and a gazebo cum potting shed, designed and built by David.

Water from a Japanese figure softly trickles through moss-covered rocks into a large water-lily pond. A miniature bridge leads to a dry riverbed that winds between sculptured topiaries, shrubs, and over a hundred carefully chosen small trees. Pathways invite you to stroll as you admire the wealth of detail in this tranquil haven; look for Japanese ornaments and select perennials amid the myriad of greens.

▯▯▯ Phyllis Stewart
416-469-5211 ext. 199

Conditions   zone 5; sandy loam; level
Plot size   80 x 80 feet
Open through Woodgreen Community Centre, first Saturday in July, 10 to 4

❧ Folk art, cottage garden, herb garden and pergolas

The dark green gate, its little window framing an enticing glimpse of the garden beyond, invites you to step through a cedar pergola into the whimsical world of Phyllis Stewart. An antique dealer and collector of folk art, she describes her garden as "a blowsy lady who puts on a green skirt with a pink blouse, then dons a strand of red beads."

The "lady" in question is perfumed with the scent of roses and surrounded by gauzy poppies, giant delphiniums, bright yellow daisies, lilies, larkspur and voluptuous pannicles of phlox. From the herb garden a turquoise gate opens to an overgrown path through clematis-covered arbours, past a water garden into the "cool room," shaded by crab and lilac.

Jaunty birdhouses old and new pop up like Jack-in-the-boxes throughout the garden. Watch for folk-art figures peeking out from unexpected corners. This naïve yet sophisticated place is full of fantasy and fun. One cannot help but be captivated by this artful place.

Parkwood Estate
270 Simcoe Street North, Oshawa, ON, L1G 4T5
905-579-1311
Corner of Simcoe and Alma, downtown Oshawa
Open June through August 10:30 to 4; daily except Monday; open holidays;
September through June, Tuesday to Friday and Sunday, 1:30 to 4 (call for
seasonal evening hours); wheelchair access

Parkwood House is one of Ontario's best-kept secrets. The impressive grounds were designed by H. B. and L. A. Dunington-Grubb during the 1920s, and since that time the beauty and scale of Parkwood have endured. Velvet lawns, mature trees, manicured shrubs and flower beds are enhanced by the strategically placed statuary, works of art of European and Canadian origin. The Italian garden is screened by an elaborate trellisage supporting roses, wisteria and morning glories. This tranquil, secluded space is centred by a lily pool with a strikingly beautiful fountain of the Three Graces. A sundial garden has the dial itself centred in bright annuals. Across the lawn a carved-stone girl with a shell sits in the centre of a small pond, surrounded by moss-covered rocks and shade-loving plants. A sunken garden has dry-stone walls and all-weather shrub borders, and a charming white garden edges the circular rose garden. A wide, elevated terrace with a massive art deco wall overlooks the formal New Garden, reminiscent of Versailles, with its 225-foot-long pool and several illuminated fountains. Overlooking one end of the pool is the Tea House, where an excellent lunch and afternoon tea is served during the summer season.

WHITBY

Cullen Gardens and Miniature Village
300 Taunton Road West, Whitby, ON, L1N 5R5
905-668-9906 or 905-294-7965; fax: 905-668-0510
From Highway 2 or 401 take Highway 12 north; west on Taunton Road West

Open daily from 10 a.m., closing time varies; extended hours in summer and from mid-November to early January, call for details; entrance fee; wheel-chair access throughout, except Lynde House

Len Cullen has transformed this scenic valley of meadows and giant cedars into a miniature village complete with replicas of existing Southern Ontario buildings, and ponds, streams, covered bridges, floral carpets of annuals and a nature trail. Floral displays take place here throughout the year — in May when the tulips are in bloom, in June and July when the roses are at their peak, and from July through September for the annuals, perennials and chrysanthemums. The winter carnival and Christmas festival of lights are very popular.

Oshawa

Parkwood Estate
905-579-1311
Luncheon and afternoon tea,
daily in the Tea House,
June through September 10:30 to 4.

Whitby

Cullen Gardens
300 Taunton Road West
905-668-6606
Luncheon and afternoon tea daily.

The Old Country Tearoom and Bakery
124 Athol Street
905-668-5775
Coffee, tea and light luncheon, Monday 10 to 4, Tuesday to Friday 9 to 6, Saturday 9 to 5, closed Sunday.

Brampton / Mississauga / Oakville

BRAMPTON

IIIIII David and Margaret Barham, *The Oasis*
905-792-1556

Conditions	zone 5 to 7 depending on snow cover; heavy sweet clay amended in raised beds with mushroom compost, peat moss and topsoil
Plot size	55 x 110 feet

Open weekends; phone at least two days ahead

Rock garden, ponds, fountains and large plant collection

When the Barhams moved to Canada in 1968, their modest suburban lot sported nothing but concrete-like clay. They battled with grass, vegetables and annuals, until finally deciding to put in raised beds filled with topsoil and compost. They edged them with limestone, which suggested a rock garden; one thing led to another, and they now have one of the prettiest small gardens in Ontario.

Clever emphasis of the diagonal view in the intimate space of the back garden gives the illusion of a much larger space. Water features in each of the four distinct areas that have been created here — a Bruce Peninsula rock garden, an English rock garden, a cottage garden and a woodland garden. They contain over 700 plants comprising some 400 species.

Under an apple tree, pruned for shape and shade, the lush woodland garden brims over with hellebores, primulas and hostas, as well as many native wildflowers. Alpine campanulas and dwarf astilbes seed themselves among the ferny Irish moss in the flagstone walk, and in spring hundreds of bulbs bloom from every nook and cranny. Paths meander behind flower beds, through trellises and arbours covered in more than forty varieties of clematis. At the edge of the lily pond the statue of a small boy admires his reflection; crimson Japanese maple is surrounded by *Lobelia syphilatica*; white *Campanula porschskiana* and dwarf aruncus mingle with pretty but invasive miniature bamboo, planted in pots to contain its exuberance. Across the lawn, pastel-coloured borders bloom from spring to late autumn.

This is indeed an oasis in the desert of suburbia.

|||||| Joseph Covello, *Perennial Paradise*
416-469-5211 ext. 199; 905-459-4828
Highway 410 and Steeles Avenue
Conditions   zone 6; topsoil and mushroom compost
Plot size   85 x 220 feet
Open through Woodgreen Community Centre, second and third consecutive
Sunday and Monday of July, 1 to 6; otherwise, by appointment with owner

❦ **Large assortment of perennials, lily collection, prizewinning garden**

Effervescent, idiosyncratic and joyful are all adjectives that can be used to describe Joe Covello and his garden. His energy is boundless, he can't stop creating, and there is always a project on the go, inside or out depending on the season. He moved to Brampton in May 1987 and by the fall had already prepared, dug and staked out this extremely large lot. He can't recall the number of times he ran upstairs to look out the window for a bird's-eye view of his plan as he worked. The swimming pool was the first task, after which came an intricate network of walkways that allow him access to the myriad of flower beds without ever having to set foot in them.

His main focus is on perennials, and every week or so he pays a visit to Humber Nurseries, buying only what is in bloom at the time. This way he ensures continuous bloom and a garden awash with colour from early June to late fall. A profusion of flower, including alliums of all shapes and sizes, over fifty varieties of lilies, phlox of every hue, roses, and the bluest-ever globe thistles — the list goes on and on — assails the eye at every turn.

Arches entwined in clematis have been placed throughout the garden. The only lawn remaining is for Joe's old age, he says, when he can no longer tend the beds. By the fall he is tired, wondering whether he will be able to do it all again. But come spring, when the first tender shoots begin to show, he "feels the stirrings" as another year begins.

|||||| Rosemary Pauer
416-469-5211 ext. 199; 905-791-7022
Conditions   zone 5; solid clay, flat
Plot size   40 x 40 feet
Open through Woodgreen Community Centre, last weekend of June, 10 to 5;
no dogs; watch for changes of level, overhanging branches; otherwise by
appointment with owner

❧ Heavily planted, shade-loving plants, small pools, homemade water features

Rosemary Pauer has transformed her small suburban lot into a green bower, but not without struggle. Over the past twenty years this enthusiastic and energetic woman has amended the solid yellow clay, wet and slippery in winter, concrete in summer, using enormous amounts of humus produced by an extensive composting system, together with the leaves she piles on in the fall. This allows her to grow the shade plants that she enjoys.

The garden, which won the *Canadian Gardening Magazine* "Garden of the Year" award in 1992, has evolved into a Japanese stroll garden, using many native trees and shrubs, and providing a tranquil haven for birds and animals. Rose has managed to create a genial sense of space; secluded shady corners and small paths disappear behind borders, dragonflies dart over little pools hidden among the shrubberies where water drips down bamboo pies into homemade bowls. A small statue stands surrounded by lush damp-loving hostas, ferns and astilbes. A row of watering cans hang over a dipping well, a reminder of her youth in Britain, and trips to the cemetery! Clematis and vines, many grown from seed, climb up the trellises; with her ingenuity Rose has made extensive use of bamboo poles, which are both inexpensive and easy to use, in constructing pergolas and arbours. There are many evergreens for winter interest. Variegated ground covers brighten dark corners, and a few flowers come and go among the greenery, with the peonies and roses at the end of June being particularly lovely.

If you are looking for massed flower borders you will be disappointed, but if you want to enjoy a "green thought in a green shade," visit Rose's world.

MISSISSAUGA

▍▍▍▍ Susan Collacott, *Bittersweet*
416-469-5211 ext. 199
Conditions   zone 5; sandy soil; flat
Open through Woodgreen Community Centre, last Saturday of May, second Saturday of June, first Saturday of September

❧ Japanese garden, pond, ericaceous plants, garden viewing room

A six-month stay in Japan was the inspiration for this tranquil "villa garden," designed to achieve the sense of harmony and contrast found in Japanese wood-block prints. Susan is a painter, described by architectural critic Adele Freedman as a "thoroughgoing woman" because of her meticulous attention to detail. From the moment one views the huddle of roofs and the charming moss-covered courtyard with its earth-coloured stucco walls and dramatic hand-picked rocks, one senses the touch of a master designer.

From the *engawa* (porch) of the viewing room, the borrowed view of a graceful willow forms the perfect backdrop to the Oriental scene. The garden is dominated by a large pond filled with water lilies and fish; a miniature island houses a dwarf pine, dragonflies flit over little streams and waterfalls that fill the air with soothing sounds. A small bridge across the stream leads from the passive (grassy) side to the aggressive (rocky) side of the pond, where Japanese iris and dwarf astilbe (*Astilbe pumila*) grow. Arrangements of rocks, ferns and dwarf pines have been planted to represent mountain views. Cherry trees drop their petals onto softly mounded woolly thyme. A hidden path continues past unusual kalmias and rhododendrons to the back of the garden, where hostas and tiarellas mingle with purple-leafed ajuga. A moss-covered bridge leads over a stream to another small pool around which are planted may apples, rodgersias, fritillarias and various water and woodland plants. Concealed among the hemlocks is a little shrine Susan has made in memory of her mother.

Following the early flowering of magnolia, redbud and many varieties of rhododendrons and azaleas, the garden settles into a quiet green oasis with the occasional ping of colour. The garden has a larger assortment of plants than would usually be seen in a Japanese garden, but this is a Canadian garden with Japanese sensibilities. Susan's unerring intuition and thirst for knowledge have guided her in creating this haven in her little corner of Mississauga. "If I could spend my life tending this garden," she says, "then my life would be well spent."

Liz Primeau and Chris Zelkovich
416-469-5211 ext. 199; 905-275-9813
Conditions   zone 6, sandy, flat, formerly an orchard
Plot size   65 x 130 feet in all; rear garden, 40 x 65 feet
Open through Woodgreen Community Centre, second Saturday of June, third Saturday of July, 10 to 4; otherwise by appointment with owner

❧ Perennials, pond

One small patch of grass is all that is left of the lawn that Liz Primeau started with over a dozen years ago. Today her garden is transformed into an informal, eclectic space that invites you to wander at your leisure.

The front garden, started five years ago, was planned as a tapestry of ground covers. A haze of thymes, moss and *Gypsophila repens*, the low-growing baby's breath, mix with soft blue catmint and fluffy lady's-mantle up the side of the gravel and flagstone path to the front door. It continues round the side of the house to the charming backyard, where it gently wends its way between large, cottage-style beds, loosely planted with a mixture of easy-care perennials and plants native to Southern Ontario, including lilies, salvia, veronica, Japanese and Siberian irises, bee balm and hyssop. Tucked away in a far corner, a waterfall splashes into a small pond adjoining a peaceful gravelled seating area.

A few other formal elements give structure to the garden, such as a low clipped boxwood hedge outlining a semicircular bed of ground covers. A Japanese-style arbour at the rear of the garden is smothered in pale pink New Dawn roses, masterfully disguising the compost bins; adding to the Oriental feeling is a small inset pond and tsukubai.

Two old apple trees, together with a large maple, provide shade for a carpet of Baltic ivy and eunonymous.

Liz has a full-time job and has tried to create a garden that is relatively easy to maintain. She is a firm believer that a garden is to be lived in rather than worked in.

▌▌▌▌ Wayne Renaud and Gordon Webber, *Oakwood Cottage Garden*
416-469-5211 ext. 199
Conditions   zone 5; sandy loam; flat
Plot size   25 x 43 feet
Open through Woodgreen Community Centre, last Saturday of May, second Saturday of June, first Saturday of September, 10 to 4

❧ Outstanding design, water garden

Here, small is truly beautiful. This courtyard garden, which has been featured in many of North America's leading garden magazines, is only 25 by 43 feet in size and yet it reflects the respective talents of its owners, Wayne Renaud and Gordon Webber, illustrating that a garden can be both landscape and architecture.

The intimate and inviting space brims with soft colour and interest year-round. The lovely Arts and Crafts entrance gate, with opaque blue and peach glass insets, and the new gatehouse, with mirrored French doors, define and enclose the front yard space. These elements together with the detailed design of the garden walls, painted grey-green wooden fences, and beautifully renovated coach house facade (circa 1915), covered in wisteria, all enhance the intimate character of the garden.

The main feature of this courtyard garden is a long, narrow lily pond, inhabited by koi and goldfish, that reflects views of the garden from the house and gate entrances. Water cascades into the pond from a stone basin cantilevered over the edge; the sound of running water plays in the courtyard through all four seasons like the trickling of a woodland stream. The garden is dominated by evergreens, and though it is modest in size, an astonishing array of trees, shrubs, vines, perennials, water plants and spring bulbs have been planted here, without it seeming the least bit crowded. From the first blossoms of witch hazel Diane in mid-February to the last autumn *Crocus speciosis*, in early December, there is always something in bloom.

▐▌▌▌▌ Patricia and William Singer, *Riverview*
416-469-5211 ext. 199
Conditions   zone 5; sandy loam; flat
Open through Woodgreen Community Centre, third Saturday of July, first Saturday of September, 10 to 4

❧ **Pergola walk, perennial beds, terraced garden on the Credit River**

The visitor who ventures down the rickety pergola walk, known fondly as the "purgatory walk," is confronted with a scene far removed from that particular venue. Overhead, pink roses intertwine with a tangle of purple clematis, while underfoot a soft carpet of lime green moss spreads through the cracks in the flagstone path. Under the archways on each side, glimpses of herbaceous borders that curve away toward the river, are filled with a wide variety of flowers. Lady's-mantle, phlox and bergamot are set off by the pretty blue flowers of *Nepeta* Andre Chaudon, the perfect foil for the wine-coloured leaves of *Rosa rubrifolia*, Martagon lilies and blowsy David Austin roses and delphiniums that also grow here. Nestled in a sunbaked corner between the garage and the house is a small herb garden, almost out of control. Chives and dill scatter their progeny everywhere, and lovage grows "high as an elephant's eye" — delicious as stuffing for barbecued fish, by the way. Morning glories smother the garage wall, spilling over an old pump and through a Father Hugo rose, one of the first roses to bloom, whose stems are covered in flowers like yellow butterflies in late May.

The shady shrub borders along the top of the riverbank are crowded with plants able to survive the antisocial habits of the black walnut trees growing here. Viburnum, witch hazel, astilbe, hosta and tiarella flourish under their boughs. Purples, greys and pink dominate a mixed border on the west. *Cotoneaster delsiana* weeps over purple ajuga, spiky red flowers of *Polyganum affine* push through purple berberis, while *Astilbe tequetti*, pink phlox and monarda Blue stocking play front-line chorus to a row of white lilacs.

A flight of steps leads past a series of planted terraces to a flagstone patio where a fountain plays in a simple reflecting pool, a lovely place to sit and watch the river. Well, maybe tomorrow, if it ever comes!

||||||| Karen York and Silvio Gaudio
416-469-5211 ext. 199
Conditions   zone 6; sandy, flat, partially wooded
Plot size   100 x 190 feet approximately
Open through Woodgreen Community Centre, second Saturday of June, third Saturday of July, first Saturday of September, 10 to 4

Rhododendron garden, woodland garden, shrub collection, perennial border, pond

To Karen York and Silvio Gaudio, this beautifully designed garden is the stage where they play out their plant passions. One of the advantages of their corner lot is the amount of exposure available for growing a wide range of plant material.

The garden is relaxed and eclectic, with much of the focus on texture, pattern and colour, as is evident from the moment you enter the drive. A lovely redbud Forest Pansy, junipers, golden elders, Russian sage, ornamental grasses, sedums and artemesias are edged by a dry stream bed, while closer to the house, rhododendrons, azaleas, and other ericaceous (acid-loving) plants put on a magnificent display in late spring.

Paths wander along woodlands plantings of epimediums and foxgloves, pulmonarias and wood poppy, growing under the shade of a huge copper beech, to the back garden where hydrangea is beginning to climb the handsome privacy fence. There is an infinity of shades of green in the Japanese angelica trees, Japanese maples, and daphnes clustered round the patio and pretty pool. A tantalizing glimpse of the perennial and shrub beds curving away in the distance leads you to a rich variety of plantings chosen for different reasons — unusual form (dwarf elm, umbrella pine), all-season interest (Japanese maples, viburnum, crab-apple), colour contrast (golden grasses, purple smoke tree, variegated willow) — and some, because they "simply couldn't resist."

"Happy accident," according to Karen, "as well as design," have result-ed in lovely "incidents," such as giant purple sedum nudging blue oat grass, or creamy kniphofia rising out of tovara and the aptly named Japanese blood grass. Constantly interesting and sometimes surprising, there is something here for everyone, and the most enjoyable part of it is the infectious enthusiasm of its creators.

Rhododendron Gardens
905-279-4966
Mississauga; south of Lakeshore Road West, west of Godfrey's Lane and east of Crozier Court
Open daily, dawn to dusk; some wheelchair access; washroom facilities

The late Dr. Joseph Brueckner was a Mississauga hybridizer of rhodo-dendrons who donated many rare species to these lovely lakeside gardens. With his generosity and assistance, the City and the Rotary Club of Mississauga have created a home for one of the largest public collec-tions of rhododendrons in Ontario. The presence of pine and oak trees and several Carolinian forest species protects this magnificent collection of over 700 rhododendrons and azaleas from the effects of wind and sun. There are walking paths throughout the garden and bridges cross over naturalized Tecumseh Creek. The garden is close to the Waterfront Trail, much enjoyed by pedestrians and cyclists, and several spots offer a panoramic view of Lake Ontario and the Toronto skyline.

Woodland Nurseries
2151 Camilla Road, Mississauga, ON, L5A 2K1
905-277-2961 or 905-277-0650

Mississauga: Highway 10 to North Service Road (just north of the QEW), to Camilla Road
Open April through October, 10 to 6

❧ **Magnificent collection of rhododendron, azaleas and native Carolinian species**

I n the fall of 1930, a real-estate advertisement prompted Leslie and Dorothy Hancock to buy a farm woodlot and swampy cow pasture. Over the years, Leslie gradually turned this lot into a unique nursery and developed the woodlot, adding rhododendrons, azaleas, pieris, kalmia, dogwood, silverbell and redbud, the waft threaded through the warp of the native stand of pine, oak and beech to create the fabric of woodland garden so many have to come to know and share.

Mr. Rhododendron, as Leslie became affectionately known, has been succeeded by his daughter Marjorie, who is committed, along with the rest of the family, to maintaining the Woodland Garden and the grounds of Woodland Nurseries. Do not miss a chance to visit this beautiful haven in the midst of suburbia, particularly in late spring when the dell is awash with colour.

OAKVILLE

🏰 Richard Birkett
416-469-5211 ext. 199
Conditions   sandy
Plot size   100 x 150 feet
Open through Woodgreen Community Centre

❧ **Japanese fountain, waterfall, pond and gazebo**

W hen the rhododendrons and azaleas are in bloom, this corner lot can best be described as a glorious blaze of colour. Designed by Elizabeth Tschopp in a woodland setting, surrounded by mature trees, this lovely garden has as its focal point an unusually shaped gazebo. Other interesting features are the Japanese fountain, small waterfall and pond. Stone walkways connect several beds filled with spring bulbs, a variety of perennials and Japanese tree peonies. One raised bed allows eye-level viewing of plants from the sidewalk.

"To garden is life itself," says Richard Birkett.

John and Vi Simkins
1246 Donlea Crescent, Oakville, ON, L6J 1V7
905-845-8380
Conditions   zone 6b; sandy; sloping
Plot size   1/2 acre
Open June; other times by appointment

❧ **Peony hobby garden**

The Simkins' nursery is well known for its glorious peony collection. Just over half an acre is planted with over a thousand peonies in twenty-six beds. There are beds bright with sunny groups of yellow and white blooms and other beds hold the warmer tones of pink, coral and red. Tree peonies come in shades of yellow, dark red and yellow-orange. Early May brings forth a lively show of tulips and spring bulbs, followed by a variety of perennials.

The raised beds in the nursery conveniently display seedlings, grafts and perennials grown by John Simkins, who also lectures throughout Canada and writes "In Your Garden" for the *Oakville Beaver*.

Bronte

Bronte Bagel Cafe
2417 Marine Drive
905-825-5942
Daily, 7:30 to 5; morning coffee, luncheon, afternoon tea; outside patio.

Oakville

La Parisienne Creperie
93 Bronte Road
905-827-2378
Closed Monday, luncheon 11:30 to 3, dinner 6 to 9
(luncheon only on Sunday).

Swiss Canadian Pastry Shop
232 Lakeshore Road East
905-338-9644
Tuesday to Saturday, 8 to 5, morning coffee, luncheon and
afternoon tea.

Upstairs Downstairs Tearoom
88 Dunn Street (south of Lakeshore Road)
905-338-1973
Daily, full afternoon teas 3 to 4:30, $9.

Port Credit

The Chelsea Bun-N-Such
7 John Street South
905-271-4290
Luncheon Monday to Saturday 11:30 to 3:00;
dinner Tuesday to Saturday 5:30 to 10.

J.J.'s Cafe
83 Lakeshore Road East
905-271-8280
Daily from noon to 9 or later; homemade European food.

Lainey's Cafe
40 Lakeshore Road East
905-278-5344
Daily, Monday to Friday 11 to 10,
Saturday and Sunday 11 to 10:30.

Brantford

Joan and Garry Burns, *Reverie*
416-469-5211 ext. 199
Conditions   zone 5; sand loam (acidic), gently sloped, bordering on
Carolinian Oak Savannah
Open through Woodgreen Community Centre, first Sunday of July

**Prizewinning garden, shaded rock garden, perennial garden,
waterfall, pond**

When a piece of bureaucratic red tape landed Garry Burns in a
Sudanese jail, he put the hours of confinement to good use —
replanning his perennial border. Three years later, at the time of writing,
he hadn't quite got round to implementing the changes. Garry and Joan
Burns's beautifully designed garden is far more than just a perennial border, however. It is a place of retreat that slowly unfolds in a series of
spaces at once sophisticated and serene. The influences of India and the
Orient blend effortlessly with the Canadian landscape, and much has
been made of the "borrowed view." Indian goddesses stand shyly among
the greenery while gremlins lurk in the ivy.

Beyond the west terrace planted with vines and fragrant honeysuckle,
an arched wooden bridge crosses a dry stream to a large lily pond where a
waterfall emerges from stones and shrubs. Amur and Japanese maples and
stately jack pines make a dramatic backdrop here. Stepping stones lead
through spring-flowering bushes under the dappled shade of locust trees,
and beneath a beautifully pruned lilac, a Buddha sits in a bed of sempervivum.

A small courtyard shaded by a young dawn redwood is surrounded by
flowering shrubs and evergreens; the calming sound of water from a low
fountain, set in round river stone, can be heard from the verandah.

My favourite place is up the path that winds past witch hazel and
serviceberry, into the shaded hosta garden. A luxuriant carpet of vinca
spreads beneath the pear and apple trees, ending at a stone bench under
an old flowering crabapple. The bench, representing a dolmen, the slab
under which the chieftain was traditionally buried, is Garry's tribute to
Ireland. Behind the bench, a stone boy, slightly the worse for wear, looks
as if he's been here since time remembered. I could sit here forever.

IIIIII Margaret and John Cousens, *Robins Rest*
519-449-5837
Near Brantford: 30 minutes west, off Highway 403

Conditions	zone 6; sandy loam, hillside, northern fringe of Carolinian forest
Plot size	3 acres in all

Open by appointment, weekends preferred

Water garden, white border, shade and woodland garden, raised beds

High on a hill surrounded by forest sits a passive solar house, built seven years ago by Marg and John Cousens. A row of stately pyramidal oaks define the entrance to this prizewinning country garden. Marg based her design on a grid for overall unity before dividing it into a series of smaller, themed gardens.

Trained as a visual artist, Marg has "painted" garden pictures at every turn. A flight of stone steps covered in thyme leads to a terrace where lavender tumbles over the drystone walls filled with pink lilies and mauve phlox. A pair of greying cedar chairs are placed invitingly beside a lily pond, and an arc of *Spirea* bridal wreath sweeps gracefully around the edge of the path that encircles an ancient apple tree. Underplanted with masses of spring bulbs, drifts of purple coneflower, pink coreopsis and artemisia, this tree makes a lovely home for a hammock, but watch out for falling apples!

A silver theme becomes apparent where an archway smothered in starry flowers of *Clematis paniculata* links the grass collection to a crescent-shaped white garden that blooms continually from the daffodils onward. In early summer the woods are awash with wild phlox, a fitting background for graceful exchorda and a variety of artemisias.

A woodland garden on the south side of the property is beginning to take shape. Tiarella, pulmonaria, brunnera, hostas and ferns are all in place, and more is planned for this beautiful location.

IIIIII Marguerite Larmand, *Armoury Hall Gardens and Studio*
Box 377, 150 King Street, Burford, ON, N0E 1A0
519-449-5462

Conditions	zone 6a, sandy and flat
Plot size	90 x 150 feet

Open first Sunday of June through September, or by appointment; garden free, open house/studio $2

❧ Historic building grasses, perennials, sculptures

A line of ginkgo trees flanks the front walkway to a flight of purple-painted steps leading to the front door of the massive brick edifice known as The Armoury. Built in 1906 as a military structure for cavalry training, it was later used as a Baptist church, and then abandoned for two years before being purchased by artist Marguerite Larmand in 1981. This unique, austere building of immense size has since been transformed into studios, a gallery and a wonderful living space full of idiosyncrasies and daring colour.

Her former partner, designer Gordon Bakker, created the garden, fusing bold clumps of foliage and delicate flowers into a mass of texture and colour. Sculptural Acanthus spinosus grows through feathery astilbe; spiky red flowers of *Polygonum amplexicaule*, with stems like knobbly old knees, set off lilies of the same hue; and a great drift of cosmos backs a froth of baby's breath edging a stone walkway.

The Duchess of Alba (*Clematis texensis*) spills from an urn, spreading her cloak embroidered with dainty red flowers across a narrow path to a sea of ornamental grasses and bamboo. A flight of stone steps leads to three small pools, each with a fountain burbling a merry chorus. Ground covers create an intricate carpet under the shade plants.

Standing quietly among the greenery are Marguerite's introspective sculptures. She allows tours of the studios and house, and her work is available for purchase here.

"While the gardener is involved with the convergence of idea, place and action, the gorgeous just 'happens' again and again," says Marguerite. Take time to see "the gorgeous" in both the house and garden; they are well worth a visit.

▨ Diane and Bob Czarnik
519-753-8688

Conditions	zone 6
Plot size	65 x 130 feet

Open by appointment; entrance charge $2

❧ Water pond stocked with koi and goldfish

This beautifully designed garden started with the pond, now stocked with koi and goldfish. The Czarniks chose Colorado stone and specially selected rocks for the waterfall. Interesting beds were gradually created and planted with perennials in a free-flowing fashion. A twig arbour leads to a sitting area shaded by maple, sumach and beech. Pine needles and eucalyptus mulch form winding tracks through a raised bed where a variety of annuals join the peonies, perennials and evergreen grasses. Springtime brings a lovely show of rhododendrons and azaleas bordered by lamium.

Margaret and Harold Howe

519-756-8862

Conditions   zone 6; sandy, gently sloping
Open by appointment

Margaret Howe felt a little lost when she came here from her native New Zealand in 1987. She joined the Brantford Garden Club and a life opened up for her. Using her newfound knowledge, starting with cuttings given her by club members, she began to develop her half-acre corner plot. On a site blessed with mature trees, she has designed a garden for year-round interest that bursts with colour from spring to autumn.

Generous perennial borders spill onto pathways that meander through woodland plantings of hostas, ferns and wildflowers. Old-fashioned roses, including many David Austin varieties, combine with perennials to fill the large island beds. This organic garden attracts many birds and butterflies. Sit for a quiet moment on the wooden bench in the shade of a large maple, and enjoy sharing this tranquil place with the visiting wildlife.

The Bell Homestead

94 Tutela Heights Road, Brantford, ON, N3T 1A1
519-756-6220; fax: 519-759-5975
Colborne Street West to Mount Pleasant Street, left to top of hill
Open Tuesday through Sunday, 9:30 to 4:30; open holiday Mondays, closed following Tuesday; small entrance fee; wheelchair access throughout buildings

Once the home of Alexander Graham Bell, who invented the telephone in 1874, the Bell Homestead is now a memorial to his achievements in telephone history. Maintained by the City of Brantford, the pretty perennial gardens, a herb garden, and miniature orchard are part of a 10-acre park. Picnic tables and park benches are placed on the grounds from May until Labour Day. The house and gardens have been restored to their 1870's appearance, and costumed staff and audio-visual presentations provide visitors with a fuller understanding of how a young teacher of the deaf came to invent the telephone and of the late Victorian society in which it emerged.

Glenhyrst Gardens
519-756-5932
Brantford: west of Ava Road, north of Inwood Drive
Open year-round; some wheelchair access

The home of the Glenhyrst Arts Council, set in 16 acres of beautifully landscaped gardens, was bequeathed to the City of Brantford to be used for artistic and cultural pursuits. The Cottage, open to the public for lunches and afternoon teas from May to October, is a very special place. Each room of the Cottage was refurbished by local interior designers as a gift to the community. The artwork displayed is for sale.

Lorne Park
Colborne Street West
Open year-round; some wheelchair access

When the City of Brantford was named Canada's Best Blooming City in the summer of 1995, this outstanding garden, which won a special award for "best planned garden," was greatly responsible for that distinction. Over 5 acres of parkland set along the banks of the Lorne River make a lovely setting for the many varieties of trees, shrubs and roses, and highly manicured formal floral carpet beds.

Brantford

The Cottage at Glenhyrst Gardens
Lunch and afternoon tea from May to October; a very pleasant place.

Mount Pleasant

Devlin's Country Bistro, on the main street, Mount Pleasant (south of Brantford)
519-484-2258
Reservations are recommended for lunch and dinner.

Dunnville

Olde Tyme Country
225 Chestnut Street
905-774-5749
Daily, Monday to Thursday 9 to 5:30, Friday 9 to 9, Saturday 9 to 5:30, Sunday 12 to 5; homemade soup and Mennonite bread.

Caledon–Orangeville Region

▐▌▐▌ Jean and Philip deGruchy and their daughter Sarah
Graymalkin Farm, 16839 The Gore Road, RR 3, Caledon East, L0N 1E0
905-880-4458

Conditions   zone 5b; sandy loam; part large drumlin, part flat field
Plot size   20 acres, 5 acres under cultivation
*Open 10 to 4; second weekend of July; Saturday and Sunday only, August 31
through October 6, and Labour Day weekend, including Monday*

❧ **Working herb and everlasting flower farm; complete retail shop in
the barn**

In 1985 the deGruchys bought Graymalkin Farm with its lovely old
barn and 20 acres of rolling countryside in the Albion Hills. Although
ostensibly retired, they have never worked harder in their lives. Through
Jean's vision, Philip's labours, and the contributions of their daughter
Sarah, whose love of herbs inspired this project, the result is a magnificent herb farm and a thriving business.

The layout has been carefully planned with an eye for unity and
colour. Jean deGruchy has a remarkable understanding and knowledge of
the plants she grows, both botanically and also artistically, demonstrated
in the overall geometric design of the garden, planted in great blocks of
colour. From the top of the hill, a giant mosaic of hundreds of flowers
and over four hundred herbs stretches into the distance; these are used
extensively by the deGruchys for everything from bouquet garnis and
vinegars to bath salts, which they sell in their beautiful barn.

The huge culinary herb bed beside the barn is also a demonstration
and teaching area. Divided into quadrants, it holds at least eleven different basils and many edible herbs, both common and uncommon; these
have been woven into intricate patterns of purples, greens, yellows and
pinks. Over a hundred lavenders fan out across the east slope to the old
herb garden, which is reminiscent of a French monastry garden and now
called the Show Garden.

Across the grass path the rectangular beds of the ornamental garden
brim with mounds of pinks and purple clary sage and tufts of wine-red
Allium sphaerocephalum, bronze fennel and lime green dill. A lazy man's
knot garden serves as its centrepiece. Four formal silvery squares of fra-

grant, closely clipped hyssop and germander hedge domes of cuban oregano and feathery wormwood.

A traditional Mary garden, an invention of the seventeenth century, has been planted in the shelter of the barn. Plantings here include Our Lady's Bedstraw (*Gallium vernum*), Virgin's Bower (*Clematis virginiana*), Our Lady's Tears (Lily of the valley), roses, as a symbol of pure love, and Madonna lily (*Lilium candidum*).

You will find much to interest you in this fascinating place, so be sure to leave plenty of time for your visit.

Elizabeth and George Knowles, *Larkspur Hollow*
416-469-5211 ext. 199
Hockley Valley: 8 kilometres east of Orangeville
Conditions   zone 4b; mixed sand and gravel, some loam, clay
Plot size   11 acres, 2 acres of which are tended
Open through Woodgreen Community Centre, third Wednesday and Thursday of June, 11 to 5

English-style garden perennial borders, scree garden, bog garden

The lovely country garden of Elizabeth Knowles lies at the end of a quiet lane in the heart of the Hockley Valley. Clucking hens and barking dogs announce your arrival at her "English Garden," with its expansive lawns, clematis-covered arches and sweeping perennial borders.

Liz, who trained as an agriculturalist in Britain, grows a wide range of plants in her greenhouse from seeds acquired through exchanges across the country and beyond. The compost heaps here are something to behold, and no doubt contribute largely to the health of this thriving garden.

Mixed shrub borders, ericaceous beds, scree and vegetable gardens all pay tribute to her prowess as a plantswoman par excellence. The wide perennial borders, measuring 15 by 75 feet, are planted to bloom throughout the seasons in wave after wave of colour. Down by the pond, where bullfrogs sing on sultry summer nights, Japanese primulas, irises and ligularias thrive in the boggy ground.

Now that the garden is established, Liz aims to create a more natural transition between the landscaped area and the natural surroundings by linking them with plantings of grasses and shrubs. The backdrop of wild meadows and wooded hills is beautiful year-round, in spring with wildflowers and fresh greenery, in summer when the trees are covered in a tangle of wild sweet pea, and with autumn colour and winter tracery.

Life here is connected with nature in the most elemental way; deer are sighted almost daily on the front lawn in winter. Choice plants are generally sited near the house, and conifers, alpines and perennials are covered, but the rest has to fend for itself. The union of nurture and nature seems idyllic.

Rosemary Ross, *Bonne Entente*
Dufferin County: 15 minutes' drive west of Orangeville
519-942-0070
Conditions zone 5; sand and clay, alkaline, flat land
Plot size 70 acres, 2 acres cultivated
Open by appointment; end of May, end of June and end of July are best times to visit

❧ Formal beds, old-fashioned perennials

Built in 1872, this historic farmhouse is aptly named Bonne Entente —"Good Feelings" — and these are exactly what I felt as I stood in this garden perched on a rise 20 feet above the cool green pond, looking out to the valley and wooded hills beyond. Large formal beds are bright with old-fashioned perennials from spring to fall. Flowers for cutting and drying are grown in attractive raised beds; the rock garden becomes a carpet of colour in the spring; a blowsy rose garden sends out its fragrance on warm summer nights; shade gardens are planted with hosta, aqualigia, digitalis and masses of primroses. The huge stand of black locust trees, the grove of birch and evergreens, and the line of sumach bushes blend beautifully with the surrounding countryside.

Rosemary Ross is a painter and interior designer who has brought her talents out into the garden very successfully.

George Shepherd, *Spring Valley Gardens*
416-469-5211 ext. 199
Hornings Mills
Conditions zone 4b; sandy loam, gentle to steep slope
Plot size 5 acres
Open through Woodgreen Community Centre

❧ Spring, stream, pond and rock garden; woodland garden

Spring Valley is a truly Canadian garden, where broad drifts of colour are harmoniously interspersed with trees and shrubs amid massive limestone outcroppings. It is a place of beauty and solitude with many rock gardens, one of them a spectacular 270 feet long, developed along the natural contour lines of the landscape. The rock gardens overlooks a beautiful curving pond, which is at a much lower level. Visitors are immediately impressed with the sense of depth and precipitousness of the garden site.

Ample pathways and steps give access throughout the gardens, although some of the steps are not for the faint of heart and must be taken with care.

The gardens at Spring Valley Farm have been twenty-five years in the making for George Shepherd and his late wife Shirley. An artist and fashion designer as well as an avid gardener, Shirley brought a fine balance of colour and structure to a difficult garden site, and George is continuing to add to it as a testament to her considerable talents.

David Simmons
416-469-5211 ext. 199
Erin
Conditions   zone 5a; gravel, woodland, wetland
Plot size   3 acres wetland, 1 acre under cultivation
Open through Woodgreen Community Centre, third and fourth weekends of May, first and second weekends of June, second weekend of July, 10 to 6

❧ Large scree garden, rock garden, waterfall, pond, shade gardens

Full thirty-five feet deep their gravel lies," and all's well, I might add. Undaunted by the gravelly ground, Dave Simmons has carved out a well-designed garden in the middle of cedars and graceful whispering aspens, making the most of what nature has given him. Over the septic system, on the north side, is a natural scree garden where lush pools of creeping phlox, dianthus, sedum and sempervivum are dominated by an unusually and very beautiful specimen prostrate larch.

A ribbon of colourful pentstemons runs along the base of a 60-foot drywall that has been planted with saxifrage and various dianthus.

The raised beds and rock garden display over a hundred varieties of alpine plants and dwarf evergreens, including gentians and androsace. Thyme gives an aged appearance to the stones around the pond, which brims with aquatic plants and flashing koi, and in the bog garden candelabra primulas in many hues put on a pretty show. The shade garden is full of woodland plants and spring here is lyrical.

David and Mary Clarke, *Glen Cross Pottery*
RR 1, Orangeville, ON, L9W 2Y8
519-941-6048
Third Line and Hockley Valley Road, northeast of Orangeville
Conditions   zone 5; bedrock
Plot size   3/4 of an acre
Open weekends throughout the season

❧ Interesting use of rock, formal herb garden

A huge willow tree drapes its branches over a simple pergola, marking the entrance to the pottery and garden of Mary and David Clarke, nestled snugly in the Hockley Valley alongside the Nottawasaga River.

A sense of Celtic Britain pervades this mystical place, where the deft hand of the artist can be felt everywhere. Mary is a glaze chemist and painter, David moulds the clay, and each of them has an abiding interest in things medieval. All these interests have spilled out into the garden, where organically shaped beds have been wrested from the bedrock with nothing more than David's fierce determination and a pickaxe, then filled by Mary with loose lush plantings of perennials, annuals and wildflowers.

A visit to St. David's in Wales inspired the building of a dramatic wall of pebbles and striated rock, with an interesting arched niche added by Mary.

Hops grown for brewing beer, as well as for their ornamental qualities, cover the beautifully simple structure attached to the side of the house. The filigreed roots of upside-down cedars, suggestive of a Gothic cathedral, form a splendid support for the glass-roofed terrace, used as a tea garden on weekends during the summer. An allée of cedar posts follows the slope to a clearing in the wood, where a new, formal herb garden is in the making, and a winding path leads back through the woodland garden along the bank of the river.

⬛🦋 Erik Hogh and Barry Dimock, *Rosehill Schoolhouse*
519-941-1114
Caledon: near Orangeville
Conditions   clay, rolling
Plot size   1 acre cultivated
Open by appointment; best mid-June through mid-July

❧ **Heritage cut-stone schoolhouse (1872), herb garden**

A charming old schoolhouse, ivy-covered bell tower, greenhouse, and an old barn surrounded by a thickly planted ground cover of hosta — these are the anchors of this enchanting garden. The old maple trees were planted by the children of the school in 1897 to commemorate Queen Victoria's Diamond Jubilee. Erik Hogh is a self-confessed compost nut, and his dedication and skill are apparent in the healthy perennial beds, rose garden and rock garden, and the raised bed under a shady maple. A perfectly manicured cedar hedge encloses the herb garden, creating a room full of memories and scents, where the perfume of old roses blends with that of trailing and prostrate rosemary, basil, dill, lemon balm and the like. The kitchen garden is host to a rhubarb patch, angelica, gooseberries, kale and varieties of tomatoes. An old rose from an abandoned farmhouse close by was introduced to the garden by Barry, and he is now encouraging it to spread on up the hillside, perhaps recreating the Rosehill of old.

⬛🦋 Claude and Patricia Sang
905-936-2964
Dufferin County: 15 minutes' drive west of Orangeville
Conditions   zone 5; mostly sandy
Plot size   several acres
Open by appointment

❧ **Friendship garden, birdhouse collection**

The Sangs invite you to come and enjoy the view from the hilltop. This parklike setting is home to an interesting collection of birdhouses, a water garden and several perennial beds. Each plant in Pat's friendship garden is a memorial to a friend or relative.

Richard and Kathy Taylor, *Donaghy House*
67 Amaranth Street East, Grand Valley, ON, L0N 1G0
519-928-3332
Dufferin County: 15 minutes' drive west of Orangeville
Conditions　　zone 5; clay/loam, flat, gently sloping
Plot size　　165 x 75 feet
Open by appointment or by chance

❧ **Pond, secret garden, National Wildlife Federation's Backyard Habitat Program Certificate of Achievement**

When Rick and Kathy Taylor's garden was virtually destroyed by the tornado of 1985 they started again, determined to make their prizewinning garden even more attractive to wildlife with perennials and shrubs. As further enticement the Taylors have erected a bat box, a butterfly box, birdbaths and bird-nesting boxes. The small pond with running water is host to fish, frogs and water plants.

A white picket fence, brightly coloured perennial borders, window boxes and containers filled with annuals complete the Old World setting of the Taylor's charming Victorian house.

There is a secret garden where humans are allowed to visit in search of solitude and serenity, provided, that is, they don't disturb the critters.

Acton

The Millcroft Inn
1-800-383-3976
Luncheon, afternoon tea served daily on the terrace overlooking the mill pond.

Rosemont

The Globe
South side of Highway 89, east of Airport Road, west of Highway 50
705-435-6981

Closed Tuesdays; luncheon from noon to 2, afternoon tea 2 to 4:30, dinner 5 to 9.

Shelburne

Mrs. Mitchell's
Violet Hill, Shelburne, on north side of Highway 89 between Highway 10 and Airport Road
519-925-3627
Closed Mondays; lunch, afternoon tea 2 to 4, dinner.

Cambridge / Fergus / Guelph / Kitchener–Waterloo / Milton / Rockwood

CAMBRIDGE

[icon] Langdon Hall
RR 33, Cambridge, ON, N3H 4R8
1-800-268-1898; Cambridge 519-740-2100
Blair: Highway 401 to Exit 275; south to Blair Road, to village of Blair;
second right after town tavern; Langdon Hall is first driveway on left

A small sign to Langdon Hall beckoned us up a driveway partially hidden by trees. The sense of anticipation heightened as the driveway widened, sweeping up to the elegant entrance. Situated on the edge of Ontario's Carolinian forest, surrounded by acres of woodland, this gracious house with its extensive gardens has been lovingly restored by architect William Bennett and his partner Mary Beaton.

Their matchmaking has resulted in a brilliant marriage between house and land — an elegant American Federal-style mansion and a garden suggestive of eighteenth-century England. A series of elegant spaces have been created, divided by walls and grade changes and plantings of large trees such as ginkgo, catalpa and magnolia, which, although eclectic in style, integrate beautifully.

At the front of the house curved beds of perennials and shrub roses set a scene of relaxed formality. The fragrance of lavender fills the air; bees buzz. Some of the gardens are joined at a central axis, each approached through a covered doorway, inviting one to wander.

Down a flight of stone steps, a tranquil cloister walk surrounds a courtyard planted with modern shrub roses, garden perennials, and shrubs for winter interest. From here, meander through another gate to where a walled vegetable garden is filled with unusual and exotic vegetables. Edible and cut flowers that are long lived, zinnias, cosmos, violas, nasturtiums and ornamental grasses, these grace the tables and beautifully appointed rooms of the house.

Mathew Smerek, who presides over it all, is always developing and expanding this area. Stroll across the lawn and stop to gaze into the formal pool where carp swim lazily among the lilies. One can take lunch or tea and sip a cooling drink beside a magnificent Camperdown elm.

This is an enchanting place where the natural surroundings meld perfectly with the formality of the layout.

FERGUS

Charles and Dorothy Sturrock, *Irvine Bank*
519-846-0175
Elora: east bank of Irvine River
Conditions   zone 5b
Open: Local Horticultural Society Tour, Wellington County Museum Tour

Sunken gardens

Charles and Dorothy Sturrock's garden has two personalities. The front is landscaped; the back, bordering on the Elora Gorge, where cedar trees and wildflowers thrive, is in its natural state.

The gazebo on the upper terrace of the front garden looks down on the sunken gardens, a large perennial garden bed with a small pond and water wheel, a rose garden, and an iris and tuberous begonia garden. The perfumes of mock orange, lilacs and honeysuckle fill the air. From the eaves and cedar fences hang arrangements of variegated impatiens and throughout are moveable pots of geraniums and pansies. A birdbath and fountain offer hospitality to the many birds who visit this colourful garden.

Jean and Philip Cardinal, *Breadalbane Inn*
The Breadalbane Inn, 487 St. Andrew St. West, Fergus, ON, N1M 1P2
519-843-4770; fax 519-843-7600
Conditions   zone 4/5; good garden soil
Open: anyone is welcome; restaurant

Heritage inn, perennial garden, pond and waterfall

This charming stone inn with its white-painted wrought-iron railings was built in 1860 as a private residence by the Honourable Adam Ferguson, co-founder of Fergus. It is considered the finest example of Scottish architecture in the area.

The Cardinals, who took over in 1975, are well known for the good food and comfort they provide. At the back of the Inn, under the shade of a pretty porch, guests and visitors are welcome to eat lunch or sip a drink while enjoying the delights of Jean's lovely cottage garden.

Encouraged to garden as a child, she became one of a gallant band of young women who during the war worked as "farmerettes" in the Ontario fields for some seventy hours a week. She loved it and still finds working the soil exciting and very relaxing after a hard day's cooking.

The sunlight that falls on the garden enables her to grow some fifty roses in the northern area, which is protected by a vine-covered brick wall. Large perennial beds overflow with flowers that early Canadian settlers knew well; clumps of white obedience plant, drifts of black-eyed Susans, and blowsy phlox are wonderful. The shaded southern beds house hostas and ferns, a voluptuous show of tuberous begonias, as well as over fifty containers bearing a good cross-section of annuals. A waterfall, small fish pond and a gazebo add charm to this lovely setting.

Fergus–Elora Rotary Heritage Art Garden
Wellington County Museum and Archives
519-846-0916
County Road 18 at Aboyne, halfway between Fergus and Elora
Open weekdays 9:30 to 4:30, weekends and holidays 1 to 5; adults $2.50, seniors and students $1.25, children $0.50, family $6; wheelchair access; washrooms, gift shop

The Victorian Garden, Nature Garden and Cottage Garden were designed by Elora artist Cecily Moon. The Victorian Garden, enclosed by a white picket fence, is planted with perennials popular in the 1800s. Trees, grasses and shrubs run riot in the Nature Garden. Fruit-bearing plants and shrubs and a herb bed make up the Cottage Garden.

GUELPH

Trevor Ashbee
519-766-9881

Conditions	zone 5; flat, composted soil
Plot size	100 x 125 feet
Open by appointment	

Alpines, variety of perennials, evergreens and shrubs

Trevor Ashbee is Head of Parks for Guelph University and his father was head gardener to one of the doyens of British gardening, Christopher Lloyd.

From two adjoining small city lots Trevor has created a mini Kew Gardens; intricate pathways weave through a series of interconnected garden rooms filled with evergreens, shrubs and a wide variety of flowers, from tallest perennials to the smallest alpines. The list of plants is too long to mention here, but treasures include *Lewisia* Cotyledon, *Dianthus haematocalyx, Adonis vernalis, Ramonda myconi, Townsendia*, an interesting variety of foxgloves and the surprisingly hardy *Paulonia tormentos*, foxglove tree. What a feast is in store for those who visit these fascinating gardens.

Victor and Lillian Chanasyk
416-469-5211 ext. 199
Conditions   zone 6; flat, small flight of steps to upper level at back
Open through Woodgreen Community Centre, second Sunday of July

Strong design, statuary, pond, perennials, ground covers

Victor Chanasyk is a well-known and highly respected landscape architect, and his strong design principles have been carried through his own garden in all its aspects, from the hard landscaping to the plantings themselves. Great attention has been placed on layered plantings, starting with a lush green canopy and richly planted understorey at the curbside garden, continuing to the courtyard by the front entrance. No trace of lawn can be found here; instead a smooth, green river of ground covers, interrupted occasionally by strong accent shrubs, lends an air of serenity and an organic quality to this carefully thought-out space. Most of the colour comes from boldly hued flowers in planters.

The back garden continues in the same manner, with textures and pattern skilfully woven into an artful design of grasses, ericaceous plants and a variety of ground covers. Water and works of art, some of the sculpture created by the owner, add focus and drama to this lovely garden. A flight of steps leads to a series of gardens, including a herbaceous perennial border planted to attract butterflies, a small herb garden accommodating a medicinal collection, and a woodland garden. There is much to learn from a visit to Mr. Chanasyk and his garden.

||||||| Gary Smith

416-469-5211 ext. 199

Conditions   zone 6; clay/loam, slight slope

Open through Woodgreen Community Centre, every Sunday from second Sunday in May to last Sunday in September, except holiday weekends, 10 to 4

❧ **Orchid house, pond, rose collection, perennials**

This garden of contrasts in the old university area of Guelph was begun by Gary Smith in 1980. The raised beds in the charming courtyard entryway are planted with *Acer palmatum dissectum* and dwarf evergreens. Two towering stands of bamboo, *Phyllostachys aureosaculata* and *Pseudosasa japonica*, with its lovely yellow and green stems, grow on either side of the path, framing the garden beyond. There, a series of interrelated angular wooden structures and gazebo are balanced and softened by curving, informal beds where the form of the plants and the play of their patterns are more important than colour. Gary has created a series of specimen plantings for deepest shade to hottest sun, as well as a growing collection of David Austin roses and lilies. A splendid perennial border is backed by a high wooden fence that provides support for species clematis and climbing roses. At the back of the garden there is a tiny woodland area planted with native Ontario shrubs, providing food and shelter for the birds and other wildlife. A highlight of the garden is the unique two-tiered pond, where plantings of the huge-leaved petasitis and petaphyllum add drama and scale to the contrasting leaves of iris, water lilies and other aquatics. "No garden is complete without water," says Gary.

He has designed his modern city garden as an extension of the indoor living area, and a greenhouse where he cultivates orchids acts as an intermediary space between house and garden. This property very much reflects the trend toward informal natural gardens, and is quite lovely at any almost any time.

||||||| Sylvia Watson

416-469-5211 ext. 199

Conditions   zone 6; clay/loam

Open through Woodgreen Community Centre, last weekend of June, first Saturday of July, first Sunday of August; 10 to 6; uneven surface (gravel) but generally wheelchair accessible

❧ Various garden styles and interesting plant material

Sylvia Watson looked on her garden as a large empty canvas when she first began, and has been continually sketching and painting on it ever since. At first the emphasis was on design, but as she got more involved her interest in plants grew, along with a desire to experiment with a number of different garden styles. She has created a number of "rooms," employing very attractive trellising as dividers, which helps to break up what was basically a square yard.

The garden nearest the house is randomly planted to resemble an English cottage garden, featuring herbs, perennials, roses and some of the more fragrant annuals such as nicotiana and night-scented stocks. As you continue through the garden gate you will face the main axis; the left-hand "room" is influenced by Japanese gardens in its use of texture and leaf pattern and very little colour, in direct contrast to the more lushly planted perennial border that faces it. At the rear of the garden an informal woodland is home to a collection of viburnums, hosta, ferns and wildflowers.

Although she isn't exactly ancient, Sylvia feels that her garden gives hope to those who consider themselves "too old" to start gardening. She is convinced that anyone who has the interest can do it.

The Gosling Wildlife Gardens
University of Guelph, Guelph, ON, N1G 2W1
519-824-4120, fax 519-763-9598
University of Guelph, Arboretum Road
Open year-round, dawn to dusk; call the University for information on guided tours; wheelchair access

Here are five gardens, each one planted and designed to attract wildlife in an urban setting: a butterfly, moth and hummingbird garden; a meadow garden; a prairie garden; a suburban garden; and a small city garden. These gardens demonstrate creative alternatives to traditional backyard gardening.

KITCHENER–WATERLOO

|IIIIIʃ Rachel Flood, *Flood's Residence*
416-469-5211 ext. 199
Kitchener
Conditions   zone 5; steeply sloped
Open through Woodgreen Community Centre, last two Sundays of June, first Sunday of July, 10 to 4

❧ **Best rose collection in a private garden in Ontario**

A carnival of colour greeted me on my arrival at Rachel Flood's garden. A first glimpse of her true passion is given in the circular garden, where approximately sixty rosebushes put on a fantastic show.

As I rounded the corner I caught my breath. A green swath of grass drops 80 feet to the banks of the Grand River, glinting in the soft autumn sun. At the top of this remarkable panorama are planted three large rose gardens containing more than 800 species of hybrid teas, grandifloras, floribundas and miniature roses, underplanted with viola and ajuga.

Most of the landscaping has to work to accommodate the huge change in grade, and the challenge is to retain topsoil in the beds. The Floods have used wood framing to create more planting space on the slope. Dragonflies dart across the ponds that tier down to a pergola covered in pink-and-cream climbing rose Handel, and cleomies have self-seeded among the miniature rose Cascade tumbling in profusion over the rocks.

Down by the wide, slow-moving river, we strolled round another rose bed featuring mainly shrub roses including some David Austins and ground cover roses, planted to withstand the browsing of the deer. A covey of dancing pines, their huge sleeves sweeping the ground, and a splendid blue spruce stand guard by the vegetable patch. The surrounding fence is covered in a tangle of sweet peas and clematis, and at their feet a profuse miniature rose Victorious is interplanted with rose Champagne Cocktail. Rachel has found her garden a good friend in difficult times.

|IIIIIʃ Lawrence (Larry) Lamb
416-469-5211 ext. 199; home 519-893-1025, bus. 519-885-1211 ext. 2646
Kitchener
Conditions   zone 5b–6; sandy loam on a gentle slope
Plot size   1/5 acre

Open through Woodgreen Community Centre, second Sunday of July;
otherwise, by appointment with owner

✤ Prairie and meadow plants, including several hundred species, plus numerous species rare or threatened in Ontario

Away dull care! Out, out foundation planting! Forget genteel borders, trimmed hedges and green lawns! This garden on a conventional suburban lot is a battle hymn to the fast-disappearing landscape of Canada, being sung loudly by Larry Lamb, a passionate and extremely knowledgeable naturalist.

Four years ago he started a front yard designed to eliminate all trace of grass, replacing it with a northern meadowscape of native plantings of small shrubs such as *Potentilla simplex* and *Vibernum rafinesquianum*. A liriodendron tree and a sweet gum have just come through their first winter. Ground covers such as strawberry, cinquefoil and bearberry creep through every available space, an inspirational alternative to all those front gardens that have to be mowed, watered, fed and sprayed.

A tall grass prairie system has been established in the gently sloping backyard, modelled on the remaining Southern Ontario tall grass habitats at Windsor and Walpole Island. It also contains species from the full range of this system, made up of 60 to 90 percent grasses and 10 to 40 percent forbs, mostly deep-rooted perennials or self-seeding annuals and biennials adapted to low moisture and nutrient-poor soil. Conditions here are perfect for the requirements of a prairie garden; facing west and with good drainage, it basks in sun all day.

The focal point of the garden is a glacial rock, suggestive of a bison rubbing-rock, around which a network of paths connects a series of island beds. These beds house compatible groups of plants, more than 3,000 of them, many rare or endangered. From mid-June to winter, the meadow's changing scenes evoke the seasons of a landscape fast disappearing on the Canadian prairie. Late August till fall brings a breathtaking vision when the haze of grasses whose names are so evocative — Indian grass, big blue stem, *Elymus canadensis*, among others — are dotted with flowers: purple liatris, starry asters, goldenrod, coneflowers and black-eyed Susans, to "set budding more and still more later flowers for the bees, until they think warm days will never cease," and play host to hundreds of butterflies, savanna sparrow and meadowlarks who enjoy this habitat.

Each time he hears a lawn mower, Larry smiles. His efforts have saved him from that particular chore.

|||||| Gordon Smallwood

519-896-0549

Kitchener: near intersection of King and Dixon Streets
Conditions   zone 5; heavy sandy loam front, light sandy loam back
Open some weekends, 10 to 6, by appointment with owner; do not phone after
9 p.m.; limit of thirty visitors

❦ **Prairie, woodland and marsh/bog plants; many grasses**

This 100-by-50-foot garden is a plant lover's paradise. Gordon Small-wood has collected a wide selection of North American and exotic plants and has carefully sited them to fit their particular requirements. The plants also play host to insects and birds whose habitat is fast disappearing.

The environment differs greatly from front to back. The front garden receives full sun most of the day, and prairie plants thrive in profusion in this hot dry site. Sporobolus, *Eryngium yuccafolium*, big blue stem, with its purple-and-green leaves, and an interesting collection of grasses combine to produce an effective show of foliage, blooms and waving plumes.

Down the steps to the back garden another world awaits, 2.4 metres lower in elevation than the front, and where a mixture of sun and shade moves through all day, providing an ideal home for hundreds of woodland plants. A myriad of leaf forms and texture creates a lush web of greenery. Beside the winding grass path the blue-green leaves of *Arundo donax* reach for the sky, while in sunnier spots, moisture-loving plants, tall perennials and even taller grasses blend with the fronds of ferns. Here you will see arisaema, with its curious hooded spathes and spikes of fleshy red fruit in the autumn, together with silphium, phytolacca and many others.

Tucked away at the back of the garden, a marsh area is in progress, and alkaline plants are being collected, by way of seed gathered in the wild and at seed exchanges. Red mulberry, witch hazel, viburnums and many others can be found here.

This is a garden that changes dramatically with the seasons and is worth visiting from late spring to well into the fall when it becomes a jungle of colour.

The Joseph Schneider House
466 Queen Street, Kitchener, ON, N2G 1W7
Downtown Kitchener

Open Tuesday to Saturday 10 to 5; Sunday 1 to 5; adults $1.75, seniors $1; some wheelchair, slide presentation available to those unable to access the narrow pathways

The garden here is a recreated four square kitchen garden typical of that used by early Pennsylvania Mennonite settlers to Waterloo County.

Special events include Maitag, the first weekend of May, to promote garden themes, and the Herb Fair, to exchange seeds.

MILTON

Joan and John Linley, *Pickletree Farm*
1094 Derry Road, RR 3, Campbellville
905-336-1398
Conditions   zone 6; rocky outcroppings, undulating
Open early May to mid-November, 11 to 5, Friday through Monday; otherwise by appointment

❧ Marvellous garden ornaments for sale, perennial gardens

When the Linleys opened Pickletree Farm nine years ago, their dream of many years became a reality. Having travelled the world visiting gardens both public and private, from large estates to tiny city cloisters, they realized that the best of them had one thing in common — a strong statement in the form of ornaments. Gardeners in Southern Ontario were just beginning to recognize the possibilities open to them, and nurseries were expanding, but no one was providing artistically designed artefacts. The Linleys decided to fill the void and have never looked back.

Gracing their beautiful galleries and gardens are a marvellous selection of antique garden pieces collected from all over Europe. Here you will find iron gates from France, fountains from Italy and urns and statues from Britain, as well as limited editions designed by local artists. The search for a perfect place to fulfill their vision ended with the purchase of this beautiful small farm on the Niagara Escarpment, surrounded by rocky outcroppings and gently rolling acres. At the end of a long *allée* of 130-year-old sugar maples stands a Victorian house of great charm, with the original gingerbreading intact. A timber barn with a stone foundation is tucked into the hillside at the bottom of a stone stairway, planted on each side with well-stocked perennial beds that have been labelled for easy identification.

Described by the Linleys as "Beatrix Potter land," the silo with its mossy interior and water fountain is flooded with a mysterious-seeming light from its glass top. Beside it stands the Milk House, sensitively transformed into a magnificent gallery, its stalls and stone floors intact.

The newly created rose garden has been planted nearby, as much for fragrance as for the beauty of the blossoms. In the distance there is a spectacular view of the valley with its series of excavated ponds. A fountain made from a 150-year-old basswood stump stands at the edge of the largest of them, cascading over the rocks to the water below.

Ornaments imported from all over the world are displayed throughout the gardens to excite and inspire us, making Pickletree Farm a unique experience.

 Marion Detlor, *Rock Ledge*

905-878-7397

Conditions   zone 6: Escarpment

Plot size   1 acre, half cultivated, half woodland

Open by appointment; donation to a charity appreciated as entrance fee

❦ Rock garden, waterfall

Once a quarry, this property on the edge of the Niagara Escarpment is the perfect natural setting for Marion Detlor's rock garden. Marion has planted miniature ferns and mosses to fascinating effect in the quarry face. In contrast to the rock garden is a sunken bog garden, where springtime is announced by bright yellow marsh marigolds followed by water iris, cardinal flowers, ferns, hosta, monarda and astilbe. Look for the miniature rose garden, mixed perennial beds, and a small fountain that lends particular charm.

Linda Schafhauser

905-878-3226

Conditions   topsoil on solid rock

Plot size   1 acre

Open by appointment

❧ Waterfall and water garden

S pring is heralded by the arrival of thousands of trilliums and lady-slippers, carpeting the woodland floor of Linda Schafhauser's front garden. Walkways of perennials and colourful annuals lead to the back of the property, with its dramatic view over the Niagara Escarpment. Sweeping lawns and sculptured beds create a parklike setting, and the manmade waterfall, cascading 35 feet from the top of the rock shelf to the ravine below, is a spectacular sight. Linda's gardener, Tony Steddy, is working on a scree bed close to the house. This is his latest project, but probably not the last, as they are considering putting in a path below the falls to take further advantage of the property below.

Milton Town Hall Garden
Milton Victoria Square, next to Milton Town Hall
Open: groups by appointment, contact Marion Detlor 905-878-7397 or Jennifer Mirosolin 905-878-3597; open to the public; difficult wheelchair access

T he ruins of the Halton jail have been transformed into an inspired garden by the Milton and District Horticultural Society.
   An archway draped in wisteria leads from the rose-covered "ante-chamber" into an inner courtyard whose crumbling walls are clad in a variety of vines. Within, generous mixed borders surrounding the lawn bloom throughout the growing season. A floral urn, sundial and garden benches add to the charm of this "secret garden" in the centre of old Milton.

ROCKWOOD

Andreas Drenters, *The Old Academy Garden and Studio*
519-856-4061
Conditions   zone 6, flat
Plot size   approximately 5 acres, 2 acres of garden
Open by appointment

❧ Sculpture garden

Through the impressive iron gates at the end of the tree-lined driveway, a magnificent stone house comes into view. More reminiscent of the Yorkshire moors than Southern Ontario, it is in fact the home of sculptor Andreas Drenters and his family.

In 1960, Andreas's brother Joseph bought the Quaker school, circa 1800, after he left the priesthood to become a full-time sculptor. Over the next twenty-three years, until his death in 1983, Joseph transformed the fields and surroundings into a peaceful cloistered garden, with the courtyard walls and chapel built with stone retrieved from condemned schoolhouses in the area. He was helped in the summers by the late Murray Haigh, one of Canada's best-known garden designers. He was responsible for the rose and herb gardens, now overgrown, and his name is carved on a stone plaque in the charming chapel that he helped to build. After Joseph's death, Andreas took the property over, but it became a financial burden. He was saved, as he says, by "a shining miracle" in the guise of a film company that used it as their location for the film *Agnes of God*.

Very few of the original plantings survive, but the serenity and peace that emanates from the grassed courtyards and walkways gives a feeling of a medieval monastery. Today the garden grows Andreas's fantastic steel sculptures that imbue this mystical place with a special magic of their own. The long cool refectory and gymnasium have been turned into galleries to house some of the small works.

The final word on this garden goes to Andreas himself. "I create organic shapes. Nature is sculpting all the time, my work invites you to look for these natural connections."

Fergus

Breadalbane Inn
487 St. Andrew Street West
519-843-4770
Tuesday through Sunday
Excellent light luncheon, dinner from 5:30.

Guelph

Meridian Coffee House
91 Wyndham

519-821-0474
Open daily, 9 am to midnight; excellent for lunch and tea.

St. Jacobs

Benjamin's Restaurant and Inn
17 King Street South
519-664-3731
Luncheon served 11:30 to 3, afternoon tea 3 to 5, daily.

Durham Region

||||||| Terry Bujokas, *Down Home*
416-469-5211 ext. 199; 416-653-8804
Priceville
Conditions   zone 5; flat, sandy alkaline soil
Plot size   100 x 100 feet
*Open through Woodgreen Community Centre, last weekend of June; other
days, by appointment with owner*

❧ **Perennial borders, white garden, herb garden**

At the end of a grassy walk lined with dark evergreens and maples, in
the middle of an enchanting garden, sits a little cabin of logs weathered to a silver-grey. Over the split-rail fence an old apple tree leans into a
field of Queen Anne's lace. Paths lined with lambs ears and thyme wind
through a herb garden dominated by a graceful white rose, *Blanc double
de Coubert*, where lavender and wormwood grow out of the gravel.
Hollyhocks and soft pink day lilies mingle with monkshood, and the
scent of rugosa roses fills the air.

Deeply scalloped island borders sweep away from each side of the
front door to meet at a white trellis arbour covered in sweet peas and
clematis. The islands' generous display of bulbs in the spring is followed
by a summer parade of flowers in skilfully graded shades of pastels.
Veronicas, iris, salvias, poppies, phlox and peonies mix happily with the
original farm flowers, and in the centre, a large bed shaped like a painter's
palette is bright with splashes of flowers in a rainbow of colours.

At the entrance to the front garden a cedar hedge is a solid background
for a white shade garden, beginning in spring with the tulips and primulas
and continuing into late fall with the last fluffy flower of cimicifuga.

The garden is lovely at any time of day, but for Terry, walking among
the long shadows created by the setting sun after work is done is when
she finds her deepest pleasure.

||||||| Douglas Chambers, *Stonyground*
416-469-5211 ext. 199; 519-881-3582
Near Walkerton, Bruce County

Conditions   5b; sandy loam and clay
Plot size   2 acres
Open through Woodgreen Community Centre, last Sunday of June, 9 to 6 ; all other appointments, including bus tours, must be made through owner; photography permitted under copyright proviso

❦ Jardin potager, Jekyll border, rose garden, cottage garden monuments and inscriptions

Douglas Chambers is a man of many parts — garden historian, plantsman and professor of English — who has brought all his wit and erudition to this remarkable garden. The property has been in the family since his great-great-grandfather began homesteading here in 1850 and was inherited by Douglas in 1984. In spite of its fertile soil, he renamed it Stonyground from Yeats's "Meditations in the Time of Civil War," about the pleasures of cultivating an acre of stony ground, for no other reason than that he liked the poem.

Quotations and puns can be found all over the property. *Omne tulit punctum miscuit utile dulce*, inscribed on the lintel of the pump house, translates as "He wins the day who mixes the beautiful with the useful," Philip Southcote's dictum for his 1730 *English Ferme Ornee*, about combining agriculture and horticulture.

The journey begins near the house, with a 30-foot perennial garden, inspired by Gertrude Jekyll, planted in a spectrum of colour from blue through orange. Continue down the pergola walk and sit awhile on the lattice-covered seat, a copy from the eighteenth-century garden at Rousham in Oxfordshire. From here you can enjoy the gorgeous display of the Great Garden with its colour-graded beds overflowing with old favourites, including a lovely array of ornamental grasses.

A pleached *allée* of little leaf lindens leads up a flight of semicircular stone steps, a tribute to Edward Lutyen's vernacular style. Here Doug has placed Diana, carved from a granite boulder, with a bow, facing her brother Apollo, a limestone column 3.5 metres high, his head a metal sun decorated with arrowlike guards from a mowing machine. A terrace overlooks the ha-ha, a tribute to Lord Elgin, where giant silver thistles (onopordum), Douglas's pride and joy, have seeded themselves among artemisia and white roses.

Tucked away behind a hedge is a wonderfully whimsical *jardin potager*. Influenced both by Rosemary Verey's garden at Barnsley House in England, and the Acadian method of planting vegetables in plots, it is divided geometrically into quadrants and richly planted in formal patterns, each with a different theme. Brick pathways have been designed to represent a Chippendale design; an Ontario lattice-crust pie; the pathways at Villandry, a sixteenth-century French castle; and in honour of his ancestors, the Cross of St. Andrew. At the hub stands a wagon wheel covered in roses, surrounded by a circle of thyme. "The roses of eternity growing through the wheel of time," explains Douglas.

A long *allée* of pyramidal cedars, a clever substitute for the cypresses of Italy, connects the garden to the fields and Circuit Walk. Strange-looking boxes with quotations and dedications, both personal and literary, hang from the trees that line the network of paths to the woodlot.

Douglas is at present writing a book, *The Making of Stonyground*, to be published in the spring of 1996. There is a twinkle in his eye as he recounts the story of an "older" woman who, when looking at the Queen Anne's lace beside the roses, was heard to exclaim, "Now if that were in my garden, I'd have it out." "God knows," says Douglas, "what she made of the onopordums!"

||||||| Agnes and George Folmer
RR 1 Chepstow, ON, N0G 1K0
519-366-2366
Just west of the hamlet of Chepstow, Bruce County

Conditions   zone 5; local Harriston loam
Plot size   1/2 acre
Open last weekend of June

❧ **Ground covers, ericaceous bed, perennial gardens, pond, formal garden, Carolinian woodland garden**

The Folmers' garden is a pool of colour in golden Ontario farmland. A wealth of different ground covers, designed to blend with the surroundings and replace most of the grass which they find so tedious to mow, create a richly textured carpet throughout the property.

An avid plant collector and garden designer, Brian Folmer has laid out his parents' garden in a series of rooms to accommodate the enormous variety of specimens he has accumulated. Many of the plants are unusual for this part of Ontario. Heather and dainty yellow aconites show their blossoms with the first snowmelt; *Cyclamen neopolitanum* flutter in the autumn wind like little Dutch bonnets. Amur maple (*Acer ginnela*),

Eastern redbud (*Cercis canadensis*) and numerous vibernums are all thriving under his expert hand.

As one wanders along the paths from garden to garden, Brian's flair for combining colour and texture can be seen in the imaginative "plant pictures" that unfold at every turn. Pale mauve day lilies with pink plumes of *Pennisetum*, silver woolly thyme and the large, rounded leaves of *Bergenia cordifolia*; the bronze leaves of a Japanese maple (*Acer dissectum atropurpurium*), ringed with blue catmint and leaning over a pond filled with pickerel weed, water iris and lilies; downy lambs ears, white panicled phlox and drifts of candytuft — all a study in form and texture. *Clematis tangutica* runs free across the woodland floor, its yellow bells changing in fall to seed heads of wispy silver caught in a tangle of leaves. Dark pines and rust-red maples are lit up by starry flowers of *Clematis viticella*. In spring thousands of blooming bulbs run riot through all.

Georg and Karen Maier, *The Gardens at Greenwood*
416-469-5211 ext. 199
2nd and 3rd Concession of Glenelg Township, 4 kilometres north of Highway 4
Conditions   zone 5a; local Harrison loam, flat
Open through Woodgreen Community Centre, last weekend of June, 10 to 4

Old barn foundation, pergola walk, sculpture garden, greenhouse, peony collection, herb garden

Anyone who places a marble tombstone on the kitchen table and uses it as a chopping block, as Karen and Georg Maier have done, must have quite an imagination. Georg Maier has given free rein to his imagination in the creation of this unique garden, which he describes as a wild oxymoron — a secret garden within a well-traversed working farm.

The 1870s stone house with its white front garden flanks a greenhouse filled with exotic birds, fish and orchids. As you cross the lawn past the colourful vegetable garden and peony collection, only the walls of the old barn foundation are visible. Once you clamber through a concealed gap in the crumbling wall, a very different light suffuses the original whitewashed wall and cement floor. Turquoise and magenta benches, clay pots, and assorted cement statuary and urns set the scene for countless varieties of perennials in hues of ultraviolet and pink, immediately transporting you to a Hellenic place. The high walls and straight paths add a sense of formality to an otherwise casual arrangement of bright colours and diverse plant forms growing in the gullies that run down the stone floor.

An enclosed garden of 10,000 square feet, divided into two great rooms, acts as a heat trap, creating a microclimate in all seasons. The gnarled limbs of fruit trees are espaliered across the walls; and rambling roses and clematis vines entwined with honeysuckle clamber up the cast-iron hoops made from an old manure track that once hung suspended above the entire space. Lush day lilies and Japanese iris surround a small lily pool; the silver-grey Russian olives and graceful willows further enhance a sense of the sunbaked Mediterranean. Fragrant plantings of rosemary and rue, thyme and lavender heighten the sense of drowsy abandon. An arbour of white clematis makes a lovely shaded place for quiet contemplation in this truly memorable garden.

Jean and Ron Morris, *Crowgarth*
416-469-5211 ext. 199; 519-369-2445
Conditions   zone 5; well-drained, gravelly, hilly
Plot size   100 x 125 feet
Open through Woodgreen Community Centre, last weekend of June and July 1, 10 to 5; other times by appointment with owner; this is a terraced garden and not suitable for wheelchairs, but garden can be seen from the patio

Sunken garden with lily pond, terraced gardens, a collection of garden verses

Standing on the patio looking out over the formal parklike landscape with its sunken gardens, rockeries and steeply terraced hillside, it is hard to imagine that twenty-five years ago there was nothing here but a mountain of sand and a lone white ash tree. The Morrises brought in a bulldozer, cleared the sand, and the garden began.

The result is a labyrinth of twisting stairways, hidden paths and secluded corners — a maze of pattern and texture. A semicircular stone staircase carpeted with thymes and Irish moss divides into a dramatic series of terraces. Sculptural masses of mugho pine and unusual junipers planted with yucca, bergenia and variegated iris are thickly underplanted with purple ajuga, glossy vinca, and hundreds of bulbs for the spring. *Clematis potentini fargessi* winds itself through a hydrangea. Little benches have been strategically placed wherever there is a sheltered spot or view to be enjoyed. Tucked away in a hidden corner among the shrubbery is a pergola with an inscription over the entrance that reads "To remember old times together," one of the many garden sayings that Jean has collected over the years.

The raised stone beds on each side of the main stairway are filled with colourful blooms, including a lovely collection of lilies, punctuated with exclamations of upright junipers suggestive of a Roman hillside.

A series of trellised arches, covered in honeysuckle, ivy and clematis lead through to the plateau garden, the highest point in Durham, where a collection of rhododendrons, heathers and ferns has just begun to take shape. Roses and perennials are tended in raised stone beds clustered round a thyme garden; in the centre sits an old farm buggy, now converted into a comfortable bench. The original white ash also has a bench encircling it, an invitation to linger awhile to catch your breath, absorb the view and renew the spirit.

Penny and Peter Norwood
416-469-5211 ext. 199
1 kilometre south of Clarksburg, near Thornbury
Conditions   zone 5b; sandy loam. sloped
Open through Woodgreen Community Centre, third Saturday of June, second-last Saturday of August

Perennial and shade gardens, folly

This garden, which was designed by David Tomlinson, gives great pleasure to Penny and Peter Norwood as it continues to develop.

To the left of the long climbing driveway is a small orchard and to the right are beds filled with day lilies and hollyhocks. Throughout the garden a variety of perennial bushes, conifers and deciduous trees are lovingly cared for by Peter. Concealed by an archway grown over with ferns is the vegetable garden, and hiding behind this is Penny's little trial nursery.

A walkway around the back of the house reveals a developing rock garden, and in a far corner is Penny's folly, a mini temple of Dionysius, where a fountain splashes into the pale marble pond ... not for lilies, and certainly not for the birds, but for the Norwoods' tired feet at the end of a gardening day.

Brian Folmer, *Extensive Landscaping*
RR 3 Walkerton, ON, N0G 1K0
519-366-2366
4 kilometres west of Walkerton on Highway 9, on north side of road;
look for sign for Brian W. Folmer
Conditions   zone 5; Harrison loam, rolling topography, varied
Plot size   105-acre farm; 20 acres landscaped
Open May 1 to December 24

❧ **Formal gardens, perennial beds, wildflower meadows, water gardens, garden centre**

I have not seen this new garden of Brian Folmer's, as it will not be open until April 1996. However, he has ambitions to make it into one of the foremost gardens and nurseries in Ontario.

Thousands of ground covers have been planted in the formal gardens around the house, situated in a parklike setting with large shrub and perennial beds and mature trees; the ground covers gradually meld into the natural surrounding plantings of wildflower meadows, native trees and dense shrubberies. Trails and walkways have been laid to access the natural features of the property, including a spring-fed pond, coldwater trout stream, wetlands, pastures and hardwood forest, and thousands of spring bulbs have been planted throughout.

Brian tells me that although the gardens are relatively new, they look mature as a result of dense planting and the incorporation of mature perennials and new shrubs.

Chepstow

Chepstow Country Inn
519-366-2274
Lunch, afternoon tea, dinner, daily 11:30 to 10.

Durham

Cosy Corners
Highway 6
519-369-6556
Monday to Saturday 8 to 9, Sundays 8 to 8.

Flesherton

Munshaw's Café Restaurant
1 Toronto Street
519-924-2814
Lunch and dinner; classical music, light jazz, smoke-free.

Thornbury

Picky Palate
10 Louise Street
519-599-6548
Lunch and tea; Monday to Saturday 8 to 4, Sunday 9 to 4.

Walkerton

Dunkeld Hotel
6.4 kilometres north of Walkerton on County Road 3
519-881-0479
Lunch, afternoon tea, dinner; Sunday brunch 11 to 2:30.

Hamilton Region: Ancaster / Burlington / Dundas / Greensville / Hamilton

ANCASTER

🚪 Ron and Joan Slade

905-648-6810

Wilson Street between Highway 403 and Fiddlers Green Road

Conditions   zone 6; sandy, slight uphill grade

Plot size   70 x 425 feet

Open by appointment; donation to charity appreciated as entrance fee

❧ Woodland stream with woodland planting, waterfall and pond

Across a curving lawn, past colourful flower beds gorgeous in their array of stately delphiniums, spikes of golden lysimachia, and lilies, is a fish pond — complete with splashing waterfall — protected by a luxuriant swamp cedar hedge. Planted forty years ago, the hedge has been carefully pruned of its bottom branches to afford a tantalizing glimpse into the garden beyond, known as the woods. The sound of birdsong beckons you down a flagstone path lined with ivy and ferns, under a canopy of flowering tulip tree (*Liriodendron*) and maple, to an aviary of glinting tropical finches. A brook winds through a shadowy glade between tamarisk and spruce, its banks covered in wildflowers and ferns, astilbes, hostas and feathery *Corydalis lutea*. A weathered bench invites you to sit and observe the variety of wild birds and animals who come to drink and bathe in this enchanted place.

Through an arbour covered in a froth of silver lace vine leading from the woods the garden opens up to the full sun, to where Joan has been gradually increasing her perennial collection to create a predominantly pink, silver and blue effect. Around the fence of the large vegetable garden, deeply scalloped beds filled with lilies, astilbes, roses, bee balm and phlox are connected by a little bridge under which flows a stream of purple ajuga. Majestic cedars interplanted with spruce are a lovely foil for the silvery caryopteris and buddleia. Wherever one turns there is something pleasing for the eye. From the arrival of the first spring snowdrop till the last autumn leaf, Joan Slade finds her garden takes precedence over everything else.

BURLINGTON

Royal Botanical Gardens
Box 388, Hamilton, ON, L8N 3H8
905-527-1158; fax 905-577-0375
680 Plains Road West
*Open: all garden areas daily, mid-April through Thanksgiving, 9:30 to 6,
Mediterranean Garden daily, October through mid-April 9 to 5; wheelchair
access in most areas*

The motto of the Royal Botanical Gardens is "where art and science meet." The gardens and conservation areas, which together cover almost 2,700 acres, make up one of the great research facilities of North America, encompassing woodlands, meadows, a shallow lake, marsh, agricultural land and ornamental displays.

The Laking Garden has one of the largest and most comprehensive collections of irises in the world. Hundreds of varieties of peonies, colourful perennials and ornamental grasses fill the many beds from spring to late fall.Hendrie Park hosts thousands of roses, a scented garden, a trial clematis garden and a medicinal garden; the arboretum spreads out over 40 acres, and its stunning lilac collection attracts thousands of visitors. It is also home to a wide variety of flowering trees such as dogwood, magnolias and redbuds. The magnificent Rock Garden, with its ponds and dramatic rock formations, is planted with over 90,000 tulips for the spring show; these are followed by summer annuals, begonias and a stunning display of colourful impatiens.

Many interesting and educational programs also attract people of all ages. The Royal Botanical Garden is the finest public garden in the province of Ontario.

DUNDAS

Pamela Norman
905-627-7439
Old Dundas
Conditions   zone 6; amended soil, flat
Plot size   1/3 acre
Open by appointment

❧ Pretty country garden

The wooden house with its green and white verandah, which has been standing in the heart of old Dundas since 1915, is set off to perfection by the pretty "granny" garden of old-fashioned favourites planted in sweet disarray beside a cobblestone path.

The lush woodland garden at the back is filled with ferns, wildflowers and hostas. A procession of peonies, iris and roses wends its way down a dynamic 240-foot freeform bed, their colours and patterns reflected in the textiles that Pamela Norman dyes and prints in her studio.

Four cats, two dogs and a "mower mad" husband have not deterred her from gardening, which she sees as an extension of her art.

GREENSVILLE

Andrew and Helen Brink, *The Green*
416-469-5211 ext. 199

Conditions   zone 5a; loam over limestone
Plot size   about 2 acres
Open through Woodgreen Community Centre, last weekend of May

❧ Organic, perennial gardens, orchard, vegetable gardens, artist's studio

History fills every corner of this fine heritage property. It sighs in the wind that blows across the lawn through the old apple orchard, whispering its secrets to the lilacs and moss roses planted sometime in the middle of the nineteenth century. Situated on a rise of ground, the rubble and limestone house with its board-and-batten annex appears, except for the modern greenhouse, much as it did when it was first built around 1821.

Since moving here in 1962, the Brinks have nurtured this evocative site, gradually landscaping the garden that slopes down to a small stream, where one ancient apple tree from the original orchard still stands. Cross the wooden bridge and stepping stones over the water to the young orchard, carpeted in spring with drifts of daffodils, blue *Anemone blanda* and a gradually returning show of wildflowers. In the wet area below the springs, a bog garden is developing, as are three well-stocked perennial beds. As you walk, look for the Latin inscription on the spring wall, which translates as "Where were those who went before us in this world?" referring to the ancient inhabitants of this place as well as the more recent pioneers of Flamborough.

Produce from the vegetable garden and eggs from the hens feed the family for most of the year. Weeds are not considered the enemy, and no toxic pesticides or artificial fertilizers have been used here for at least thirty-five years. It is a lived-in garden, enjoyed but never finished.

Helen is a potter who is happy to open her garden and studio to anyone who is interested. The two other gardens in this street are also artists' gardens, and arrangements can be made to visit all three on the same day.

Mary Anastasia Crowe, *Atelier Marianastasia*
905-627-3121

Conditions	zone 5a; Niagara Escarpment, lime, clay, rock
Plot size	1/3 acre

Open by appointment

Small pond, waterfall, rock garden, gazebo

The hues of the tangle of flowers in this pretty little cottage garden are reflected in the watercolours painted by its owner, artist Mary Anastasia Crowe.

A narrow path threads its way up a gently sloping rock garden to a gazebo, fountain and shady patio surrounded by lushly planted woodland. A cutting bed and clematis-covered arbours provide many of the flowers needed for her paintings, which she often exhibits in the garden.

HAMILTON

Anna and Ed Hobson, *The Cliff*
416-469-5211 ext. 199
Hamilton Escarpment

Conditions	zone 6b; clay, flat
Plot size	2 acres

Open through Woodgreen Community Centre, last weekend of May, second weekend of June, first weekend of July and some September weekends

❧ Rose garden, formal white garden, rhododendron and primula walk

At the end of a hidden lane high on the Escarpment sits a gracious 1860s stone house, its garden an evocation of a bygone era of tea on the lawn and the gentle *click* of croquet mallets. Ed Hobson is a traditionalist with a passion for plants and Victorian antiques. Anna is an artist who, besides deciding where Ed's impulse buys should be placed, likes to "get her hands dirty." The result is in an enchanting series of enclosures, at once relaxed, sophisticated and romantic. "The garden is a personal journey both forward and back, and so full of remembrances," says Anna.

Billowing white hawthorn, purple lilac, and the blossoms of graceful dogwoods (*Cornus florida*), underplanted with hundreds of tiny bulbs, line the driveway in spring. Along the front of the house a box hedge borders a grouping of iris and yellow peonies, and curving freeform beds snake across the lawn, planted mainly for spring and autumn interest. Under a jack pine Anna has created a shade garden of trilliums, tree peonies, weigelia and hostas. Circled by a grass path edged with lilac, the statue of a shy Venus shelters under the snowballs of *Viburnum opulus*. A collection of clematis, including *Clematis montana*, its starry pink flowers draped over the tennis court railing, leads to the rhododendron dell, a breathtaking sight for the last two weeks in May. Azaleas, dogwood, and magnificent specimens of *Viburnum plicatum*, *Liriodendron* and oak are heavily underplanted with a lovely collection of primulas, heathers, bulbs and anemones.

In mid-June the rose walk comes into its own, a glorious sight with twin borders edged in lavender, stretching a hundred feet or more to a lattice pergola covered in clematis. The air is sweet with the fragrance of 150-old-shrub roses collected from all over the world.

A flight of stone steps leads to the formal garden at the back of the house, with its view over the spectacular panorama of Hamilton Bay. Tall yew hedges and symmetrical beds with clipped box edgings make a wonderful foil for the white flowers that fill the beds.

The 95-foot-long perennial border is Ed's domain, beginning its long season of colour variations in early summer with *Eremurus* (foxtail lily), onopordums, delphiniums, lilies, veronicas, coneflowers and more, continuing in quick succession. "Beware the gardener who says it is finished," says Anna. "For none of us can recreate that first and perfect Eden, but to try is at least a step in the right direction and a continuous joy."

||||||| Harvey Sobel

905-528-1913 (business); 905-528-7973 (home)
Conditions   zone 6b; amended from red clay to loam
Plot size   50 x 120 feet
Open by appointment; donation to Hamilton Aids Network appreciated as entrance fee

❧ **Beautiful design and planting, interesting ornaments**

Harvey Sobel's mother was a florist in Toronto, and it was she who encouraged him to create his first arrangement for competition at the age of five — tissue sprayed with spinach, and perfumed with her Evening in Paris cologne! It won a prize and he's been designing ever since. Now one of Canada's foremost designers, he has created with his own garden a notable manifestation of his talent.

He bought his charming Ontario cottage over thirty years ago, and created this jewel of a garden which is designed to give pleasure all year long with minimal maintenance. A deceptively simple formal courtyard of immaculately clipped box hedges, divided by formal brick pathways and lined with rhododendrons and azaleas, combines effortlessly with the natural surroundings. At the top of a flight of stone stairs, reflected in an trellised mirror, stands a magnificent bronze statue of Mercury, a single red tulip at his feet. At the highest point of the garden, hidden from view, Harvey and friends can dine by the light of a lantern suspended from the vine-clad pergola, seeming so far away from busy Hamilton.

Emphasis has been placed on the play of texture, colour and form, with trees and shrubs such as weeping beech, and graceful laburnum, with its dripping yellow pannicles. The grotesque yet charming terra cotta benches, antique fountain, and fragmented artefacts have all been chosen with the unerring eye of an artist.

Outside the bedroom window Harvey has transformed what was once a courtyard into a woodland glade. English ivy makes the link to the rest of the garden, and is a perfect foil for the white oval disks of *Viburnum plicatum*, blooming beside a crimson maple. A pink redbud glows against the dark green trellis covered in wisteria. A moss-covered rock pool has been strategically placed for birds to perch and drink. Harvey is never happier than here in this haven of peace.

||||||| Kay and Tad Suzuki
905-389-9735
Hamilton Mountain

Conditions   zone 6b; heavy clay, flat
Plot size   100 x 170 feet
Open by appointment

❧ Herbaceous perennial border, iris collection

For Kay Suzuki, gardening is a full-time mania. Describing herself as a "collector of plants," she began, twenty-five years ago, by planting her "must haves" wherever she could find a spot, and over the years the garden grew "like Topsy."

The magnificent perennial border, 12 by 100 feet blooming in full sun from May to October, is at its best in July, although when I saw it on a golden September day, it was still full of colour and interest from the sculptural acanthus leaves, jewel-like asters, boltonias, aconitums, and masses of the pink and blue lisianthus that Kay loves so much. She is an inveterate seed collector and grows many unusual annuals. I particularly like the soft red pompoms of *Gomphrena* Strawberry Fields, but her pride and joy is *Salvia patens* Oxford Blue, glowing like a stained-glass window in the afternoon light.

From early May onward, the extensive iris border at the north end of the property swells with wave after wave of colour. As the charming miniatures fade, standard dwarf beardeds take their place, and then in June the breathtakingly beautiful tall beardeds bloom along with the Siberians, and finally the Spurias continue the display. A raised acid bed houses the elegant Japanese irises, followed by acid-loving Oriental lilies.

A stroll around the central island bed reveals roses of every kind, shade-loving primulas under a canopy of a *Euonymous alatus* that is smothered in alpine clematis and intertwined with *Codonopsis clematidea*. In the early spring hundreds of bulbs and wildflowers gladden the eye. Petasites, a Japanese delicacy, is grown and harvested not only to keep it under control, but also for the delicacy of its stalks, which bear a marked resemblance to rhubarb.

Kay's husband, Tad, who claims to be her "two-legged mule," looks after the compost mountain and vegetable garden. For Kay the work is endless but well worth it; visions of sipping mint julep on a lazy summer afternoon will have to wait for another year.

Jean and Bruce Wright, *Elysium*
905-627-0353
Dundas

Conditions	zone 6b; clay, ravine
Plot size	18 acres, 2 acres cultivated

Open by appointment, two weeks' notice for groups

Pond, streams and waterfall, perennial beds, woodland

Toward the end of an undulating country road lie 18 glorious acres of Carolinian ravine valley property. Spring flowers and bulbs and then ferns and hostas line the steep clay-banked driveway that sweeps up to the Bavarian-style house, the home of artist Jean Wright and her husband, Bruce.

Two acres of gardens with almost 400 cultivars of perennials are set off by ponds, bog gardens and streams. Espaliered apple and pear trees, bittersweet, Japanese wisteria and silver lace vine decorate the large hexagonal pergola that overlooks the lily pond and stream. On a knoll not far from the house, look for an old beech tree carved with the initials of early settlers who lived here.

Jean has applied her talent as a watercolourist to her garden, and nowhere better than in her imaginative use of the "leftover" perennials. The colours and textures of Jacob's ladder, bergamot, monkshood and lilies blend perfectly with the indigenous woodland plants lining the paths that wind down through the three ravines to a fast-flowing stream and waterfall.

This is an ongoing project, combining the preservation of birds, animals and forest plants with the cultivated gardens. The next challenge is to build a Japanese garden. "The fun," says Jean, "is in the making."

Whitehern Garden
41 Jackson Street West, Hamilton, ON, L8P 1L3
905-546-2018
Jackson Street and McNab Street
Open June 15 to Labour Day, daily 11 to 4; Labour Day to June 14, 1 to 4, closed Mondays, Christmas and New Year's Day; small entrance fee; limited wheelchair access

Once described as an oasis in a downtown desert, this garden has been evolving since the late 1840s. The present layout of the garden was developed by H. B. Dunington-Grubb in the 1930s. Distinctive iron flowers "growing" from the stone walls surrounding Whitehern draw the attention of passers-by. Within these stone walls is a terraced garden of shrubs and fruit trees. A friendly and knowledgeable costumed staff conduct seasonal and educational programs and garden tours year-round.

Ancaster

Old Mill Inn
548 Old Dundas Road
905-648-1827
Buffet luncheon, Monday to Friday.

Burlington

Royal Botanical Gardens
680 Plains Road West
905-527-1158
Cafeteria in Rose Garden, Turner Pavilion, April 24 to Thanksgiving 9:30 to 6; Rock Garden Tea House, June to Labour Day 9:30 to 6; Garden Cafe in Main Centre open year-round.

London

▦ Shirley Andreae

416-469-5211 ext. 199; 519-657-3919

Conditions   zone 6; edge of a moraine, flat pasture, valley, woods

Plot size   56 acres

Open through Woodgreen Community Centre, Saturday before last in June; and September, by appointment with owner

❧ **Lovely setting, extensive perennial borders, shade garden**

Early in the morning, as the mist rolls away from the meadow and the sun comes up over the pond, Shirley Andreae likes to take her cup of coffee and sit in the peony garden watching the deer nibbling at the fruit trees. This idyllic country garden reflects the gentle, gracious personality of its owner.

As the days becomes warmer, meals are taken in the shade of the gnarled old grapevine that twines its way along the verandah, beside the lovely borders filled with larkspur, day lilies and glowing Oriental poppies. From spring to late frost a procession of perennials makes a continual show of colour, attracting a great diversity of birds and butterflies.

A stroll down a shady path in the early evening leads to the romantic garden, where Shirley relaxes under a canopy of lilac and crabapple. Continue through fern and astrantia, meadow rue and feathery astilbe to where a lichen-covered bench is surrounded by a pool of periwinkle. An ancient willow weeps here, and the fields beyond stretch away to the distance, making this the perfect spot to enjoy the setting of the sun. Across the lawn, a sequestered garden offers up its charming secrets, including *Lilium regale* and wine red spheres of *Allium cerecephalum*.

"It's the physical and mental challenge of it all that add to my joy of gardening," says Shirley, who has created a truly magical place.

▦ Sally Bryant

519-433-3317; summer weekends 705-635-3877

Conditions   zone 6; sandy, flat

Plot size   100 x 200 feet

Open by appointment

❧ Summer house, arbours, shrubs, hedges

The Bryants began to garden here in 1981, and ten years later involved the talents of the late great landscaper David Thomson to "pull it all together." Flagstone and grassy paths have been used extensively throughout the garden to demarcate the various enclosures. An arbour on the west side of the house is covered in New Dawn rose and leads to the long shrub border, adorned with a show of blossom in the spring from flowering dogwoods, laburnum and the lovely magnolia Rikkii. Halfway down the border Sally has planted a semicircle of young pleached lindens, otherwise known as "stilt hedge," interspersed with yew. Below the large terrace at the back of the house is a boxwood parterre interplanted with lavender; beside it another mature box hedge circles a white rose garden filled with Little White Pet rose and the graceful everblooming Iceberg rose.

Further on, a sunny oval lawn is bordered by pastel-coloured perennials that are, in turn, set off by a dramatic arc of tall clipped yews. The formality of this planting is accentuated by topiaried holly and four elegant urns planted with blue-flowered agapanthus.

The garden is full of lovely features: garden seats, wooden trellises and frames to support the many climbers, as well as a charming summer house half hidden by the hops and climbing roses.

Cuddy Farms
519-245-1592
Strathroy: 20 minutes from London

Conditions   zone 6; heavy clay, compost and mulch, flat
Plot size   20 acres gardens, 120 acres landscaped grounds
Open by appointment, contact The Foreman, Cuddy Farms (519-245-1592, fax 519-245-5916); advance notice required; large groups can be accommodated; donation to the Strathroy Horticultural Society appreciated

Water garden, formal gravel garden, rock garden, perennial border

This magnificent property is a private estate with the atmosphere of an English country manor. Designed by David Thomson, the garden is planted and maintained by Mike Pascoe and a staff of six who have filled the extensive grounds with 30,000 narcissi; approximately 20,000 minor bulbs and 2,000 species of plants have currently been catalogued.

At the side of the house, behind a rose-covered trellis, the sound of water from a fountain can be heard as it cascades into the pretty courtyard pool. Across the sculpted lawns and past plantings of rare magnolias, an elegant sunken garden and rock garden have been created with natural stone for the low stone walls and steps — a perfect foil for the ornamental grasses, herbs and foliage plants planted here. Just beyond this point, a long herbaceous border houses a lush collection of day lilies together with a wide variety of perennials.

Take time to wander through the lilac dell and shady woodland garden where wildflowers grow between hostas and ferns, and notice the cedar benches, vine-clad pergolas, rose arbours and English statuary that add beauty, grace and architectural interest to this gracious property.

▦ Lee Goossens
519-663-9377
Conditions   zone 6; flat
Open by appointment

❧ **Perennial borders, lovely design, interesting water feature**

T his marvellous house was built in the 1930s as a replica of an English parsonage, and almost all the materials were imported from England, except for the beautiful slate roof, which came from Scotland. With its mullioned windows, angled bricks and stone gables, and leering gargoyles, it could be mistaken for something out of a gothic novel.

Lee Goossens worked together with the late David Thomson, the highly talented garden designer, to plan a garden that enhanced the English atmosphere. Care was taken to ensure that the full view could never be seen at the one time, allowing the mystery of the place to unravel slowly. A white redbud (*Cercis canadensis alba*) and a graceful silver bell stand on ivy-carpeted slopes that curve away from each side of the front door. A Japanese maple turns a brilliant red in autumn, and the straplike leaves of *Hosta lancifolia* planted throughout add lushness.

The original wooden gate, with its distinctive design and copper flashing, leads to the back garden where a very different story unfolds. Between the gate and the slope stands a magnificent magnolia, a banner of spring for the whole neighbourhood when it unfurls its flowers at the end of May. A sense of nostalgia fills this charming garden, where urns are filled with lilies and white geraniums and herbs self-seed among the pebbles. On either side of the cedar arbour edging the green lawn, two borders — one hot, one cool — are filled with showy perennials. Through an arch in the charming stick fence, an old-fashioned pebble walkway planted in silvers and soft pastels leads to a sunken stone garden. Here, ingeniously, three Chinese egg bowls, filled with water, seem to be floating in a sea of lilyturf (*Liriope*). The walkway continues through ivy and periwinkle under the shade of a Norway spruce.

In the middle of it all sits an antique iron bench. Where better to sit and enjoy the flowering dogwoods, statuary and other hidden delights of this place? Lee walks through his garden several times a day; he sees it as a testament to his childhood memories and his heritage.

Harry and Joyce McGee, *Rosebank*
41 Outer Drive, Lambeth, ON, N0L 1S3
519-652-5728

Conditions   zone 6b; topsoil over sand; level terrain
Plot size   1/2 acre
Open by appointment; admission charge for large bus tours

 Roses, lilies, irises, pergolas, lily pond

E verything's coming up roses." At Rosebank there are more than 350 of them, of every shape and size — the passion of Harry McGee's life — English Austin roses, climbers, shrubs, old damasks, albas, bourbons and two that are extremely rare, known only in Tadjikstan, *Rosa aitkinsonii* and *Rosa maracandia*.

The garden is designed on the Celtic cross, laid out in flagstone; the principal view north reflects the McGees' ancestry, while at the centre, a circle, signifying eternity, encloses a water-lily pool stocked with koi and goldfish. The formal design of the garden is as interesting in winter, when the blood-red hips of the roses drip into the snow, as it is in summer bloom.

The cross effectively divides the main garden into quadrants, each planted in a different colour spectrum. June brings a gorgeous bouquet of pinks, blues, apricots, dazzling oranges, shrimps and salmons; the pergolas, sheltering three sides of the property, are covered with climbers and a rare rambler, *Rosa* Patricia Macoun, repatriated from Germany in 1995.

Roses are not the only thing growing here, however. Joyce McGee loves perennials and has developed a pair of crescent-shaped gardens, one focused on a bubbling fountain and the other on a sundial, filled with a magnificent collection of lilies and irises, alstroemeria and hundreds of bulbs that bloom from spring, beginning with the snowdrops and fritillarias and ending in late fall with a flourish of *Colchicum* Autumn Major.

Sitting in the evening under an arbour covered in pink wisteria and Concord grape, listening to the sound of the splashing fountain, the McGees look back at the glowing colours, admiring the fruits of their hard work, and know they're alive by the garden's continuing existence.

Louise Weekes

439 Pinetree Drive, London, ON, N6H 3M9
519-471-2235

Conditions	zone 6; clay, loam; flat
Plot size	80 x 180 feet

Open by appointment; plants for sale

❧ **Perennials, pool, troughs, peony collection, alpines and bulbs**

From the moment you arrive at Louise Weekes's unique front yard, you know that an addicted gardener has been at work. A narrow grass path, the only remnant of lawn remaining, snakes between rectangular beds packed with colour. Lining the driveway, eighty or more peonies and tree peonies make a stunning sight in early summer.

Over the past twenty years Louise has had to use all her ingenuity to create enough space on this average-size suburban lot to house her extraordinary collections of day lilies, hostas, alliums, ornamental grasses, hardy geraniums and bergenias. Despite the fact that she "crams it in," as she puts it, the plants are arranged so that their similarities and differences are revealed, and some very interesting and unusual plant associations have evolved.

As well as importing large number of bulbs, she raises many perennials and alpines from seed when they are difficult to find, and has had great fun trading with people of like mind over the years. A few of her favourite plants worth looking for are *Acanthus spinosus*, *Begonia grandis*, *Brunnera* Hadspen Cream, *Clematis macropetala* Maidwell Hall, *Nepeta phyllochlamys*, *Gillenia trifoliata* and *Primula* Kisoana.

A very large vegetable garden is jealously guarded by her husband from any encroachment by Louise — a very real threat, as there is absolutely no more space. Some may call it a magnificent muddle but Louise calls its heaven. She is an inspiration to garden lovers one and all.

Marlene and Cameron Colquhoun, *The Lavender Path*
416-469-5211 ext. 199
Conditions   zone 6/7; sandy loam
Plot size   city lot
Open through Woodgreen Community Centre, third weekend of August

Formal trellised garden

Situated at a busy intersection in Dorchester, these colourful gardens surround three sides of a picture-postcard 1910 Edwardian home and are a real showstopper for passersby. A spectacular sweep of Munstead lavender skirts immaculate beds full of imaginatively chosen annuals. The theme of the annuals changes every year, and any lawn that remains is fast being replaced with more and more flower beds.

In 1994 the Colquhouns designed an original and stylish formal court-yard garden on the west side of the house, fulfilling many of Marlene's dreams. Enclosed by a lovely white lattice fence modelled after the one they saw at Butchart Gardens in Victoria, BC, generously proportioned raised beds house perennials and shrubs together in one of the prettiest vegetable gardens I have seen. Gladioli, for cutting, line the back fence where runner beans have been allowed to twine through roses and clematis that are beginning to cover the lattice. Boulders covered in sedums and nasturtiums surround a central quadrant that can be entered from either side through vine-covered arches. At the moment it is full of fragrant herbs, but as with so much of this garden, they are still experimenting. Cameron is planning a peony border along the boundary of the fence, and lilac trees have been planted in the hope that when they have matured, Marlene can lie under them to dream some more.

Eldon House
481 Ridout Street North, London, ON, N6A 2P9
519-672-4580
Open Tuesday to Sunday 9 to 5; closed Mondays and Christmas Day;
nominal entrance fee, no charge on Tuesdays; some wheelchair access

Eldon House is the oldest residence in London. Biennials and perennials fill the long borders at the front of the house, and the cutting garden at the back is devoted to annuals and perennials. The rose garden bursts with the colours and scents of traditional roses. Look for the gold-fish pond in the rock garden.

In this romantic setting under the magnolia trees, staff in period costume serve traditional afternoon tea with scones and all the trimmings. Watch for special events in the garden, from June to September.

Harvey and Irene Wrightman, *Wrightman Alpines*
519-247-3751
Conditions   zone 6b, rock with stone mulch
Open: visitors are welcome by appointment only; the garden is part of the nursery business

Alpine nursery, crevice garden, rock garden

Some years ago Harvey Wrightman gave up a career in teaching and he and his wife opened this interesting garden and nursery, specializing in alpines and rock plants.

For Harvey, the most fascinating of all the different areas that have been created here is the Crevice Garden, which he built with the help of Josef Halda from the Czech Republic, one of the leading lights in the world of alpine plants and their propogation. It is constructed on an incline of stacked, paved limestone, and pockets in the vertical fissures of the rocks created have been planted with many unusual species as well as with stock plants sold in the nursery. These include *Dionysia* alpine convulvulus and alpine daphnes, as well as dwarf conifers, saxifragas and other precious gems.

Beside the house is an impressive dryland granite rock garden with a stone mulch and a small reflecting pool. Growing here are drought-loving dwarf penstemons, dwarf irises, both the junos and the onclocyclus, and the pretty campanula-like flowered edraianthus.

Josef Halda's expeditions to Central Asia, Siberia and Mongolia in search of new material furnish Harvey with new plant and seed materials that share the same latitude and climate as this area. These are used in extensive trials carried out in the nursery, and the ones that succeed in braving the Ontario climate are eventually propogated and sold here.

If you're looking for something a little out of the ordinary, then Wrightman's is the place to go. A detailed catalogue is available, listing the extensive selection of rock and alpine plants the Wrightmans sell by mail order.

London

Eldon House
481 Ridout Street North
519-672-4580
Traditional afternoon tea is served June 25 to September 5, Tuesday
through Sunday, 2 to 4.

Home Restaurant
King Street
519-438-5122
Lunch 11:30 to 2, dinner 5:30 to 9:30; closed Sunday and Monday.

Tapas on King
King Street
519-679-7800
Lunch and dinner; closed Sunday.

Sunflower Café
King Street
519-645-6488
Outdoor café; daily in summer 8 to 7:30.

Marysville / Morrisburg / Napanee

MARYSVILLE

**|||||| Harlan and Maureen House
RR 1 Marysville, Village of Lonsdale, ON, K0K 2N0
613-396-3513
Conditions   zone 5; limestone, slightly sloped
*Open garden and studio tour first two weekends of May, by appointment;
photography by permission only*

❧ Bedrock gardens

Harlan House is one of Canada's finest potters; Maureen is the plantswoman who, according to Harlan, is "the memory and brain" of the pair. Both their talents are evident in this organic garden. If they had to do it all again, they would ask for good soil and water; it is, however, the lack of these elements that makes their garden so unique.

The fissures in the limestone rocks at the bottom of the studio steps overflow from spring to the end of July with a succession of bulbs and perennials. The bright flowers enhance the beautiful jade green pond, in the centre of which lurks a fierce porcelain fishlike creature, one of Harlan's extraordinary creations.

Harlan built a large vaulted structure as a birdhouse where peacocks and guinea fowl roam, and beside it, a large, free-flowing perennial bed spills into the lawn, stocked with a diversity of plant material. A ceramic sculpture of Neptune holds a boat above his head while guarding the raised peony bed — as good a place to guard as any, I suppose.

At the side of the property, limestone terraces are complemented by prostrate Colorado spruce and flowers of white, silver and palest pink, including lilies, Japanes anemones, artemisias, delicate acidanthra, day lilies and a mass of white cleomes.

The Houses are constantly amazed as they walk round their gardens at just how much is possible in their garden despite its limitations.

MORRISBURG

▦ Jeff Arsenault, *The Garden*
17 Casselman Road, Box 1329, Morrisburg, ON, K0C 1X0
613-543-3960
Morrisburg: South of Highway 2, east of Highway 31,
Open mid-May to end of first weekend of October, 8:30 to dusk

❧ **Gazebo, bridge, fish pond, found objects**

"Welcome to the Garden," boldly proclaimed on the sign hanging from a bed headboard, invites callers in at the entrance to Jeff Arsenault's inventive garden.

Jeff's original vision was of a garden on a much larger scale than he could fund, and since necessity is the mother of invention, the vision became a reality by filling the garden with finds from "shopping" trips to landfill sites and dumping areas and visits to the banks of the nearby St. Lawrence River to collect rocks. A wooden footbridge spans a large fishpond, whose surface is decorated with lily pads. Well-defined pathways made from old house bricks lead through colourful beds crammed with perennials and annuals. Giant baskets of geraniums hang from a gazebo handcrafted from cedar wood, and across the lawn a generous rose bed is framed by a pergola draped in grape vines.

Jeff's "old backyard" has been tranformed into a showcase, and as a result of television and newspaper coverage, this unique garden has attracted many visitors.

🏛 Queen Elizabeth Gardens
Crysler Farm Battlefield Park, Morrisburg, ON
613-543-3704
11 kilometres east of Morrisburg, off Highway 2, near the entrance to Upper Canada Village
Open Victoria Day weekend to Thanksgiving weekend, dawn to dusk; wheelchair access

To commemorate the visit of Queen Elizabeth II to Ontario in 1984, the Province and the St. Lawrence Parks Commission presented these gardens as a gift to Her Majesty. A sunken rose garden, antique rose garden and wildflower area have been created in Crysler Farm Battlefield Park, where, in 1813, a Canadian contingent joined British Regulars in a battle against American forces.

NAPANEE

Allan Macpherson House and Park
Box 183, 180 Elizabeth Street, Napanee, ON, K73 3M3
613-354-5982
Open gardens accessible at all times; house open March through June and September through December, Monday to Friday, 12 to 4:30; no fee for gardens; limited wheelchair access

The white picket fence and pots of cheerful pansies at the front door of this charming home welcome you into a bygone era. Hollyhocks and other old-fashioned perennials grace the borders around the property, and the well-tended vegetable garden with its fragrant herbs is a replica of the garden that existed in the 1800s. A sundial was recently installed in the Lady's Garden, renamed the Helen Hutchison Memorial Garden in recognition of her work in restoring this lovely park.

Standing in the meadow looking down on the windfall of lime green apples, my eyes were drawn to the algae-covered pool and the river beyond stretching away into the distance, a scene little changed, I should imagine, from the one the Scottish settlers first set eyes on all those years ago.

Morpeth

▥ Keith McLean
RR 1, Morpeth, ON, N0P 1X0
519-674-2225
From Highway 401 at Exit 101, travel south 13 kilometres to Highway
51; farm is near entrance to Rondeau Provincial Park
Open anytime; wheelchair access is limited

❧ **Ponds, lotus, rock garden, chrysanthemums**

K eith McLean is well into his seventies and as energetic as ever. He
has transformed the wetlands behind his farm buildings into four
huge lotus-filled ponds, surrounded by rolling lawns. Boardwalks and
observation decks have been built over the water, providing excellent
viewing of both the plants and the abundant wildlife.

The arboretum, rock garden and many flower beds, together with a
spectacular chrysanthemum show in the autumn, make for an interesting
outing, and Keith welcomes visitors.

Morpeth

The Plaza Restaurant
Intersection of Highways 3 and 21, northwest corner
519-674-3112
Open 9 to 8, closed Mondays.

The Old Lumber Yard
Highway 21 just north of Highway 3
519-674-1055
Open 8 to 9, closed Tuesdays.

Niagara Region: Grimsby / Niagara Falls / Niagara-on-the Lake

GRIMSBY

Steve and Darlene Allen-Roxburgh
11 Birchpark Drive, Grimsby, ON, L3M 4L4
905-945-9810
Conditions   zone 6; sandy
Open: Grimsby garden tour, Hamilton Spectator *garden tour, or by appointment*

Ponds, waterfalls, and strong design

A towering oak tree 100 feet tall with a circumference of 13 feet stood alone here when the Roxburghs first moved to this home; it was their inspiration and the beginning of their love affair with gardening.

A sense of mystery pervades this garden of deep shade and few flowers. As you stroll through the intricate network of flagstone walkways, horse sculptures, hand-painted fences and Japanese ornaments confront you at every turn. Toward the back of the garden, a subtle shift in attitude takes place, from the strict control of strongly sculptured plant material to a more natural, free-flowing environment. Water is everywhere, gushing from a hole in the rocks, trickling down a stream, spouting from a three-tiered fountain, and filling a large fishpond, home to a variety of life, including rosi reds, turtles and Japanese koi. An additional pond contains a large variety of plants, and last but not least, a single freefall of water cascades approximately 5 feet into a catch basin, creating a dramatic punch bowl effect. This garden is a fine demonstration of the ingenuity and imagination of two talented landscapers.

NIAGARA FALLS

Centennial Lilac Gardens
2.5 kilometres north of Niagara Parks Botanical Gardens, just north of
the Floral Clock
Open daily, dawn to dusk; limited wheelchair access

There are 1,000 lilac shrubs representing over 250 varieties planted in
this 10-acre garden. A recent addition to the garden is a rhododendron collection, which blooms contemporaneously with the lilacs. A
prairie grass meadow is developing around the park. May and June are
the best months to visit.

Fragrance Garden
South of Canadian Horseshoe Falls, just north of Niagara Parks
Commission Greenhouse
Open daily, dawn to dusk; wheelchair access

A great variety of flowers chosen especially for their fragrance are
planted in this garden. The wide pathways accommodate wheelchairs. Braille labels are used for plant identification.

Niagara Parks Botanical Gardens
Niagara Parks Commission School of Horticulture and Butterfly
Conservatory
Box 150, Niagara Falls, ON, L2E 6T2
905-356-2241
8 kilometres north of the Falls
Open daily, sunrise to sunset; wheelchair access

With its heavy clay soil and rock outcroppings, this 100-acre property is a challenge to the students of horticulture who developed and
maintain the grounds as part of their studies. The Visitor Reception
Centre has a gift shop, washrooms and telephones. There you can pick
up a self-guiding map for walking tours that lead along pathways from
the centre. These include a rose garden; others include the annual gar-

den, lilac collection, iris border, rhododendron collection, woodland garden, rock garden, vegetable garden, white garden, perennial border, herb garden, specimen trees and the arboretum.

In the fall of 1996 an exciting addition to this location will be an 11,000-square-foot showcase butterfly conservatory, which will operate year-round. A network of pathways will wind through the building, allowing visitors to observe the butterflies feeding on nectar-producing flowers such as lantanas, pentas and passion flowers.

Oakes Garden Theatre and Rainbow Gardens
On the Parkway at Niagara Falls
Open year-round, dawn to dusk

There is an air of mystery to the sloping terraces of this amphitheatre with its stone walls, well-defined boxwood and yew hedges, vine covered lattices and lindens with their branches bent and intertwined. The rock garden, pool and stone bridge are of Oriental design. The Rainbow Gardens adjoining the theatre continue in the same formal fashion.

Queen Victoria Park
500 metres south of Canadian Horseshoe Falls
Open daily, dawn to dusk; wheelchair access

From spring until fall this park generates a blaze of glorious colour. Five hundred thousand daffodils bloom among the specimen trees in the spring. The rose garden in the centre of the park is home to an impressive 2,000 plants of all varieties. Dahlias, delphiniums and hollyhocks are a few of the other perennials to bloom before the fall show begins.

Rock Garden
South of Park Police Headquarters
Open year-round, dawn to dusk; wheelchair access

This garden, planted on limestone, changes with the seasons. The exquisite details of the tiny narcissus and snowdrops, the glorious colours of the dwarf iris, the miniature evergreens and the rich colours of the ground phlox are but a few of pleasures that unfold here each year.

Wayne Renaud and Gordon Webber, Mississauga

Barbara Bell, Toronto

Harvey Sobel, Hamilton

Spadina, Toronto
— WITH PERMISSION OF THE TORONTO HISTORICAL BOARD

Amanda McConnell, Toronto

Lee Goossens, London

Joyce and Harry McGee, London

Susan Collacott, Mississauga

Olivia and Chris Mills, Burritt's Rapids

Douglas Chambers, Durham

Parkwood Estate, Oshawa

Louise Weekes, London

Turid Forsyth, Elgin

Merike Lugus, Cobourg

Gerald Whyte, Riverdale

Gunhild and Johannes Dutt, Burritt's Rapids

Patricia and William Singer, Mississauga

David and Margaret Barham, Brampton

Phyllis Stewart, Oshawa

Joseph Covello, Brampton

Georg and Karen Maier, Durham

NIAGARA-ON-THE-LAKE

Isobel and Dick Davis
905-468-3548

Conditions   zone 6; good with green manuring
Plot size   double lot
Open fourth weekend of June, second weekend of September; 10 to 5

⁂ Fruit trees, evergreens and perennials

As a child Isobel Davis loved being outdoors gardening with her mother, and so she was quite up to the challenge of making a garden from this property, a treeless, neglected yard cluttered with years of refuse. More than just a green thumb was needed, however; tons of manure and a daunting amount of hard work have transformed this garden into a place of tranquillity and elegance. Symmetrical plantings of boxwood along the pathways, low stone walls, and an *allée* of Bradford pear trees are the bones of its strong design. An old apple tree spreads its lichen-covered branches over a flagstone patio, and an attractive weathered shed lend a rustic air. Eunonymous surrounds the ancient well, which has a ship's bell on top adding its charm. A stroll across the lawn brings one to the fishpond, hidden away in a shady spot among hostas, where ferns mix attractively with grasses. The Davises have created a sanctuary that seems light years away from the madding crowd.

Alan and Jeanette Earp
905-468-2606

Conditions   zone: 6b/7a; clay, flat
Plot size   75 x 100 feet
Open fourth weekend of June and second weekend of September, 10 to 5; otherwise by appointment

⁂ Strong design, lovely pond, original use of ground covers

The Earps planned this lovely garden in 1992 to complement architect David Snell's innovative house design. Their unerring sense of design and colour has resulted in a garden of masterly layout and skilful planting that encompasses every square inch of this corner lot.

Tightly woven ground covers carpet the Earp's unique front garden where tufted mounds and ferny fingers of foliage create a kaleidoscope of fast-changing colour and pattern. A drystone bed "flows" beside the house. The series of cleverly angled free-standing trellises planted with clematis along the boundary adds a vertical dimension, as well as valuable growing space.

A small screen of hedged hornbeams, whose russet leaves and interesting silhouette bring much to the winter landscape, shields the entrance to the English-style garden beyond, where a sense of gentle order prevails. The clever emphasis of the diagonal axis enlarges the sense of space as it thrusts out from the living room into the garden, across the diamond-shaped pond. The eye is drawn to the focal point of a four-seasons shrubbery, whose glorious display of bulbs, flowering dogwoods, rhododendrons and Japanese maples can be enjoyed from the house.

Odd touches of quirkiness, so much a part of British gardens, comes from plants chosen deliberately for their "wiggle." Two crooked pines, *Pinus takiosha* and a Temple hawk, were found in the orphanage area of a local plant nursery, and have been used as strong architectural features. The magnificent borrowed view makes a perfect backdrop for the David Austin roses that grow along the back trellises, including lovelies such as the slightly wild Lucetta, apricot Evelyn, and the dainty St. Cecilia Perle d'Azure. Arbours are covered in the rose Awakening, together with the silvery-blue clematis Perle d'Azur. Perennials of similar hues overflow the beds bordering the lawn, and unruly herbs near the back door are curbed by a neat box hedge. The attention to detail is meticulous, with imaginative touches such as pots filled with the fuzzy pink plumes of Pennisetum grass or an interesting chair used as a sculpture adding to the strong sense of design that runs through the entire garden.

Alan tells the story of a young woman, interested in how much time he spends in his garden. "I just enjoy puttering a little each day," he told her. "My father likes dithering in his garden," replied the young woman. "Madam," said Alan, with all the aplomb he could muster, "I can assure you there is a great deal of difference between dithering and puttering!"

Virginia and Jamie Mainprize
905-468-0000
Conditions　　　zone 6
Open fourth weekend of June and second weekend of September, 10 to 4; otherwise by appointment

❧ Pond, shade garden, perennial beds

This exquisite bed and breakfast has a garden to match. The flower beds of pink, white and blue perennials are interspersed with annuals to continue the flow of colour into late summer. A small pond with a low waterfall is surrounded by ferns, hosta, heuchera and primroses. A high trellis fence supporting roses and clematis separates the sun garden from the pool area, approached through an attractive wisteria-covered archway. Across the lawn a bench is invitingly place in the shade garden, a cool oasis of dark evergreens, the perfect companions for bulbs, pulmonarias, hostas and palest pink astilbes.

Virginia says she is a novice gardener but her success so far has encouraged and inspired her. As her knowledge increases she is spurred on to ever more ambitious plans.

▦ Lydia Szukis

905-468-2300

Conditions	zone 7a; deep sand, level land
Plot size	3/4 of an acre

Open by appointment; charge for organized tours

❧ Spring bulbs, perennials, flowering shrubs

A severe hailstorm nine years ago persuaded Lydia Szukis to remove the badly damaged peach orchard and realize her dream of creating a "park" of flowers and ornamental trees. Redbud, catalpa, paulownia, metasequoia, blue atlas cedar, Carolina silverbell and many more wonderful trees benefit from the climate of this area and the loving care of Master Gardener Lydia Szukis.

Everything here is lush and large. Pastel-coloured iris flank the drive, followed by a splendid collection of hosta; blooms of vivid blue *Clematis* Ramona and white *Clematis* Henryi climb the garage wall, and tight drumheads of *Primula denticulata* fill a bed in shades of pink and mauve. Apricot, deep wine and yellow rhododendrons present a stunning sight in front of the house and lining the long driveway. Huge beds brim with foxgloves, asphodels, poppies, penstemons and fat lupins, lovely companions for single peonies, thalictrums, and alliums. There is something in flower here for every season till the end of November, when the last rose drops its petals.

Lydia looks on the garden as a memorial to old friends and relatives who have given her seeds and snippings over the years. When day is done she to likes to walk the grassy paths in her "park," reacquainting herself with fond memories through the plants that thrive so well under her loving care.

[butterfly icon] Donald L. Combe
905-468-4175
Conditions   zone 7a; garden soil
Open by appointment

❧ **Pool, pollarded sycamores**

D onald Combe's gem of a garden is beautifully designed as an extension of his living space. As the pollarded sycamores change with the seasons, so does the appearance of this charming room, bright in springtime with bulbs and early blooming flowers, shaded in the summer with a canopy of green and carpeted in golden leaves in the autumn. The white blooms favoured by Donald accentuate the strong texture and tone of the rich greenery. High trellises and mature trees make this a private place, and the gentle sound of water in the tiny reflecting pool enhances the sense of tranquillity and beauty.

[butterfly icon] Lyall and Betty Crober
905-262-4331
Conditions   zone 7a; predominantly clay, very rocky, sloping
Plot size   100 x 350 feet
Open by appointment

❧ **Rhododendrons, evergreen and deciduous azaleas**

I n spite of the hazards of several large black walnuts and a butternut tree, Lyall and Betty Crober enjoy an interesting variety of rhododendrons in this mature garden sheltered by the Niagara Escarpment. After the forsythia and daffodils have finished, the rhododendrons and azaleas growing up the steeply wooded slope put on a magnificent show. Scattered among the evergreens are the charming flowering dogwood, redbuds and the graceful *Cornus alternifolia*, which seeds itself so readily. A variety of wildflowers provide colour all summer long.

Tom and Sharon Laviolette

905-468-3005

Conditions   zone 6; heavy clay, flat

Open second weekend of September 10 to 5; please phone; otherwise by appointment only; May is best for bulbs, August through November for grasses

❧ Bulbs and grasses

Tom Laviolette is the senior instructor for the Niagara School of Horticulture and is well known for his informative appearances on "The Guerilla Gardiner."

His is a garden for all seasons. Some 15,000 bulbs both major and minor celebrate the arrival of spring. Summer and fall sees a wealth of ornamental grasses and other perennials. Annuals and vines are allowed to self-seed. The garden is of low to medium maintenance, requiring minimal irrigation. If you visit you will have the added reward of an expert to answer any questions you may have concerning your own garden.

 Campbell Scott

905-468-3925

Conditions   zone 7; flat

Open by appointment

❧ Japanese water garden

Campbell Scott is an exceptional artist and designer who has created his own unique house and Japanese-inspired courtyard garden. The focal point in this tranquil setting of geometric pools is the glass gazebo with its canopy of Chinese blue wisteria. The fence is lined on one side with clematis, and on the other with trumpet vine and Oklahoma redbud. Pathways of polished pebbles set off Campbell's unique begonia-filled chimney-pot planters and a collection of Japanese violet, verbena, juniper and hostas.

 Angie Strauss

178 Victoria Street, Box 445, Niagara-on-the-Lake, ON, L0S 1J0

Conditions   zone 7; flat

Open any time, to be viewed from the street

❧ Japanese tree peonies, ferns

Angie and Hartley Strauss's turn-of-the-century Gothic farmhouse with its wisteria-covered porch and overflowing front garden is a real showstopper.

A white picket fence surrounds beds burgeoning with flowers of the richest shades, diverse in texture and pattern. Masses of tulips, daffodils and violets announcing the arrival of spring are followed by voluptuous Japanese tree peonies. Arbours covered in wild clematis and glorious perennials vie happily all summer long with masses of ferns, hostas, vinca and sweet woodruff. They are the inspiration for Angie's well-known paintings, reproduced on many products sold all over North America. Do pay a visit to her shop a block away on the main street.

 Bruce and Cheryl Cumpson
RR 3, Niagara-on-the-Lake, ON, L0S 1J0
905-937-6758
Lakeshore Road

Conditions	zone 7; sandy, sloping
Plot size	2 1/2 acres

Open every day except Mondays

❧ Hosta specialists

Cheryl and Bruce Cumpson have created a lovely demonstration garden and garden centre, backing onto a creek filled with solomon seal, trilliums and wild geraniums.

Interesting mixed plantings surround the house, showing off the extensive collection of hostas, premium perennials and grasses to their best advantage. Most of what you see is available in the nursery.

Niagara-on-the-Lake

Epicurian Fine Foods
84 Queen Street
905-468-3408
Light luncheon daily.

The Oban Inn
160 Front Street
905-468-2165
Luncheon daily from 11:30, afternoon tea every day except Saturday.

Ottawa Region: Almonte / Arnprior / Braeside / Burnstown / Burritt's Rapids / Carp / Dunrobin / Elgin / Kemptville / Kinburn / Merrickville / Ottawa / Perth / Portland / Woodlawn

ALMONTE

Sandy and Suzanne Patry, *Whitehouse Perennials*
Rae Side Road, RR 2, Almonte, ON, K0A 1A0
613-256-3406
Between Almonte and Carleton Place, on Rae Side Road, 1 kilometre off Highway 15

Conditions   zone 4; very rocky; sandy soil
Plot size   2 acres, formal and field gardens
Open weekends May 1 to July 1, day lily display last Friday and Saturday of July; for other times, phone for hours

❧ Bog garden, scree garden, extensive woodland gardens, shade and sun perennials, two ponds

The Patrys set themselves a daunting task when they began constructing the garden around their house, built on very rocky, sandy soil. They selectively cleared an area in the existing hardwood forest, and then transformed an abandoned hayfield, fallow for twenty years, into a spectacular demonstration and trial garden.

Suzanne's incurable obsession for collecting plants, combined with Sandy's design and building abilities, has resulted in a remarkable garden. The property is filled with hundreds of varieties of hostas, day lilies, perennials rhododendrons, azaleas, primulas, antique roses, unusual shrubs, grasses and herbs, and their plant odyssey takes them all over the world. I have never seen hostas used more effectively than at the Patrys'. Grown in generous beds carved out in the shade of the extensive woodland, their favourite cultivars have been combined for maximum effect, giving customers and visitors an imaginative vision of the plants that are sold in the nursery. Ponds have been carved out of the limestone rocks. In the field area, reminiscent of Monet's garden at Giverny, there are row upon row of peonies, Siberian irises, hundreds of day lily hybrids and other sun-loving perennials a vivid display for most of the season. The garden is a must, but if you can't get there, do the next best thing and send for their catalogue.

ARNPRIOR

Gillian Danby
613-623-8538

Conditions   zone 3b/4; rock, fill and topsoil imported
Plot size   approximately half an acre
Open by appointment; $5 donation to a charity of owner's choice appreciated

❧ **Beautiful setting on the Madawaska River, unusual rock garden**

On a rocky peninsula that juts out into the sparkling waters of the Madawaska River this idyllic garden with its stately old trees awaits discovery. The first thing you see on a midsummer's day are the blue spires of delphiniums standing tall behind a white picket fence covered in roses and clematis. The garden has a distinctly English feel to it, which is not surprising, since Gillian Danby is British.

Hundreds of perennials, herbs and bulbs have been carefully considered with a view to warm and cool plantings, textures and continuation of bloom. Imaginative colour combinations brighten border and island beds throughout the property. Pale mauve penstemons soften deep red yarrow, pale pink campanula Loddon Anna is surrounded by lavender, and butterfly lilies in apricot and white rise out of a haze of blue catmint. A charming latticed arbour covered in starry flowers of *Clematis paniculata maximowiczian* is perfect for a romantic white garden, at its peak in August.

Along the river, willows provide shade for hostas, ferns and wildflowers. Sumacs edge the extensive natural limestone garden, where a growing collection of alpines and sedums is slowly creeping over the lichen-covered rocks to the water below.

Gillian feels that her job is to enhance what nature has provided, and is forever experimenting with new plants and ideas; the result is always memorable.

BRAESIDE

|||||| Norma Moore, *Norma's Garden*
613-623-6389
Carmichael Side Road, McNab Township, Renfrew County
Conditions   zone 5; hillside, rock base
Plot size   5 1/2 acres
Open by appointment; donation for charity appreciated as entrance fee

❧ **Rose garden, pond with small waterfall, gazebo**

One of Norma Moore's greatest pleasures is to stand at her garden gate in the evening after work and drink in the scent of peace and serenity. This large country garden overlooking a wooded hillside to a splendid view of the Dochart Valley is sited on a base of shale and limestone with little natural soil. Truckloads of manure have been brought from the Moore's farm to fill the raised beds that have been built directly over the rocks. The result is an extremely pretty garden featuring over seventy roses and hundreds of the perennials that Norma loves so much. The shale and limestone has been put to good use, however, in elegant garden pond and pathways that wend their way through the property.

Flowers in pinks and blues fill the wide, curving bed that leads to a trellised gazebo, a Mother's Day present from her sons. The lovely rose Frau Dagmar Harstrup is a highlight of the yellow-and-blue-themed centre bed. Large-leafed rodgersias ferns and the white shrub rose Iceberg cluster round the lily pond, and along the house, a shrub rose border glows with Norma's favourite Grahame Thomas roses, whose warm yellow tones are set off by bright blue annual daisies underplanted here.

After teaching high-risk adults all day, Norma recharges her batteries and her patience in the garden. "On a trying day," she says, "it is certainly my sanity and my salvation."

BURNSTOWN

|||||| Valerie Roos Webster and John Webster,
Touch of Sky Garden and Studio
Burnstown, ON, K0J 1G0
613-432-8406

Conditions   zone 4/5; on a small plateau, mostly flat, sandy
Plot size   50 acres, 1 acre cultivated
Open open studio and garden last weekend in May; otherwise by appointment

❧ Perennials, Mediterranean garden, formal water garden, bog garden

The road to the Touch of Sky winds along a gorgeous stretch of the Madawaska River, then turns away up a wooded hillside. On entering the Websters' property, a red pine plantation envelopes you in a haze of soft silvery green; step out into the clearing and you find yourself in an enchanting garden, situated on a plateau overlooking a wooded valley.

Valerie and John have put their talents as painters and artisans to good use in the design and building of their nineteenth-century-style farmhouse and the landscaping around it.

The view from the front porch looks out over what was once the front lawn, now transformed into a formal water garden. Patterned gravel paths wander around the large, rectangular lily pond; at its corners, four L-shaped beds are planted symmetrically with day lilies, iris and plumed grasses. A 10-foot-long hedge of hardy rugosa roses, chosen to withstand the baking heat and fast-draining sandy soil, separates this area from the Mediterranean-style garden beyond. Approximately 40 by 60 feet, this garden is surrounded on three sides by the pine plantation, making it very sheltered, creating a unique microclimate on the property. Valerie is experimenting here with temperamental plants, such as lewisias. The patterned gravel paths continue here, dividing the protected area into sections: a cactus garden with, at the present time, six assorted Opuntias; a tall bearded iris section; and herb beds, including several varieties of thyme, sage, artemisia and lavender. In the spring this garden is covered with masses of flowering bulbs, including fritillarias, species tulips and species crocus.

On the south side of the house a clematis- and rose-covered arch leads into a traditional English-style garden, consisting of two long borders with a central path. Valerie grows a large selection of named perennials, including over eighty varieties of iris (including Touch of Sky, after which the property was named), as well as peonies and Japanese tree peonies, poppies and lilies (Asiatics, trumpets and Orientals), all underplanted with hundreds of spring bulbs.

The garden gradually blends into the surrounding landscape with a path that leads to a natural pond through the woodland where hostas have been planted to mingle with the ferns and wildflowers.

Valerie's exquisite watercolour flower paintings are inspired by her gardens, which she considers a work in progress. Various projects are in the planning stage, a pleasant state of affairs, especially as Valerie feels that the anticipation is one of the most exciting aspects of gardening.

BURRITT'S RAPIDS

You can arrange to coordinate a visit to the following gardens in Burritt's Rapids on one day; a $3 contribution to the Community Hall is appreciated as entrance fee to each garden

Gunild and Johannes Dutt, *Rideauwood Gardens*
613-269-3212
South side of the Rideau River between Burritt's Rapids and Merrickville
Conditions　　zone 4/5; sandy loam
Open by appointment; $3 donation to Community Hall appreciated

Perennials, shade gardens, vegetable garden

Gunild Dutt wasn't afraid to roll up her sleeves and wade into the weeds when she and her family moved to their 130-year-old farm in 1986. She comes from a long line of gardeners, including a grandfather who looked after the Duke of Furstenberg's estates on Lake Constance for many years.

Existing terraces have been planted with perennials chosen for hardiness, colour and size. Lovely combinations of vivid blue *Campanula glomerata* and yellow loosestrife, pale pink phlox with blue perovskia, lilies, baptisia and veronica are massed in perennial beds around the pool. Her favourite area is the summer house, where a charming yellow and white bed overflows with *Coreopsis verticillata grandiflora*, euphorbia, orange marigolds, feverfew and airy dill. Great use is made of annuals, particularly purple heliotrope, whose tightly clustered flowers blend well with the yellow and pink themes Gunild favours. Pots bursting with vibrant colour are everywhere, some placed directly into the garden to extend blooming time as the perennials fade. A perfectionist, she makes life easier for herself by using only plants that do well in this part of the world, especially those with good leaf texture and pleasing flowers. The shade garden on the east side of the house is particularly successful, with drifts of astilbes and monardas, goatsbeard snakeroot and hostas, under-planted with the pretty foam flower (*Tiarella cordifolia*).

Gunild's impressive vegetable garden is of the utmost importance to her. "It should be as aesthetically pleasing as my flower garden," she says, "besides providing my family with good healthy food." Constantly learning through trial and error, she does all the work herself, but is very careful to keep her gardening efforts in balance with the rest of her life.

Jean and Al McKay, *Balnakeil*
613-269-3115
Regional Road 23, between Burritt's Rapids and Merrickville
Conditions   zone 4/5; Grenville sandy loam; flat
Plot size   3 1/2 acres
Open by appointment; $3 donation to Community Hall appreciated

❧ Perennial borders, scree garden

This waterfront property in the Rideau Corridor is part of land granted by the Crown to United Empire Loyalist Solomon Jones in 1797. The garden surrounds a stone cottage dating to about 1835.

The McKays bought Balknakeil in 1985, and the planning and planting of this lovely garden, surrounded by rolling fields and the river beyond, have kept Jean and her husband busy ever since. Some distance from the house on the river side, an impressive border curving in broad sweeps follows the line of a split-rail fence bounding the perimeter. Plant shapes, drifts of foliage and flower colour have been repeated at intervals for continuity, and the wildflowers in the surrounding fields have been cleverly echoed with plantings of their cultivars. The wall of evergreens provides shelter from the wind, while shrubs such as viburnums, dogwoods and mock orange add substance to the masses of perennials. "The mixed border without a few roses would be unthinkable," says Jean, but she only includes hardy species such as *Rosa rubrifolia*, one of the loveliest of all rose species, and rugosa hybrids *Double blanc de Coubert*, Adelaide Hodless and Therese Bugnet.

Spring brings fountains of *Spiraea arguta* underplanted with black and white cottage tulips, and *Geranium sanguineum*. Narcissi carpet the orchard and species tulips push up from the beds around the house.

A visit to Beth Chatto's garden in Essex provided inspiration for use of drought-resistant plants including *Iris pallida* with its superb striped foliage, *Genista vancouverii*, *Dianthus deltoides*, sedums and cranesbills.

Ever adventurous, Jean is developing a gravel garden as well as the pool area. "In order to keep a garden vital," she says, "it must keep changing. We have to take risks, try new things, break out of old formulas and pattern — this is what makes a garden truly one's own."

▌▌▌ Olivia and Chris Mills

613-269-3257

Conditions	zone 4/5; light, gravelly
Plot size	200 x 100 feet

Open by appointment; $3 donation to Community Hall appreciated

❧ Perennials, sunken garden

I n 1894, Somerville and Ross, in one of their many books set in Ireland, wrote that one of the "absurdities of Irish life is that the ladies of the house should enjoy doing the gardener's work for him." Having spent her early years in Ireland surrounded by gardeners — especially her father — Olivia Mills soon developed a great love of gardens … and of gardening.

The property sits high up on the banks of the Rideau River, open to the northerly winds and shady on much of the south side. "Not a great site to start a garden," says Olivia, but over the years she has toiled ceaselessly to turn it into the charming garden it is today, with many of the original tulips, peonies and other plants rescued when she cleared the site surviving the rigours of time.

The garden has gone through many phases over the years. The children's recreation area has been transformed and in its place a lovely sunken garden has been created. Along one side, against a weathered stone barn, leans an old wagon wheel half-hidden among the ferns and cornflowers. Poppies and the variegated obedience plant stand tall beside the purple and yellow faces of little Johnny-jump-ups. Through all the many changes, however, there are always roses in Olivia's garden, and although there are not the "masses" that she would like, she succeeds in growing a good show of rugosas and even some less hardy varieties such as David Austins, which she tends carefully.

A wave of colour draws you across the back half of the garden, over to the billowing perennial beds rich with the flowers and fragrances of her youth. Sweet peas, dianthus, phlox and roses mingle with the yarrows. Delphiniums and an arbour beckon you through to a shade garden, planted for the minimum of maintenance.

It is very rewarding for Olivia to see a great burst of colour or a pleasing group of plants, but in the end, she says, "It's the doing of it that brings the most pleasure."

|||||| Renée and Brad Smith, *Burritt Farm*
613-269-4785
Burritt's Rapids

Conditions   zone 4/5b; clay mixed with thirty years of barnyard
              manure and much straw

Plot size   5 acres

Open by appointment; $3 donation to Community Hall appreciated

❧ Cutting garden

Thirty years of muck and manure and Renée Smith's hard work have transformed the garden at Burritt Farm from a sow's field to a beautiful bower, creating a fitting setting for a handsome 1830 stone house on the banks of the Rideau River, carefully restored to its former glory.

Renée has had to work around a great deal of traffic from horses and tractors on this hobby farm, creating colourful shrubberies round the barn, planting only those varieties that will survive the climate. "No pampering" is her motto. Northern bayberry, late lilacs, potentillas, and wild roses are all thriving. She loves exciting "look-throughs," and has planted an enormous spruce hedge that divides the garden into an inviting series of views. Arbours lead to the riverside, where large island beds are filled with good old favourites: peonies, shasta daisies, phlox, delphiniums, campanulas, cosmos and many more have been massed in drifts for greater effect.

Renée runs a small flower-arranging business, and the attractive cutting garden, traversed by gravel paths, has rows of oblong beds of statice, zinnias, larkspur and straw flowers that, because of the constant cutting, look good for most of the summer. Hops have been set to climb up over the tennis court fence; these she grows mainly for their seed heads, which are also excellent for drying and decorative all season. This lovely garden is the result of Renée's inherent good taste and boundless energy.

CARP

Georgina and Geoff Goodinson
613-839-2354

Conditions   zone 5; sandy, flat
Plot size   1/2 acre
Open last Sunday of May, 9 to 5, third Sunday of June, 10 to 4, last Sunday of August, 10 to 4

❧ **Dried-flower beds, large borders, pond**

I f it isn't set in concrete it can be moved," says Georgina Goodinson. When a large tract of her front lawn succumbed to drought, she transformed it into a magnificent bed of flowers used mainly for drying. Salvias, larkspur and clary sage rub shoulders with frothy baby's breath, delphiniums and hollyhocks, and the wide bed in front of the house is crammed with flowering shrubs and roses.

Beyond an opening in the clematis-covered trellis, the natural rockery of the Canadian Shield provides a lovely backdrop for the lily pond and shade garden, particularly in the spring when it is awash with colour from the primula, trillium and foxgloves.

Georgina grows from seed hundreds of stachys and cornflowers in pink, blue and white, which she then plants out in several large oblong beds in her cutting garden at the side of the house. Most of these are dried and used for arrangements in great demand at the local farmers' market, open from August to October. Look out for charming little garden ornaments that peek out from corners of the garden — ducks, hedgehogs and turtles that she makes out of rubber moulds.

Rhoda and David Lemke
613-839-3270

Conditions   zone 5; granite outcropping, acidic soil
Plot size   2 1/2 acres
Open by appointment

❧ **Manmade ponds with waterfall, bedrock gardening**

The Lemkes have been developing their spectacular garden over the past twenty years and there is still no end in sight. Dramatically situated on granite rocks in an area known as the Carp Ridge, and surrounded by an umbrella of magnificent white pines, the garden has been created where parts of the forest have been selectively cleared to create beds in the rocky outcroppings. Great care has been taken to ensure that the plantings are as natural as possible, although Rhoda smiles when she says "as possible," since the collector in her wants everything.

There is little soil depth, so drought conditions are a concern. In order to preserve moisture and nutrients, the Lemkes have been filling the crevices and beds with silt from their natural pond. The drainage, however, is excellent and the rocks provide microclimates for semihardy plants. Both the white- and blue-flowered speedwell, saxifrage and the aptly named dragon's blood sedum weave their way over the lichen-covered granite, through wild juniper spiked with yucca, fern and white lychnis.

Paths crisscross the property through mossy boulders, over lawns, and past perennial borders to the far side of the house. Here, where David has built a dramatic series of ponds and waterfalls, carved out of the bedrock and surrounded by pines, he is establishing a wildflower garden.

According to Rhoda, all the water in the world empties itself into her bog garden, where pink-plumed *Filipendula rubra*, *Rodgersia pinnata*, androsace (bog rosemary) and *Iris pseudocarus* thrive in such conditions. "Everyone is welcome here," says Rhoda, "including the numerous critters — except when it comes to slug and raccoons — then it's total war!"

DUNROBIN

Lois Anne Addison and Dorothy A. Richardson,
Bedrock Gardeners
201 Wagon Drive, RR 1, Dunrobin, ON, K0A 1T0
613-832-4202 Please call for directions

Conditions   zone 5a/4b; challenging: less than 2 inches of soil above bedrock

Plot size   5 acres

Open by appointment; plants for sale

❧ Rock scree garden, marsh and bog gardens, woodland garden and wildflower meadow, heather and heath collection

I take my hat off to Lois Addison and Dorothy Richardson, who have single-handedly battled through illness, drought and flood to drain, dig and plant 5 acres of land that is basically bedrock. "We want to show what two aging and increasingly arthritic women can still do," says Lois.

When they moved here six years ago, these feisty women set to work moving hundreds of rocks to build the alpine and scree garden. The next project was a large hill, built to house the heathers and heaths that Lois loves. "The element of excitement and surprise when you see their beautiful flowers peeking through the spring snow is tremendous," says Lois. The collection is now expanding to include autumn bloomers.

Ditches were then dug and the run-off used for a new bog garden, which they are filling with mainly native plants. Enormous satisfaction is derived from the evolution that has occurred here in such a short time, beginning with the tiny insects and microscopic organisms to the frogs and dragonflies that dive and dart among the varied plant life.

While they enjoy their well-stocked perennial borders, it is the alpines and wildflower habitats that are their passion. In the dappled shade of their sweetly scented conifer forest, Dorothy scouted for existing wildflowers and has become quite an authority on the subject. "Don't lay the paths with anything the critters can eat or dig up," she says. "We put hay and then woodchip, and that was fatal, they dug up everything and got fat on the hay!" The woods are dotted with collections of robust hostas and unusual ferns, jack-in-the-pulpit, shooting stars, prettily clumped ginsing and rattlesnake plantain, as well as early spring bloomers.

One of their major projects has been the preparation and planting of moist and dried-flower meadows. "No one ever tells you how much work and time goes into a meadow," says Lois. "There's no such thing as just throwing it in and letting it happen. This has taken us two years of back-breaking preparation."

As if this weren't enough, they also run a home-based micro-nursery. The potted plants for sale are divisions of flourishing clumps, self-sown seedlings, cuttings or seeds from the plants growing on their 5 acres.

There is a great deal to learn from these two courageous women who call their garden "the field of dreams." "Build it and they will come," says Lois, and judging from the incredible array of life, both animal and vegetable, already here, their dream is well on the way to becoming a reality.

ELGIN

|||||| Turid Forsyth, *Garden in the Woods*
613-359-5061

Conditions: zone 4; from bedrock to swamps
Plot size: 230 x 260 feet
Open by appointment

❧ An ever-changing landscape

At the tiny hamlet of Chaffey's Lock, the road crosses a narrow bridge spanning the Rideau Canal; look for houseboats floating lazily down its quiet waters. Continue along the country road through lofty forests, beaver swamp and sparkling lakes to a rusty mailbox that marks the entrance to Turid Forsyth's garden — don't blink or you'll miss it.

Stands of hollyhocks — "roses on sticks" in her native Germany — and Queen Anne's lace line the driveway to a rustic pine house on a hill looking out over treed valleys, jade ponds and fields of oxeye daisies and goldenrod that stretch away into the distance. It is here that Turid Forsyth reinvents her magical garden each year, primarily for use in her shimmering photos, which can be seen in many Harrowsmith publications.

A screen of feathery asparagus, turning a pale yellow in autumn, peeks over the wall of the main enclosure at the top of this terraced garden. The crumbling grey foundation wall glows with fluttering poppies spiked with brilliant blue larkspur. This is the experimental garden, where a permanent invitation is extended to native wildflowers to settle among the perennials, annuals and vegetables.

"This is my controlled wilderness," says Turid, "and all I do is give it a little push." I would rather call her efforts "a firm hand on a brilliant vision." Whimsical yet practical, this remarkable enclosure is dug and reshaped each year according to the project she is working on.

When I visited her last summer, it was a "sunflower," housing members of the vast *Compositae* family, a company of more than 20,000 species and 1,000 genera. Cos lettuce were planted under dahlias to keep them shaded, edible chrysanthemums combined with cosmos and straw flowers, deep red raddichio with cardoons, and chicory was "cooled" by silvery artichokes. A blazing rosette of sunflowers, chrysanthemums, marigolds and zinnias planted in tight circles made up the centre of the gorgeous sunflower.

As well as being a photographer, Turid is a talented watercolourist, and she worked as a botanical illustrator at Harvard University for many years. The canvas of her garden is painted in the bold strokes of a master: magenta lychnis with a touch of orange marigolds, combined with blue stalks of viper's bugloss; red poppies and corydalis with purple clary sage, beds of deep wine-coloured lilies. It is a feast for the senses. Fireweed and golden willow glow in the early evening sun, when the deer and snapping turtles come out of the woods to nibble at the raddichio. This little Eden will linger in the memory long after you leave.

Janet Baird Weisiger, *Paradise Hill Gardens*
613-359-6545
Sand Lake on Rideau Waterway
Conditions   zone 3/4; rocky, sandy soil
Plot size   gardens comprise about 1/2 acre of this 6-acre property
Open by appointment

Wonderful setting, perennial beds, spring garden, gazebo

The Rideau Lake district has to be one of the most beautiful spots on earth. As I drove up the bumpy track through a sun-streaked forest of majestic oaks, white pines and silver birch, the Weisegers' unique post-and-beam home came into view. Perched high on the hill, its terraces command panoramic views over Sand Lake and the surrounding woodlands, as well as colourful perennial beds located to the south and west of the house.

When Janet Weiseger starting gardening here in 1992 she found that not only were they sitting on granite, but also that it was impossible to get a tractor up the long, winding drive. Undaunted, she brought in soil "teaspoon by teaspoon," filling the crevices in the rocks, which she then proceeded to plant with sedums and sempervivum, lilies and penstemons, all good plants suiting the natural surroundings.

Past beds filled with hardy roses, astilbes, lilies, herbs and carefully chosen annuals, a grassy track slowly merges into the rocky outcroppings and a natural woodland, carpeted with daffodils in the spring and a rainbow of wild lupins in June. A vine-clad gazebo perched at the tip of the promontory overlooks a spectacular view. Take time to sit a moment and watch the sailboats as they glide across the sparkling waters of Sand Lake.

KEMPTVILLE

▌▐▌▌▌ Larry and Anstace Esmonde-White, *Evergreen Farm*
Evergreen Farm, RR 5, Kemptville, ON, K0G 1J0
613-258-5587
On Bedell Road between Kemptville and Oxford Mills

Conditions: zone 4; loam
Plot size: 5 acres
Open weekends 10 to 4, Tuesday to Friday 2 to 4, closed Mondays; plants for sale; teahouse

❧ **Many different gardens, including a maze**

E vergreen Farm lies along a quiet country lane whose verges are rib-
boned with wildflowers. An imposing avenue of maple trees line the
driveway to the old stone house, home to the Esmonde-Whites since
1971. This interesting couple will be familiar to those who watch "From
a Country Garden" on PBS, and the CBC show "Midday."

The garden owes much to the grand estates of Ireland where they were
brought up. Memories of those childhood days began with the recreation
of a cedar maze, much like the one through which Larry used to chase
Anstace, some sixty years ago.

Cedar hedges take the place of Irish yew, acting as windbreaks
between the "rooms" of this nostalgic garden. The blue-and-white garden
brings to mind a Wedgwood plate. The formal rose garden is edged with
lavender and old-fashioned "granny" flowers fill the perennial beds.
Bounty from the beautifully ordered vegetable gardens is served at the
excellent café on the premises. Paths meander through meadows of wildflowers; ducks swim in a pond beside an old log cabin, one of several
rescued and reassembled on the property by the Esmond-Whites. This
"little bit of Ireland" is quite at home in rural Rideau.

KINBURN

Carole and Phil Reilly, *Reilly's Country Gardens*
3328 Diamondview Road, RR 2, Kinburn, ON, K0A 2H0
613-832-2965
Between Kinburn and Carp
Conditions   zone 4/5; clay, flat land
Plot size   1 acre
Open: "If we're in, we're open."

❧ Fifteen demonstration gardens

I f a perennial survives here, it has to be tough" is the Reillys' criterion.
Mature maple trees border the lovely century home and garden.
Perennials fill the demonstration beds. Three tear-drop-shaped shade gardens have been carved out under the maple trees; and a variety of plants, 250 of them, each with its own sign detailing soil, light and water requirements, are displayed in large island beds edged with picket fences.

This family cottage industry is a source of joy to the Reillys, and they are happy to share it with you.

MERRICKVILLE

Diana Beresford-Kroeger and Christian H. Kroeger, *Carrigliath*
Box 253, Merrickville, ON, K0G 1N0
Conditions   zone 4/5b
Open: write for an appointment; usually open for the daffodils, and Sundays in July

❧ Bioplanned garden, rare plants, very large collection of daffodils

D iana Beresford-Kroeger can often be heard on CBC Radio Noon's
weekly gardening show, where she has gained a reputation as a pioneer ecological gardener. She is, among many things, a student of classical botany, medical biochemistry and organic and radionuclear chemistry. All this knowledge has been brought to bear over the past twenty years in her 5-acre bioplanned garden.

The largest collection of daffodils in North America makes a breath-taking sight in the spring, when over 5,000 species burst into bloom. As a result of Diana's botanical searches across the world, many rare, heritage and exotic plants can be seen here, among them, Manchurian apricot, rare *Primula violaceae* from Ireland via the Himalayas, and Japanese platy-codon (*Lilium* Thunderbolt), to name but a few. She is very fond of her nut tree collection, which includes a plantation of northern Shadbolt hickory (*Carya obulata*), now nearly extinct. Diana runs her own trials and has just developed a species of mildew-resistant phlox.

Habitats for all sorts of creatures are fostered here, including damp areas for the amphibian population, which is particularly important to her. As we stood at the edge of the pond, a wizened little face with a wrinkled neck peered out of the water. This was "Shakey," a twenty-five-year-old Eastern painted turtle, come for food and affection, in response to Diana's soft Gaelic endearments. "Thirty percent of these creatures have disappeared from our planet," she says.

It is the synthesis of the ecology that is important here at Carrigliath, as she has recorded in her informative, beautiful book, *A North Temperate Garden; Bioplanning for the Next Millenium.*

▌▌▌▌▌ Joyce Devlin

613-269-4458

St. Lawrence and Drummond Streets

Conditions   zone 5b; flat, local topsoil

Plot size   50 x 150 feet

Open by appointment, or by chance

❧ Delight in the unexpected

Joyce Devlin is a well-known painter whose magical garden is full of happenstance. This is a garden in motion, where plants are pushed around like paint on canvas. The emphasis changes year by year, with a new arch here, a texture or a colour there, or maybe just a simple circle of stones or plants. A thick cedar hedge encloses the blue-shuttered house with its grey plaster walls covered in single pink roses. Through the undergrowth, a path leads to a hidden glade where a basin of blue water sits in a bed of ajuga. The hand of the artist is everywhere, from purple clematis clambers through burnt red lilies and pale pink phlox, to a tiny white garden that she calls her miniature Sissinghurst, where sweet peas grow in pots and white roses creep into the cedar hedge.

Memories abound — on a brick circle, known as the desert garden, an orange tree in a terra cotta pot to remind her of Greece; a birch tree from her grandmother's garden; sweet night-scented stocks from her youth — each contributes to the sense of place.

It is the owner's remarkable imagination that makes this garden unique.

OTTAWA

▨ Billings Estate Museum
2100 Cabot Street, Ottawa, ON, K1H 6K1
613-564-1363, fax 613-564-1365
From Bank Street, Riverside Drive East to Pleasant Park and follow signs
Open May 1 to October 31, Sunday to Thursday 12 to 5, May 1 to August 31, also open Thursday 6 to 8 p.m.; closed Thanksgiving weekend; entrance from $1 to $2.25; wheelchair access throughout

W e began the world 40 miles from any house on one side and 7 on the other, no road either way, not one house in the town but our own." Thus wrote Lamira Dow Billings, the seventeen-year-old bride of Braddish Billings, as she and her husband established themselves as the area's first settlers in 1813. They built their home in the 1820s on this site, aptly named Park Hill, with its sweeping grounds overlooking the Rideau River. The Billings Estate Museum, situated on 8 acres of historic parkland, includes the neoclassical house, several outbuildings, and a cemetery. A collection of Billings family items contains records spanning two centuries and five generations.

The Billings family were long associated with botany, agriculture and horticulture, and each generation has made its contribution to this picturesque woodland retreat. Ornamental trees and shrubs are planted around the house, and winding pathways lead between the lawns and the twentieth-century perennial beds. Herbs in the demonstration garden on the south side of the house are grown for use in the tearoom. Wander the grounds of this lovely place, across lawns, past flower beds and wooded slopes, as others have done for so many years, and you feel a real kinship with those first garden enthusiasts.

Tea is served on the lawn Sunday through Thursday, from 1 to 4, June 1 to Labour Day.

Dominion Arboretum

Agriculture Canada, Building 72, Central Experimental Farm, Ottawa, ON, K1A 0C6
613-995-3700; fax 613-992-7909
Preston Street and Carling Avenue, south of the city centre
Open daily from dawn to dusk; wheelchair access

This farm is a research facility of Agriculture Canada, governmental advisor to the nation's farmers. Among the many attractions are the magnificent gardens.

Three adjoining gardens, the Macoun Sunken Garden, the Rock Garden, and the Ornamental Garden, display many varieties of flowers and shrubs, including lilacs, peonies, hostas, geraniums, Explorer roses, weigelas, forsythia, mock orange and a large selection of perennials.

Over 500 varieties of tropical plants, orchids, cacti and banana trees among them, grow in the greenhouse; the chrysanthemum show here in early November is stunning.

A hedges garden demonstrates the use of shrubs and trees best suited for hedging in the Ottawa area. This outstanding arboretum is planted with over 2,000 woody specimens, including magnolias, rhododendrons, azaleas, crabapples, Ponderosa pines, metasequoia, and a wisteria. A floral sundial greets visitors at the entrance plaza to the astronomical observatory, built in 1902.

Fletcher Wildlife Garden

Central Experimental Farm, Ottawa, ON, K1A 0C6
613-230-3276
At Preston Street and Carling Avenue, south of the city centre, at the south end of Dominion Arboretum
Open daily from dawn to dusk; wheelchair access

This wildlife garden encompasses 18 acres. The plot of wildflowers is a butterfly meadow; there is a sedge meadow pond and a woodlot, and many bird boxes are in place. The grasses grow as they will, except for the grass on the pathways.

PERTH

Heritage House Museum
Old Sly's Road, Box 695, Smiths Falls, ON, K7A 4T6
613-283-8560
Just off Highway 43 from Perth on road to Merrickville
Open May 1 to December 31, Tuesday to Sunday, and holiday Mondays 11 to 4:30 ; nominal admission fee; wheelchair access limited to main floor of house

A variety of lilacs and perennials are planted around the house, including a yellow rose bush, a cherished antique over a hundred years old. There is a replica Victorian herb and vegetable garden and a pretty picnic area. A short walk through parkland brings you to the Rideau Canal. Gift shop, tearoom and washroom facilities are all wheelchair accessible.

Perth Museum, Matheson House
11 Gore Street East, Perth, ON, K7H 1H4
613-267-1947
Open year-round, Monday to Saturday 10 to 5, Sunday 1 to 4; adults $1.50, children $0.50

After the War of 1812 many families came together from far afield to make their homes in Perth, and of course a home in those days had a garden, a hedge and a sundial. These requirements and more have been recreated within the stone walls and white picket fence enclosing this charming restored 1840 Scottish garden. Two circular grassed areas are bordered by pathways and a variety of unusual and colourful flowers grow around the perimeter. The stone bench placed under a shade maple and the plantings of ferns, evening primrose, hostas and damask roses are pleasing reminders of days gone by.

The Round Garden for the Blind
Box 438, Perth, ON, K7H 3G1
For guided tours: Sylvia Van Oort 613-267-7365, Margaret Graham 613-264-8599, Renai Rennick 613-267-7272

From Highway 7 south on Wilson Street to Sunset Boulevard
Open daily, dawn to dusk; donation welcomed as price of entrance; wheel-chair access; washroom facilities at adjacent County Buildings during regular business hours

Although this garden was specially designed for the pleasure of the blind, the elderly and the handicapped, it is worth a visit for anyone. The plants in the waist-high planters are chosen for their texture and perfume as well as colour and are all identified in English, French and Braille. They are arranged in a circle surrounded by a variety of shrubs. A splashing fountain and song birds bring music to this delightful place. Linger awhile at picnic tables under oak trees and pergolas.

To continue operations, the Garden depends on donations from the community and visitors. The Friends of the Garden for the Blind, a group of dedicated volunteers, tend the garden and act as tour guides. To arrange a tour please phone or write one week in advance.

PORTLAND

Susan Young
11 Colborne Street, Portland, ON, K0G 1V0
613-272-2579
Conditions: zone 4; compost-enriched topsoil, terraced
Plot size: 60 x 120 feet
Open by appointment, by telephone or mail

Water garden, perennial borders

This little gem of a garden is on a terraced village lot. It features a waterfall and a watergarden, perennial beds and an herb garden. A shade garden is in the works, and with the threatened addition of a rose garden, the grass will disappear, as will the lawn mower. Susan describes this garden as a source of "sanity, satisfaction and pride to its caregivers."

WOODLAWN

▐▊▊▌ Donald and Jean Collier, *Windseuch*
613-832-3650
Buckham's Bay West, off Dunrobin Road
Conditions   zone 5a; sandy loam, cleared land and bush,
                gentle slopes
Plot size   1 1/2 acres
Open by appointment

A circular laneway through woodland leads to the Colliers' garden.
Bright flower beds all around the house are planted with a large
collection of lilies and dahlias, and they like to experiment with new
perennials. Shade perennials and ground covers surrounding the garden
create a gradual transition from the cultivated landscape to the wilderness
beyond.

▐▊▊▌ John and Lynda Soper
613-623-6498
Conditions   zone 4a; limestone and a little sandy loam
Plot size   25 acres, garden 1 1/2 acres
Open daily; please call ahead

❧ Water garden

Limestone rocks, cedars and white pines set the scene for a magical
water garden and fountain carved out of the limestone, its craggy
shoreline planted with many rock-loving plants. Shady areas under
spruce trees are planted with primulas, hostas and astilbes, and Lynda,
an accomplished potter, is gradually creating perennial beds around the
swimming pool, which is also built from the natural rock.

▣ Audrey Bloedow
102 Harry MacKay Road, RR 2, Woodlawn, ON, K0A 3M0
613-832-2227
North end of Stonecrest Road

Conditions   zone 5b; sandy loam, limestone near surface in places
Plot size   1 1/2 acres
Open any day, by appointment.

❧ Shade garden, deciduous woods, trilliums

Audrey and Ed Bloedow built their home with 120-year-old-logs; these provide the backdrop for beds of hostas, ligularias and many other shade-loving plants growing in the shadow of the house. In the surrounding deciduous woods, hepatica, trillium, wild columbine, wood lily and single-flowered hollyhock grow in profusion. Audrey and her sister-in-law have transformed an acre of sunny meadow into a nursery of flowers, including tall bearded iris, cranesbill, yarrow, delphiniums and poppies. Some of these are grown for dried-flower arrangements and bouquets and some are sold bare-root. There is also an extensive vegetable garden and pick-your-own berry garden.

Arnprior

Bonnie Jane's Scones
148 John Street North
613-623-0552
Monday to Saturday, 8:30 to 5; tea, coffee, light luncheon; browse in the adjoining bookstore and art gallery.

Burnstown

Burnstown Cafe
County Road 2, opposite the post office
613-432-8805
Open May 1 to November 30; breakfast, lunch, tea.

Carp

The Swan at Carp
108 Falldown Lane
613-839-7926
English-style country inn open year round; luncheon and dinner.

Kanata

The Glen Café
262 Hazeldean Road
613-836-5622
Luncheon and dinner,
closed Sunday.

Kemptville

Evergreen Farm
Badell Road, RR 4, Kemptville
613-258-5587
Garden Tea House open summer weekends 10 to 4.

Merrickville

The Baldachin
111 St. Lawrence Street
613-269-4223
Open daily; luncheon,
dinner.

Country Corner Tearoom
106 St. Lawrence Street
613-269-4204
Daily 9:30 to 4:30, light luncheon.

Sam Jakes Inn
110 Main Street
613-269-3711
Daily 7:30 am to 9, breakfast, luncheon and dinner; snacks in the bar.

Tearoom Café
224 St. Lawrence Street
Merrickville
613-269-2233
Luncheon served daily 11 to 5, dinner 5 to 9.

Ottawa

Billings Estate Museum
2110 Cabot Street
613-247-4830
Traditional afternoon tea on the lawn Sunday to Thursday, 1 to 4, June 1
to Labour Day.

Perth

Courtyard Tearoom
91 Gore Street East
613-267-5094

Perth Manor
23 Drummond Street West
613-264-0050
Daily, 8 to 9; breakfast, luncheon and dinner.

Portland

Gallagher House Lakeside Inn
14 West Water Street
613-272-2895
Luncheon, tea, dinner.

Steam Boat Landing
Colborne Street
613-272-2992
Open daily, breakfast, luncheon, supper.

Smiths Falls

Heritage House Museum
Old Sly's Road (just off Highway 43)
613-283-8560
May 1 to December 31, Tuesday to Sunday and holiday Mondays; 11 to
4:30.

Peterborough Region: Bewdley / Buckhorn / Omemee / Orono / Peterborough / Warkworth

BEWDLEY

|||||||| Vivian and Paul Parkin, *Justa View*
Box 425, Oak Hills Road, Bewdley, Ont. K0L 1E0
905-342-3477
From Highway 28, east on County Road 9, north on Oak Hill Road,
then west on Bamsey Drive; house is 1 kilometre on left
Conditions   zone 4/5; hilly and gravelly
Plot size   120 x 420 feet; a third is cultivated, balance is woodland
*Open 2 to 4 most Sundays, otherwise by appointment; small donation
appreciated for upkeep of garden*

❧ Strictly organic with over 600 different plants; featured in 1994/95
Plant and Garden magazine

S urrounded by woods and blessed with a panoramic view of Rice Lake
— the Parkins certainly couldn't have chosen a better spot to build a
house. Paul, a bricklayer by trade, and his wife, Vivian, a retired musi-
cian, semi-retired professional photographer and master gardener,
designed their property round a giant oak tree, known affectionately as
"The General." They didn't have much ambition for the garden when
they first started, but it wasn't long before the idea of a few flowers here
and there developed into a full-fledged organic garden. There are now
more than 1,500 plantings of more than 600 different varieties, species
and cultivars, most of them chosen for zone 4 hardiness and tolerance to
the wicked winds from the lake, intermittent snow cover and summer's
frequent drought conditions.

The sweeping flowers beds start at the side of the long fieldstone driveway that curves to the house, and continue along the raised stone bed
at the front of the property. Perennials, evergreens, flowering shrubs and
trees bloom successively from late March until October. Spring brings
over a thousand bulbs, followed by iris, lilies, day lilies and vines. These

lavish plantings are continued in the terraced back garden, where the sound of splashing water emanates from a set of rapids and a waterfall cascading into the fishpond. Narrow paths edging the terrace below the woodland are lined with ever more plants, including a large collection of winter-hardy Canadian shrub roses, rugosas and antique roses. In a separate bed a small group of tender modern roses are treated as annuals if they don't come through the winter.

BUCKHORN

Fenny and Henry Spitse
RR 1, Buckhorn, ON, K0L 1J0
705-657-9554
First mailbox on right side of Highway 36, just north of Buckhorn
Conditions   zone 4; peat-granite, wooded hill, flat ponds and marsh
Plot size   56 acres, 3 acres cultivated
Open by appointment or by chance; donation box

❧ **Extensive water gardens, large collection of bulbs, woodland gardens, rock garden**

Great drifts of colourful flowers line the banks of the these beautiful water gardens, dug out of the black peaty marsh that makes up much of this property. Each year the marsh has been drained a little further to accommodate more and more perennial gardens, including the 4,000 "friends" that the Spitses brought with them from Windsor in 1988. An extensive network of paths meanders past streams and on through the many shady moist areas ideal for growing a large selection of primulae, various bog plants and astilbes, for which Henry has a soft spot. A hosta garden leads to a woodland full of rhododendrons, and the natural granite hills harbour a large rock garden behind the house. In May the garden is a truly lovely sight to behold, with thousands of bulbs in all their glory throughout the property.

Nearly everything here is grown from seed, something that Henry knows much about, as he worked for twenty-nine years as a retired greenhouse manager. His wife, Fenny, is the "weed patrol," but all work stops in the evening when they take their drinks and venture out to sit by the babbling brook and listen to the birds.

OMEMEE

Linda Friend, *Rural Roots*
705-799-6972
Hay Line, just southeast of Omemee
Conditions   zone 5; clay loam, level lot in region of gentle hills
Plot size   1 1/2 acres
Open by appointment, closed Sundays

❧ **Nursery and perennial beds, roses**

This is a dream of a perennial garden, although Linda Friend says that most days she feels on a less rarefied plane as she battles wind, drought and sometimes poorly sited plants.

Starved for colour during the long winter months, her aim is to have seven months of bloom in this hardy and varied garden. She has filled the three main "rooms" with exciting and imaginative plant combinations, such as the silver-blue heads of *Eryngium cerulean* intermingled with purple coneflower, and soft pastel-coloured lilies surrounded by clouds of gypsophilia spiked with purple allium.

Linda is no garden snob when it comes to annuals, which she grows from seed, and her "happenings" from the likes of zinnia spiced with salvia Red Lady, salvia Victoria and dwarf nicotiana are well worth remembering. She uses petunias and marigolds, rusty old hollyhocks, barnyard golden glow, cosmos and brilliant blue larkspur mixed in with her huge selection of perennials. "I even welcome yellow," she says, much to the disdain of her more artistic cohorts. She figures that any plant willing to brave our wretched and intemperate climate deserves an enthusiastic welcome. Blowsy beds of summer phlox, fleabane, Shasta daisy, the towering *Nicotiana sylvestris* and self-seeded *Malva moschata* have been edged with cosmos, whose blooms keep coming long after everything else has faded. A flagstone path leads through a clematis-covered arbour to a 40-foot bed massed with roses, predominantly David Austins, shrub and moss. Underplanted with a haze of lavender and dianthus, their fragrance permeates the air. That sweet scent and the steady hum from busy bees epitomizes all that's best on a summer's day.

Besides a small orchard and a large vegetable garden, Linda also runs a flourishing nursery on the property, with her partner, Ann Greer-Wootton, from which they sell young surplus plants. "It's a matter of choose, dig and bag," she says. This spring they should have masses of dianthus, campanulas, and silene, probably 60 to 70 varieties in all. She works nonstop six days a week in the season. I do hope that on the seventh day she has time to sit awhile and enjoy the fruits of her labours.

ORONO

David and Sandra Hinton, *Rhododendron Woods*
3384 Taunton Road, RR 2, Orono, ON, L0B 1M0
905-983-5528
West off Highway 115/35 on 4th Concession, north on Pollard Road
Conditions   zone 5; sandy loam, rolling land
Plot size   5 acres
Open first Saturday and Sunday of June, 9 to 4; other times by appointment

Rhododendrons and magnolia collection

This lovely country garden is a magnificent sight to behold in June, when hundreds of rhododendrons burst into bloom. Under lofty stands of pine and oak, sandy paths wind between the growing collection of flowering magnolias and azaleas, and the woodland floor is carpeted with spring flowers. A primeval feeling pervades this part of the garden where many of the rhododendrons have grown to a great size; it's hard to believe that David Hinton started them from mere seedlings back in 1976.

Rhododendrons are not the only points of interest here. Take time to wander through the impressive grounds and lovely gardens and view the new fishpond, rock gardens and large perennial beds planted with interesting species, including unusual ligularias, various rodgersias, many different primulae, cacti, stately eremurus and inulas, mostly all grown from seed. There is much to learn from your hosts, who are very knowledgeable, particularly when it comes to the growing of rhododendrons.

|||||| Douglas Lycett and Henry Lorrain, *We're in the Hayfield Now*
(Day lily gardens)
4704 Pollard Road, RR 1, Orono, ON, L0B 1M0
905-983-5097
West off Highway 115/35 on 4th Concession, north on Pollard Road
Conditions   zone 4b; sandy loam
Open garden second-last weekend of July; closed Mondays and Tuesdays

❧ **Thousands of their own seedlings; hundreds of hybrid day lilies from U.S.**

You can't help being swept away on a tide of enthusiasm by Doug Lycett. Life for him and his partner Henry Lorrain is a "bowl of lilies," day lilies, to be precise. Over 17,000 seedlings are nurtured under lights each winter, of which just a handful will be tagged for propogation. This is virtually the only place in Canada where new strains of day lily are being developed on this scale — and at half the price of anywhere else.

Doug Lycett was first introduced to these wonderful plants by his friend Eleanor LeFave, founder of Mabel's Fables children's bookstores, who told him to buy one at a nursery. The bloom "knocked his socks off," and when he and his partner Henry Lorrain moved to their small farm in Orono ten years ago, they made their foray into propogating, producing 120 seedlings in the first year, which Doug says were "quite dreadful." They have become friendly with Bill Munson in Florida, who is the world's leading hybridizer of day lilies. Every May they visit him to work and observe his methods, and have learned how to make their selections. "It's as much an art as a science" says Doug.

Expansion has been steady. Out went the raspberry canes, away went the vegetables, and in marched the day lilies, slowly filling the garden, until finally, with nowhere else to go, they took over the surrounding hay fields. "Well," remarked a friend, "that's it. You're certainly in the hayfield now," and the rest is history.

It is a sight to behold — acres of these robust plants, their crimped waxy petals of every hue, from palest yellow to deepest maroon, turned to face the sun for one brief brilliant day. We are indebted to these two men who are bringing their vision and dedication to the gardeners of Canada with a plant that adapts to almost every corner of this country. Long may they and their day lilies flourish!

PETERBOROUGH

[gate icon] Ann Greer-Wootten

705-743-2343

Conditions	zone 5b; clay, flat
Plot size:	1/3 acre

Open by appointment only

❧ **Pond, collections of clematis, lilies, roses and hostas**

Elegant antique iron gates usher you into Ann Greer-Wootten's garden where long curving borders are filled with spring-flowering bulbs, hundreds of lilies, delphiniums, phlox, bergamot and her favourite David Austin roses. Clematis-covered arbours define "rooms," some sunny, some shady, the latter planted with a large collection of hostas, ferns and cranesbills. As the saying goes, "chance is a fine thing" for the wildflowers that seed themselves in Ann's garden. No matter that their colours might clash with the neighbours, they are welcome, especially the froth of Queen Anne's lace that blends beautifully with everything.

Under the shade of a huge old maple a peaceful sitting area has been created. From here you can see the pond and listen to the fountain as it trickles into the water. Ann helps to run a nursery with her colleague Linda Friend, whose garden is described above.

[icon] Hutchison House

270 Brock Street, Peterborough, ON, K9H 2P9

705-743-9710

Open May 1 to December 31, Tuesday to Sunday; January to March, Monday to Friday; 1 to 5; adults $2, seniors and students $1.50, children $0.50; limited wheelchair access

The house and gardens are owned and operated by the Peterborough Historical Society. There are many things to do and see here and knowledgeable costumed guides on duty to assist you. The period gardens are planted in the style of an 1860s cottage garden, with iris, peonies, hosta, bleeding heart, balloon flowers and many more. Colourful shrubs thrive; old-fashioned roses and a Canada moonseed vine trail around the fence overlooking the rail-trail bicycle pathway. Some of the harvest from the herb garden is used in the museum kitchen, while the cutting garden provides flowers for the arrangements in the charming old stone house and on the tables in the terrace where Scottish Teas are served daily during the summer.

Ecology Park

Peterborough Green-Up
209 Simcoe Street, Peterborough, ON, K9H 2H6
705-745-3238
Highway 7 and Ashburnham Drive; from the main gates of Beavermead Park walk to the southeast corner
Open May through October; limited wheelchair access

Peterborough Green-Up and the City of Peterborough are the sponsors of this ecological adventure. Included in the park is a children's garden, a wildlife garden, food gardens, a heritage garden, backyard theme gardens (settlers', medicinal and wildlife gardens, and an edible landscape), native tree nursery, nature trail and compost and garden clinics.

Fleming Park

Brock and Aylmer Streets, Peterborough, ON
Open daily, year-round; wheelchair access

The garden is the pride of the Peterborough Horticultural Society, whose members chose this location as its public project in 1993. A large variety of old-fashioned flowers were selected when the perennial bed were created. There are two annual beds, a shrub border, a shady wildflower nook and an herb garden.

Margaret and Robert Burley

705-745-8322

Conditions	zone 5b; clay
Plot size	2 acres

Open by appointment

❧ Pond, fountain and stream, garden shop

The Burleys are always thinking up something new to add to their spacious garden, situated on a gently sloping hill and full of interesting features. A "secret" rose garden is the newest addition, where David Austin roses mix with old-fashioned shrub roses. Robert has built one of the most unusual water gardens I have seen — a forty-foot raised stone trough has a stream running along its length, finally cascading into a lily pool. Margaret grows from seed many interesting annuals such as Flocks of Sheep in lovely pastels as well as vibrant corals, purple heliotrope and the trumpet flowers of Asarina. The many beds are edged with stones from a local quarry. A large shade garden is thick with hostas, ferns and wildflowers. Look for the water-barrel fishpond.

WARKWORTH

Schoolhouse Gardens
RR 1, Warkworth, ON, K0K 3K0
705-924-3255
North of Highway 401, east of Highway 45, on southeast corner of Highway 25 and County Road 29
Conditions   zone 5
Plot size   3 acres
Open last Sunday of May, third Friday of July, thereafter Sundays at 1:30, guided tours, $5

Heritage property, perennials, herbs garden

Schoolhouse Gardens nestles in the beautiful Northumberland Hills not far from the Trent Waterway.

Dennis and Tom have lived in this converted circa 1847 schoolhouse since 1987. Their dream was to have their own park, and they have put their hearts, souls and a huge amount of work into restoring the old grounds and creating new gardens that cover some three acres.

Accessed by a network of paths, the terraced hill behind the house overflows with perennials that have been planted to the perimeter of the natural woodland surrounding the property. Lilies in their hundreds, delphiniums, onopordums, and Shasta daisies are but a few of the varieties that fill this dramatic space. Around the house, flower beds filled with sweet peas tangle with gladioli and roses. An old school bell hangs over the well, used by the school until it closed in the 1950s.

A wisteria covered-bridge leads over a little brook whose banks are covered in hostas, primroses and iris that flourish in the spring. Across the water is the formal garden, where a lovely collection of peonies have been planted. The original herb garden has been resurrected, as has the vegetable garden used by the school for many years. These enterprising young men are now turning their attention to a new rose garden, and the bush beyond is being naturalized with early spring bulbs to blend with the trilliums, hepatica and the like.

You are invited to explore the Friendship Walk and bring a smooth pebble, which will be placed in the walk as a memento of your visit.

The Woodshed Gift Shop open during Garden Tours sells all sorts of goodies from the garden — relishes, dried herbs, salad dressing and fresh-cut flowers.

Peterborough

Hutchison House
270 Brock Street
705-743-9710
Scottish Teas served weekend afternoons in June and daily in July and August; also by special arrangement any other time.

Bagels Unlimited
Corner of Water and Parkhill
705-740-2802
Open daily 7 a.m. to midnight; infusion tea, savouries and sweets.

Picton

▐▐▐▐ John and Pauline Burton
613-476-6731
11 kilometres east of Picton (opposite Gloria Condie's property)
Conditions   zone 6a; limestone, sandy
Plot size   20 acres, 3 acres developed
Open June only; by appointment

❧ **Raised beds, formal garden and fishpond**

When the Burtons moved here in 1985, the property was nothing but 20 acres of tired, worn-out pasture land and limestone shale. Ten years later the Burtons seem to have worked a miracle, creating a flowering desert in this drought-ridden area.

Water is plentiful in spring, filling the natural ponds and bogs, bringing lushness to the dried-out bush. Pauline has planted a "host of golden daffodils" to naturalize through the groves of white ash and silver birch; lilacs are massed in the dell, wild phlox cover the fields in a pale mauve wash. With the arrival of summer and dry weather, self-seeded poppies dot themselves among yuccas and iris. Lilies, lavender, statice, sedums and other drought-resistant plants fill the heavily mulched beds, allowing the Burtons to enjoy their gardens till the fall rains.

John's passion for rocks, together with his talent for design, can be seen in the many stone walls and large raised beds, connected by an intricate network of gravel paths that run throughout the 3 acres of developed land. Wander through the parklike setting enjoying the shrub borders and abundant perennial beds. Recently added are a cutting garden for Pauline's flower arranging and a large goldfish pond centred on a formal garden, where vivid petunias and creeping portulaca have been planted en masse, to combine with sculptured junipers. Banks of rugosa roses and beds of lilies have been sensitively set into the natural environment, creating a garden that is relaxed, harmonious and varied.

▐▐▐▐ Gloria Condie, *The Lord's Garden*
613-476-6108
11 kilometres east of Picton
Conditions   zone 6a; sandy loam rocky and hilly, by lake

Open by appointment

❧ Cottage garden in the woods, biblical theme

A steep path leads down through a dense wood of white ash and silver birch; the branches above are hung with biblical sayings. Around the last bend, Lake Ontario stretches out before you, its sparkling blue waters lapping the flower-filled banks of Gloria Condie's lovely garden. This charming and deeply spiritual woman came from Cuba twenty-seven years ago to be with her husband and has enjoyed gardening here ever since.

From spring to late autumn there is something in bloom. Thousands of daffodils, wildflowers, ferns, hostas, colourful annuals and hundreds of perennials light up this unique garden, extending deep into the woods behind the house.

For the past fifteen years she has been alone. No longer a young woman, Gloria says she needs all the help she can get. Her strength comes from her deep belief in God, to whom she attributes all the glory of this special place.

▦ Ellen and Stan Jablonicky, *Garden Cove*
RR 1, Cherry Valley, ON, K0K 1P0 (bed and breakfast)
613-476-7030
5.6 kilometres west of Cherry Valley; from Picton, take Lake Street for 14 kilometres; look for white trellis heart
Conditions   zone 6a; sandy and clay, hillside, meadow and rock
Plot size   5 acres
Open daily 12 to 7, any other times by special request, groups by appointment

❧ Garden rooms, perennial beds, woodland garden, water feature

A large heart-shaped gazebo announces the entrance to the Jablonickys' very comfortable bed and breakfast, set in 5 rolling acres that stretch down through woods and fields to a sheltered cove at the waterside.

When the Jablonickys arrived here in 1987, Stan wielded his trusty sickle and cleared the land, securing the hillside with loads of rocks before building their large perennial beds and pond areas. Hundreds of seedling trees were planted, and hanging from their now mature branches, are many unusual birdhouses, from little stone churches to brightly painted gourds, all built by Stan.

Different garden rooms have been created. Wisteria-covered arbours lead to the country garden, sweeping perennial beds curve away to the fields bright with hollyhocks, lupins and Asiatic lilies; a Japanese garden overlooks the east lake sunsets, and tucked in among the flowers, a sundial inscribed with the words "Every hour brings death nearer" silently ticks away the time.

Ellen's favourite place is the mystical woodland garden, where ferns and wildflowers grow beneath gnarled old trees. Iron bedframes have been turned into benches, and a grotto is guarded by the statue of a lady surrounded with flowers. "If you listen closely," says Ellen, "you might hear the sound of goblins dancing in the nearby meadow."

Her latest ambitions are to plant a Bible garden; a tea garden, to include plants that may be used to make a variety of teas, listing their beneficial effects; and a healing garden, with plants offering medicinal properties.

"Plant for future generations," advises Ellen. She echoes the sentiment taught by Native peoples, "We do not inherit the land from our ancestors; we borrow it from our children."

Macaulay Heritage Park
613-476-3833 or 3836; fax 613-476-8356
Church and Union Streets
Open June 1 to Labour Day, Monday to Frida, 10 to 4:30; Saturday and Sunday 1 to 4:30; closed Tuesdays; phone for spring and fall hours; entrance fee for Macaulay House and Museum; no charge for park; picnic area and washroom facilities

This heritage complex explores the rich history of the County of Prince Edward, and the atmosphere is that of the mid-nineteenth century. The gardens have been carefully restored. The old apple trees in the orchard have been replaced and are now bearing fruit, and a fine collection of butternut, black locust, black walnut, sugar maple, common lilac, white oak has been planted.

I walked from the old church, now the Prince Edward County Museum, with its neatly mown lawns and white picket fence, toward Macaulay House, an elegant mansion built in the Georgian style in the mid-1800s. The spacious garden has two large herbaceous beds cut out of the lawn, one a circular bed facing the house and surrounded by a pathway planted with old-fashioned flowers such as lady's bells, phlox, fern, tiger lilies and roses. Behind the house are more pleasures. There is a limestone bed full of roses and alyssum edged in silvery artemisia, with a view of the park and a hardwood-treed hill beyond.

Through a chain-link fence lies the conservation area, with its "living walkway," so named in memory of those who shaped the destiny of this county town.

Bloomfield

Angeline's
Bloomfield Inn
29 Stanley Street West
613-393-3301
Located at Highways 62 and 33

Central Prince Edward County

Food for Thought
613-393-1423
11:30 to 4, closed Monday; luncheon and tea, all homemade; Highway 62 south from Belleville, east on Schoharie Road, house on left.

Milford

Milford Coffee Gallery
King Street
613-476-7251
Not open until Easter.

Picton

Cornucopia
172 Main Street
613-476-2702
Monday to Saturday 9 to 5, morning coffee, luncheon and afternoon tea.

Port Dover Region: Norwich / Otterville / Port Dover / Tillsonburg

NORWICH

Gloria McMillen, *McMillen's Iris Garden*
McMillan's Iris Garden, RR 1, Norwich, ON, N0J 1P0
519-468-6508
6.4 kilometres west of Norwich, 1.6 kilometres south
Conditions   zone 6; sandy loam
Plot size   15 acres
Open May 1 to mid-August, daily, dawn to dusk; bus parties call ahead

Iris and day lilies

Once a dairy farm, these 15 acres have been transformed into Canada's largest iris garden. Imagine row upon row of 1,200 varieties of iris — starting with a rainbow of colour from the charming early miniatures, followed by the medians and finally the tall bearded Siberians, from 4 inches to 40 inches tall. As the iris season comes to an end, Gloria McMillen and her sons prepare for the appearance of the 100 varieties of day lilies in glorious hues of yellow, gold, orange and red.

More energetic visitors view the blooms at close range by walking the rows while others prefer to sit in the shade of the country garden or in the gazebo by the Japanese garden. Orders for plants are taken by August and can be picked up at the garden. A coast-to-coast shipping service is also available.

OTTERVILLE

Marilyn Edmison-Driedger, *The Herbal Touch*
30 Dover Street, Otterville, ON, N0J 1R6
519-879-6812
Conditions: zone 6a; sandy, slight
Plot size: approximately 1 acre

Open: shop open May 2 to December 23, 10 to 5; not easy for wheelchairs, but help is given, garden visible from patio; plants for sale

❧ Herb nursery, friendship garden, shop for herbalists and gift hunters

S et in the lovely countryside of Oxford County, the charming old mill town of Otterville is home to the Herbal Touch. This magical place is the inspired brainchild of Marilyn Edmison-Driedger, lecturer, writer and artist, well known for her appearances on "The Gardener's Journal."

Through the gate in the grey picket fence, the air is sweet with heady fragrance from the luxurious-smelling herb gardens that spill down the terraced slope. Stroll along lavender-lined paths past lily ponds and beds crammed with favourites, old and new. Beside the courtyard, the quaint old barn houses a delightful gift shop that stocks the harvest from the garden. Here you will find herbal teas, unique all-seasons botanical wreaths, everlasting bouquets, as well as books, garden accessories, essential oils and a "to die for" hot sauce known as the Herbal Touch meltdown.

Across the road lies the relatively new Friendship Garden. Marilyn has taken an Ontario field and turned it into a sea of colour. Old-fashioned roses fill a long border; rows of lemon verbena, eleven types of basil and many varieties of hot peppers share bed space with hundreds of perennials and everlasting blooms. Special bouquets of fresh flowers can be cut on request, and Marilyn supplies floral arrangements for any occasion worth catering for.

PORT DOVER

Cathy and Dennis Boyko, *Laser Garden*
RR 9, Dunnville, ON, N1A 2W8
905-774-8360

Conditions	zone 6
Plot size	3/4 of an acre

Open by appointment

❧ Iris and day lily collections, scree and water gardens

W hen Kathy Boyko's plan to buy a Laser sailboat was quashed, she named her garden "Laser." An L-shaped driveway lined with perennials leads through native woodlands to a 50-by-12-foot iris bed bordering the front lawn and rhododendrons framing the house. To the east is a hosta collection and a trial garden where Cathy experiments with special plants in raised beds; these are surrounded by gravel walkways that lead through to the back garden. The south lawn is flanked on three sides by perennials, peonies, narcissus, shrubs and herbs. Masses of irises and day lilies and a variety of perennials are planted in large, sweeping beds. A scree bed is filled with alpine plants and miniature irises; a waterfall splashes into a kidney-shaped water garden stocked with koi. The gazebo is fashioned on an Oriental theme. If you feel energetic you are invited to walk around the 14-acre woodland, where wild geraniums, hepaticas, wood anemones and trilliums grow.

Cathy's impressive iris collection includes beardless, tall bearded and historical. She is happy to take orders and have them ready for pickup or shipment at a later date.

Jim Cruise
519-428-9929

Conditions   zone 6; clay loam, rolling terrain
Plot size   200 acres (2 acres of garden, 6 acres of lake)
Open by appointment

❧ Uncommon trees and shrubs, perennial beds, birds and animals

I couldn't help thinking of Dr. Dolittle when I visited Dr. Jim Cruise, who shares his large country property with a large assortment of dogs, cats, a variety of exotic birds and two llamas, Carlos and the amorous Don Juan, who is not backward in coming forward for a kiss.

The house was built by his grandmother in 1905, and looks out over a peaceful valley. Jim has lived here all his life, and his interest in gardening goes back almost as far; he laid out the first lawn on the property when he was twelve. A plant physiologist and taxonomist, he is continually experimenting with unlikely specimens for this climate, as is evident in the many unusual trees and shrubs that are planted throughout. A 6-acre lake, Lake Marburg, is home to three species of swans and an array of wildlife; over the years he has raised and sold some fifty mute swans.

Accompanied by a lolloping Hungarian sheepdog, we walked through the parklike grounds where peacocks and guinea fowl roam free among the flowers and other ornamentals, which must be tough and resilient to withstand the birds' rigorous attention.

An extraordinary structure, known as "The Monument," was created by Jim and his brother. Assembled from hundreds of welded cast-iron pieces, found inside the house and around the farm, it towers 20 feet high, a fitting monument to the family and its life here over the past century.

Jim hopes that he will live long enough to see some "knees" in the lawn from the false cypress he acquired in Florida last year. Away in the distance two bald cypress flourish in the valley along with several interesting species of beech, including fern leaf beech, a weeping full-skirted European beech, fastigiate beech and tri-colour beech. These are interspersed with many unusual conifers, including the lovely dawn redwood, which he received as a cutting from one of the original group, discovered in China in 1940. *Hydrangea petiolaris* and its lesser-known, but, in my opinion, more beautiful counterpart, *Schitzophragma*, grow up the trunks of many of his trees, emphasizing the exotic feel of the place. Sculpture plays an important part in this garden; and lording it over all stands the steel sculpture of an enormous eagle, master of everything he surveys.

Large perennial beds house collections of hostas, day lilies and peonies. Behind a pair of charming iron gates a lushly planted enclosure contains a water wheel churning beside a lily pond; here the most beautiful lotus I have ever seen, great shower-head blooms of pink and white, provide a dramatic finale to a fascinating visit.

Frank Schaefer, *Schaefer's Mini Arboretum*
40 Lakeview Avenue, Port Dover, ON, N0A 1N8
519-583-0389
Just east of Port Dover off Highway 6
Conditions   zone 6; clay topped with sand
Plot size   140 x 135 feet
Open by appointment or by chance

Unusual trees and shrubs

I could scarcely believe my eyes! A monkey puzzle tree, a *Magnolia grandiflora* and pampas grass thriving happily in Southern Ontario? It's true, thanks to Frank Schaefer, who has created a mini Kew Gardens in his modest-sized backyard. When he and his wife bought the cottage as a holiday home in 1961, it sat in the middle of a ploughed field. Today, enveloped in lush greenery, the garden has come a very long way from the first tentative planting of silver birches.

"You don't see straight lines in nature," says Frank, pointing to beds that sweep in graceful curves round the green lawns. Beckoning paths lead off under arches of golden hazel through luxuriant woodlands, where he has tiered the plantings for a naturalistic effect. Thickly planted ground covers hug the base of a middle canopy of shrubs, which in turn are backed by trees, including thriving Carolinian and exotic genus. Among them can be found sassafras, cucumber tree, *Halesia* (silverbell) and a large variety of magnolias.

The extraordinary collection of broad-leafed evergreens hails from far and wide. A Chitalpa, a cross between catalpa and desert willow, came from south Russia in 1988. Sweet bay, hardy orange (*Poncirus*), Chinese parasol tree (*Firmiana simplex*) Japanese cedar and Himalayan pine, photinia, and moosewood (*Acer pennsylvanica*) with its interesting tropical bark, all thrive in this botanical heaven, as beautiful in winter against the white snow as they are in summer in all their finery.

Frank has been able to nurture his plants through the worst of winters, helped by a proximity to Lake Erie, which produces constant humidity and moderates the climate. The tenderest of them are placed in a charming round gazebo cum greenhouse. He has a strict routine for any new exotic plants that he acquires, exposing them to the elements very gradually after their first winter, until by the fourth year they are "on their own." His success rate is remarkable, growing things that most people wouldn't even dream of in this part of the world. For Frank Schaefer, no challenge is too great.

TILLSONBURG

Carole and Henry Reimer, *Reimer Waterscapes*
Box 34, Tillsonburg, ON
519-842-6049; fax 519-688-LILY
5 kilometres west of Tillsonburg, on the Bayham Ninth Line,
Open April 15 to September 30, Monday to Saturday noon to 5; extended hours May and June, Monday to Friday noon to 7, Saturday and Sunday 10 to 4

Water lilies, bog and shallow-water plants, fish, snails and frogs

The Reimers are water garden specialists. Their display gardens are well worth strolling, especially for those interested in pond settings.

There are six large ponds, each one demonstrating the Reimer flair in the use of water and nature. From small tubs to large natural ponds, all stocked with the prettiest water lilies, the variations are endless. When the sun goes down, the hardy day-bloomers take a nap and the tropical night-bloomers take over. Floating water hyacinths, lavender-coloured in flower, and tropical bog plants of infinite hues and textures make an elegant vision. Enjoy a picnic in the Japanese garden that overlooks the ponds.

"Our souls know we came from water," says Carole, happy in this aquatic paradise she and Henry have created.

Port Dover

Trifles
Gift Shop and Tearoom
326 Main Street
519-583-1313
Open daily.

The Erie Beach Hotel
10 Walker Street
519-583-1391
Open daily.

Port Hope Region: Brighton / Coburg / Grafton / Kendal / Newtonville / Port Hope / Welcome

BRIGHTON

Marg Fleming and Glen Parsneau, *Cedar Valley Gardens*
RR 7, Brighton, ON, K0K 1H0
613-475-0535
6 kilometres north of Brighton on Highway 30, 4 kilometres west on Northumberland Road 21

Conditions   zone 5; sandy loam, rolling hills
Plot size   150 acres, of which 5 are cultivated
Open May through October, every day except Tuesday; 8 to 6; plants sold

❧ Scree, Japanese, perennial and bog gardens; water-lily pond

Marg Fleming is a horticultural expert whose enthusiasm and hard work are infectious. She has, almost singlehandedly, built Cedar Valley Gardens into one of the most extensive perennial display gardens in Eastern Ontario.

Under the trellised archway, hundreds of perennials fill sweeping island beds cut into a rolling expanse of lawn that stretches to the gazebo. From this shady platform you can view large collections of bearded iris and peonies that make a kaleidoscope of colour in early summer. The tour continues past the Japanese garden, with its five islands covered in brilliant green Irish moss, to an expanding scree garden, where *Clematis virginiana* grows over the pergola walk. Paths wander through woodland groves of hostas and wildflowers to the natural ponds, where a large waterlily collection floats among the reeds. Along the banks, Marg has planted a graceful array of grasses; the bog garden here is home to many damp-loving plants, including *Lobelia cardinalis*, *Iris pseudocarus* and stately ligularias.

The gardens are accented with statuary and Victorian hand-blown glass gazing balls; these are available for sale, as are the top-quality vigorous plants. A comprehensive catalogue is available, and Marg will happily order in anything that she doesn't sell herself.

COBURG

Ⅲ Merike Lugus, *Swallow Hill*
905-372-2410
Just north of Lake Ontario, east of Coburg
Conditions zone 5/6; clay, alluvial fill
Open by appointment

✤ **Magnificent setting, rock garden, perennial garden, sculpture, studio**

The view that stretched before me, as I stepped through the narrow opening in the cedar hedge, was stunning. Situated on a drumlin overlooking the Northumberland Hills, the garden was started in 1989 and grew according to three considerations: the first, to hold on to the magical feeling Merike Lugus had when she first entered the property; the second, to lead the eye toward the lake; and the third, not to involve her husband's time and energy.

Through the craggy limestone fingers that form the large rockery near the house, thyme mixes with heuchera, a maple lies prostrate across the stones, autumn-blooming clematis clambers through juniper and tangles with the soft blue flowers of caryopteris. Paths wander through fields of goldenrod, asters and milkweed pods, to ponds where willows lean into jade green water splashed with magenta waterlilies.

The garden is full of what she calls "consequential stuff like love, joy and sorrow" — the first thing to catch my eye was Merike's strong yet tender sculpture of a woman, known as the Madonna of the Tulips, gazing out over the garden to the lake in the far distance. As I rounded the corner I was stopped in my tracks by the sight of a great steel arch of brilliant blue, a Matisse-like cut-out, its flamboyant shape echoing the billowing clouds and undulating hills captured forever in its frame. Merike created this special structure for the occasion of her daughter's wedding, and with the erection of the arch came the birth of the garden beyond. All her artistry comes into play here with plants of exquisite shapes, colours and scents skilfully combined, blooming in endless succession, from the first snowdrop and Iris reticulata in spring to the last Japanese anemone, snakeroot and rose in the fall.

Newly planted roses took on a special significance in the last months of her mother's life, especially the *Rosa mundi* and the warm yellow Graham Thomas. As long as she is their caregiver, she says, these plants, like others associated with people she loves, must never die.

GRAFTON

▥ Pat Poisson, *1812 Heritage Garden*
1812 Heritage Antiques, Danforth Road, Grafton, ON, K0K 2G0
905-349-3756
Between Port Hope and Coburg on Highway 2; at the corner of
Danforth Road; entrance to garden behind Heritage Antiques
Conditions   zone 5; loam, flat
*Open daily 10 to 5, garden open May through September Sundays 12 to 5;
plants for sale*

❧ **Folly, sculpture for sale, cutting garden, pond, cut-your-own flowers**

This heritage building has been transformed into a charming row of
shops, well worth stopping to explore, and the garden at the back of
Pat Poisson's delightful 1812 antique shop is an added incentive.

Soaring maples, their branches hung with whimsical birdhouses, pre-
date the venerable building by several years, providing welcome shade in
the heat of the summer. Around their base, a ground cover of smooth
pebbles dotted with found objects leads to a stream that trickles into a
pool where fish dart beneath yellow water lilies. A tin sheep beside the
twig arches marks the entry into an Alice in Wonderland world. From the
midst of a magical cutting garden rises a folly in the form of a huge metal
pergola, grown over with morning glories and backed by a dense arc of
giant sunflowers. Pretty terra-cotta brick pathways wander between beds
overflowing with cottage flowers; poppies, daisies, larkspur, towering delphiniums, and lilies are sumptuously arranged in rich colour harmonies.
The heady perfumes of nicotiana, lavender and night-scented stock perfume the air here.

Pat has turned this section of her garden into a unique resource, a
public cutting garden where, for a modest charge, you can come and fill
your trugs with these lovely flowers, either for drying or to place fresh in
your vases.

▣ Judy and Neil Baird, *Griffindale Farm Bed and Breakfast*
905-349-2940
3 kilometres north of Grafton; phone for directions

Conditions   zone 5b; silty loam, rolling farmland
Plot size   130 acres
Open fourth Saturday in May, second and fourth Saturday in June, first and third Saturday in July; 10 to 5; $5 per car to be donated to the Haldimand Township Horticultural Society

❧ **Perennials and a variety of rosebushes**

This lovely heritage farmhouse, its weathered barn restored to its former glory, is run by Neil and Judy Baird as a bed and breakfast. Set in the Northumberland Hills, it is surrounded by two acres of lawn and lovingly tended flower beds filled with perennials and roses.

From the first early spring anemones to the last rose of summer, this garden is forever changing in appearance, with each season bringing its own special delight. Judy is passionate about her garden and enjoys the "doing and the redoing" in anticipation of whatever changes the next year might bring.

KENDAL

The Ganaraska Countryside Adventure
All three of the following gardens are open for viewing on the Great Ganaraska Countryside Adventure, organized by Elva Reid and Kristin McCrea. This event runs the weekend before Labour Day each year. The cost is $10 for each adult, which gives you access to sixty-five farms and gardens over the two days. For more information on the many gardens open in the Ganaraska, call 905-983-9339 or e-mail redwing@osha.1gs.net

▥ Ed and Lorna Audette
905-983-8241
Oak Ridges Moraine, between Kirby and Kendal
Plot size   50 acres, 2 acres cultivated
Open through the Great Ganaraska Countryside Adventure, 905-983-9339; otherwise, by appointment only

❧ **Perennial gardens, antique shop**

This lovely property sits comfortably in a valley backing onto the Ganaraska Forest, an idyllic setting for the Audettes' garden and the Georgian clapboard home they have been restoring for the past five years.

The original veggie gardens now produce food for the family and seeds for the birds. Flowers were never a focus on this property, but that has changed recently, and ever-expanding perennial gardens frame the house and restored barn, from which the Audettes run their antique business.

Luke and Cynthia Prout, *"Kiss me over the garden gate"*
905-983-9865
Oak Ridges Moraine, outside Kendal
Open through the Great Ganaraska Countryside Adventure, 905-983-9339; otherwise, by appointment only

Located on a tributary of the Ganaraska River, this garden carved from the woods is home to a collection of herbs, heritage perennials and old roses. The English-style garden is not only named after an unusual flower, it is also home to many unusual plants.

Elva Reid and Kristin McCrae, *Redwing Farm*
905-983-9339
Oakridge Moraine, between Kirby and Kendal
Open through the Great Ganaraska Countryside Adventure, 905-983-9339; otherwise, by appointment only

Birdhouses

The garden at Redwing Farm has evolved over the past seven years, and the intent of Elva Reid and Kristin McCrae was to reclaim their piece of rolling pasture land and marsh. They, as others in the Ganaraska, are fortunate in having a good supply of water water as the backbone of their garden and have no difficulties with drought.

Neither Elva or Kristin have time to tend two-plus acres of flowers and vegetables. They decided to create a "wild garden" as an interesting experiment in low-maintenance gardening. They transplant seedlings from the bush to the vegetable garden; as the plants grow stronger these are transferred into the wild garden, where it becomes a matter of the survival of the fittest. The result has been beyond their expectations, rewarding them with a glorious tangle of colour and form from the flowers, leaves and seed heads that have triumphed!

The rolling topography, pond and small streams are enhanced by the trees that Elva and Kristin have planted. Much of what changes here is influenced by Kirsten's fascination with birds; this has led her to build the most interesting birdhouses, including replicas of old barns, country houses and historic churches. Some can be seen around the property, but they don't stay for long, as they sell almost as quickly as she makes them.

NEWTONVILLE

John A. deWitt, *Long John's*
RR 1, Newtonville, ON, L0A 1J0
905-786-2014
From Highway 401, north at Exit 18 north of Highway 2
Open: not Victoria Day weekend; any other weekend, or by appointment

❦ **Lily ponds, perennials, shrubs, antiques for sale**

The redbrick farmhouse with its red barns to match make a charming courtyard and entryway for John deWitt's garden in rolling Ontario farmland. Meander around the flagstone pathways beside a series of lily ponds for a close-up view of the large selection of colourful perennials.

John is a dealer in antiques, and his interest in the beautiful and unusual is reflected in his garden.

PORT HOPE

Michael and Shirley Harrison
73 Bramley Street North, Port Hope, ON
905-885-2142
Port Hope: last house at north end of Bramley Street
Conditions   zone 5, slightly sloping
Open by appointment or by chance, "Just come on by"

❧ **Perennials, annuals, rock garden, lilies, wildflowers**

I f variety is the spice of life, then Michael Harrison has surely found a fine flavour in this lovely old garden. Each year he plants over 3,000 seedlings, all of which he carefully nurtures from seed. Enormous beds cut out of the rolling lawns are filled with a vibrant display of annuals and perennials that put on a colourful display for months on end. Both the garden and his love of it were inherited from his mother.

WELCOME

Kathryn McHolm
RR 1, Port Hope, ON, L1A 3V5
4749 Highway 2, Welcome
905-753-2196
1 kilometre from the 401 on left or west side of Highway 2, look for Artist's Garden and Studio sign

Conditions   zone 5; good loam, flat with a gentle slope
Plot size   approximately half an acre
Open: art show second weekend in July; weekend hours for June through August are 10 to 4 Saturday, 1 to 4 Sunday; call ahead for appointments during the week; box for donations

❧ **Large heritage garden, herbs, studio, shop; plants for sale May and June**

K athryn McHolm lives and works in the sleepy village of Welcome. Her charming mid-nineteenth-century house with its beautiful grey barn provides just the right background for the exuberant mass of perennials, wildflowers and herbs that proliferate here. The backbone of the garden is the collection of heritage plants: peonies, verbascums, hollyhocks, giant thistles, black-eyed Susans, larkspur, poppies, phlox, campanulas and lilies have been allowed to run riot, seeding themselves at will in every available space.

Nothing in this garden goes to waste. Morning glories and sweet peas climb through strange-shaped prunings from the neighbour's apple trees, a wild grapevine pulled from the birches is woven into her inspired wattle fence, and a red osier dogwood becomes a basket. The shed housing her bric-a-brac shop is stocked with everything from lacy ribbons to dried herbs, wreaths, floral arrangements and handmade paper, all created from ingredients culled from her joyful garden.

A rustic cedar arch covered in clematis leads to the unusual "home" garden. Paths like tributaries of a river flow round dirt islands planted with herbs and vegetables — an idea, she owns, that was copied from Martha Stewart.

Dragonflies flit across the pond, now turned into a giant bath for the birds; together with the continual parade of butterflies and bees, they provide inspiration for the lovely watercolours she paints and sells. "It's my pleasure," says Kathryn, "to be able to share it with visitors." Once there, I guarantee you'll find its peaceful magic difficult to leave behind.

Port Hope

The Beamish House
27 John Street
905-885-8702
Luncheon and dinner, daily 11 to 1 am.

The Carlyle Inn
86 John Street
905-885-8686
Luncheon served 11:30 to 4, and dinner from 4.

The Owl and the Pussycat
127 Walton Street
Pub lunch served daily 11:30 to 5; closed Tuesday and Wednesday.

Sault Ste. Marie (Hilton Beach)

|||||| Russell and Eleanor Adcock, *Adcock's Woodland Gardens*
RR 1, Tenby Bay, Hilton Beach, ON, P0R 1G0
705-246-2579
Hilton Beach: St. Joseph Island, 50 miles southeast of Sault Ste. Marie;
Highway 17 east to Highway 548 south to Tenby Bay; garden is just
north of the U Line and Fifth Side Road

Conditions	zone 4b; humus and sand, marshland
Plot size	98 acres, 4 acres landscaped

*Open May 15 to September 30, by appointment, or just drop in between 10
a.m. and dusk; freewill donations accepted*

❧ **Landscaped, naturalistic, three large excavated ponds**

Adcock's Woodland Gardens is one of the main attractions on picturesque St. Joseph's Island at Tenby Bay. After they retired, Russell
and Eleanor Adcock decided to try to grow something on their "little
inland marsh." With designs by Russell and one of their sons and ideas
from the rest of the family, nearly 4 acres of gardens, ponds and lawns
have been developed in this natural setting. Rustic walkways meander
through the grounds, with benches conveniently placed to encourage you
to linger awhile. The variety of beautiful native and imported plants,
flowers and shrubs is impressive. Swathes of iris surround ponds filled
with many species of brightly coloured water lilies.

The Adcocks' intention was to create a place of beauty to enjoy and to
share with other garden lovers.

Stratford Region: Baden / Sebringville / Stratford

BADEN

||||||| Gwynedd and Ewart Brundrett, *Wanakiwin*
519-634-8500
13 kilometres west of Waterloo to St. Agatha, first woodlot on the left;
left-hand lane through the woodlot, left turn in the woods, to the top
of the hill

Conditions   zone 5; sandy, hilly
Plot size: 25 acres, over 1 acre under cultivation
Open by appointment

❧ **Various plant collections especially lilies, pond**

When the Brundretts bought Wanakin, a 25-acre woodlot, in 1966,
they were unaware that it was one of the richest woods for flora
in Ontario. Wildflowers bloom in abundance here, starting in the spring
with hepaticas of every shade, and literally hundreds of thousands of
trilliums; to date they have identified fifty-four species of wildflower.

Carved out of this natural scene, the garden spills down a sunny slope
from a prettily paved knot garden filled with herbs, past shrub and shade
borders. A series of terraces and island beds bursting with perennials and
organic vegetables, fall away to where a fountain and trickling waterfall
recirculate between two large ponds, where the statue of a heron waits
patiently for a glint of fish. A fan-patterned fence made by Gwynedd's
husband Ewart, who calls himself "the Grunt," is covered in species
clematis. The drystone wall around the lower pool is planted with a new
collection of alpines and a Japanese maple (*Acer dissectum atropupurea*)
whose red leaves offer a brilliant contrast to clipped boxwood.

In the ruins of a recently torn down greenhouse and hidden behind a
Chinese-style fence, another rockery is in the making, where she hopes to
indulge her passion for alpines.

The Brundretts say it is their good fortune to have a son who shares in
their enthusiasm and has a degree in botany, the happy result being this
interesting garden with its diverse collection of flora.

SEBRINGVILLE

Sherry and Leo Van de Wetering, *Sherry's Perennial Garden*
519-393-6661 (business); 519-393-6602 (home)
Conditions   zone 5/6
Open by appointment

❧ **Gazebo, ponds, perennials, herbs**

L eo the builder, Sherry the floral designer and their ten-year-old son —
the willing helper — have created a garden of pleasant places. Lush
green plants and colourful perennials line the driveway leading to the
back garden. Mandivilla, gardenia, jasmine and hibiscus fill the planter
boxes on the deck and around the gazebo. Comfortable twig furniture is
placed invitingly by two fish ponds. Clematis and honeysuckle vines surround a sunny flagstone patio. Among the unusual trees in Sherry's
collection are an Asia pear, corkscrew hazel, lilac standard, weeping larch
and copper beech. Trilliums carpet the apple orchard. The delphinium
collection is especially beautiful.

Gerald Brickman, *Brickman's Botanical Gardens*
RR 1, Sebringville, ON, N0K 1X0
519-393-6223
At Sebringville O.P.P. station turn right (north) onto County Road 12, to
Wartburg intersection (Ellice 6 and 7), turn left and travel 1 kilometre
Conditions   zone 5; flat
*Open mid-April to Thanksgiving weekend, daily, Monday to Friday 8 to 8,
Saturday and Sunday 8 to 5; wheelchair accessible; no pets please; all garden
tours are self guided; $4.25 per person, children under twelve $0.50*

❧ **Many specialty gardens, garden centre, mini zoo**

S urrounded by a sea of corn and grain where cattle graze under whispering poplars, 11 acres of farmland have been transformed into a
series of specialty gardens housing a treasure trove of plants, as well as a
mini farm zoo with rare breeds of animals and birds not seen on the typical Ontario farm. These spectacular botanical gardens are the inspiration
and life's work of Gerald Brickman, who was born here some forty-four

years ago. It is interesting to note that "botanical" is defined by Gerry as "a garden where our plants are tested and studied for hardiness."

When I visited this fascinating place on a golden afternoon in August it seemed I had walked into a Bonnard painting. Drifts of heleniums, hazy blue Perovskia, eupatorium, kniphofias, deep blue Bella Donna delphiniums, species phlox, roses, eryngiums, asters, at least ten different crocosomias — the list goes on and on — put on a breathtaking show.

A maze of stone paths winds past long island beds crammed with over 3,000 bulbs and perennials both rare and familiar that have been collected by Gerry from all over the world. He refuses to be thwarted and has succeeded with many species that defy both the Ontario weather and sceptics alike; even Agapanthus overwinters here.

The new scree garden, a "lunar landscape" of mounds and craters, has a cactus-shaped pond, grasses, sedums, sempervivums and cactus. The old-fashioned rose garden features many plants that date to the Middle Ages, such as the lovely striped *Rosa mundi*; the Queen Mother's Garden is filled with "her favourite" flowers, and a Bible garden is devoted to over a hundred plants mentioned in the Bible. Sit in the all-white garden and drink in the perfume of the rugosa rose *Blanc double de Coubert*, or beside one of the several hidden water gardens. The latest ventures are a hosta bed and a humongous formal area laid out like a wheel, whose gravel paths are lined with over a thousand lavenders. Gerry doesn't believe in doing things by halves.

This is a great outing for all the family or for those of you looking for a break from the theatre. There's also a very nice English tearoom, where you can have a light lunch or a wonderfully fattening cream tea before browsing in the gift shop or purchasing a "treasure" from the nursery.

STRATFORD

Gerard Brender à Brandis
249 Ontario Street, Stratford, ON, N5A 3H6
519-273-7523

Conditions   zone 5; mellowday, much improved, flat
Plot size   42 x 133 feet (including house and driveway)
Open: Garden visitors welcome same hours as studio is open, Wednesday to Sunday 10 to 6 from mid-May to mid-November

❧ **Small city garden, wide variety of perennials, bulbs, shrubs, vines**

Gerard Brender à Brandis designed and maintains this delightful little city garden as a source of inspiration for much of his outstanding work as a botanical artist. It is crammed full of all the elements usually found in a large garden.

There are semi-shade woodland beds and sunny beds; each filled with unusual and beautiful plantings. The stately foxtail lily (*Eremurus robustus*), *Kirengeshoma palmata* with its dangling yellow bells, and *Skimmia japonica* are some of the more unusual plants found here. Raised beds contain a small kitchen garden and another of tea herbs. A trellised arbour and fence are hidden by the climbers they support, and "pictures" have been created within the garden by the careful use of conifers, interesting shrubs, grasses and flowering plants.

A bookwright and engraver, Gerard has made this garden a lovely setting for his studio/gallery located here. His exquisite prints and handmade books and gifts, some printed on paper made from iris leaves or other plants from the garden, are on display in the front room gallery of his 1877 Ontario cottage.

Shakespeare Gardens
Huron Street Bridge, downtown
Open year round, dawn to dusk; wheelchair access

The long oblong beds filled with rue, rosemary, phlox, lilies and roses are carved from the lawns that lead down to the River Avon. A bust of William Shakespeare stands beside a small garden that has been planted with flowers mentioned in his plays; read the engraved plaques for the associated quotations. This is the perfect setting for a picnic on a summer day.

Stratford Festival Theatre Gardens
55 Queen Street, surrounding the Theatre
Open daily; wheelchair access

The sweeping lawns surrounding the main theatre and the rich plantings of perennials and shrubs conform to the original plans of H. B. Dunington-Grubb. A rose garden has been added to this charming garden.

Sebringville

By the Garden Gate
Brickman's Botanical Gardens
Wartburg
519-393-6223
English tearoom at the entrance to the gardens in an English country garden setting. Herbs from the garden are used for the specialty teas and in
sandwiches. Light lunches and teas served daily from 10 to 5.

Stratford

Down the Street Bar and Café
30 Ontario Street
519-273-5886
Excellent lunch and dinner menu from 11:30.

Toronto: Cabbagetown / East York / Etobicoke / North York / Riverdale / Rosedale / Scarborough / Central Toronto / Toronto Islands

CABBAGETOWN

Aileen Harris
416-469-5211 ext. 199; 416-323-3520

Conditions   zone 6; 12 to 14 inches garden compost, underlying sand base

Open through Woodgreen Community Centre, fourth Sunday of June; otherwise by appointment with owner

❧ **Espaliered fruit trees, small pool, unusual containers and plants**

The late and great landscaper Murray Haigh helped to design the bijou garden of Aileen Harris, a fantasy courtyard reflecting her experiences and her dreams. To the east, fruit trees espaliered like a Sultan's fan are underplanted with roses and lavender. To the north, a devil's walking stick vies for attention with a contorted and recalcitrant wisteria. Will it ever bloom? The west wall, sunny in the afternoons, plays host to a collection of clematis, the unusual and the familiar woven together. A small pool and fun planters are filled with blue plumbago and standard lantana, a reminder of her winter home in Mexico. Aileen's vigorous composting and constant redesigning guarantee that this garden will continue to be one of the gems of Cabbagetown for years to come.

Robert Packham and Jamie Graham
416-469-5211 ext. 199; 416-944-8041

Conditions   zone 6; garden loam underlying sand base
Plot size   15 x 125 feet
Open through Woodgreen Community Centre, fourth Sunday of June

❧ Unusual design and architectural features, plant collections

This is the latest garden venture for the duo of Robert Packham, well-known landscape architect, and his partner, Jamie Graham. They have really gone to town in this delightfully eclectic space, making it rich with nuances of the great gardens of the classical tradition, and yet still paying attention to a wealth of detail in the hard landscaping as well as the plantings.

Robert calls himself a collector, and continues to ferret out the "rare and unusual," which he has worked into the intricate overall design. Trees and shrubs abound: Katsura, weeping purple beech and the Forest Pansy redbud grace the backyard, and in the front he has planted an exotic fern grove and magnolias such as Elizabeth and *sieboldii*. Here you will find foxgloves from all over the globe, species clematis, chocolate cosmos, and many varieties of hardy geraniums and Kaffir lilies.

Sit on the amusing thyme throne and study the stone compass at your feet, each "point" featuring a different mint or thyme. Many varieties of buddleia and day lilies have been planted en route to the laburnum walk, where those weeping yellow racemes live up to their name, "the Golden Rain tree." In this witty knowledgeable garden, the more you look the more you will see; it is truly an original work of art.

EAST YORK

Janet Bedali

416-751-0685

Conditions   zone 6; clay, flat
Plot size   30 x 100 feet
Open by appointment; plants for sale

❧ Day lily specialist, peonies

A double peony hedge, over a hundred day lilies, an extensive perennial mixture, vegetables and a collection of hostas are all growing on this little corner lot. Every inch has been employed, both vertically and horizontally. The organization is casual but ordered, with the back garden laid out like an allotment, for maximum growing space. But for Janet, the undisputed stars of the show are the day lilies. "They are one of the best-kept secrets around," says Janet, who does much of her own hybridizing. "It's thrilling that such an amazing assortment of shade and colour could result from one little pod."

Gardening started out as a pleasurable hobby, but with retirement has become the focus of her life. She likes the contact with the people who come to buy her plants or simply stop to make inquiries and admire.

Laura Grant

416-422-2164, 416-250-9000 (business)

Conditions   zone 6; sandy, table land

Plot size   40 x 160 feet

Open by appointment; some plants for sale to offset the cost of the garden; a small donation to the East York Garden Society appreciated as entrance fee

❧ Pond, rock, scree, woodland

Laura Grant, President of the Rhododendron Society of Canada, is a committed gardener who certainly knows her plants.

The emphasis in her immaculate mini botanical garden is on unusual trees and shrubs, planted for interest and low-maintenance. Species chosen are either dwarf, espaliered or pruned to suit the scale of a small garden, with particular attention given to the dynamics of control through shape and texture. Azaleas and rhododendrons put on a gorgeous spring display along paths that meander through tall grasses and bamboos, alpines, scree and herb gardens, to a little bridge over the pond where bullfrogs sing and fish swim among the lilies.

Glen Hutzul

416-469-5211 ext. 199

Conditions   zone 6; clay, flat

Plot size   18 x 45 feet

Open through Woodgreen Community Centre, second Saturday in July

❧ Excellent small garden design

Glen Hutzul's "pocket handkerchief" is a marvellous example of how a keen gardener makes the most of what he hasn't got. The exuberant front garden of his little cottage is surrounded by a low grey picket fence, brimming with old favourites. In complete contrast, the shaded backyard is beautifully designed and cleverly divided to give the illusion of space. Glen uses standard plants and recycled materials in a truly original way. A clipped Austrian pine grows out of a rectangular pond in the centre of the garden, drawing the eye across the diagonal to where a group of flowering shrubs adds colour to a quiet corner. Three-foot-wide beds are thick with a mixture of perennials, ornamental grasses vegetables and herbs, including tarragon and sage. Campanulas grow among the lettuces, and beans interwine with clematis. Silver lace vine and hanging pots on the pretty porch complete the picture in this unique garden.

Anna Leggatt
416-755-2325

Conditions zone 6; clay and garbage fill over deep sand; part flat, part ravine

Plot size 50 x 250 feet

By appointment with owner; donation to the Church of St. Columba and All Hallows

Alpines, woodland, scree, new crevice garden, large pond, peat garden

A powerhouse of energy, Anna Leggatt is forever tearing down walls, digging, propogating and planting. Well known in Canadian gardening circles as a writer, lecturer and extremely knowledgable plantswoman, Anna has a garden that is a testament to her never-ending quest for new discoveries, and growing beautiful plants in the best possible setting. She is gradually melding an amalgam of ideas from gardens she has visited, together with inspiration from the wild areas that border the property. Her task is not easy, as her time and the space available are both limited. However, this blowsy romantic garden is full of lovely corners and a wealth of material.

Among her favourite groups are the alpines, from the tiny ones for troughs to those that tumble in profusion over the rock garden walls. The front garden has been transformed into an Ontario woodland, rich with bulbs and wonderful spring wildflowers, and she has a fondness for practically every member of the foxglove family. The lovely pond, filled with water plants, is surrounded with rock plants and perennials, while a small scree garden and crevice garden near the patio are in their early stages. It is impossible to name everyone of Anna's all-time favourites, but here are a few: *Acer japonicum dissectum* and cultivars, double bloodroot, trillium, mottle-leaved hepaticas, the late *Tulipa batalinii* Bright Gem. In the rock garden, various penstemons in pinks, blues and mauves, and gentians grow alongside various campanulas, her favourite being *Campanula alpina* (*bughetti*). Colchicums and crocus bloom in the fall, with the splendid *Cimicifuga racemosa* Atropurpurea followed in November by the waxy flowers of *Helleborus niger* Praccox, which continue undaunted thoughout the winter, under the snow. You will glean much from a visit with Anna Leggatt.

Ⅲ Pauline and Joseph Marmina
416-757-8607 (home); 416-691-8892 (business)
Conditions   zone 6; clay, flat, backing on to ravine
Plot size   55 x 226 feet
Open weekends, by appointment

❧ Japanese-Canadian courtyard, extensive use of rock, English-style perennial garden, woodland

The Marminas' garden offers a complete contrast to that of their neighbours, the Leggatts. Designed by their son Joel, the Japanese-inspired front courtyard garden, which they regard as a spiritual sanctuary, abounds in symbolism, with its Zen dry-landscape elements, including simulated riverbeds, a raked gravel "seascape" and handcrafted bamboo entry gate. A roofed "viewing" bench invites you to sit and enjoy the more traditional hill and pond while listening to the soothing sound of water. Plantings were primarily chose in shades of green to preserve the Japanese aesthetic and to temper the harshness of the abundant stone. This weathered rockery, chosen for patina of age and beauty of vein, anchors the garden. The grasses are particularly lovely from September and December, and the garden is open then so you may enjoy them at their best. Noteworthy for its novelty is the streetside riverbed that courses out from under the courtyard fence, created with the intent of both exciting the viewer and persuading them that when the rains come, the river will flow again.

Through the garden gate a very different scene awaits. Generously curving beds snake away to the wooded ravine in the distance, where, hidden from view, the Marminas have sited their extensive composting system. Spring-flowering bulbs and shrubs are followed in quick succession by colourful perennials that fill the beds until the late fall. A large pond is in the making, and a rhododendron garden is beginning to grow. This is a garden full of sensual delights and inspiration for all.

|||||| Lucie and George Simons
416-696-7217

Conditions　　　zone 6; ravine soil, mostly leaf mould with patches of sand, tableland

Open by appointment

❧ **Shade plants, ravine, stream**

A clematis-covered archway marks the start of the descent into paradise. Five springs join forces to stream down the ravine where jewelweed and marsh marigolds grow in abundance, under a leafy canopy of Ontario woodland. This is the setting for the lyrical garden of artist Lucie Simons, who has carved a series of terraces out of the hillside and tangled underbrush, filling them with shade-loving plants. A series of paths and narrow bridges lead past terraces lush with yellow bells of Kiroshegama, tall ligularias, hostas, and *Lobelia syphilitica* in reds and pinks. Lucy is keeping her fingers crossed for the rhododendrons and pieris that have been newly planted in the undergrowth. A gazebo sits hidden in the trees, overlooking the water where the sound of windchimes plays eerie accompaniment to the trickling of the stream. In spring a miniature forest of horsetails makes a lovely foil for the generous clumps of marsh marigolds beside the stream bed, spiked with the young shoots of bamboo and slender reeds. The first tight-fisted flowers to appear are those of petasites, whose dramatic umbrella-like leaves unfurl later on. The blossoms of a wild pear tree show up the fragility of the emerging leaves. Autumn brings fields of goldenrod and wild aster glowing in the far distance, and wild grasses bloom on Lucie's ravine where the trees are burnished russet and palest yellow.

ETOBICOKE

Humber Arboretum
205 Humber College Boulevard, Rexdale, ON, M9W 5L7
416-675-5009
Rexdale: Highway 27 and Humber College Boulevard
Open dawn to dusk; wheelchair access limited to Ornamental Gardens and Dunington-Grubb Gardens

From the Nature Orientation Centre, follow the pathway system, which connects over 250 acres of ornamental gardens, woods, meadows and wetlands with the Metro Cycle Pathway. The Dunington-Grubb Gardens adjacent to Humber College feature wonderful plantings of perennials, hardy shrub roses and rhododendrons, and over a thousand species and varieties of woody and herbaceous plants.

James Gardens
Edenbridge Drive, near Scarlett Road and Eglinton Avenue West

A formal garden with terraced flower beds. In springtime follow the trail leading to Lambton Woods, famous for its wildflowers.

NORTH YORK

Ellen and Bobby Eisenberg
416-449-4976; fax 416-449-5190
Plot size 100 x 269 feet
Open by appointment

❧ **Glorious perennial beds, forested front garden**

The Eisenbergs' house lies hidden behind a mysterious green forest, where one might well imagine creatures with great shy eyes looking out from the undergrowth. A log path winds its way through a carpet of ivy periwinkle and sweet woodruff, past a little pool and benches placed beside shaded beds, where wildflowers grow beneath viburnum, cutleaf stephanandra and dogwood. Huge rhododendrons crowd the alley to the back garden where a very different world awaits.

Dappled shade leads into sunlit spaces that seem to go on forever. No part of this garden is visible at the same time. The next view beckons enticingly over lawns, round trees, past beds with flowering shrubs that fill the air with fragrance in spring and early summer. The breathtaking perennial bed is a huge island divided into a myriad of smaller beds, connected by a narrow brick pathway that snakes everywhich way. Form, colour and texture are totally understood, each plant considered for its overall effect. A trellis burgeons with clematis; chives mix with coreopsis and hostas; roses, poppies, peonies and soft yellow lady's-mantle, who holds a dewdrop in her leaf, lupins, feverfew, and hundreds more create wave after wave of watercolour washes from early May to fall. Ellen Eisenberg is a master in the art of gardening.

Edwards Gardens, Civic Garden Centre
777 Lawrence Avenue East, North York, ON, M3C 1P2
905-445-1552
North of Toronto's city centre, at Lawrence Avenue East and Leslie Street
*Open: gardens, daily, dawn to dusk; Civic Garden Centre, Monday to Frida,
9:30 to 4:00, weekends 1 to 4; wheelchair access*

Edwards Gardens and the Civic Garden Centre (CGC) share the same home. The Gardens are maintained by Metro Toronto Parks Department, and the CGC, which is run by volunteers, offers tours of the Gardens throughout the summer. The formal beds at the main entrance greets visitors with thousands of spring bulbs, then summer annuals, followed by a blaze of colour from fall chrysanthemums. To the west are the perennial beds and huge formal rose garden, all set off to perfection by mature deciduous and evergreen trees. Down the ravine slope is a beautiful wildflower area, where hollies, azaleas and rhododendron thrive in the shade of hemlock and birch trees. A rockery soaks up the sun on the more exposed western slope of the ravine. Wilket Creek tumbles through this very beautiful place, and by damming up chosen spots, a series of picturesque pools and waterfalls have been created.

The CGC has earned a reputation world-wide as a leader in the advancement of horticulture. Workshops are offered on gardening and flower arranging, and there are over 6,000 books and publications in the horticultural library. The CGC Trellis Garden Gift and Book Shop is a pleasant place for browsing.

RIVERDALE

|||||| Judit and Peter Adam
416-469-5211 ext. 199
Conditions   zone 6, garden soil, flat
Plot size   double lot
Open through Woodgreen Community Centre, fourth Saturday in June

❧ Interesting plantings, unusual pool

Judit Adam knew exactly what she wanted when she designed her garden, a lyrical and fitting addition to an 1885 Victorian house.

Everything is touched by her romantic wand, including the "natural" swimming pool. This velvety green grotto, open summer and winter, is surrounded by rockery that climbs many feet above it. A mass of blue in the spring, with virginia bluebells, scillas and iris, its colour graduates to shades of magenta and pink as summer wears on. Heuchera, azaleas, and Martagon lilies combine with Japanese maple, weeping larch and contorted pine to subtly suggest an Oriental sensibility in this part of the garden.

Judit spends hours selecting the plants and deciding where to place them, ensuring that each month brings a differently coloured picture and another "story." The little woodland area has been planted in multiple layers. Hellebores, white redbud and deep pink quince are lovely with pale, lily-flowered tulips, while sweet-smelling *Daphne* Nora Barlow makes a fragrant companion for mahonia. Around the pool masses of *Lythrum* Robert set off the chestnut-shaped leaves of *Rodgersia asclepias*; white and maroon lilies shimmer in the early morning sun, the perfect foil for the rust-pink rocks, each one hand-picked by Judit.

Soft grey pots full of oleander surrounded by scaviola, plumbago blue as a bird's eye, and urns planted with graceful sprays of potato vine sit on a moss-covered patio, and later are overwintered in the solarium. Alyssum seeds itself among the fairy roses, and wisteria flowers along the house. *Hydrangea petiolaris* covers the front fence wall, overhanging a mass of brilliant orange poppies that Judit has combined with clear blue iris, delphiniums, and cranesbill. This is a garden of great originality and beauty, with an intensely personal vision.

 James Edmond
416-469-5211 ext. 199; 416-466-4701
Conditions   zone 6; ordinary garden soil, good topsoil, flat
Plot size   small city lot
Open through Woodgreen Community Centre, fourth Saturday in June; otherwise by appointment with owner

 Unusual design, large collection of roses

Warm yellow roses, dainty threadleaf coreopsis, lupins and purple pansies line the path to the little yellow cottage, its blue front door and lovely wrought-iron verandah covered with the white blooms of *Clematis* Henryi. This city garden is so small that Jim feels his aspirations for it, along with his assumption of its capabilities, are a bit absurd. I don't agree.

Formal gravel paths bisect a series of raised beds, bringing depth and order to the wonderful profusion of planting. Lavender, delphiniums, lilies and roses, in shades of purples, reds, pink and white, fill every square inch of space, with obelisks and trellises supplying extra support for a myriad of climbers and vines. Unimpeded sunshine for as long as twelve hours a day means that almost everything Jim grows flourishes.

He likes his plants to express themselves — he admits to talking to them, commending them for doing well, and apologizing if he bumps them — but if they don't stay within bounds, they're yanked out. Surrounding the stone patio, a semicircle of trellis is covered with more clematis. Optimism shines through in the planting of a not-very-hardy Mermaid rose, one of the most beautiful of all climbing roses, on the warm south wall of the house. Three cedar posts, painted a surprising pillar-box red, an idea from a Japanese garden, contain the patio, where Jim likes nothing better in his old age than to sit "swanning and swooning" among his roses on warm summer nights.

▐▌▌▌ Juliet Mannock
416-469-5211 ext. 199; 416-463-5334

Conditions   zone 6; amended clay
Plot size   27 x 80 feet
Open through Woodgreen Community Centre, fourth Saturday of June, 10 to 4; otherwise by appointment with owner

❧ **Cottage garden, summer house, ornamental pool, fish out of water!**

Juliet Manning is a fun lady and so is her garden. From childhood to seniorhood, Vita Sackville-West has greatly influenced her taste, and although her "plot" would probably fit into Sissinghurst a few million times, it certainly has its own sense of place. Once through the gate into her front garden, you are assailed by the fragrance of herbs and scent of roses. Beds have been laid out in a Greek Key pattern; blue and grey flowers predominate, with a touch of yellow and white for contrast, tomatoes and veggies jostling for space among the perennials.

At the side of the house, what Julia calls "a rather snotty patio" houses a large coffinlike planter and a bath from a horror movie. The latter serves as a nursery site for young seedlings grown indoors under lights. A blaze of gold and yellow meets the eye as you walk under the arch into the garden proper. Divided into four or five "rooms," its walls are covered in a tumult of vines. A pretty pool and rock garden can be enjoyed from the charming summerhouse. Beyond lies the compost heap, upper patio and the wild garden, which Julia dismisses as an area of "mistakes" — whatever the problems, I'm sure she'll rectify them.

The garden is in bloom from the first aconite of spring till the last David Austin rose in mid-November. Her only real "no-nos" are bicoloured plants, which are a complete anathema to Julia, who reckons that "two-toned jobs" confuse the bees and butterflies, as well as bugging her.

Vita Sackville-West once wrote that she "liked to think the flowers in her garden were enjoying themselves," a sentiment that Julia surely shares. She once asked a friend to describe her garden. "Full," came the unflinching reply. An understatement, I think.

|||||| Jacob Verkade

416-469-5211 ext. 199

Conditions   zone 6; mainly paved, flat
Plot size   city plot
Open through Woodgreen Community Centre; fourth Saturday of June

❧ High design

A visit to the tennis club at Newport, Rhode Island, was the guiding influence in Jacob Verkade's design for his stylishly elegant garden. The dark green trellised walls, complete with "portholes," divide a series of "cool" room within rooms. Ivy and bittersweet clamber everywhere, and architectural elements such as the Newport-inspired divider and neo-classical pergola form a quiet ferny courtyard, reminiscent of a Greek villa, with artefacts and mementos adorning the walls. Lie in the hammock or sit on the Rockwood-style bench listening to the splashing of a small fountain. Morning glories tangle with blue hydrangea, and Irish moss mingles with thyme through the flagstone floor. For the most part, this is a green garden, given texture and pattern with plantings of plumed grasses, white azaleas, ferns, cotoneaster and Emperor Taro. Charming statues and pillars are placed throughout, and a recycled Victorian bathtub has been transformed into a whimsical pond. White perennials line the beds surrounding the large stone patio, with its Moroccan tent providing shade for meals al fresco. Jacob Verkade has created a world where Victorian England and Classical Greece have happily married.

|||||| Gerald Whyte, *Calpurnia's Garden*

416-469-5211 ext. 199

Conditions   zone 6; sandy, level
Plot size   narrow city lot
Open through Woodgreen Community Centre, fourth Saturday of June

❧ A glorious conglomeration

Each spring when the garden awakes from winter with a blossoming of crocus, tulips, hyacinth and daffodils, Calpurnia the family cat prowls through the many stages of her inner city sanctum, designed as a retreat from the whirl of city life.

As you enter through the narrow flower-laden alley, the fantasy world of Gerald Whyte immediately embraces you. A gnarled old grapevine spreads shady tentacles over the bamboo beams of a large pergola, and a Victorian child's cot, flanked by terra cotta lions, invites you to sit and wile away the time among the pots and planters overflowing with perennials and annuals. Through a clematis-covered archway, a flagstone path tours a lucious landscape of huge grasses, exotic sunflowers, giant thistles, peonies, poppies and lilacs, interspersed with shaded seating areas, sculptures and containers. Two hidden ponds are connected by a small stream, and the sound of the waterfall washes over the garden. The pond excavation and the rubble from the uprooted concrete walk provided the material for a small hill and a second small pond, as well as a planting of raspberry canes. The delicate blossoms of plum and apricot trees afford a fragile contrast to a variety of evergreens and leaves of clump birches.

At the rear of the garden, the former garage is now a summer dining and reading room. Transformed into a rustic Greek temple, it is overgrown with vines, hanging baskets, planters filled with perennials and colourful annuals, and more than a hint of mint. An exotic second-floor balcony is filled with palms and huge blooms of hibiscus, bougainvillia and scented jasmine. This magical oasis is the epitome of what English landscape and garden writer Stephen Lacey describes as "the Startled Jungle" in his book of the same name.

William Gilpin

416-469-5211 ext. 199; 416-466-5490

Conditions zone 6; garden soil, flat
Plot size small city lot
Open through Woodgreen Community Centre, fourth Saturday in June (house and garden), 10 to 5; otherwise by appointment with owner

Historic house

The fascinating house of William Gilpin is currently acknowledged as the oldest continuously occupied house in Metropolitan Toronto. The rusticity of this pioneer-era dwelling has been well concealed with many additions and alterations, the last one in the 1870s. It is one of the only surviving examples in Toronto of a classic Ontario Regency cottage, a high Victorian porch a sympathetic addition to the facade's otherwise sober symmetry. William is restoring the house to its former glory, uncovering original log walls and reinstating old wallpaper. He is a fund of knowledge, and I guarantee an interesting afternoon if you to visit both house and garden.

The front plot began four years ago with one windswept lawn. William set about designing a garden that would be appropriate for a house such as this, with formally composed narrow borders and whimsical paisley-shaped island beds, inspired by nineteenth-century Canadian watercolours and the illustrated 1870s atlases of Ontario. The general impression is of mid-to-late Victorian ideals, in spite of the dense planting and some choices of plant materials that are clearly twentieth century.

Camperdown elm, Egyptian onion, ornamental rhubarb, valerian, prickly pear cactus and dozens of other species add up to a very eclectic collection, one that would have been coveted on such a site a hundred years ago, in the golden age of plant discovery.

ROSEDALE

▌▌▌▌ Cecily Bell
416-469-5211 ext. 199; 416-926-0484
Castle Frank
Conditions   garden loam, steeply terraced
Open through Woodgreen Community Centre, fourth Saturday in June, 10 to 4; otherwise by appointment with owner

❧ Terraced garden, perennials, woodland garden

Hidden away on a lovely cul-de-sac, this charming house with its trellised walkway covered in pale blue *Clematis* Vivian Penell has a very pretty front garden dominated by a magnificent Himalayan birch.

A tender yellow Mermaid rose flanks the sheltered flagstone patio at the top of the steep, south-facing slope in the backyard that has been transformed into a series of terraces and raised beds, filled with romantic flowers. Lilies, delphiniums, roses and many other favourites spill out over the paths, with the last terrace devoted to vegetables and caged to keep out the critters. Steep steps on each side of the yard are bordered by trellis, planted for privacy with eunonymous, clematis and the annual cup-and-saucer vine (*Cobea scandens*). Pots are filled with hostas, squirrels sit on the base of an art deco sundial, and an elegant iron urn is planted with marguerites and "spilly things," as Cecily calls them. Her husband has made an interesting feeding station for the birds, a focal point for the garden that can be enjoyed year-round. Sweet Cicely and the nodding yellow bells of Kiroshegama combine with masses of pink and white Japanese anemones in the fall to form a memorable impression. At the bottom of the slope, a mysterious woodland of dark pines and blue-flowered periwinkle beckons you into its cool depths, where you might find welcome relief from the sun-baked terraces.

IIIIII Susan and Geoffrey Dyer

416-469-5211 ext. 199

Conditions	zone 6/7 micro-climate; amended clay, sandy area, new loam
Plot size	35 x 100 feet

Open through Woodgreen Community Centre, fourth Saturday in June, 10 to 4

❧ **Perennials, architecture, formal Roman garden**

Two adjoining gardens, the Dyer and Zakuta gardens, are perfect foils for one another. The Dyer's English-style garden was designed by David Tomlinson of Merlin's Hollow in Aurora, but the choice of plants is their own. This garden is of elaborate scope, and its elegant trellises in soft grey-green show off to perfection the abundant array of pastel-hued perennials and flowering shrubs, which Susan is slowly pepping up with the introduction of more vivid colours. "If you don't plant yellow in this country," she says, "you end up with a 'nothing' garden by August." Paths lead from the prettily planted shade area into "rooms" displaying an enormous variety of shape, texture and fragrance. This is a truly romantic garden in the heart of the city.

IIIIII Douglas and Barbara Wilkins

416-469-5211 ext. 199

Conditions	zone 6; sandy loam, hillside, south-facing

Open through Woodgreen Community Centre, last Saturday in May, first Saturday in June, 10 to 4; wear flat shoes for hillside walking

❧ **Rhododendrons, woodland garden**

The enchanting garden of Barbara Wilkins, considered by many one of the loveliest in Toronto, has developed slowly over the past thirty years. Her first enthusiasm was for alpine plants, to take advantage of the sunnier slopes at the top of the garden. In the seventies, however, she discovered rhododendrons and azaleas. The tiny specimens she planted have grown to a fair size, which, together with magnolias, mountain laurel and many shade lovers, put on a glorious show in the spring. The garden is long and narrow, sloping fairly steeply to the south, and heavily shaded to the east and north, giving the overall impression of a long winding path that beckons you into the woods, lovely throughout the year.

Robin Wilson, *Robins Nest*
416-469-5211 ext. 199; 416-926-9464
Conditions   zone 6b/7; flat, topsoil on clay base
Plot size   150 x 30 feet
Open through Woodgreen Community Centre, fourth Saturday in June, 12 to 5; otherwise by appointment only (strict adherence to times appreciated)

Courtyard with fountain, perennials, good small garden design

In the early 1900s this property was the clubhouse for the Rosedale Golf Club course; today it is a charming bed and breakfast with a delightful garden. Designed by Robin's husband, who has an excellent eye for shape and structure, it is enhanced by Robin, who has a flair for colour and a passion for plants. The front garden, which receives full sun, is choc-a-bloc with perennials, in pink, blue white, silver and pale yellow shrubs, rugosa roses and fifty-year-old irises from her mother's garden.

Silver lace vine runs rampant over the archway and fence into the unusual back garden. Water from a small pool cleverly links the two levels of this elegant garden, splashing into a semicircular sunken brick patio. Surrounding a small lawn is a pretty woodland garden of hostas, fern and wildflowers, and another small pool with a backdrop of flowering crabapple is planned for 1996.

Leo and Annette Zakuta
416-469-5211 ext. 199
Open through Woodgreen Community Centre, fourth Saturday in June, 12 to 5

Formal green garden

An arch in the cedar hedge from the Dyer garden leads into a green oasis where a completely different scene awaits. The Zakutas had no interest in gardening when they bought the house, and it was sheer fluke that they ended up with this large backyard. However, they both have a keen interest in art and wanted a garden strong in design and very low in maintenance. Reminiscent of the ancient Roman gardens with their long walks and simplicity of planting, this cool, serene space looks lovely in all seasons, its clean, low lines emphasized by hedges of flowering currant and box, edging vast green pools of ivy. Ajuga underlies the shrubs planted along the narrow walkways, and the only colour comes from the white flowers in containers on the back deck. The original design by Brian Bixley was later modified by Judith Adam, who helped them to achieve their objective, bringing to this peaceful place a sense of order and clarity, and demanding only minimal maintenance.

SCARBOROUGH

Sheila Cule and Peter Keeping
416-292-4955

Conditions   zone 5/6; clay, flat
Plot size   Scarborough lot
Open by appointment

Pond, clematis and perennials

Sheila Cule's garden is a marvellous example of how pretty an ordinary suburban lot can be with clever planning and imaginative planting. The garden is divided into three main sections by a long oval bed that runs down the centre and has reduced the lawn to a narrow grass path, inviting a stroll between beds flower-laden from spring to late fall. Shrubs and fruit trees, perennials, annuals and vegetables all have a place. Everyone who visits is amazed by the amount of plant material there is here, much of it grown from unusual seed that Sheila brings back from her trips to the United Kingdom.

April and May bring the crocus, tulips, fritilarias, cheerful doronicums, euphorbias and Persian carpets of polyanthus. The flowering shrubs refuse to be outdone, showering the garden with blossoms, and following hard on their heels come the perennials of June, plump and preening, showing off their gorgeous colours. Peonies, Anemone pulsatilla, delphiniums, salvia, thalictrums and, of course, roses come to call, while the trees and fences are covered in over seventy species of clematis collected by her husband. Seven years ago, a pond was added beside a weeping mulberry tree, framed by an arbour covered in wisteria and many different vines.

Sheila and Peter have managed to create beautiful vistas from wherever you look in their prize-winning garden.

The Guild Inn Sculpture Garden
201 Guildwood Parkway, Toronto, ON,
416-266-4449
Morningside and Lawrence Avenue East, south of Guildwood Parkway
Open daily, dawn to dusk; wheelchair access

Once a country estate, this property on the Scarborough Bluffs became home to the Guild of All Arts in 1932 and under the patronage of Rose and Spencer Clark it became a thriving artists' colony. The demolition of many of Toronto's most beautiful and historic landmarks in the sixties and seventies to make way for the skyscraper takeover caused Spencer Clark to collect and preserve what he could of old Toronto. He and a devoted team of architects and stonemasons were responsible for the collection of architectural fragments salvaged from more than fifty buildings in Toronto's business district. These architectural monuments are installed in the gardens of the Guild. Cultivated plantings and mature trees complement the monuments. Trilliums, trout lilies and many other wildflowers add to the charm of this unique collection of "things beautiful."

The Guild is currently maintained by the Municipality of Metropolitan Toronto Parks and Culture Department as a public park and inn with dining facilities. Phone for information on customized tours of the outdoor collection.

CENTRAL TORONTO

|||||| Barbara Bell, *Miro's Eye*
416-469-5211 ext. 199
Conditions   zone 5
Open through Woodgreen Community Centre, third and fourth Saturday and Sunday in June, 10 to 12 and 2 to 5

❧ **Interesting design and pond**

Tucked away in an unsuspecting corner of the city lies a garden with a fascinating design concept. Its long, narrow lines, inspired by the paintings of Jean Miro, are based on a series of intersecting arcs — the perfect marriage of the geometric and the organic. Two of the arcs create a small eye-shaped island bed — hence the name of the garden. Various vertical elements serve to visually enclose the space and make it very private. The sound of water fills the garden, cascading down a fieldstone face into a pond alive with koi, goldfish, water lilies and other aquatics.

The garden is relatively shady and foliage is of paramount importance to Barbara, who is particularly fond of plants with bronze and purple foliage, especially when planted with the silver artemisias. Many of the shrubs are variegated, to light up the darker corners. Ferns, pulmonarias and hostas mingle with soft-coloured plantings of clematis, heuchera, lilies and Michaelmas daisies. A large deck off the house is protected by a grape-covered pergola, providing a romantic place to dine al fresco.

|||||| Zora Buchanan
416-469-5211 ext. 199
Conditions   zone 6; long, narrow city lot
Open through Woodgreen Community Centre, third Saturday in July; other open days through Toronto Gardens newspaper (see Other Garden Tours and Resources, page 204)

❧ **Arbour, perennials, pond**

Zora Buchanan's mother used to vie with the neighbour to see who could get to the coalman's cart first to shovel up the "goodies" left by the horse, which she then proceeded to mound onto her precious strawberry barrels. Zora doesn't wait for the coal cart, but her garden is a veritable flower bower, so she's certainly doing something right.

With no formal plan, and sod-on-clay from fence to fence, she has created a veritable silk purse out of a sow's ear. Today she has a rich perennial garden, with many features added over the years.

Her husband plays barber once a week to the silver lace vine that covers the entrance arbour. Every evening in the good weather they dine on the patio, among morning glories and nasturtiums enhanced by white Datura lilies.

A curving "river" of leftover bricks and red stone chips leads past voluptuous beds of delphiniums, roses, lilies, hollyhocks, blowsy phlox and many others to a little pond filled with water that trickles from a huge rock. Zora is enchanted by the thought of the koi, comets and frogs born right in the pond among the water lettuce and water hyacinths.

One of her flower beds became so wide that she made a path around the back where she plants trillium, Solomon's seal and other wildflowers, watched over by a little sculpture of a child called the Scholar. This is where she tells her granddaughters that "there are fairies at the bottom of her garden," and I have to say I wouldn't be a bit surprised if it were true.

Amanda McConnell
416-469-5211 ext. 199
Conditions   zone 6; flat, alkaline
Plot size   40 x 190 feet
Open through Woodgreen Community Centre, third Saturday and Sunday in June 10 to 4

❧ **Herbaceous garden, shrubs, pond**

For ten years Amanda McConnell gazed longingly at the double lot across the road. Although the plot had been completely decimated, she saw the huge potential for her to create the garden of her dreams. When the For Sale sign went up, she bought it within a day. It's the rashest thing she has ever done in her life, she says, but she couldn't bear the thought of someone getting their hands on the garden she had coveted for so long.

Long winding paths lead through a series of romantic rooms which are at once luxuriant, wild and impulsive. Shell-pink flowers of New Dawn rose cover the arbour, and silvery Russian olive, bridal veil spirea and a dramatic stand of plume poppy (*Maclya cordata*) add to the sense of careless abandon. Hot-coloured zinnias set off the golden solidago around a small pond, and red *Lobelia cardinalis* shows up vividly against a deep green carpet of ivy, Solomon's seal, sweet woodruff and ferns. A great umbrella of elderberry shades the path, and fragrant thyme and portulaca grow through the cracks of the stone terrace.

The garden has been described as "the domain of a woman who can't make up her mind." It took time, however, for her to understand that this kind of effect is not achieved by neglect, but by choosing plants that enhance the feeling of timelessness, understanding their habits and nurturing them accordingly. Her abiding hate is the climate: too cold in the winter and too hot in the summer. "I like plants that thrive," says Amanda, "because it gives me hope that I will too."

Mary and Terry Mills

416-469-5211 ext. 199

Conditions	zone 6; clay, gradual slope, deep shade and full-sun borders
Plot size	35 x 40 feet.

Open through Woodgreen Community Centre, third Saturday in June

Courtyard garden, perennials, pool and fountain

Framed by a weathered vine-clad fence, this small flagstone courtyard garden is a haven of peace in a central city neighbourhood, and links the house to the borrowed view of the city park to the south. The tranquillity of this garden comes from its strong architectural "bones," sense of scale, and sensual, soft-coloured plantings, carefully chosen to give a lush romantic feeling to this very precisely defined space. Although the garden is small, it is designed in such a way that it has to be "discovered." Built on several levels and divided symmetrically, it gives the impression of a much larger space. The focal point is a central island bed with a Red Jade crabapple surrounded by dwarf vibernums and ground covers. Behind it a charming bench invites you to sit and listen to the sound of water pouring from a fountain of Pan into a small octagonal pool, hidden away behind the angled path. The mixed borders contain over 130 plants, small shrubs and vines chosen for their vigorous foliage, extended flowering and overall good manners.

At the top of the wide stone steps, adjoining the sunroom, is a lovely pillared pergola; how lovely to sit under its wisteria- and rose-covered roof, sipping a glass of wine and drinking in the peace.

|||||| Josie Szczasiuk and Mark Abbott
416-769-8942

Conditions   sandy soil, valley
Open fourth weekend in June, 11 to 4; because this property is on a hillside and has many stepping stones, it is not wheelchair accessible or recommended for people with canes

❦ **Terraces, fishponds, water fall, perennials, roses**

Part of the charm and challenge of this garden is its hilly location. The owners have come to terms with their valley, and enjoy the different rooms and levels accessed by a network of stepping stones. It was originally landscaped in 1924 with humberstone retaining walls and evergreen shrubs. Mature cedar and juniper hedges now surround the front yard, where grass has been replaced with scented ground covers, including thymes, limonium and lavender. Flourishing on the east side of the house is a pale pink New Dawn rose intertwined with purple *Clematis jackmanii*, a graceful *Acer japonica* Butterfly and a Dutchman's pipe. In the terraced border at the back of the house, a raised bed of irises, roses and other fragrant flowers is enhanced by a fishpond and waterfall. Rhododendrons and azaleas grow under a mature pink crabapple. Further down the garden, the ground cover is magenta-flowered purpurea, and periwinkle. A charming Friendship Gate entwined with wisteria leads to the neighbour's garden. In the shade of mature oak trees grow ferns, phlox, Dame Rocket, trillium, and in the spring, a carpet of blue scilla. On the west side of the house another small hillside is planted with euonymus, veronicas and thymes.

Josie is a garden designer, the planner and the plantsperson, while Mark is the intrepid wrought-iron, pond and fountain authority.

▦ Spadina
285 Spadina Road, Toronto, ON
416-392-6910
South of St. Clair Avenue West and north of Davenport Road
Open dawn to dusk, year-round; no fee for gardens; house, $5 adults, $3.25 seniors and youths, $3 children; limited wheelchair access

One of Toronto's best-kept secrets, Spadina is perhaps Toronto's finest historic garden. The Garden Club of Toronto and the Toronto Historical Board have worked together to restore the grounds to resemble the garden as it was when first landscaped in the early 1900s. A splendid 6-foot perennial border surrounds the large kitchen garden, which is divided into quadrants edged with paths. The centre of each quarter has a cutting garden where attractive vegetables such as purple hyacinth beans, cardoons and rhubarb chard and tomato plants are combined with the flowers. The less attractive vegetables are grown behind a cedar hedge, out of sight from house guests. Lilacs, peonies, day lilies, irises and an old rambling rose are just a few of the flowers that have been restored. The apple trees in the ancient orchard bear fruit no longer considered practical in today's market. Formal flower beds and ornamental planters add grace to the mansion they surround. With more than 300 varieties of plants throughout the grounds, there is much to see and enjoy on a walk around Spadina.

Call to confirm times of tours of the house and garden, conducted during the summer months on Sundays and Wednesdays.

Casa Loma

1 Austin Terrace, Toronto, ON, M5R 1X8
416-923-1171
South of St. Clair Avenue West, north of Davenport Road
Open daily 9:30 to 4 from May through October; adults $8, seniors $6; price of admission to the castle includes viewing the gardens; group tours are available, $50 per hour per group; limited wheelchair access (terrace and building only)

Sir Henry Mill Pellat, a prominent Canadian financier of the early twentieth century, built Casa Loma in 1914. When his financial empire crumbled, the castle fell into disrepair and became known as Pellatt's Folly. Thanks to the Kiwanis Club of West Toronto and the volunteers of the Toronto Garden Club, it has been transformed into an enormously popular tourist attraction and a centre for special events.

The sweeping driveway leading to the house through formal gardens reveals little of the romance and elegance of the mansion and the terraced gardens beyond. One terrace overlooks a woodland falling steeply away, revealing glimpses of the Toronto skyline and Lake Ontario beyond. The lower terrace is a pleasant spot with its small pool and fat perennial beds.

A curving pergola leads down to the new Secret Garden and its lush plantings of aromatic catmints and lavender and shrub roses. The rhododenron dell is ablaze with colour from April to June. A woodland path fringed by ornamental grasses leads to a reflecting pool surrounded by astilbes, marsh marigolds and water irises. Budding maples on a carpet of daffodils fill the woodland area in spring. The landscapes within this 6-acre estate are grand and varied and well worth a visit.

TORONTO ISLANDS

Hop on a ferry at Queen's Quay terminal and in ten minutes or so you will disembark in a world far from the one you left behind. Wander through a myriad of tiny streets no wider than a sidewalk. Shaded by huge old sycamores overgrown with ivy, higgledy-piggledy houses, reminiscent of a once brightly coloured toy town, are now slightly chipped, and utterly enchanting. Faded turquoise, hot pink, yellow and blue colour the buildings and gardens alike, where giant sunflowers, delphiniums, artichokes, thistles and roses are grown in orderly tangle along with tomatoes, beans, strange sculptures and children. Enjoy a picnic or have lunch at the café situated on the equivalent of the village green.

▌▌▌▌ Steve Aikenhead and Halina Bregman, *West Meadow Garden*
416-203-3205
West Algonquin Island
Conditions   zone 6a; sand base, rejuvenated with compost
Open by appointment; freewill donation appreciated as entrance fee

❦ **Stone work, statuary, North Carolinian trees, interesting design, perennial, bulbs, evergreens**

Steve Aikenhead and Halina Bregman have learned that when it comes to gardening, compromise — with each other's ideas and with the natural environment — is the name of the game. These two artists, one a professional landscaper and sculptor, have been tending their lush mini-jungle the past seventeen years.

One of their main priorities is privacy, and this has been attained by extensive plantings of trees and shrubs, bulbs, perennials, and a large variety of wildflowers that have obligingly seeded themselves from all over the island and beyond. Giant hostas, left over from the fifties, line the front pathway, their purple flowers making a gorgeous sight in late August after the soft peach day lilies have faded.

Steve's sculpture has played a large part in imbuing the place with a special magic. He is constantly striving for a balance between his structures of wood and stone and the textures, forms and colours of the abundant plant life growing here.

Shrubs that develop quickly offer an opportunity for topiary, and those that need special nurturing and encouragement are especially rewarding, although they are struggling with the increasing shade from the cottonwood canopy. Steve and Halina are interacting and "co-aging" with their plants, trying to work with nature, rather than control it.

Grahame Beakhust, *Third Street Parkette*
416-203-0859
Numbers 1 and 3 Third Street, Wards Island (two vacant lots)
Conditions   zone 6b; flat sand; compost, leaf mould and
                  enriched
Open: "Just come by"; plant exchange; entrance fee: "Leave a plant."

Spring bulbs — more than 3,000 of them

Here is a garden full of fascinating contradictions, with private spaces that are quite public, as well as shared spaces full of hidden corners. There are no barriers here. Children are encouraged to explore and play as they learn about the many perennials, trees and thousands of bulbs that fill the garden. For Grahame Beakhust, well known as the Discovery Channel's "Guerilla Gardener," the garden is first and foremost a place of beauty, repose and fun. Raised beds are filled with all sorts of junk for drainage, and then planted with seedlings from his greenhouse as well as plants from his father's garden in Bayfield. Many of the gorgeous irises, poppies and columbines in the gardens around the island come from Grahame, but of all the things he is attached to in his garden, the trees are the most important. Aiming for year-round interest, he likens his "corral," as he call it, to his interest in jazz. "It's a jazz garden," he says, "with a strong rhythm section and some great solos."

|||||| Sheila Murray and Jim Belisle, *Belisle/Murray Cottage Garden*
416-203-2221
Toronto Island "Annex" (Ward's Island)
Open anytime, or phone ahead

❧ **Interesting use of found objects, lovely ambiance, pretty planting**

Two weeping birches and the scent of lavender welcome you to this sensual garden, enclosed by an old hedge of privet, chinese elm and highbush cranberry. Sheila Murray and Jim Belisle are well-known landscape designers who have put their artistry to work here with the witty and ingenious use of recycled material.

A Mediterranean feel with a touch of the Orient pervades the garden. Brilliant pink and purple adorns the windows and doors of the house. "Hernia," a garage-sale statue named in honour of the men who succeeded in lifting her, stands in an arc of reclaimed yew, with vinca and white snowdrops tickling her feet. Heavy chains hang from the eaves, transformed in winter to a sculptural frozen waterfall, suspended over the dramatic boulders at its base. Five dead cherry trees serve now as a framework for morning glories and sweet peas; unusual birdhouses have been created by local children and neighbours; foxgloves seed themselves between the cracks in the paving, while luxuriant plantings of climbing roses and clematis clamber over the entrance arbours. A free-standing porch column, found in the garbage, has a trumpet vine flowering around it from June through September. Richness and texture abound in the plantings of rhododendrons, eunonymous, and seed heads from Annabel hydrangea, as well as pampas grass and Japanese maples. Spring, summer and winter are all well catered for in this fascinating garden.

|||||| Diana Rowland
416-203-0995
Algonquin Island
Conditions   zone 6b; sand
Best times to visit: July, August
Open: drop by, or phone ahead

❧ **Two ponds, stream, perennials and wildflowers**

Diana Rowland's garden has evolved from years of being loved and lived in, as opposed to being laid out by a professional with designer taste. To her it is the same difference that distinguishes between a house and a home, indefinable, yet unmistakable. All the neighbourhood children play in Diana Rowland's yard, amusing themselves for hours along the pathways, over the bridge and stepping stones, hiding in the bushes or watching the tadpoles and fish in her charming pond, cramming their mouths with raspberries. Many of the perennials come from friends' gardens, serving as a reminder of special people. If something cannot grow here, she does not allow it to struggle, hence the lack of roses, which she loves. This has not, however, precluded a rich variety of vegetation from growing in this enchanting place. Water lilies and wildflowers, dahlias, delphiniums, lilies and Michaelmas daisies and more can all be found here, providing food and shelter to many birds, butterflies and insects, as well as the youngsters who thrive in this organic environment.

The Guild Inn
201 Guildwood Parkway (Morningside and Lawrence Avenue East)
416-261-3331
Daily, luncheon 11:30 to 2:30, dinner 6 to 10; the beautiful grounds of the Inn, on the Scarborough Bluffs, enhance the pleasure of dining here.

There are countless restaurants throughout the Toronto area; ask for local recommendations at the gardens you are visiting.

VISITING ARRANGEMENTS THROUGH WOODGREEN COMMUNITY CENTRE

The list below provides a quick overview of open days for gardens accepting visitors through Woodgreen Community Centre. Please be aware when you phone Woodgreen (416-469-5211 ext. 199) to book your visits that these are private gardens, and dates and times may change occasionally. And don't forget, there may be other gardens in the same neighbourhood whose owners, though not booking through Woodgreen, would be happy to see you on the same day.

Aurora
Lumsden: May through July, by appointment
Nobleton (Aurora)
Harris: Monday through Thursday, fourth week of July
Richmond Hill (Aurora)
Chater: third Saturday of June and July
Bowmanville
Edey: first weekend of July
Oshawa (Bowmanville)
Belfour: first two Saturdays of July
Derham, Stewart: first Saturday of July
Brampton
Covello: second and third consecutive Sunday and Monday of July
Pauer: last weekend of June
Mississauga (Brampton)
Collacott, Renaud-Webber: last Saturday of May, second Saturday of June, first Saturday of September
Primeau: second Saturday of June, third Saturday of July
Singer: third Saturday of July, first Saturday of September
York/Gaudio: second Saturday of June, third Saturday of July, first Saturday of September
Oakville (Brampton)
Birkett: by appointment
Brantford
Burns: first Sunday of July
Caledon–Orangeville Region
Knowles: third Wednesday and Thursday of June
Shepherd: by appointment
Simmons: third and fourth weekend of May, first and second weekend of June, second weekend of July
Guelph (Cambridge)
Chanasyk: second Saturday of July
Smith: every Sunday from second Sunday of May to last Sunday of September except holiday weekends

Watson: last weekend of June, first Saturday of July, first Sunday of August
Kitchener–Waterloo (Cambridge)
Flood: last two Sundays of June, first Sunday of July
Lamb: second Sunday of July
Durham Region
Bujokas, Maier: last weekend of June
Chambers: last Sunday of June
Morris: last weekend of June, July 1
Norwood: third Saturday of June, second-last Saturday of August
Greensville (Hamilton)
Brink: last weekend of May
Hobson: last weekend of May, second weekend of July, some September weekends
London
Andreae: second-last Saturday of June, some September days
Colquhoun: third weekend of August
Cabbagetown (Toronto)
Harris, Packham: second-last Sunday of June
Central Toronto
Bell, B.: third and fourth weekend of June
Buchanan: third Saturday of July
McConnell: third weekend of June
Mills: third Saturday of June
Szczasiuk: second-last weekend of June
East York (Toronto)
Hutzul: second Saturday of July
Riverdale (Toronto)
Adam, Edmond, Gilpin, Mannock, Verkade, Whyte: second-last Saturday of June
Rosedale (Toronto)
Bell, C., Dyer, Wilson, Zakuta: second-last Saturday of June
Wilkins: last Saturday of May, first Saturday of June

OTHER GARDEN TOURS
AND RESOURCES

Canadian Wildflower Society
4981 Highway 7 East, Unit 12A, Markham, ON, L3R 1N1
Nature walks and garden visits. For information call Carolyn King at
416-222-5736 or Paul McGaw at 416-261-6272.

Central Ontario Garden Railway Association
RR 3, Georgetown, ON, L7G 4S6
Gardens with miniature railways, of interest to young and old.
For information on tours, contact Ross Webster at 905-877-5381.

Civic Garden Centre
777 Lawrence Avenue West, North York, ON, M3C 1P2
416-444-1552

Municipality of Metropolitan Toronto
Metro Parks and Culture
For a calendar of events, including Spring Walks, Gardens in Bloom, Heritage Walks, Meadows,
Bobolinks and Butterflies, and Fall Colours, call 416-392-8186.

Ontario Rock Garden Society
c/o Andrew Osyany
Box 146, Shelburn, ON, L0N 1S0
519-925-5331
Organizes tours for its members to some of Ontario's best gardens.
Call for information on joining the society.

Royal Botanical Gardens
Box 399, 680 Plains Road West, Burlington, ON, L8N 3H8
905-527-1158

Toronto Gardens
1560 Bayview Avenue, Suite 302A, Toronto, ON, M4G 3B8
416-481-1955
A monthly newspaper, published March through September, and distributed to all libraries,
White Rose nurseries and other garden centres, provides information on tours in the Greater
Toronto area.

*Contact local art galleries, horticultural societies and libraries for information on garden tours in
your area.*

ACKNOWLEDGMENTS

First and foremost I would like to thank my husband, William, for his love, faith, encouragement and patience through thick and thin.

Next I would like to mention Irene Rowley, my assistant, cook, bottle-washer, and above all friend, whose help in the research and writing of this book has been invaluable, and Dorothy Hartsell, who has guided me to myself over the past years.

A very special thank you to Fiona Finch, without whose help and enthusiasm at its inception this book might have remained nothing more than a dream. I would like to thank Rachel McHenry for her organization of the project.

I am indebted to all the gardeners I have visited, in particular Audrey and Ed Bloedow, Judy and Neil Baird, Jeanette and Alan Earp, Turid Forsyth, Bela Gross, Juliet Mannock, Margaret Howe, Cathy Renwald and Gerald Whyte.

I am honoured to have the photographs of John de Visser, Sidney Feitelberg and Turid Forsyth gracing the pages of this book. A big hug and thank you to my friend Sidney Fietleberg for guiding me through my many computer crises, to my publisher, John Denison, and Noel Hudson for saying "yes" to the idea, to designer Gillian Stead, and last but not least to my editor, Kathleen Fraser, for her eagle eye and discerning pen.

GARDEN INDEX

H Historic, P Public, N Nursery

Praise for *Irma Voth* and Miriam Toews

#1 NATIONAL BESTSELLER
Winner of the Writers' Trust Engel/Findley Award

"There is something quite mesmerizing about Miriam Toews's prose. It's to do with the rhythm of her language, with the seeming effortlessness of it and, when combined with her quick, offhand wit, it can enliven even the darkest of moments." *Toronto Star*

"Miriam Toews must surely be among the most beloved contemporary Canadian authors." *Quill & Quire*

"As brisk and believable as tomorrow's news. . . . The characters of *Irma Voth* pulse with individual feeling." *The Globe and Mail*

"[By the] outrageously original premise alone, Miriam Toews should have you. Next, by her dialogue, then by her setting and, finally, by her style. . . . Toews imbues Irma with a naïve but unsentimental voice, a crucial distinction that makes the character believable, admirable and irresistibly lovable. . . . A deliciously rapid read." *The Chronicle Herald*

"Miriam Toews has a remarkably light touch. She combines a playfully sardonic humour with crushing pathos." *Times Literary Supplement*

"The mood is typical Toews, as slyly comic as a Jim Jarmusch film, but there is a core of loneliness in Irma, along with a buried family secret, which adds gravity to the humour. And there are many pinpricks of joy, like points of starlight, along the way, too." *Maclean's*

"Toews has depth and knows funny." *NOW* (Toronto), Books of the Decade citation

"She's again able to dislocate herself and still be very located somehow with her comic vision. . . . Her work resonates with people who don't have any knowledge of Mennonites. . . . One thing I would certainly emphasize is that Miriam Toews didn't come out of the blue. . . . But being a brilliant artist she just makes a leap. She's doing fascinating new things with comedy." Magdalene Redekop, quoted in the *Globe and Mail*

"Toews . . . is clearly an artistic powerhouse." *Times Colonist*

"A trademark tragicomedy. . . . Toews's quirky and authentic voice shows increasing range and maturity. She is well on her way to fulfilling her promise as an important and serious writer." *The Gazette*

"*Irma Voth* shifts between dream and cruel reality [with] vivid colour." *The Times*

"The story's heavy emotional content is intensified by the cruel humour of Irma's world. . . . An engaging, deceptively simple tragicomedy of considerable emotional heft. . . . Toews never loses focus on the core of her story: one girl's authentic effort to understand her family and herself." *Irish Examiner*

"A wonderful canvas for Toews's mood-rich writing. . . . Funny and skilfully drawn." *The Guardian*

"Beautiful, heartbreaking. . . . Toews's four previous novels . . . have earned her a reputation for unflinching honesty and keen insight into both the tragedy and comedy of human existence. *Irma Voth* continues this exploration. . . . She explores the father-daughter relationship in a new light, giving it a tough and clear-eyed treatment here. . . . This novel also calls to mind Ann-Marie MacDonald's . . . *Fall on Your Knees*." *Winnipeg Free Press*

"Strong and skilful. . . . Rich with oddball observations and arresting images." Annie Proulx

"A provocative and highly affecting story of a young woman's rejection of religious repression and search for freedom. . . . An impressive and well-wrought work." *The Vancouver Sun*

"Toews's prose has always been fast-paced and readable, and there is a kind of joy in finding oneself unmoored in it. . . . Beautiful, strange and fascinating, and readers wise enough to trust in the author's sure hand will be rewarded with a novel that takes them someplace altogether unexpected." CBC Books

"Elegant, insightful writing with a dark psychological edge." *Red Magazine*

"Toews . . . combines an intimate coming-of-age tale with picaresque and extremely effective prose." *Publishers Weekly*

"A crystalline vision. . . . A stark, beautiful and mature work, one entirely comfortable within itself, its scope and its sadness." Jared Bland, *The Walrus*

"The nicely drawn contrast between what Irma knows and suspects and what the reader understands about her world gives *Irma Voth* a suspenseful charge from the first pages. . . . Daring." Jane Smiley, *The Globe and Mail*

"A stunning culture clash between the Mennonite and art communities. . . . The internal conflict over when to reveal hard information, in life or in art, is one of Toews's key themes. A sequence about how it feels to tell the truth is a knockout." *NOW* (Toronto)

Irma
Voth

MIRIAM TOEWS

VINTAGE CANADA

VINTAGE CANADA EDITION, 2012

Published in Canada by Vintage Canada, a division of Random House of
Canada Limited, Toronto, in 2012. Originally published in hardcover in
Canada by Alfred A. Knopf Canada, a division of Random House of
Canada Limited, in 2011. Distributed by Random House of Canada Limited.

Vintage Canada with colophon is a registered trademark.

www.randomhouse.ca

LIBRARY AND ARCHIVES CANADA CATALOGUING IN PUBLICATION

Toews, Miriam, 1964–
Irma Voth / Miriam Toews.

ISBN 978-0-307-40069-7

I. Title.

PS8589.O6352I76 2012   C813'.54   C2010-907643-5

Book design by Kelly Hill

Cover image: JH Pete Carmichael/Getty Images

Printed and bound in the United States of America

2 4 6 8 9 7 5 3 1

for my mother, Elvira

ONE

JORGE SAID HE WASN'T COMING BACK until I learned how to be a better wife. He said it's okay to touch him with my arm or my leg or my foot, if it's clean, when we're sleeping but not to smother him like a second skin. I asked him how could that be, I hardly saw him any more and he said that's a good thing for you. He said people always lie about their reasons for leaving and what difference does it make?

I blocked the doorway so he wouldn't leave and I begged him not to go. He put his hands on my shoulders and then he rubbed my arms like he was trying to warm me up and I put my hands on his waist.

I asked him how I was supposed to develop the skills to be a wife if I didn't have a husband to practise with and he said that was the type of question that contributed to my loneliness. I asked him why he was trying to blindside me with answers that attempted only to categorize my questions and I asked him why he was acting so strange lately and where his problem with the way I slept with my leg over his leg had come from and why he kept going away and why he was trying so hard to be a tough guy instead of just Jorge and then he pulled me close to him and he asked me to please stop talking, to stop shivering, to stop blocking the door, to stop crying and to stop loving him.

I asked him how I was supposed to do that and he said no, Irma, we're not kids anymore, don't say anything else. I wanted to ask him what loving him had to do with being childish but I did what he told me to do and I kept my mouth shut. He looked so sad, his eyes were empty, they were half closed, and he kissed me and he left. But before he drove off he gave me a new flashlight with triple C batteries and I'm grateful for it because this is a very dark, pitch-black part of the world.

The first time I met Jorge was at the rodeo in Rubio. He wasn't a cowboy or a roper, he was just a guy watching in the stands. We weren't allowed to go to rodeos normally but my father was away from home, visiting another colony in Belize, and my mother told my sister Aggie and me that we could take the truck and go to the rodeo for the day if we took the boys with us so she could rest. She might have been pregnant. Or maybe she had just lost the baby. I'm not sure. But she didn't care about rules that afternoon so, miraculously, we found ourselves at a rodeo. Maybe it was the pure adrenalin rush of being away from the farm that made me feel bold but I noticed Jorge sitting there by himself, watching intently, and kind of moving his body subtly in a way that matched the movements of the real cowboys, and I thought it was funny, and so I decided to go up to him and say hello.

Are you pretending to be a cowboy? I asked him in Spanish.

He smiled, he was a little embarrassed, I think.

Are you pretending to be a Mennonitzcha? he said.

No, I really am, I said.

He asked me if I wanted to sit next to him and I said yes, but only for a minute because I had to get back to Aggie and the boys.

We had a conversation in broken English and Spanish but it wasn't much of one because as soon as I sat down beside him my boldness evaporated and my knees started to shake from nervousness. I was worried that somebody would see me talking to a Mexican boy and tell my father. Jorge told me he was in town buying something, I can't remember what, for his mother who lived in Chihuahua city. He told me that he had a job delivering cars over the U.S. border from Juárez to El Paso and that he got paid forty American dollars a car and he didn't ask questions.

3

Questions about what? I asked him.

Anything, he said.

But about what? I said.

About what's in the cars or who's paying me or when or just anything. I don't ask, he said. He seemed a little nervous, so we both looked around at the people in the stands for a minute without saying much.

Some people are staring at us, he said.

No they're not, I said.

Well, actually they are. Look at that guy over there. He was about to lift his arm and point but I said no, please, don't.

He told me he thought it was strange that a Mennonite girl was at a rodeo and I told him that yeah it was. I tried to explain the rules my father had but that he was out of town and my mother was tired and all that and then we started talking about mothers and fathers and eventually he told me this story about his dad.

All I really understood was that his father had left his mother when he was a little boy and that one day his mother had told him he was going to meet him for the first time and he better look sharp and behave himself. She said she was going to drop him off on this corner by their house and his dad would be there waiting for him and then they could have a conversation, maybe get a meal together, and then the dad would drop him back off on that corner when they were done. So Jorge, he was five years old, decided he had better clean up his sneakers, especially if he wanted to look sharp for his dad. He washed them in the bathtub with shampoo and then he put them in the sun to dry. When it was time to go, his mom dropped him off at the corner and said goodbye and left and Jorge stood there for a long time, waiting. The sky got darker and darker. Finally it started to rain and Jorge started to worry. Where was his dad? Some men in cars drove past him but nobody stopped to pick him up. It started to rain harder. Then Jorge looked down at his shoes and noticed that they were foaming. Bubbles were floating around by his shoes and he didn't know what was going on. He was too young to understand that he hadn't rinsed his sneakers when he washed them with shampoo and now the rain was rinsing them for him and the soap was bubbling out of them and making them foam. Jorge felt like a fool. Like a clown. He was mortified. He was just about to take them off and rub them in the dirt on the sidewalk to try to make them stop foaming when a car pulled up and a man got out and introduced himself to Jorge as his father. He asked Jorge what was going on with his sneakers and Jorge told him that he didn't know. That they had just strangely started foaming like that and his father looked at him and told him that shoes didn't normally do that. Jorge had wanted to tell him that he had only been trying to look good and clean for his dad but he didn't really know how to say that and so he just started crying out of shame.

And then what happened? I asked Jorge.

My father told me that he loved my shoes that way, that they were great, that he wanted a pair just like them, said Jorge. That made me feel a lot better. And then we went and had some shrimp cocktail. Afterwards he dropped me back off at the corner and I never saw him again.

Oh, I said. Where did he go?

I don't know, said Jorge. But I was sure it was because of my stupid shoes that he never came back. I realized that he had lied to me. Obviously he didn't want a pair of shoes that foamed up. Who would want that? So eventually I made this decision not to act like an idiot in life.

But you weren't trying to be a clown, I said. You just wanted to have clean shoes to meet your dad. Your mom had told you to.

I know, he said, maybe it's not rational. But after that I decided I would try to be a cooler boy and not try so hard for things.

I told Jorge that I was sorry about that but that I had to get back to Aggie and the boys.

I guess I'll never see you again either, he said. He was smiling. He told me it was nice meeting me and I said he could visit me in our field, maybe, beside the broken crop-duster that had crashed in it, and I gave him directions and told him to wait there later that evening.

Make sure you look sharp and behave yourself, I told him. But I didn't really say it correctly in Spanish so he didn't get the little joke which wasn't funny anyway and he just nodded and said he'd wait all night and all year if he had to. And I wasn't used to that kind of romantic speaking so I said no, it wouldn't take that long. I wanted to tell him that I had tried most of my life to do things that would make people stay too, and that none of them had worked out, but then I thought that if I said that our relationship would always be defined by failure.

———

Jorge came to visit me a few times, secretly, on his way between El Paso and Chihuahua city. We would lie in the back of his truck and count the number of seconds it took for jet streams to evaporate. If you happened to fly over this place you'd see three houses in a row and nothing else for miles but cornfields and desert. Mine and Jorge's in the middle and on one side of us my parents' house and on the other side an empty house where my cousins used to live, the space between them approximately the size of a soccer pitch or a cemetery. On a clear day I can see the Sierra Madre mountains way off in the west, and sometimes I talk to them. I compliment them on their strength and solidity, and by hearing myself talk that way I am reminded that those words exist for a reason, that they're applicable from time to time. It's comforting. There are a few little villages around here. Some are Mexican and some are Mennonite, we're sorted like buttons, and we're expected to stay where we're put.

If Jorge visited in the evening he and I would lie in the back of his truck and stare at the stars and trace the shapes of various constellations and touch each other's bodies very gently like we were burn victims. Jorge told me that I didn't have to be so nervous. Don't you want to leave this place? he said.

I think so, I said.

So even if your father finds out about us the worst thing that can happen is we go away.

I know, but, I said. But then we can't come back, really.

So, he said. Why would you want to?

Well, I said. I would miss my mother and my sister and—

But Irma, he said, you could visit them secretly just like what we're doing right now.

I don't know, I said.

But you and I are in love, he said. We're eighteen now. We don't need our mothers so much.

He told me that it was like a star museum out here, there were so many of them, every different kind from all the ages, stored right here in my campo for safekeeping. He said I could be the curator of the star museum.

I'd rather not.

I was just saying stuff.

I know, I said, but I'm not good at keeping things safe.

I know, he said, I didn't mean it for real, it was just a thing to say.

I know, I said, but I can't be the curator of anything.

Okay, Irma. I understand. You don't have to take care of the stars, okay? That was just stuff to say. It was stupid.

I had meant to tell him, again, that I wasn't good at keeping promises or secrets or people from leaving. I kept meaning to tell Jorge things.

On our wedding day nobody came except the justice of the peace from the Registro Civil in Cuauhtémoc, who finished the ceremony in under a minute. He got lost trying to follow Jorge's directions to our campo and it was dark by the time he finally showed up. Jorge had brought a candle with him and he lit it and put it next to the piece of paper we had to sign and when I leaned over to write my name, Irma Voth, my veil caught on fire and Jorge pulled it off my

head and threw it onto the ground and stomped the fire
out. We were in a sheltered grove near my parents' farm.
The justice of the peace told me I was a lucky girl and Jorge
grabbed my hand and we took off, running. He wore a
white shirt that was too big on him and hard plastic shoes.
We didn't really know what to do but after a while we
stopped running and we walked around for a long time and
then we went to my house and told my parents that we
had got married and my mother went to her bedroom and
closed the door softly and my father slapped me in the face.
Jorge pinned him to the wall of the kitchen and said he'd
kill him if he did it again. I went into my mother's bedroom
and we hugged each other and she asked me if I loved
Jorge. I said yes. I told her that he and I were going to go to
Chihuahua city now and that we would live with his mother
for a while until we found jobs and our own place to live.
Then my father came into the room and told me that Jorge
and I weren't going anywhere, that we were going to live in
the house next door and work for him and that if we didn't
he'd turn Jorge over to the cops and that the cops would
sooner put a bullet in the head of another greasy narco than
bother with the paperwork of processing him. He didn't say
it in a fierce or menacing way, just in a way that made it clear
and final. And then he left the house and my mother went
into the kitchen and put some buns and cheese onto the
table and a rhubarb *platz* that she cut up into small pieces.
Jorge and I sat down with her, on either side, and she held
our hands and prayed for our happiness and for an everlasting love. She spoke quietly so the other kids wouldn't wake
up. After that she whispered congratulations to us in Low

German and I told Jorge what she had said and they smiled at each other, I had forgotten how pretty her smile was. Jorge thanked her for the gift of me and she asked him to protect and cherish that gift. Then my father came back into the house and told us to get out and that we were no longer welcome in his home. Jorge and I walked down the road to our house and he took my hand and asked me if I believed what the justice of the peace had said, that I was a lucky girl. I looked west towards the Sierra Madre mountains but I couldn't make them out in the darkness. Jorge's hand was a little sweaty and I squeezed it and he was kind enough to let that be my answer.

We lived in the house for free but worked for my father for nothing. We looked after the cows so that he could work the fields and travel around from campo to campo imploring people to continue with old traditions even though the drought was killing us. The plan was that when my little brothers were older they would help him with the farm, and Jorge and I would be booted out of the house. Jorge said he wasn't worried about that because he had other opportunities to make money and eventually he and I could follow our dream of living in a lighthouse. We didn't know of one but he said he knew people in the Yucatán who would help us. I didn't even really know exactly where the ocean was.

But none of that actually matters now and it's embarrassing to talk about because Jorge is gone and I'm still here and there's no lighthouse on my horizon as far as I can see.

———

Jorge came and went all that year and I never knew when he'd show up but when he did it wasn't for long so I really saw no one, except the cows.

One morning my little sister Aggie snuck over and gave me some news. She told me that filmmakers from Mexico City were moving into the empty house next to mine and our father said she wasn't supposed to talk to them or in any way whatsoever to acknowledge them.

She also told me that she had a new dream of becoming a singer of canciones rancheras, which are ballads of love and infidelity and drunken husbands. She had new dreams every day.

I missed Aggie. I missed her big laugh and her little tricks. I missed listening to her practice her swearing deep under the blankets so our parents wouldn't hear. She has white-blond hair and a brown face from the sun and blue eyes that are so light they're almost translucent, like a wolf. She told me that the sun and the moon are the two eyes of God and when one disappears the other one pops up to keep spying on us. When we can see them both at the same time we're in big trouble and all we can do is run. Since I married Jorge she hadn't been allowed to talk to me, which is why she had to sneak over, but it wasn't really sneaking, not entirely, because our mother usually knew when she was coming and sometimes sent things along.

According to my father, Jorge was more interested in searching for sensations in Chihuahua city than taking care of the cows and the corn in Campo 6.5. He had other reasons for not liking Jorge but the real reason was that I'd married a non-Mennonite. A long time ago, in the twenties, seven Mennonite men travelled from Manitoba to the Presidential Palace in Mexico City to make a deal. They'd been offered this land for cheap and they decided to accept the offer and move everyone from their colony in central Canada down to Mexico where they wouldn't have to send their kids to regular school or teach them to speak English or dress them in normal clothing. Mennonites formed themselves in Holland five hundred years ago after a man named Menno Simons became so moved by hearing Anabaptist prisoners singing hymns before being executed by the Spanish Inquisition that he joined their cause and became their leader. Then they started to move all around the world in colonies looking for freedom and isolation and peace and opportunities to sell cheese. Different countries give us shelter if we agree to stay out of trouble and help with the economy by farming in obscurity. We live like ghosts. Then, sometimes, those countries decide they want us to be real citizens after all and start to force us to do things like join the army or pay taxes or respect laws and then we pack our stuff up in the middle of the night and move to another country where we can live purely but somewhat out of context. Our motto is from the "rebuke of wordliness," which is from the Biblical book of James: *Whosoever will be a friend of the world is the enemy of God.*

I once made the mistake of asking my father if it didn't make sense that in all those years from then to now some Mennonite girl would fall for a Mexican boy and want to marry him. It's called integration, Dad, it's not a big deal.

I mean if you accept their cheap offer of land . . . But he had stopped listening to me ages ago. The last real thing we talked about was the absurdity of life on earth. He was thinking about something he'd read in an old newspaper that had somehow managed to float into our field from El Paso or somewhere. We were in the truck on our way to Cuauhtémoc and he asked me how I thought it was possible that a crowd of people could stand on the street in front of a tall office building and cheer a suicidal man on to his death by encouraging him to jump. I was surprised by the question and said I didn't know. What does that say about us? said my dad. That we're cruel, I said. Then my dad said no, he didn't think so, he thought it meant that we feel mocked, that we feel and appear stupid and cowardly in the presence of this suicidal man who has wisely con-cluded that life on earth is ridiculous. And we want him to die immediately so that the pain of being confronted with our own fear and ignorance will also, mercifully, end. Would you agree with that? my dad asked. What? I said. I didn't know what he was asking me. It's a sin to commit suicide, I thought. I said no, I still think it means we're cruel. My dad said no, it doesn't mean we're cruel. He got a little mad at me and stopped talking to me for a while and then as time passed never got back into the habit.

My father had lost his family when he was a little kid, when they'd been driven off their farm near the Black Sea. His parents and his sisters had been slaughtered by soldiers on a road somewhere in Russia, beside trees, and buried quickly in the ditch. My father survived by singing some songs, German hymns I think, for the soldiers, who thought it was cute, this little blond boy, but eventually the novelty of that wore off and they foisted him onto some other fleeing Mennonite family who adopted him and brought him to Canada to help with the animals and baling. He hated his adopted family and ran away when he was twelve to work on some other farm where he met my mother and eventually married her. That's all I know about that because by the time it occurred to me to ask him questions about it he had stopped talking to me. I tried to get more details from my mother but she said she didn't know any more than that either.

We'd had fun, me and him, you know, typical farm fun, when I was young. He made me a swing that I could jump from into hay and he understood my grief when my favourite chicken died. He even brought me to the fabric store to buy some flannel to make a burial suit of little trousers and a vest and hat for my chicken and he let me bury it outside my bedroom window rather than tossing it into the rubble fire like the other dead ones. But it was colossal and swift like the sinking of the *Titanic* the way all that disappeared when he moved us overnight to Mexico.

Two weeks after we moved here my mother took me to the doctor for the first time in Cuauhtémoc and told him that I thought I was dead and nothing she or my father said could convince me of the truth. I was thirteen years old, the same age that Aggie is now. My father stayed outside in the truck. The doctor spoke to me in Spanish and I didn't understand him very well. His office was in a big barn and the nurse was his wife. He had a small revolver in his pocket but before he examined me he took it out and laid it on his desk. He asked me what my life was like when I was alive.

I don't know, I said.

Is this your life after death? he asked me.

Yes, I said. I think so.

How did you die? he asked.

I don't know, I said.

Food poisoning? he asked.

Maybe, I said. I don't know.

Snake bite? he said.

No, I said.

Heart attack?

I'm not sure.

Do you feel that you were born and lived and then you died or that you have never lived at all? he asked.

I was born and lived and then died, I said.

So, he said, do you think that you're in heaven?

I don't know, I said.

What makes you feel like you're dead? he said. Are you numb in some parts of your body?

No, I said. I don't know.

Did you see yourself die? he asked.

Yes, I said.

How did you die? he asked.

I'm not sure, I said.

But you saw yourself die? he said.

Yes, I said.

In a dream? he said.

I don't know, I said.

If you still feel that you are dead in six weeks will you please come back to see me? he said.

I looked at my mother and she nodded. She didn't like his question about food poisoning. The doctor thanked her for bringing me to see him and patted her arm. He put his pistol back into his pocket. My father was still sitting in the truck, waiting for us. He asked my mother if I still thought I was dead.

I don't know, she said.

Why is it so important to you whether I'm alive or not? I asked them.

It's not whether you're alive or not, said my father. Clearly you're alive. It's what you believe. He pinched my arm. Do you feel that?

I nodded.

You need to stop playing games, Irma Voth, he said.

Someday you'll be a wife and mother, Irma, said my own mother. Will you come alive for that? I didn't know what to tell her. How was I supposed to know? On the way home I put my head in her lap and she undid my braids and combed my hair with her fingers. I like to remember how that felt. She was so gentle. I still don't understand how she managed to take out my tight braids without any tugging or pain. Irma, she whispered to me, just begin. I didn't know what she meant. When we got back she stayed with me in my bed even though I was thirteen and rubbed circles on my back slowly.

———

Aggie and I sat on the fence and talked. We were surrounded by nothing but three farmhouses in a neat row, sky and corn. How are the boys? I asked.

Annoying, she said. We had two little brothers, Doft and Jacobo, who liked to connect everything with rope.

Are they still tying shit together? I asked.

Yeah, and hiding shoes, she said. She told me that already my father was fighting with the director of the movie.

He's here now? I said.

He came early, said Aggie. Mom and I listened to him talking with Dad in the kitchen. Dad said he'd shoot his dog if it attacks the cows or even if he sees him in the cornfields. He's a fighting pit bull from Mexico City, Irma, and the director said he's got a haunted soul and a natural sweetness, and he'll play in the movie as a dog of the family. Dad told him that no family here has a fighting dog from Mexico City and especially not one with a soul and that's the first sign the director doesn't know what he's doing.

Aggie told me the director said he had invested almost all of his own money into his art, into making this film about beautiful people in a beautiful part of the world, and that he has nothing but respect and admiration for the Mennonites. My father asked the director if the dog was really there purely for protection. He accused the director of lying to him. That the dog was there to protect his expensive camera equipment. The director denied that and said no, the dog would be an integral part of the film. Aggie said that our father told the director that films were like beautiful cakes, filled with shit.

How can he say that when he's never seen them? I
asked her.

He says art is a lie, said Aggie.

We sat on the fence and stared at things. Artless things.
Things that were true. Things that belonged to ourselves
and to each other. The clouds, our clothing, my hands. A
bird flying over us had two long twigs in its mouth and he
dropped one so that it landed directly at our feet like it was
a gift. Here you go, Mennonite girls, prepare a nest. Or
maybe it was an attack.

Dad says you believe in God but not an afterlife, said
Aggie. He says that's impossible.

That's not remotely accurate, I told her. I never said
that.

Frieda's dad drove his truck the wrong way down the
highway to Cuauhtémoc, said Aggie.

What a moron, I said.

No, she said, he killed himself.

On purpose? I said.

I don't know, said Aggie. Didn't he drive there all the
time? Did they secretly reverse the directions?

What are they gonna do? I said.

Who knows, said Aggie. Get a new truck? Katharina at
school said he owed money to narcos.

Aggie, I said.

Well, how should I know? she said. Oh, I have this for
you. She pulled a tiny infant's undershirt out of her pocket.
There was a small faded flower on the collar. You wore it in

Canada if you were a baby, she said. Mom told me to give it to you.

Thanks, I said. *When* I was a baby.

When you were a baby? said Aggie. English is such a prick.

You're pretty good at it, I said.

Oh, and this is from her too, she said, and kissed me on the cheek.

Get lost, I said.

Can I come live with you, Irma? said Aggie.

Well, I said, are you looking for a quick and easy way to complicate your life forever?

Maybe I could live with you secretly, she said.

We sat quietly. We heard cows practising their English, trying with no luck to form words.

What's he trying to say? said Aggie.

Help, I said. Our own stupid joke.

I told her to go before it got so dark she'd fall into the ditch on her way home but she didn't move. Aggie ignores all my advice, as though she were determined to live successfully, and we sat on the fence for a long time. Then we started to get stiff from sitting and began to kick each other lightly in the dark.

When are they moving in? I asked Aggie.

I don't know, she said. Tonight.

My power was still off and I couldn't find the flashlight that Jorge had given me. I thought about bringing a cow into the house for company, just one. A small one. Or I could sleep in the barn like Jesus but without the entourage or the pressure to perform. I lay in my bed thinking of ways I could make Jorge happy if he ever came home again. One was: wash my feet before going to bed and dry them completely. The other one was: be hotter. It was true, what Jorge had said, that we weren't kids anymore. I loved chasing him around fields and having dried turd fights and hiding in the corn while he looked for me and planning our future together in the Yucatán in a lighthouse with round rooms and a pole in the middle that we would use to slide down from the top floor directly into a boat that with one shove would put us out to sea. I told him we could call the boat Katie but he said he'd have to name it after his mother and even that was okay with me, I didn't argue. I knew I would be alone for the rest of my life if Jorge didn't come back to me. No boy from any of the Mennonite colonies would want a woman who'd been married and abandoned and especially one who'd been married to a Mexican.

I decided to go out and spy on my family from the roof of their grain shed. I could see directly into their large room. I thought about throwing myself off the roof of the grain shed and onto the roof of the outdoor kitchen which they're not using now and lying there, dead, for months, invisible but toxic.

I wondered how long it would take them to find me. Then I remembered that they wouldn't be looking. Well, maybe Aggie would be looking, but that's the thing that stopped me from doing it. I had one question of myself: how do I preserve my dignity when nobody else is watching? By believing in a happy ending, I told myself. I had to get out of the house.

I stood in my yard and noticed the lights on at my cousins' old place. The filmmakers had arrived. And then I heard voices and music and laughter and I had never felt more alone and strange in my life, which is something. I went back into my house and lay in my bed some more and tried to pray. God, I said, help me to live. Help me to live, please. Please God, help me to live. God, I need your help. I need to live. Please? I need help living. God. Help. I had never learned how to pray properly. It didn't make sense that God would require me to articulate my pain in order for him to feel it and respond. I wanted to negotiate a deal. I knew I wasn't supposed to talk to the filmmakers but wondered if it would be acceptable to observe them from a distance. I punched myself on the side of my head. What difference did it make what my father had said? I posed another question to myself. How do I behave in this world without following the directions of my father, my husband or God? Does it all end with me sleeping in a barn with cows and creeping around the campo spying on people from the roofs of empty grain sheds?

I got up again and went outside and crept along in the darkness towards the filmmakers' house. I leaned against the water pump in the side yard and watched while several guys unloaded a million black boxes from a truck and a car and a van and carried them into the house. All the lights were on and the filmmakers were laughing and talking loudly and music was playing from somewhere inside. A dog was barking. In fact, a dog was barking and running at me in the dark and it looked like his eyes were on fire and I could see sparks flying out of them. I thought, well, I should run now, but I couldn't move, I was galvanized to the pump, and then I heard a man yell, Oveja, Oveja!

Which is how I met Diego, the director of the film.

Vive aquí? he said. He was kneeling, looking up at me, and holding on to Oveja's collar.

No, I said. Well, yes. Over there. I pointed. I tried to smile. I shook with fear. I may have bitten off a piece of my own tongue.

Me llamo Diego, said Diego.

Irma, I said.

Mucho gusto, Irma.

Mucho gusto.

Diego released Oveja and the dog wandered back to the house and Diego and I stood in the dark by the pump. He spoke quickly and precisely but his voice was soft, as though he were helping me through an emergency. He told me that Oveja, the pit bull, used to be a champion fighter in Guadalajara. He told me that Oveja, like every living thing, needs to love and be loved. And that his eyes tell a story of pain and suffering, and that he is haunted by his criminal past, a life he would never have chosen for himself.

Oveja and I are blood brothers, Diego said. We were

soldiers and now we are artists. He explained that before he became a filmmaker he was involved in armed conflict, though on the legal end of things.

Oveja will eventually play the part of the family dog in my movie, said Diego.

I know, I said.

Ah, you do? he asked.

He suggested that we move closer to the yard light so that we could see each other's faces. He smiled and I looked at him closely. He wore a thin thread around his neck and attached to the thread was a small piece of paper the size of a postage stamp. It had writing on it but I couldn't read it. He had a red dot in the white part of his left eye, like a tiny pilot light.

Which languages do you speak, Irma? he asked me.

German, Spanish and English, I said.

Do you want a job? he asked me.

I don't know, I said. I think I have one.

What is it? he said.

The farm, I said. I glanced over at the barn behind my house. And . . . wife.

How old are you, Irma?

I'm nineteen years old, I said.

And you're married? he said.

Yes, I said, for one year already.

Have you been here all your life?

I was born in Canada, I said.

Where is your husband? he said.

He's in the city.

Which city?

Chihuahua. Or Juárez.

For how long?

I don't know.

Would you like to make some extra money as a translator? he said.

Diego said he'd explain to me in Spanish or English what he wanted his German actress to say and do and I'd tell her, in German, what it was. He told me that it didn't really matter what the actors were saying because nobody watching the film would understand the language anyway. It wasn't really German that they'd be speaking, it was Low German, which is the unwritten language of the Mennonite people and hardly used in the world anymore. And besides, he said, there will be subtitles.

My actors could be saying I have worms, you have worms, we all have worms, he said, and nobody would know the difference. Do you understand, Irma?

I do, I said.

But I want *them* to know what they're saying, he said. So that they'll feel the words and produce the appropriate emotional response.

He told me that Miguel, a sixteen-year-old production assistant, will pick Marijke the German actress up at the airport in Chihuahua city tomorrow and bring her here to Campo 6.5 and we'll begin to shoot the movie the next day after she's had some time to rest.

I'm looking for internal energy and presence, Diego told me. I travelled around the world searching for the woman who would play this role. I want her to be beautiful, but not beautiful.

I understand, I told him.

I want her face to feel at home on an ancient coin, he said. I want her eyes to harm me. I want her, I mean *her*, to be too big for her body, a living secret, so that she is squeezed out through here, he said. He touched my forehead.

And here too, he said. He put his hand on my throat. And here, especially. He covered my eyes for a second.

And you found her? I said.

Yes, he said. In Germany. In a very small village. There was a woman in France but she was too beautiful.

Are you from Mexico City? I asked him.

Yes, but I've been living in Europe for the last few years. How long have you been living here? he asked me.

We came six years ago, I said.

It's very beautiful, he said.

It is? I said.

Yes, it's astonishing, he said.

What's Mexico City like? I said.

Ah, it's heaven and hell, he said. Are you nervous? You're shaking.

No, I said. I'm cold.

Why don't you come inside and meet the crew? he said. It's warm in there. I'll make you an espresso.

No, I have to get back to . . . there, I said. I pointed behind me.

The cornfield? he said.

I pointed again, towards the shadowy assortment of metal and concrete that housed my belongings. Diego smiled but I couldn't tell if he was sad or happy because he hadn't stopped smiling since rescuing me from his blood brother.

Okay, he said. But, quickly, let me just explain a few things to you about the job. We have a small crew, he said, and we are investing in time, not equipment and salaries. We all have specific responsibilities but everybody will be required to help out with everything. It's very necessary. Do you agree with that, Irma?

Sure, I said.

I hate stories and photographs, he said. They scare me. They freak me out. They're dead. I want emotion, the feeling, the emotional resonance of the person, the character coming out of a shot, a painting. I hate narrative. I hate actors. It's very important that your translation of my words is precise. Will it be?

Yes, I said.

And Irma, do you feel that we can rebel?

I don't know, I said. I had no idea what he was referring to, or on which word of the question to put the emphasis.

Do you feel that we can rebel against our oppressors without losing our love, our tolerance and our ability to forgive?

I don't know, I said. I looked around towards nature for a clue. A bird, a gust of wind, a star? But there was nothing, as though nature had noticed me trying to cheat and quickly covered up her answers. Diego put his hand on my shoulder and continued to smile.

Perfect, he said. You will be perfect.

———

The next morning Aggie and I met on the road between our houses and had one of our speed conversations. It's a silly thing we do together to make it seem like our imposed separation is not the source of continuous heartbreak and an abomination of what is just and loving but one long ridiculous joke like the Berlin Wall.

You're working for the filmmakers as a translator? That's crazy! Dad'll kill you! He already hates them!

I know, I said, so don't tell him. Diego will pay me and then I can use the money to go to Chihuahua or Juárez to find Jorge. Here, I have something for you.

What is it?

A switchblade. I brought it from Canada. Open it.

It's a comb!

It's a joke!

Drag.

Okay, then give it back to me!

No, I'll keep it.

I gotta go or you'll be in deep shit.

Irma, she said. But I had started to walk away. I heard her say some more things but by then I had yanked my skirt up and was running down the road away from her and begging the wind to obliterate her voice. She wanted to live with me. She missed me. She wanted me to come back home. She wanted to run away. She was yelling all this stuff and I wanted so badly for her to shut up. She was quiet for a second and I stopped running and turned around once to look at her. She was a thimble-sized girl on the road, a speck of a living thing. Her white-blond hair flew around her head like a small fire and it was all I could see because everything else about her blended in with the countryside.

He offered you a what? she yelled.

An espresso! I yelled back. It was like yelling at a shorting wire or a burning bush.

What is it? she said.

Coffee! I yelled.

Irma, can I come and live—

I turned around again and began to run.

TWO

I SPENT THE REST OF THE DAY cleaning the house and milking the cows and embroidering dangerous words onto the inside of my dresses, words like *lust* and *agony* and *Jorge*, and baking bread and yanking vegetables out of the ground, and making apple sauce with the apples that my aunt from Campo 4 had left for me at the end of the drive-way with a note that said even sinners need to eat and a religious magazine with a headline that read the only way to heaven is to admit that you are a complete failure, and washing the windows and burning stuff and poisoning snake nests and killing rats. I didn't see Aggie for the rest of the day. I knew she was mad at me. I could picture her stomping around the house and being sassy to everyone and brandishing her useless weapon.

That night I took off all my clothes and examined my body. I had forgotten about it. I poked at it like a doctor would and asked myself did I feel this and did I feel that? Then I looked at my face in a small mirror and tried to make the two vertical lines between my eyebrows disappear by stretching the skin away on either side. I brushed my hair until my arms ached and then I draped it over my breasts like Eve when she was being flirty in the Garden.

I still had no power. I couldn't find the flashlight. The silver eye of God was right outside my bedroom window. I heard music coming from the filmmakers' house, by now Marijke the German actress would have arrived, and I fell asleep alone and naked in my bed.

The next morning there was a knock on my door. It was a boy wearing narrow black jeans and enormous white sneakers. He said he was Miguel, Diego's assistant, and I should come to the house immediately. Diego needed to explain things to Marijke before they began shooting and he needed me to help him do that. Miguel was very polite. When you are ready, he said. I told him I had to milk the cows first and he frowned. He asked me if he could help because Diego was already vibrating and we needed to hurry. There are sparks flying off him in every direction, he said.

What's that? I asked him. He was holding something in his hand.

A two-way radio, he said. Listen. He pushed a button on the radio. He put his finger to his lips.

We heard voices, one in particular.

Who's that? I said.

It's Diego, said Miguel. He pointed at the filmmakers' house.

Is he angry? I asked.

No, said Miguel, it's a motivational speech.

I told Miguel I'd do my milking fast but alone and be at the house in half an hour. I told him that if Diego needed to tell me things before that he could come see me in the barn and talk while I milked. He could bring Marijke if he wanted to.

Roger, said Miguel. Is that how you say that?

Roger? I asked.

Yeah, in Canada. They said you were from Canada?

I left when I was thirteen, I said. Maybe over and out?

Over and out, Irma, said Miguel.

Okay, I said.

Miguel took off and I stood in the sunshine for a couple of warm seconds trying to think of other coded ways to say yes, I understand, goodbye.

Half an hour later I averted another attack from Oveja by befriending him with wieners and applesauce. For a soldier turned artist he was still surprisingly aggressive.

The filmmakers had tied plastic bags filled with water all around the front porch of their house to keep the flies away. The bags of water sparkled in the sunlight like little chandeliers. I stood outside the door poised to knock while Oveja lay on the ground beside me devouring my leftovers. Then the door opened on its own, well, not on its own but from the inside and all the shouting stopped and Diego came over and kissed my cheek and took me into the huge kitchen to meet the crew.

The house that used to belong to my shy farmer cousins was now inhabited by tattooed artists who lay around smoking and drinking espresso and arguing about politics and camera angles. Diego asked me if I liked the music. I nodded. Have you heard of Tuberculosis? he asked. I nodded again. They're my favourite band, he said.

One by one they all got up and kissed me on the cheek and introduced themselves to me in Spanish or English or both. I didn't see Miguel anywhere. Diego explained to me each of their responsibilities. The camera, the sound, other things I had never heard of. We are creating a small world, he said. A world that is more real than the one we know. He told me that he had just discovered that a very important piece of the camera was missing. Show me your thumb, he said. I held it out to him. It's this small, he said. But it's the difference between life and death. Can you do your farm work without your thumb? he asked me. I shook my head. I thought of how annoyed Jorge would be if I lost my thumbs. Diego told me that two of the filmmakers, including Miguel, had driven to El Paso to pick up a replacement part that was being sent from Los Angeles.

It's an old Russian camera from the sixties, he said. It's difficult to find parts. Now we have to wait for them to come back. It's excruciating but we must be Zen about it.

I was so nervous. I felt like a moron. I stood there staring at them. I felt conspicuous in my long dress. I could feel the bobby pins from my *doak* stabbing me in the head. I could smell the cow shit on my shoes. I felt like Jonah after he'd been spit out of the whale onto dry land en route to wicked Nineveh. I didn't know what to say. There were no women in the house.

Where's Marijke the German star? I finally blurted out.

Diego whispered in my ear. She's in her room, crying. Let's go speak to her now. We walked down the long hallway to the back of the house. There were six or seven bedrooms that we passed to get to the very end. Diego pointed at each bedroom and told me which of the crew it belonged to. Somebody has painted an upside-down cross on mine, said Diego. Irma, did you know that Saint Peter asked specifically to be crucified upside down?

Nope, I said. I looked at Diego and smiled. It was a long hallway that led from Biblical times to the present and back again.

Out of humility, said Diego. To differentiate himself from Jesus Christ. The blood would have pooled in his head. I nodded. But I think, said Diego, that my crew meant it to be the sign of the Antichrist. They're funny guys.

Marijke had been given my aunt and uncle's former bedroom, the biggest one. Even the furniture was the same, and the bedding. My cousins had left in a hurry, apparently, and according to my dad it was because Wilf, the older boy, was a narco and about to be eviscerated by some rival narcos. My dad thought everyone who left Campo 6.5 was automatically a narco because why else would they be running away if they weren't narcos. If my dad's assessment was accurate this place was teeming with narcos, and not just garden-variety narcos but narcosatanics in search of sensations (like Jorge, allegedly), bored with drinking blood from skulls and poised to bolt for bigger thrills while the rest of us were in it for the long haul, working hard and honestly for very little money, the way God meant for us to be. But I didn't believe it. I think my uncle got a job selling cars in Canada and Wilf wanted to study the violin and my aunt thought it would be cool to get a perm. But who knows. Maybe they're a family of drug lords now, throwing bodies out of helicopters and bowling with the heads of double-crossers. That would be my father's theory.

Marijke was beautiful, strangely beautiful, like Diego had said. Everything about her seemed elongated, firm and far-reaching, like a tower crane or a tall, flightless bird. I imagined cowering under her wing in the rain. She was a Mennonite but she dressed differently than me. She dressed the way I had dressed in Canada, sort of. She had on skinny black jeans, like Miguel's, and a green T-shirt. She wasn't crying anymore. She was sitting cross-legged on her bed, on my aunt and uncle's bed, and smoking a slim Vantage cigarette. Diego greeted her in Spanish and kissed her cheek and she murmured something and smiled at me and asked me, in German, if I was the translator. I told her yes and we shook hands and then Diego said he'd leave us alone to talk.

What did he say? she asked me.

He just said hello, how are you, I said.

He's very polite, isn't he? she said.

Yes, I said. She looked around the room and then she walked over to the window and stared out at the yard. She was quiet, looking, and then she turned around and smiled at me again.

How old are you? she said.

Nineteen, I said. How old are you?

How old do you think I am? she asked.

I don't know, I said. Thirty?

I'll be forty-one in three weeks, she said.

You don't look forty-one, I said.

That's because something very traumatic happened to me when I was fourteen and as a result of that trauma I was prevented from moving forward, she said.

Oh, I said. But you will be forty-one in three weeks?

Technically, she said. On some level I've been alive for forty-one years but on other levels I stopped progressing at fourteen.

What happened to you when you were fourteen? I asked. I sat down on the bed beside her and she handed me her pack of cigarettes.

I'll tell you another time, she said. I have a son who isn't much younger than you.

How old is he? I asked.

He's sixteen, she said. But spiritually he's much older. I'd say closer to eighty.

I hope that someday somebody asks me where I was when I smoked my first cigarette so that I can tell them that yeah, well, you know, I was in my aunt and uncle's bed with this fourteen-year-old German actress who had an eighty-year-old son. No big deal. Marijke talked about her son, about missing him. She told me that she was worried that maybe she had been too much of a friend to her son lately and not enough of a parent.

Friends are good, she said, but sometimes a kid needs someone just to say hey, don't inject that, or whatever.

Are you from Russia? I asked her.

Yes, she said. I was born there but the place where I was born doesn't exist now.

What do you mean? I asked her. I was having a hard time following this conversation. I knew more about the social significance of birdsong, I realized, than I did about human interaction.

We talked about Diego and the crew and we talked about the script which I hadn't seen but which she told me was full of little drawings that accompanied the text and that she thought she'd be expected to take off her clothes for one or two scenes.

Do you want me to tell Diego that you don't want to take off your clothes? I asked her.

No, no, she said. That doesn't bother me. It's his story.

What is the movie about? I asked her.

Agony. And swimming. I don't know. I can't quite figure it out from the pictures and it's written in Spanish.

She asked me if I wanted to see the script and I said yeah but then she couldn't find it in her room and didn't want to go out to the main room to see if she'd left it there because she'd be expected to socialize with a bunch of people she couldn't communicate with beyond tequila and *danke schön* or learn how to juggle devil sticks or whatever they were doing in there.

I should go, I said. I was worried that Aggie would come looking for me here.

Why? said Marijke. You're nineteen years old! Are your parents that strict?

No, no, I said. My husband.

What? said Marijke. You're married?

Yeah, I said.

Does your husband mind that you're working as my translator?

No, I said. Not really. Well, actually, he doesn't know about it. He's been away for a while.

Well then, how would he be worried? she said. Why should you go home? She put her finger gently on the bumpy ridge between my eyes. Where your source of energy begins, she said. She kneaded the bumpy ridge gently with her long finger. I tried to speak and she said don't speak now, notice the light. Do you notice the light?

I don't know, I said. I have to do the milking or the cows will explode.

Is your husband a good kisser? she asked.

What? I said. Jorge? I don't know. I have nothing to compare him to.

We were quiet then, smoking, thinking about Jorge. At least I was. I think he might have been a good kisser. I pledged to tell him that if I ever saw him again. The cigarette was making me feel dizzy and I was trying not to cough.

Have you heard of the four-part cure, Irma? she asked.

No, I said. Cure for what? I stood up and looked around for a place to put my cigarette.

Here, said Marijke. She took it and put it in a glass of water next to her bed.

She said she had googled a new philosophy, a four-part cure, that would help her to live life on life's terms. She laid it out for me:

Don't fear God, she said.
Don't worry about death.
What is good is easy to get, and
What is terrible is easy to endure.

I'm quoting, she said. It's Epicurean. From a thousand years ago. People misinterpret Epicureanism these days. They misinterpret everything.

Plus, she said, I've learned that thoughts are atoms flying around in totally random patterns.

Oh, I said. They are?

That's all they are, she said. It'll help me in the desert. And I do believe in my soul. Anxiety's the killer.

Yeah, I said. That's true. Can I ask you a question?

Anything, she said. She squeezed my red, chapped hands and the room suddenly smelled like milk.

Why were you crying before? I asked.

Oh, that, she said. Okay, here's the thing. It's true that I have a new cure that I'm counting on to get me through life and it's true that I'm a little bit tough but the reality is that I'm a middle-aged woman in the middle of nowhere, a Mexican desert for God's sake, about to do something I have no experience doing and I'm feeling very, very alone and unsure and ridiculous and afraid.

Well, why did you agree to be in the movie? I asked her.

I'm not really sure, she said. Why did you agree to be my translator?

I'm not sure either, I said.

Well, I think I do know, actually, she said.

Yeah? I said. Why?

Because we were asked to, she said.

Oveja was stoned and following me from a distance. Elias, the cameraman, had told me on my way out that Oveja had eaten his stash of pot and that it had made him more philosophical. He'll think twice before he attacks, he said. Elias made me laugh. He didn't stop talking, like he didn't care that silence was supposedly golden, his currency was different. He had bought himself some clothes from the store in town, Wrangler jeans and a plaid shirt and work boots. Now I'm a Mennonite, he said. He told me that when he was a boy in Mexico City he had learned about Mennonites. He had seen some of them selling cheese on the streets and he had wanted to be one. Elias told me that he had even drawn a self-portrait of himself as a Mennonite in a bathtub. It's remarkable, he said, that now I'm making a film about them. He showed me a photograph of himself as a little boy on a beach in Acapulco. See that? he said. He told me that when he was a little boy he had an ass but that somehow, along the road to adulthood, he had lost his ass. Do you see? he said. He turned around so I could look at him. I thought he did have an ass but a small one. Look at Wilson, he said. He's got two asses and I have none. That's not fair.

Wilson ignored him completely. He was writing something down. Then he looked up and smiled at me and shrugged his shoulders. I'm Wilson, he said. That's fine, I said. Why did I say it was fine for him to be Wilson? I wanted to go back and tell him that I was Irma. But he knew that.

Diego asked me, before I left for home, if Marijke was okay and what we had talked about. She's fine, I said. Diego told me that the others had returned with the essential camera part and that tomorrow morning, early, we'd start shooting.

I was less afraid of Oveja now that he was a philosopher but I was nervous when he followed me home. I imagined his brown teeth sinking, pensively, into the back of my leg in search of something elusive. I thought about what Marijke had said. Oveja, I said, would you please stop following me? Asking didn't change anything with dogs.

Aggie was standing like a thief in the night at the dark end of my driveway. Her hair was tied back tightly, viciously. Her head shone like an egg.

What's wrong? I asked her.

What's that? she said, pointing at Oveja.

What's wrong? I asked her again.

Everybody hates you, she said. She kicked a bit of sand in my direction. Oveja sighed. What was the point. Stars fell.

That's not true, Aggie, I said. They don't care enough about me to hate me. You're the only one who does.

I don't hate you, said Aggie.

I know, I said. How do you like my new friend?

He's hideous, said Aggie. He's an asshole and he stinks like shit. I hope he gets run over by a baler.

We stood quietly and stared at the night. We were living in a dark, empty pocket. Not even the Hubble telescope could spot us on the earth's surface now.

Oh, c'mon, Aggie, I said. Stop crying. I wanted to tell her about the four-part cure. I wanted to convince her that everything good was easy to get and all that was terrible was easy to endure.

Hey Aggie, I said, you know what?

What? she said.

Oveja's stoned right now and thinks he's a philosopher. When it wears off he'll go back to attacking people. I don't think we have a lot of time. Then Aggie told me that her friend Aughte's dad, Alfredo, was going to play the husband in the movie. That Diego had promised him and his wife and kids a two-week all-inclusive resort package in Cancún when it was over and now everyone was mad at him too, and maybe after the movie they'd all move to a colony in Veracruz and she'd lose her best friend and Alfredo would find out that I was working for Diego too and tell our dad and that would be it, curtains.

And Mom's pregnant again, said Aggie. And doesn't want to get out of bed and doesn't smile anymore and I have to do everything now and Dad just yells and prays and I have chigoe bites all over my legs. So, why did you have to be such an idiot and go and marry a cholo?

He's not a narco, Aggie, I said. Let me see.

She lifted her dress a bit. There were ugly red sores all over her ankles and shins where the fleas had burrowed beneath her skin.

Let me sleep at your place tonight, Irma, please?

That night I had a dream about my mother and the next morning I saw her for the first time in months. I was up early, ready to start my new job, and I was standing in my yard waiting for the sun also to rise and warm me up. In my dream I was thinking about my dad yelling and praying and wondering if he got them mixed up sometimes and forgot who he was talking to. In my dream I looked at the road and there was my mother walking slowly, proud and majestic, or maybe just exhausted, like one of those giraffes you see briefly in shimmering sunlight on the savannah. She didn't look real and for a second I thought my mind had conjured up the thing it craved, the way a pregnant woman cries so she can taste the salt her body needs. Which is actually a lie my mother told us to explain away all her tears. But I was thinking about that stuff while I was running and then I was hugging her and I knew she was real because she was holding me so close to her it hurt and I was coughing trying to catch my breath and I could smell fresh bread and soap. I touched her stomach. She was farther along than I had thought.

Another one? I said.

Is Aggie with you? she said.

She's still asleep.

Send her home now, Irma, quickly.

I wanted to tell her about my dream but she had already begun to walk away and I stood there, like always, like forever it seemed, in the middle of the road waiting for something or someone to revive me, God or a parent or my husband or any of those things or people or ideas or words that by their definition promised love.

Diego suggested I keep a diary of "the shoot" after I mentioned a few things that Marijke had wondered about. For instance, why her character would be serene all the time. Was she in a depressive fog or not quite human or just plain stupid? He told me that he found it easier to understand certain ideas when he wrote them down or captured them on film and that I could try to do the same thing by keeping a diary of the shoot rather than by worrying about *his* ideas. Or something like that. He gave me a black notebook and a pen with a small light bulb on the tip.

Does this pen light up? I asked him.

Yes, there's a switch, he said. It doubles as a flashlight.

Thank you, I said.

The first thing I wrote down in my new notebook was:

YOU MUST BE PREPARED TO DIE!

That's what Diego told us this morning before we headed off to our first location. This is commando filmmaking, he said. The little red dot in the white of his left eye shone brighter than usual, like fresh blood on snow.

This is guerrilla filmmaking, he said. When it's time to work, it's time to work. If you're not prepared to risk your life, then leave now.

Irma, he said. Are you afraid?

Of dying? I said. I laughed out loud.

What is he saying? asked Marijke.

He wants us all to have fun, relax and be brave, I said.

I ran my fingernail over the leathery cover of the notebook and tried to carve my name into it. Then I thought to use the pen. I wrote my name on the inside cover and then crossed it out. I was afraid that my father would find it. I traced my left hand on a blank page and then filled it in with lifelines that somewhat resembled my own.

Diego has put Marijke into a dress like mine and tied her hair back with a kerchief and scrubbed off all her makeup. I explained to her that the first scene we'd be shooting was the family in their farmyard checking out a new tractor. We'd have to drive about an hour to the farmhouse where the scene would be shot. She stood in the yard like a smoking tree while the rest of us carried the equipment to the trucks.

Then Alfredo showed up with his wife and kids from Campo 3 a mile away, and they were not happy. I waved to them because I've known them all my life and Peter, the little boy who doesn't know any better, waved back. His older sister, Aggie's friend from school, pulled his hand down. They stayed in the truck and stared away at something. Alfredo ignored me and went over to Diego and told him that he had to quit.

What do you mean, quit? said Diego. What are you talking about? We haven't even started!

Alfredo told Diego that he was getting too much pressure from his wife and his parents. They didn't want him to act in a movie and it was taking him away from his work digging wells and his wife was jealous of his movie relationship with another woman.

Como lo arreglamos? said Diego. He wanted to know how they could work things out. Alfredo shrugged.

Diego smiled at me and then took Alfredo's arm and led him away behind the barn to talk about it and everybody standing around heard them yelling at each other in Spanish. Oveja went running around to the back of the barn to see what was going on and I heard Alfredo say he'd rip Oveja's jaw out and crush it under his truck tires if he came any closer. Then Diego yelled at Wilson to come and get Oveja and tie him to the pump.

What's the problem? Marijke asked me.

Nothing, I said. Diego is preparing Alfredo for his role.

At first Diego pleaded with Alfredo and then he was shouting, saying he had thought they had an understanding, and then he changed his strategy and appealed to Alfredo's ego (There is nobody, NOBODY, but you who can give this part the depth and humanity that it demands) and then he shifted his position again and offered him some more money and shortly after that they stopped yelling at each other and emerged from behind the barn and Alfredo went over to his wife and kids and talked to them and they drove off without waving and without Alfredo.

I don't want him to yell at me, said Marijke, if that's what it takes to prepare me. I can't handle that.

He won't, I said, your role is different.

We all piled into the trucks and drove off to shoot the first scene. Elias was driving the truck that Marijke and I were in. In Rubio, the closest village to our campo, he smashed it into a fence trying to back up and Diego, following behind, radioed him to let me drive because I knew the roads around there. We had to wait for a while so that Diego could negotiate something with the owner of the fence. Alfredo came over to where Marijke and I were standing and asked me if my father and my husband knew I was working for Diego.

When Diego came back he suggested that Alfredo change trucks and sit next to Marijke so they could get to know each other because they did speak the same language, but Marijke said that in fact their dialects were entirely different, she was a Russian Mennonite living in Germany and he was a Canadian Mennonite living in Mexico, and Alfredo was drunk and reeked of booze and was completely unintelligible and so . . . no.

She just wants some time to herself to organize her thoughts, I told Diego.

What thoughts? he said. Is she unhappy again?

I drove for a long time past various campos, clusters of barns and houses here and there, and down dirt roads and through cornfields and little streams and mud and desert. Elias and Sebastian, the sound guy, were sleeping in the back seat and Wilson sat in between them writing in his notebook.

What's he writing? Marijke asked me.

What are you writing? I asked Wilson, in Spanish, and he said stories, small stories. He said he'd like to read them at a festival in Guadalajara but he can't now because he's been commandeered to work for Diego and he needs the job.

Marijke, I said, does your husband mind that you're here in Mexico working on a movie?

No, she said, not at all. I don't think he does. Do I mind if he goes to work? Do I mind if he shits and breathes?

I thought, that's what I should have told Alfredo when he asked me about Jorge.

Elias woke up and lit a cigarette. I forgot my light meter, he said. I'm a dead man. Wilson looked up briefly from his writing.

We drove through clouds of dust in silence. We passed a few Tarahumara Indians on the road, a mother and her daughters clad in beautiful colours. They didn't seem to be walking anywhere. They were just there, standing brightly. I turned around to look a few times to see if they would move. I did it quickly, trying to catch them moving, but they had my number.

Marijke and I sat in an empty shed on upside-down feed buckets talking about the script and sex and the nervous system. She asked me if Jorge had wanted to have a baby with me.

I'm not sure, I said.

You didn't talk about it?

I don't think so, I said.

Would he make a good father, do you think? she said.

Well, I said, I'm not sure. What do you mean?

I mean would he be helpful with the baby and love it more than himself.

I was quiet, thinking of fathers, of my own and of Jorge's, who had watched his small shoes bubble over and then disappeared.

Well, what do you think? said Marijke. Are you crying?

Diego had asked me to do Marijke's hair like mine. I started combing it and a few chunks of it, long strands, fell onto the dirt floor. Those are my extensions, she told me. She told me they had been welded to her head with a heat gun and glue. She told me that mostly her hair would have to be braided and stuffed under her doak when she was acting but she thought there was one scene where it was required to tumble out of her kerchief and that's when she'd need the extensions.

I had that dreamy feeling of falling, for a split second, and then losing my footing again. To regain it, I tried quickly to remember the meaning of the word *samizdat*. And then I heard screams. A kid came running into the shed and grabbed my hand and dragged me outside into the yard where a bunch of other little kids were standing around a four-foot tiger snake. I grabbed a rake from the shed and neatly (not to brag, but you know) sliced the thing in two and the kids stared for a while, a couple of the boys kicked at it, and then went back to their game. Marijke came outside and asked me what was going on. Well, this thing is dead now, I said.

We stood with our hands on our hips and looked at it. Marijke's hair was half done and billowing out from one side of her head like the flag of some beautiful and indefinable region. She moved her fingers gently over the tight braids on the other side. Good job, she said.

Check this out, I said. I picked up a piece of the snake and peeled off its skin. I crushed the hard shell in my hand and showed Marijke the powder. You can sprinkle this over your food like salt, I said.

She licked her finger and dabbed at the crushed bits in my hand.

Hmmm, she said. Are you sure?

Diego called to say he needed Marijke then, to just shove the rest of her hair under the kerchief and come right now because the light was right and the Mennonites who owned the house were getting restless. The crew had set everything up and the Mennonite kids playing the Mennonite kids were in their places and their parents, Alfredo and Marijke, were supposed to talk about stuff while checking out the new tractor with the family. One of the kids didn't want to be there and Miguel was trying to cajole him in Spanish, which the kid didn't understand yet, and then to bribe him with chocolate. Eventually Miguel just said okay, go play, and he went out and plucked a different, more pliable blond-haired, blue-eyed kid from the crowd that had gathered around and set him down next to the tractor for the scene.

Diego asked Alfredo to remove his beer can from the hood of the tractor so it wouldn't be seen in the shot and then he took me aside and said that this was the scene of the family together, pivotal and establishing, and must be perfect. Alfredo will tell Marijke that he has to go to town on some kind of business and Marijke will indicate through her body language that she does not believe him but that she will accept what he is saying for the sake of peace in the home. Alfredo will take a few steps then come back and put his hand on her shoulder and tell her that he loves her. Marijke will tell him that she loves him too. Okay? he said. It's simple, right?

I nodded. Yeah, I said. Should I tell her now?

Yes, Irma, please, said Diego. We're ready. And can you also tell her to please not look into the camera.

I went over to Marijke and told her what Diego had said about not looking into the camera.

And when Alfredo tells you that he loves you, I said, you smile a little sadly and put your hand softly on his hand and tell him quietly that you're tired of his bullshit. In fact, no, not tired, but very close to being *defeated* by his bullshit.

That's what I tell him? she said.

Um, yes, I said. Quietly and sadly.

Okay, she said.

And remember the camera, I said. Not to look at it.

On the way home Elias and Sebastian smoked Faros and shared headphones.

Irma, said Elias. Do you know Neil Young?

Yeah, I said.

You do? said Elias.

No, I said.

He's from Canada! said Elias. He handed me his head-phones and I put them in my ears and listened. I heard Neil Young singing about a sky about to rain.

What does that last part mean? said Elias.

I don't know, I said. Then I thought about it. I don't know, I said again.

It comes out of fucking nowhere but it fits perfectly, said Elias. I don't know what it means either but it's fucking brilliant. He took the headphones back and listened to another song. When it was finished he took them off and told us that the song was about this guy, he loses his way, his map, he loses his telescope, he loses his coastline! It's so great, he loses everything, he loses his words! So he keeps singing but just this la la la la la la la la and it gets more and more joyful and builds into this incredible cre-scendo, it's so happy, because he's finally free and he's lost but he's free!

Marijke slept with her rubber boots up on the dash and Wilson wrote in his notebook.

Hey Wilson, said Sebastian. What are you writing about?

Nothing, said Wilson. He closed his notebook and put it on the seat beside him.

C'mon, you're writing something, said Sebastian. What is it? A love letter? Is it about us?

No, said Wilson. Fuck off.

C'mon, said Sebastian. What are you writing? Tell us.

I'm writing about how dreams are like art and how both are sort of a conjuring up of the things that we need to survive.

That's why I always dream about sex, said Elias.

Even if it's an unconscious or subconscious act, said Wilson. Art, of course, is a more wilful act than a dream, but it comes from the same desire to live.

I once had a dream that I was fucking the world, said Elias. Like, I don't know how old I was but I was in Montevideo in a house somewhere and I was bored so I wandered around and then I got this idea so I went to the back door and I opened it and stepped outside and took my dick out and started banging the night. Like, I was just banging away at the night. But the night was dark, obviously, so there was no stopping it. I mean I couldn't see where the night ended, because of the horizons or whatever, so it was like the night was the whole world and I was fucking it.

You weren't fucking the world, said Sebastian. You were jerking off in the dark like every other night.

No, man, said Elias. It seemed like that but it was different in my dream.

I'm talking about dreams of guilt and dreams of redemption, said Wilson.

We don't know it but we direct our own dreams, said Sebastian. A restructuring or an un-structuring of ideas and experiences that allow for our own salvation.

Give that to me, said Wilson. You're an asshole.

Our dreams are little stories or puzzles that we must solve to be free, Sebastian said. He was reading out loud from Wilson's notebook. My dream is me offering me a solution to the conundrum of my life. My dream is me offering me something that I need and my responsibility to myself is to try to understand what it means. Our dreams are a thin curtain between survival and extinction.

Sebastian, said Wilson. Can I have that, please?

I like it! said Sebastian. No, seriously, that's heavy shit that clarifies a thing or two for me.

Sebastian, said Wilson. Please?

Sebastian handed over Wilson's notebook and apologized for reading from it. Wilson waved it all off and smiled at me as if to say, would you help me blow up the universe?

Well, said Elias, my dream is me telling me to fuck the world. That's my art. What can I say.

Wilson stared out the window and Elias and Sebastian went back to listening to their music. I looked at Marijke. She was still sleeping. Then she opened one eye halfway and looked at me as though she was incorporating me into her dream and closed it again. I drove slowly, trying to relate everything to a dream, hoping to see my Tarahumara family again before the dream ended.

THREE

IT WAS LATE WHEN WE GOT BACK to the filmmakers'
house. Wilson invited me in for coffee and I said no, I couldn't.
Then I changed my mind and said yeah, okay. He told me
he wanted to show me something. Marijke had gone to her
room and closed the door—we could hear her laughing or
crying—and Diego was busy talking on the radio. Wilson
asked me if I would come into his bedroom. I stood still

and quietly panicked and then he said that it was okay, he didn't mean it in that kind of way, he just wanted a little privacy from the others. So I followed him into his room and he closed the door and I went and stood by the window and he sat on his bed.

I'd like to read you something if you don't mind, Irma, he said. He opened his notebook and read a story, half in Spanish, half in English, about an angry circus clown who was going through a divorce.

All the people in my stories are awful, he said. I agreed with him.

Why don't you write about people who aren't such ass-holes? I asked him.

Because, he said, that would be too painful.

I looked around the room. I remembered playing with my cousins. I remembered trying to climb out the window of this room and breaking the window frame. I got up and went over to the window and it was still cracked and crooked.

I used to play here all the time, I said.

Really? said Wilson.

Yeah, my cousins lived here.

One family? said Wilson. There are so many bedrooms in this house.

Lots of kids, I said. A soccer team.

Or a film crew, said Wilson.

They didn't make movies, I said.

I know, said Wilson, I was just kidding. They probably didn't play soccer either.

Of course they played soccer, I said. That's mostly what we did all the time.

Oh, said Wilson. Are you any good?

Not really, I said.

Do you want to kick a ball around sometime? said Wilson.

Well . . . I don't know, I said. I'm a married woman now. So? said Wilson.

I could see Elias and Sebastian standing on the road talking to each other and passing a cigarette back and forth. Elias was waving his arms around and Sebastian was perfectly still. Corn was behind them. Endless corn. Then Elias crouched down to the ground and picked up some stones and threw them at the corn and there was a dark explosion of crows.

Why is it so painful to write about people who aren't assholes? I asked Wilson.

Because I would start to love them, he said.

I was still looking through the broken window. I didn't know what to say. I heard Wilson sigh. Can I show you something now? he asked. I went over to the bed and stood beside him and he lifted up his shirt. There were scars all over his chest and stomach, some of them looping around to his back.

What happened? I asked him.

I'm dying, he said. I sat down beside him on the bed.

From what? I said.

My veins won't stay open, he said. They sometimes just collapse. The doctors have cut me open so many times to work on a vein but after a few months another vein quits and they have to go back in. Then they gave me this super-industrial-strength medicine that I had to squirt into my body through a tap in my stomach. They drilled a hole right here above my belly button and stuck a little faucet in there that was attached to a long cord and a pump which I could hold in my hand and every hour or so I'd have to squirt another drop into my body and it would go through the long cord and then through that little tap into my gut. It was basically like TNT blasting through my veins trying to wake them up so the blood could move.

You don't have the tap anymore? I said.

No, said Wilson, because I kept getting infections from the incision and they had to replace it every three weeks and that was excruciating. So now it's just a matter of waiting. But I try not to think about it.

Are you afraid? I asked him.

He told me he was scared shitless, actually, who wouldn't be? And then I told him about all the stupid things I'd done in that room when I was a kid and a little bit about my old life in Canada, how we couldn't recognize even our own mothers in the winter because we were so bundled up trying to stay warm, which he thought was funny. And I told him about the hockey rink that my father built for us little kids in our backyard by first of all clearing away tons and tons of snow and then using that snow to build towering walls around the rink and then by packing down the surface until it was as smooth as glass even though it was only rock-hard snow and how once I woke up in the middle of the night and the yard light was still on which made me wonder what was going on so I looked out the window at the glistening hockey rink in our backyard and

I saw my father on his hands and knees in the middle of it next to a perfect red circle and he was all hunched over and concentrating, painting lines, red ones and blue ones, on the hard snow to make the hockey rink official and the lines were so even and perfect and bright against the white snow. I watched him paint for a long time and finally he stood up and put his hands on his hips like this and stared at his circle and his lines and he had this huge grin on his face.

Did he see you in the window? said Wilson.

No, I don't think so, I said.

Was it supposed to be a surprise for you guys? said Wilson.

Yeah, I said. The next morning we went downstairs and we went outside and he was there with new hockey sticks for all of us too. We had to make up names for our teams and sing the national anthem.

Beautiful, said Wilson. Did you play on it?

Yeah, we played forever, I said. Not with skates or anything, just in our boots. Sometimes, my older sister, Katie, would referee for a while before she got bored and went off with her friends. Every night until way past everyone else had gone to bed. So it was me and my mom against my dad and Aggie. She was little and he made sure she got a shot every once in a while and me and my mom would fake trying really hard not to let it in.

But somehow it got in, said Wilson.

Yeah, I said. And then she and my dad would do their victory dance.

Do you think it's still there? said Wilson.

Well, I said. You know what happens to snow, sometimes, right?

Two things happened when I got back to my house. Somebody was sitting at the kitchen table in the dark. I thought it was Jorge and I was about to jump on top of him but then I realized it was my father.

That was the first thing. And the second thing is that he spoke to me. But not until after a long period of spooky silence. Just sitting there and looking at me or looking around the house.

So what's up? I asked him finally. Is mom okay?

You're involved with the filmmakers? he said. I didn't say anything.

And Aggie is also spending time with you? he said.

She's my sister, I said.

She's my daughter, he said. I'm thinking of selling your house.

Well, where will I live? I asked him.

He suggested I talk to God about that and reminded me that the house belonged to him and that he had only allowed Jorge and me to live in it because we were also taking care of his cows but now I was getting Aggie to do the work and running around with artists, and my husband should be the one to take care of me and now I was humiliating everyone, my mother, my father, my relatives, the entire campo, the church and God.

What about the cows? I said. You forgot to mention.

You're not funny, Irma, he said.

Well, you're not either, I said. I guess the apple doesn't fall too far from the tree.

What apple? he said.

Me, I said. I'm the apple and you're the—

You're a lunatic, he said.

Jorge hasn't left me, I said. My father looked around the house pretending to search for Jorge like it was a joke. I stood up. I wasn't afraid of him for myself, only for Aggie, but I was going to leave.

Irma, said my father, what do you want from this life?

I sat down next to him and touched his arm for half a second. It was a surprise and he didn't flinch. He didn't expect an answer. It was a kind gesture for any man from around here to ask a question of his daughter. I felt like touching his arm again but I knew he'd be prepared this time and pull away.

You don't have light in here? he said.

Sometimes, I said. I can't get the generator to work. I had a flashlight but I lost it. He didn't say anything. For a second I was sure that he would promise to come back to fix the generator. I knew he wanted to. I waited for him to say the words. Then he got up and left. It felt like a scene in the movie. I imagined my father saying hey, how was that? Was I okay? And I'd say well, it wasn't bad, but let's do it one more time.

We were in an apple orchard with an old, slimy swimming pool in the middle. An ancient Mexican woman in a Nike T-shirt had opened up the wire gate for us and led us to the pool. I had wandered off into the trees to pee and while I was squatting in the dappled sunlight a huge horse appeared out of nowhere and tried to push me over with its nose. Fuck off, I said, and then apologized. I picked up a rotten apple that had fallen onto the ground and tossed it gently at the horse and it moved a foot or two away from me and snorted like it was planning to charge and then changed its mind and came back and stood next to me, over me really, while I finished peeing. If I could only interpret my dreams I would know what I wanted from this life and then I'd be able to explain that to my father. I felt sleepy, so tired. I thought about having a short nap while the horse watched over me. Horse, I said, what are you doing here? He let that question dangle between us and I left.

It was another shot of the family, this time swimming together but with undercurrents of tension. On the surface the shot was supposed to be serene and warm and show the hard-working family having a nice little break. Diego was having a heart-to-heart conversation with Alfredo about the necessity of him taking his clothes off in the abandoned change room.

Marijke doesn't have a problem taking off her clothes, said Diego.

She's European, said Alfredo.

It will be a long shot, Alfie, said Diego. You'll be this big. He held his fingers up an inch apart. And it's dark in there. It will be one brief second in the film.

Marijke was lying in the sun reading a book called *You Are Not a Stranger Here* and smoking and Miguel was running around with the Mennonite children, trying to keep them from getting bored while the others set up the shot. A crowd of people from the nearby campo, including the mothers and siblings of the kids acting in the movie, had found out where we were shooting and were standing around watching.

One of the mothers came up to me, her name was Tina, and she asked me how my mother was and I said I didn't know really but that she was going to have another baby and then Tina asked me if I knew that Aggie had quit school to help out at home.

When did that happen? I said.

I think today, she said.

I thought of my father making a long slit in the stomach of a hog and draining its blood and guts onto the ground in minutes. In seconds. In one second. Which was the length of time it took for news to spread around here.

I wasn't surprised at all and I wanted to talk to Tina some more about Aggie just to be able to form the shape of her name with my lips and my tongue, Aggie, but Diego called *my* name and I had to go.

Tina, I said, will you ask Abe to talk to my father about Aggie staying in school?

What would I say? said Tina.

I don't know, I said. But my father has always liked Abe and maybe he can say something.

Tina nodded and touched my shoulder. She told me she would pray for our family. She told me that Abe liked my father too, but didn't like how strict he was. She said that she and Abe were grateful to my father for not involving the police when their son shot one of our cows just for fun.

Thanks, I said. Can you please tell my mother hello and how are you.

Diego called me again and Tina and I said goodbye. He was still trying to convince Alfredo to get naked and Alfredo was sitting on a rock enjoying another vampiro and smoking and shaking his head and Diego told me to tell Marijke that when Alfredo told her what a good mother she was, in the scene, that she should tell him that he was a good father, too. And that when Alfredo commented on her soap-making abilities that she acknowledge him gratefully with something appropriate.

I began to walk over to where Marijke was and Diego began yelling at Alfredo that okay, fine, he'd take his clothes off too, for the shot, no sweat. And then he told the crew that they should take theirs off too so that Alfredo could see that he wasn't the only man in the world with a cock and balls and they said sure, no problem, and began to strip down to their underwear and Marijke was looking at them all calmly, smoking, and I started to panic and ran over to Diego and told him that they couldn't do that, that all the Mennonites watching would seriously freak out and the crew would be herded up and shot and left in a field to rot and their faces sewn into soccer balls.

All right, said Diego, we'll shoot that part another time when nobody is watching. He put his pants back on but by this time Elias, Sebastian and Wilson were all in the pool in their underwear trying to keep the camera from slipping off the inner tube that they had tied it to. Some of the women watching had taken their kids away and a few of them were standing with their arms folded laughing at the half-naked crew and whispering. I ran back to Marijke and sat down with her in the sun and she put her arms around my shoulders and asked me how things were going.

Life is a bitter gift, no? she said.

So, now, in this shot, I said, when Alfredo tells you that you're a good mother you smile softly, like this, and look at him and say thank you, but how would you know? And when Alfredo tells you that you make good soap or whatever his line is you nod and say yes, but you're sick of making soap and thinking of just buying it in the store from now on. And again, I said, try not to look directly at the camera. Marijke nodded and got up. Thanks, Irma, she said.

No sweat, I said.

We smiled and I told her she was beautiful. Radiant. I told her I thought her neck was as long if not longer than my forearm, like Nefertiti. She told me she felt like shit in the dress she was wearing and then looked at mine and apologized and said that it was weird that her dress was a costume and mine was just a dress even when they were virtually identical and then she apologized again, she put her hand on her throat as though that was the place where regrettable words sprang from, and I waved it all away, it didn't matter. I had befriended a horse wearing this dress. For some reason I thought it would be funny for me to tell Marijke that but she was already gliding away towards Diego and the others.

The next day everybody was sick, probably from the dirty water in the pool and nobody had anything to say. Through the kitchen window I could see Oveja napping under the truck. I pulled the notebook from the pocket of my dress and pressed it to my forehead. It felt cool on my warm skin.

Diego has asked me if I'd be willing to clean the house and do the crew's laundry. Marijke and the crew are huddled around the TV watching something with no sound and looking green and exhausted. I don't know how to ask Diego if he'll pay me extra for cleaning. In addition to the word *samizdat* I'm now pondering the meaning of the word *despondent*. My English is fine. I lived in Canada for thirteen years and went to a normal school with normal kids. But there are words that drift around in my head like memories from the Jazz Age or something. I want to say them but they're not really mine to feel. Here comes Diego again. The end.

Okay, I said. I'll clean the house.

He said he'd still take the crew out to shoot some stuff but that Marijke could have the day off and stay in bed or do whatever she wanted to do.

Where's Wilson? I asked.

He went back to Caracas, said Diego.

Why? I said.

We had a fight, said Diego. I keep forgetting how sensitive he is. He erupts like shrapnel and then goes psycho still, like numb inside. His eyes go like this. I don't understand him. He wants me to write an introduction to his book of stories. But now we all have extra work. Irma, I have a question to ask you. Do you know that song "A Hard Rain's A-Gonna Fall"? Do you know this? *A-gonna?*

No, I said.

Diego went back into the living room to talk to the others and I wandered into Wilson's room and looked around. He wasn't there. So, that was true at least. I sat on Wilson's bed and felt the mattress sag a bit beneath me. He hadn't forgotten to take his notebook.

After the others had left, Marijke went into the yard and threw up next to the pump. She washed her face and then stuck her whole head under the water and then took off her T-shirt and lay on the grass on her back with her breasts exposed to the sun and the wind and God. I lay down in the grass on my side with my back to her.

Marijke, I said, what kind of a Mennonite are you? I said it quietly and in Spanish. In fact, I may not have said it at all.

Irma, she said, do you have any real idea of what this movie is about?

Well, it's about the meaning of life? I said. I mean not life, life, but some lives? That's all I can think of. Leave-taking.

What did you say? she said.

Leave-taking, I said. I wasn't sure how to use that word in a sentence. Our leave-taking from Canada was abrupt and permanent. Our poignant leave-taking left me breathless and . . . I wasn't sure.

You miss Wilson, she said. I didn't say anything. I couldn't see her. She put her hand on my back and I went stiff like a stillborn calf. I felt like I was being branded. I thought I'd start to cry.

No, I said, I miss Jorge.

When we first got married Jorge was at home all the time but then he went to his mom's place in Chihuahua city one weekend to visit and he met some guys who offered him real money. All he'd have to do was store their boxes of *hierba* in our grain shed because we lived in the middle of nowhere but only a few hours from the border and it was all perfect, and Jorge said sure, that sounded good, all he'd be doing was storing it, and he had held my hands and told me it would be a great opportunity for us, that it might help us to make enough money to leave the campo so he wouldn't have to work for nothing for my father anymore and he'd take care of me and we'd have babies and move away from here and get that boat we'd been talking about. And then he started bringing stuff back to our place.

I think Diego might want to sleep with me, she said.

What? I said. Why do you think that? You don't even know what he's saying.

I don't have to know what he's saying, she said.

Well, I said. I wouldn't if I were you.

Why not? she said. What if I'm feeling lost and lonely? Are you? I said.

Of course I am, Irma! she said. Look around. Can I talk to anybody but you? Do I have my husband and son here with me? Do I have friends? Do I know what I'm doing? Do I understand this story? Do I have anything to do but lie around and try to remember not to look directly at the thing that's always looking at me?

No, I said. I guess not.

I'm trying not to let my anger bubble to the surface and infect my mood, she said. Have you ever stomped down on a ceramic tile on your kitchen floor? It keeps popping up. I'm not going to sleep with him, don't worry.

I'm not worried, I said.

My anger, I said to myself. I liked the sound of that. I needed something of my own, something I could keep. My anger. I'd embroider these words into my underwear. I felt like Frankenstein. I punched myself in the forehead. My mother thought I was retarded when I was a baby because I'd bite myself and pull my own hair. Well, whose hair was I supposed to pull? I'd ask her.

Marijke lit a cigarette and started humming.

Well, the tile just needs to be glued down, I said.

Hey, she said, do you mind asking Diego if it's possible to get more leafy vegetables around here? I was looking at the whites of my eyes this morning and I think I'm developing anemia.

I turned around and looked deeply into the whites of her eyes and tried to detect a problem.

Then she told me she'd like to meet my family and I told her why that was pretty much impossible and then just at that moment as though we'd conjured her up like a dream Aggie was standing next to us with a suitcase and there we were, three Mennonite girls in an empty field, one bare-chested, one bewildered and one on the run.

Diego and the crew came roaring back into the yard in two trucks and Elias and Oveja ran over to us and Elias said we had to go shoot right then, immediately. Because the light, he said. And we had to bring Oveja with us for some reason

I couldn't quite understand. Either because we would need protection or because he, Oveja, needed protection.

What did you say? said Aggie.

Who is this? said Elias. He smiled and kissed Aggie on the cheek.

Aggie, I said. My sister. This is Elias. He's a cameraman. This is Marijke.

Did you come from the airport? said Elias. He pointed at her suitcase.

No. Just from over there, said Aggie. She pointed at her house.

Come with us, said Marijke. She put her T-shirt back on and grabbed Aggie's suitcase. It'll be fun.

No, I said, she has to go back.

No, I don't, said Aggie.

Yeah, you do, I said.

Well, I'm not, she said.

Agatha, I said.

Irma, she said.

We rode in the back of the truck this time. while Diego drove and had a money talk with one of the film's producers, José. We could see their arms flying around in the cab while they talked. Elias told us that José had come from Mexico City with some concerns about the amount of money Diego was spending out here in Chihuahua. Diego was having to shell out dough like crazy to the various Mennonites he'd enlisted to help him realize his dream. Elias explained Diego's rationale with the campo dwellers. This is what he says, said Elias. I understand and respect your religion's stance on photography and artificial images but I also believe that by making this film we can help to preserve your culture and prevent it from disappearing. This presented a conundrum that stopped the Mennonites in their argumentative tracks. Diego then added that he was willing to pay them for letting him shoot on their land, or in their house, or wherever it was that he wanted to shoot, and that got the Mennos nodding again and shortly thereafter the deal was done.

That's what they're talking about, said Elias. Diego is trying to explain to José the reason why the Mennonites are being truculent. No offence.

I had stopped listening, really, because now Aggie and I had started to argue.

Marijke and the crew smoked and stared politely into the desert pretending not to notice me and Aggie hissing at each other in the wind. She kept her hand on the handle of her suitcase but she turned her head away from me when I tried to talk to her.

So, where do you think you're going to go? I said.

Don't worry about it, she said.

Well, obviously I'm going to worry about it, I said. Are you a total moron or what?

Let's enjoy the moment, Irma, she said. She was quoting Marijke. José and Diego were shouting and throwing cigarettes out the windows. A spark skittered off the metal and landed on Elias's arm and he swore in Spanish, *puta*, and extinguished it with his spit. Trucks packed full of Mexican or Mennonite families were passing us and they were all waving and smiling or very determinedly looking away, like

Aggie when I tried to tell her that she was risking her life by leaving home.

I know, she said. So what. I didn't know what to say then and wished that I smoked for real or that sparks would land on me.

Because the light, said Aggie.

What? I said.

Because the light, she said. What that guy said. She pointed at Elias who blew her a kiss. It's funny, she said.

Stop taking my things, I said. I pointed at her ratty suitcase.

I'm returning it to you, she said.

We're standing, lying, sitting in an empty field waiting for the rain. This time Aggie is with us, learning how to play Frisbee with Miguel and Elias, and apparently enjoying the moment as though it were her last. Oveja has now become her best friend thanks to a dozen zwieback she had in the suitcase. Alfredo has come here in his own truck, by himself, but he's sulking and Diego is worried about him leaving before the rain comes. Alfredo says he is wasting his time and losing money that he could be making from his real job and that there's so much stress at home because of this movie. Diego has taken me aside and asked me, again, to ask Marijke if she would spend more time with Alfredo. If maybe now she would agree to drive with Alfredo in his truck so that they can get to know

each other and so that Alfredo won't feel lonely
and ignored.

I took Marijke aside to tell her what Diego had told me. I
handed her my bottle of water.

He would like you to spend more time alone with
Alfredo, I said.

Why? said Marijke.

To strengthen your relationship.

What relationship?

Your movie relationship.

That's Diego's job, she said. She drank the water that
was left in the bottle and gave it back to me.

Diego jogged over to us. He looked worried. He was
wearing white, gauzy pants that billowed out like sails
when he ran. From a distance his head was a crow's nest.
He asked me if I had told Marijke what he had said about
spending time with Alfredo.

Yes, I said, but she has reservations.

Please tell her that it's important for the energy of the
film, said Diego. Please tell her that when I see a beautiful
fish I immediately have feelings for it. I wait until the last
possible moment to cook it. And it's that connection that
makes the meal delicious.

Marijke, I said, Diego wants you to know that he sometimes has feelings for beautiful fish before he eats them and
that makes them taste better.

Is he stoned? said Marijke.

Hang on, I said. I spoke to Diego in Spanish. Yeah, I
said, she understands. But she doesn't want to drive with

him because he's always drunk and she's not prepared to die.

Irma, said Diego, when I said we must all be prepared to die for this film, I didn't mean in a car crash because of drunk driving. If that's what you're implying. Tell her I'll talk to Alfredo about his drinking.

Well, I said. And she's worried about having anemia. She needs more leafy vegetables.

We continued to wait in the field for rain. José and Diego played a game that involved slapping each other hard in the face. José seemed to be winning and Diego refused to give up. Why are they doing that? Aggie asked me.

Elias heated up some sausages on a filthy grill over an open fire. I taught Marijke how to make a type of kissing sound that would keep the rattlesnakes away when she went into the trees to pee. José and Diego ended their strange game with an embrace. The sun scorched us. Diego tried to get Marijke to rehearse a kiss with Alfredo and eventually became so angry with Alfredo's clunky attempts that he grabbed Marijke and did it himself. Is that so difficult? he asked Alfredo.

Afterwards Marijke came up to me and asked me if I knew what she meant about Diego having the hots for her and I said yes. We sat on the ground and flipped through the pages of the script. It was clear that Diego had started to make things up along the way.

Aggie came to sit with us and had a look at the script too, and I asked her what she thought. I don't understand all the Spanish, it's a bit majestic, I guess, she said. I liked the offhanded way she neutered words that were meant to be powerful. Then all the men started yelling at each other about the new Mexican president and the fraudulent election. The Zócalo in Mexico City was filled with thousands and thousands of protesters. They've been there for a week already, said Diego, and they refuse to budge. He said he thought it made more sense to wait for rain in the desert than for justice in Mexico City.

The clouds were moving around, bulging and darkening here and there but nothing else. It was getting late and I had to get Aggie home before my dad got back from the field or from town or wherever he was. She and I were still arguing. I told her that she was risking a lot by being out here with the film crew and that she was being foolish. I told her how much her brazenness bugged me because she didn't have a clue what she was doing.

Well, why are you here then, Irma? she said. You're a hypocrite.

I'm here because it's a job and I have no money and no family. Nothing! I said. I have nothing to lose. You should go home and stay away from me.

I was starting to sound like Jorge.

You can't tell me what to do, she said.

You're an idiot, I said. You have no idea.

Most of the crew had fallen asleep on a tarp, surrounded by equipment and empty water bottles, and Diego and José were talking quietly in the truck. I knocked on the window.

I need to get Aggie home, I said.

Diego got out of the truck and stood there squinting

up at the sky. We'll give up on today, he said. I thought it was the rainy season now.

It's supposed to be, I said.

Do you think God is punishing us? said Diego.

Why, what did you do? I said. He told me he was just joking.

Will you be able to make a meal for the crew when we get back? he said. A woman from the village was supposed to come but she took my money and never came. Her brother told me she went to America. Or she is dead. I'm not sure.

I'm not sure I have time, I said. Aggie has to get back and I'm worried—

Now you're worried, said Diego. First Marijke, now you. You girls are professional worriers, I'll say this.

I'm not going back, Irm, so don't worry your pretty little head over me, said Aggie.

You don't know that expression, I said.

You don't know everything, said Aggie.

We'll stop and buy some food and it'll be green and good for your anemia, said Diego.

Not mine, Marijke's, I said.

Okay, said Diego. I could make it myself but José and I have paperwork to fill out and the guys are still feeling a little sick. Plus, I promised in their contracts there would be meals and I'm worried about a mutiny. Please, Irma, I really need your help.

I didn't say anything. I waited to feel that old familiar pain in my chest, my cue to continue.

I'll do it, said Aggie.

No, you won't, I said. She can't.

Why not? said Diego. It makes no difference, you or her.
I want to do it, said Aggie.

No, I'll do it, I said. It's fine. No sweat.

Aggie started to say something to me in German, but
Diego cut her off in English. You and Aggie can sit in
the cab with José and me, said Diego. Marijke will drive
with Alfredo.

What? I said. I told you, remember, that Marijke doesn't
want to drive with Alfredo. She's worried that—

It's all right, said Diego. I talked to Alfredo. I ran
four times around the pasture with him and afterwards
he was healthy.

José opened the passenger door for Aggie and me and
we got in. Oveja jumped up and down throwing himself
against the window, crying and howling. Aggie said we had
to let him in and Diego said no, not possible, he had to ride
in the other truck and Aggie said fine, let her out then, but
the other truck had already taken off so Diego had to let
Oveja ride with Aggie. The truck got stuck in the muddy
field and we had to push ourselves out and José helped but
fell and was covered completely in mud and very angry
because he hadn't brought extra clothes from Mexico City.
We had to stop all over the place to buy supplies, food and
water and beer and gas and some new pants for José.

Aggie and Oveja and I sat on a box outside a store in
Rubio and looked around. Aggie couldn't remember the
last time she'd been to town. She was making some jokes
and goofing around but I was trying to ignore her. Did you
know that there's this country that nobody really knows
about that's kept in an office building in Paris? she said.

A girl wandered over to us and asked if she could sit down too, and we all moved over a bit and waited. She didn't look much older than Aggie. She was drinking some juice out of a plastic bag. She told us her name was Lindsay Beth and that she was from Indianapolis. We told her we were Irma and Aggie from nearby and that the dog was Oveja.

Why are you dressed like that? she said. We shrugged and looked around some more. That a pit bull? she asked. We nodded.

Are you here all by yourself? said Aggie.

Yeah, she said. They had to keep me in a cage.

Who kept you in a cage? said Aggie.

Rehab, she said. She told us they had thrown a box of soap in her cage and she was supposed to use it to carve her urges into shapes and she'd carved a giant key.

I would kill for OxyContin, she said.

Then how are you allowed to travel all by yourself? I asked her.

It's about establishing trust, she said.

What is OxyContin? said Aggie.

This is the last time my parents are going to bail me out, said Lindsay Beth. I'm not actually by myself.

She was wearing pyjama bottoms that said *dark side of the moon* all over them. A little boy who had been playing around in the dirt came over and practised his reading on her legs. He poked at her pyjamas. His small finger traced the words. Dark. Side. Of. The. Moon, he said. Dark side of the moon. Dark side of the moon. Dark side of the . . . He pulled the fabric a bit where it had crinkled . . . moon.

This is my brother's kid, she said. We waved at him.

Where's your brother? I asked her.

Inside, she said. We're on our way to the last ditch hotel. They're supposed to make excellent smoothies there, that's all I know, and that's all my stomach can absorb. My brother will drop me off and only pick me up again if I'm clean at the end of it. Otherwise I'll just be released into the atmosphere like a toxic gas. I'll just wander around the desert like Neal Cassady or whatever and eventually lie down for a nap on railway tracks.

She told the kid to go and find his dad. She told us that her brain had disintegrated to the point where her eyeballs had minds of their own and that even when she knew she was staring straight ahead her eyeballs would do their own thing and look elsewhere, off to the side or up towards the sky. She told us that even her one-thousand-dollar-a-day rehab facility in Malibu with equine therapy had failed to take. They think my brother will help me but he won't. He's fed up. She pointed at the store. I have to want to stay alive or not. I told her it looked like she wanted to.

Do you? said Aggie. She had stood up and was facing Lindsay Beth with her hands on her hips.

Well, she said, I want my hair to stop falling out. She pulled out a chunk of her hair and showed it to us. She held it tenderly in her hand like a wounded bird. Aggie stared at it for a long time and seemed distressed when the girl finally threw it into the wind and it flew off towards El Paso. We talked for a while about things and played a little hide-and-seek game with the boy and waited and waited.

FOUR

BY THE TIME WE GOT HOME a little apocalypse was brewing. I saw smoke coming from the field behind my house and told Aggie to stay put and then ran over to investigate. I saw the car. I saw the fire. I saw Jorge.

You're home! I said. I ran up to kiss him and hug him. I wanted to touch him. I wanted to feel the hard slope of his back. I wanted to put my head under his shirt and pin him to the ground and listen to his heart beating but he was busy throwing stuff into the fire.

Where were you? he asked.

Where were *you*? I said.

Help me put this shit away, he said. We carried his boxes into the back shed and he hoisted them up into the rafters. After that he relaxed a bit and smiled and even made a few jokes and was almost like his old self and we went into the house and I made him something to eat and he gave me a new pair of sunglasses which I put on and then he gave me a new pair of jeans which I also put on under my dress.

We fooled around for a while, throwing grapes into each other's mouths and then bouncing them off the wall and seeing if we could still catch them in our mouths.

How's your mom? I asked him.

Good, he said. Says hi.

Jorge said he wanted to teach me some dance move he'd learned in Chihuahua city. You stand like this, he said. He turned me around so he was behind me.

How'd you learn this dance? I said.

Then slowly grind down to the floor by moving your hips like this, he said. He demonstrated.

But where'd you learn to dance like this? I said.

Like a rotor, he said, and while you're doing that, I'll stand behind you with my hands on your hips like this and I'll grind down too. Okay, go. Slowly.

I tried to remember the instructions. I knew the objective was to get down to the floor in a squatting position.

No, he said, you're dropping way too fast, like you're dodging a punch or something. You have to make small,

slow circles with your hips, like gradually, until you're down.
I tried again.

Irma, he said, it's not that hard. What's your problem?
Look. He showed me what to do.

See? he said. Stop laughing. Try again.

I stood up and shook my head. I can't, I said. I'm sorry,
but—

Take your dress off, he said. Okay?

I don't have a top on under, I said.

Yeah, I know, he said. That's okay, it's nice. It'll be nice.
I took my dress off and stood there topless in my new stiff
jeans and sunglasses.

Yeah, he said, you look good. That's nice. Okay, let's try
it again. He stood behind me and put his hands on my hips
and we began to grind. He whispered in my ear. Slowly,
Irma, he said. Even slower. He slid his hands up to my
breasts and played with my nipples. In circles, Irma, he said.
Move your hips in circles. Yeah. Do you feel me? I could
hear him breathing. Okay, and down now, Irma, but slowly,
really— Fuck! Irma. What the hell is your rush? Look, I'm
up here still and you're down there crouching like you're
taking a dump.

I don't know, I said. I don't get the move. I'm sorry. It
feels weird.

Jorge sat down at the table and rubbed his eyes and
sighed.

Irma, he said, I'm trying to improve our lives.

I know, I said. I'm sorry. Can we try it again?

I'm so tired, he said. He took my hand and kissed it.

I'm sorry, I said again.

I'm sorry too, he said.

I miss you, I said.

Irma, I'm so tired now, he said. But I can't sleep anymore.

Why don't you try sleeping now? I said. I could lie down with you until you fall asleep.

I'm not a little kid, he said. He put his head down on the table and I rubbed his back and kissed his hair.

Are you tired of being a man? I asked him.

Why would you say that? he said. That's so messed up. Are you tired of being a girl?

Yeah, sometimes, I said.

Well, why would you even think that? said Jorge. Irma, you have to stop talking that shit. Do you want to become a man?

No, I said. It's not that. I'm just asking if—

Fuck it, he said. Never mind.

I told you I was sorry, Jorge, I said. I can't do that dance. These jeans are—

Just stop talking, he said. I don't give a shit about the dance, okay?

Why should I stop talking? I said. How can I explain things if I don't talk? I can't move in these stupid pants and—

Why don't you just go sit in the corner and breathe, he said.

What? I said. That's kind of a dumb thing to say when—

There was a knock at the door and I grabbed my dress and put it back on and whipped off the sunglasses and went to see who was there. It was Miguel. He was leaning against the door frame, smiling and shy in his skinny black jeans and giant white sneakers.

Crap! I said. I forgot about cooking. I saw this fire in my yard and had to . . . I'm sorry. I'll be right there. Is Aggie still at the house?

No, no, I'm the one who's sorry, Irma, said Miguel. I don't mean to bother you. He looked around me and into the house.

No, no, it's fine, I said. But is Aggie still there?

Diego asked me to come, he said. Aggie is there, yes, she's fine. She's learning how to juggle devil sticks.

Jorge came to the door and I introduced him to Miguel in Spanish. Then Miguel left and Jorge closed the door and said. So, Irma, who the hell is that and what the hell is going on?

As questions go, they were good ones. Jorge took off. Jorge's gone again. I tried to tell him that my father was threatening to sell the house and I'd need to have a place to live, preferably with him, he was my husband, maybe we could live with his mom in Chihuahua city, I could sell cheese, I could get a job, I could learn to dance, but Jorge said those were just words.

Well, then this is just a situation, I said. And you're just a man.

You don't even know how to argue properly, said Jorge.

Well, I think your age is starting to show, I said. You didn't even fix the generator.

What do you mean by that? he said. We're the same fucking age. You're just saying stupid things to keep me here.

Why would stupid things keep you here? I said. I want you to stay. You're my husband. You're supposed to stay here. I'm probably stronger than you are.

What is that supposed to mean? he said. I was running along beside the car now. He was leaving.

I was yelling. Why do you want to know what everything means? I said.

Take your hand off the wheel, he said. Irma. Please.

I ran for a long time, like a dog, like Oveja. Stupid. I was stupid. But not stupid enough to keep Jorge from leaving. I had options. I could have stood perfectly still like the Tarahumaras, and waited. But all I wanted was to run. I fell a few times and ripped my new jeans, stovepipes the label said, no wonder they were so stiff, and scraped my legs and got back up to run some more. When I stopped to catch my breath I realized I was on the road in front of my parents' house and the lights were on and I could see my mom in the kitchen and it looked like she was cutting something with a knife and she kept looking down and then up and then down again and I guessed she was giving some bits of food to my little brothers. But they were too short for me to see them in the window and she was talking to them too. She was out of bed. I wondered if she was okay. Then I turned around and passed my house, mine and Jorge's, and there was nobody in the kitchen, nobody handing anybody anything. I finally made it to the filmmakers' house and walked right up to the front door and knocked my head against one of those plastic bags filled with water to keep the flies away and I punched it hard and broke it and the water sprayed out of it and drenched me and I didn't care, I opened the front door and walked in. Everybody, including Aggie, was watching TV and didn't really notice me but I said hello in a few different languages and then walked into the kitchen and yanked a pot out of the cupboard and slammed it onto the stovetop and hauled some food out of the fridge and turned on the tap to boil water and grabbed the sharpest, biggest knife I could find and cut up the vegetables and the meat and flung all the pieces into the pot to cook. Then I took some other pieces of meat and went outside and flung them at Oveja so he wouldn't forget that we were friends and then went back to my cauldron.

Irma, said Diego. He was calling me from the living room. He was shouting over the TV.

Sí, I said.

More rain is forecast for tomorrow, he said.

Hallelujah.

I heard Elias talking about some girl's rock-hard ass. He said it was so hard he could play "Wipeout" on it. He made some strange sounds. I heard Diego call Elias an idiot. They insulted each other's mothers, playfully. Then Elias started impersonating a woman. I threw more stuff into the pot and stirred so hard it slopped over the sides and onto the stove and made little hissing noises.

I could hear Aggie laughing, pretending to know what was going on. Go home, I said. Too quietly for anyone to hear. You should go home. Diego came to the kitchen to talk to me.

Oh my God, he said. Irma, I cannot believe this.

I'm sorry, I whispered. I'm not . . . This is ready to eat, I think. I pointed at the pot on the stove.

What are you doing? he said. He put his arm around my shoulder. What's wrong?

I don't know, I said.

Please stop crying, he said. Irma. Please?

He sounded just like Jorge, calm and sincere, when he asked me to stop screaming and chasing him down the road. He stood behind me. He put his arms around my waist and his chin on my shoulder. I kept stirring the slop I'd created hoping he wasn't expecting me to grind down to the floor right there at the stove.

I went outside and walked to the barn and sat down on the concrete pad and leaned against the door. Diego came outside and talked to me. He asked me how I was doing. He asked me what was wrong. He told me that his parents had died in a terrible car accident twenty years ago and after that his brother had decided to walk to America. He was fifteen years old. He left the house and started walking north and he hasn't seen him since.

Do you think he's alive? I said.

Yes, said Diego.

Why do you think that? I said.

Sometimes my phone rings and nobody talks, he said.

You think it's him? I said.

Yes, he said. I know it's him. I talk to him about things. Simple things. My life. My work.

And he never says anything? I said.

That's right, he said. He listens and then when he's heard enough he hangs up.

But why doesn't he want to talk to you? I said.

I don't know, said Diego. But it doesn't matter. It's not important. I'll talk to him and he'll listen. That's how it is now. Like a prayer.

Eventually everybody ate except for Marijke and José who were fucking in her room, according to Diego. She is very angry with me for making her ride with Alfredo in his truck, he said. So she is trying to make me jealous with José. I know her astrological sign well. Very intense. Have you ever been dumped by somebody you didn't even know you were dating? That has happened to me. It's surprising.

Oh, I said. So are you jealous?

Only a little, said Diego.

Where's Alfredo? I asked.

He went home to his wife and kids, said Diego. He and Marijke had a fight.

About what? I said.

Well, said Diego, from Marijke's body language I think that Alfredo made a pass at her in his truck. I spoke to him about it and he said it was nothing. He put his hand on her leg, like this, she could have been his sister, but she became inordinately angry. She said she wanted to break the truck's side-view mirror and use the shards to slice Alfredo's hand off and then throw his hand out the window for the condors to feed on.

But she didn't, I said.

No, said Diego. She hit him in the face. Now he's very mad and I'm a little frustrated with her, but don't tell her because I'm afraid she'll leave. European women are difficult, he said. They overreact. For instance, French women hate papaya. They say it tastes like urine. I know this. So, if she wants to sleep with José I don't care.

Diego went outside to stare at the sky. He needed rain. I wished I was a difficult European woman. It occurred to me that Marijke was the same age as my mother. Elias gave me a beer to drink when he saw that I'd been crying. It tasted awful. I had another one. We were outside sitting on the bench in front of the house because I didn't want Aggie to see me drinking beer. Elias taught me how to smoke marijuana from his vaporizer. He asked me if I wanted him to sing and I said yeah.

Frankie Valli or Van Morrison? he said. I don't know, I said. I don't care. Frankie Valli.

He started singing. He stood up and pretended to be holding a microphone.

I passed him his vaporizer. *Like heaven to touch*? I said.

Yeah, he said.

He sang for a while. You can't be in a bad mood if you're singing, he said. If you sing a song it's important that you sing the living shit right out of it. With this part of you. This part here. You should sing with me.

I don't know any real songs, I said.

How can you not know any real songs? he said. I thought about the songs I had vaguely known in Canada.

Your love is lifting me higher and higher, I said. Is that a song?

He told me he was going inside to finish watching the movie. I looked through the window and saw Aggie sitting very close to Miguel on the couch. Their knees were up like little kids. They had their arms around their knees. They looked like Russian dolls. I tried to think. I needed a plan. I closed my eyes and saw only vines and waterfalls. I got up and walked back out into the dark yard so I could see the stars a little more closely. They didn't give a shit about my plans. I was trying to figure out what I was going to do with Aggie and then I heard some scuffling and a familiar voice.

Buenas noches, chiquita, said Wilson. *Cómo estás?*

What are you doing here? I said. I can't believe you're back! Where did you come from?

I got a ride to Rubio and walked the rest of the way.

That's a long way to walk, I said. Are you okay?

Yeah, yeah, he said. A little tired.

Why did you leave? I asked.

That's obvious, isn't it? he said. Diego and I had a fight but we worked it out.

What were you fighting about? I asked.

I don't know, said Wilson. His recklessness. It makes me mad. I've worked for him before and we've had the same fight. He's a genius but he taxes me. I feel that he extorts from me. Painful feelings. And then I'm happy to be extorted. I don't know. I just want to make some money and go live in Paris or something for a while and write. Or just read, for like a month. Nothing else.

What do you want to read? I asked him.

Jung, he said. I want to read his journals and everything

else he's ever written. The way he understands the human mind. But not just the mind. Do you know him?

Let's go over there by the fence and talk, I said. It's darker. Irma, I told myself, try to make sense when you speak.

He walked ahead of me and I watched him. When we got to the fence I put my arms around his neck and kissed him. He smiled and leaned back.

Is it electric? I said.

I don't think so, he said, I didn't feel a shock. He put his hand on the wire fence and held it there for a few seconds. No, he said. Or it's burnt out.

That's good, I said. I kissed him again and took his hands and put them on my waist.

Do you have a girlfriend? I said.

No, but you have a husband, he said.

Yeah, I guess, I said. Would you like to make love right now? Or something like that? Do you think you could or are you too tired from walking?

Here? said Wilson. He looked around at more of the same. Grass, darkness, stars.

Well, maybe just . . . like, over there a bit, I said. I pulled him slightly farther away from the fence.

We lay on the grass and Wilson peeled my jeans off and lifted my dress up over my arms and then folded all that clothing neatly and put it under my head as a pillow. He sat cross-legged beside me and ran his hands lightly up and down my body. I barely moved. I stared at the stars, mostly. I looked at him once or twice.

Your knees are all scraped up, he said.

Those jeans are . . . they're called stovepipes, I whispered.

You have an on/off button, he said. He touched the mole in the centre of my sternum.

Aggie says it's Zacatecas, I said. If my body was a map of Mexico.

What's this?

Mexico City? I said. I smiled and looked away.

And this? He touched my eyebrow.

Juárez, I said.

You're beautiful, he said.

I like the way you walk, I said.

I like the way you moan, he said.

After all that, Wilson asked me if there was something I wanted to tell him, anything at all, because he would keep it a secret for me.

No, thanks, I said. I smiled. I put my clothes on.

I told you that I was dying, he said.

Is that a secret? I asked him.

Well, mostly, he said. Around here it is.

Okay, I said. Well, I used to have another sister.

The one who refereed your hockey games? he said. What happened to her?

Yes, her. She died, I said. In Canada. That's why we moved here.

How did she die? he said.

I don't know, I said. Nobody would tell me.

Are you sure she's dead? he said.

Well, yeah, I said. Otherwise, where would she be?

How old was she?

Sixteen, I said.

Did she look like you? he said.

She was far prettier, I said. And braver. I had this dream about her a while ago. I dreamt that I was in a van with a bunch of people, I didn't know who they were, and we were driving along the highway in Canada, in Manitoba, and we noticed that there was some kind of fair going on along the side of the road with different food stands and games and some rides and all that stuff so we stopped to check it out and we were walking around and a little bit beyond where everything was going on there were a few chairs so I walked over there because I felt like sitting down and then there was Katie, that's my sister, sitting in one of those chairs and she was a fortune teller! I was so happy to see her. She was happy to see me too. I had this date square in my hand, my mom calls it a matrimonial square, which was her favourite dessert, so I gave it to her and asked her how she was doing and she said great and that if I wanted she could read my palms. So I put my hands out for her to read and she held them and then she smiled and she looked up at me and that was the end of the dream.

Wilson took my hand. That's a good dream, he said. Jung would say it was positive, I'm pretty sure.

But that still doesn't mean that she's not dead, I said.

That's true, he said. Have you heard of the song of Nezahualcoyotl?

No, I said. I was thinking about Marijke. I was thinking about how she had asked me if I knew what the four-part cure was but said not to worry if I didn't because not worrying was part of the cure.

With flowers You write, said Wilson,
O giver of Life,
With songs You give colour,
with songs You shade
those who must live on the earth.

Later you will destroy eagles and ocelots;
we live only in Your book of paintings,
here, on the earth.

Can you say that again? I asked Wilson. I got him to say
it five or six times until I had memorized it and could say it
along with him in my head. We didn't hold hands when we
walked back to the house but we had exchanged secrets.

The living room was empty except for Aggie and Miguel
who had fallen asleep and toppled over in tandem, arms
still locked around their knees, mouths open.

Who is that? whispered Wilson, pointing at Aggie.

My sister, I said.

She's alive! he said.

It's a different one, I said.

I touched Aggie's arm and told her that we had to go,
we needed to do the milking, but she didn't move and she
didn't open her eyes.

Ag, I know you're faking, I said. C'mon. You have to
go home.

Miguel woke up and cleared his throat loudly and
blinked and focused and stretched out his legs and high-fived

Wilson and said you're back. *Qué tal?* He got up and gave both of us a hug.

Está bien, said Wilson. He smiled and rubbed Miguel's head.

Aggie, I said. Get up. Now. You have to go.

I drugged her, like Roman Polanski, said Miguel, in slangy Spanish he thought I wouldn't understand.

Only way you'd ever get a girl, said Wilson.

At least *I'm* into girls, said Miguel.

Your sister doesn't count, said Wilson.

Aggie opened her eyes. We actually understand that, she said. Me and Irma.

Shit, sorry, said Wilson. Say sorry, asshole, he said to Miguel.

Yeah, sorry, said Miguel. We were just kidding around. Your Spanish is not very bad.

Aggie, I mean it, let's go already, I said. Get up. I pulled her arm and she yanked it back and nestled into the couch.

Why can't she just sleep here? said Miguel. She can use my blanket and pillow. Hang on.

No, she can't, I said. Miguel had rushed off to get his bedding. Wilson said he was going to get a beer, did I want one?

C'mon, Aggie, I said. Stop fooling around, okay? We have to go.

I told you I'm not going back, she said.

Yes, you are, I said.

I'll have a beer, please, she told Wilson. She asked for a pint but mistakenly rhymed it with *mint*.

What does she want? said Wilson.

Aggie, I said. Seriously. You have to go. I grabbed her arm this time and pulled her halfway off the couch.

Why are you so mad? said Aggie. Leave me alone. Let go of me.

I let go of her arm and she rearranged herself on the couch. I sat down next to her and stared straight ahead. I breathed deeply. I spoke to her in Low German. I made a promise.

She was quiet for a few seconds and then got up and said good night to Wilson and Miguel and foul Oveja, who had been let in for the night, and I followed her out the door and watched her walk down the road towards home, hers, and the bright yard light, and her own bed, and our parents, and I stood there for a long time because I didn't know where else to go. I stood there long enough to feel the chill of the night. The sky was a blanket of stars. Indifferent. I repeated the ancient song of Nezahualcoytl. I stood there long enough to hear my family singing. Why were they singing at two in the morning? I heard the high, creaky voice of my mother and the off-key but persistent voices of my little brothers.

Gott ist die liebe
Lest nich erlosen
Gott ist die liebe
Er liebt auch dich.

They sang another verse and I listened. And one more verse and I listened to that too. And then, finally, I realized what was missing, which were the voices of my dad and

Aggie, and I wondered why they weren't singing and then I knew and I ran to the house. My mother was wiping tears from her face and my little brothers were pale and stricken. They were sitting at the table holding hands and singing hard with the same energy you need to clear a field of rocks.

Where is she? I said. My mom pointed to the back of the house, towards the summer kitchen, and I ran over there and broke the flimsy hook and eye and ripped the screen door off its feeble hinge and told my father to stop hitting her, he was whipping her with a belt, and Aggie to come with me right then. Right then. My father and I looked at each other. His eyes were wild with fear and despair and he began to cry and he asked me to forgive him. He begged me to forgive him.

Gott ist die liebe
Lest nich erlosen
Gott ist die liebe
Er liebt auch dich.

That's a lie. My father hadn't said anything. But it's true that we looked hard at each other, briefly. I saw his eyes. I remembered Diego's words. I want her eyes to harm me, he had said when we met for the first time. I want her to be too big for her body, a living secret, squeezed out through here, here, and especially here.

FIVE

AGGIE AND I WALKED FOR A FEW HOURS, all the way to San Juan, a tiny village a few miles away. We didn't walk right into the town, that would have caused more problems, but to the frayed edge of it. It was still very dark, the village was silent, but we wanted to see the small, twitchy boy who'd built himself a very high unicycle and had to come up with ingenious ways of getting on and off it. We didn't see him. We hadn't seen him in years actually but we thought that life was messed up enough that night that it could happen. And then back to my place. When we got there Aggie asked me to remind her of the cold in Canada. How parts of your body go numb and all you can do is keep moving or you will definitely die.

I want that, said Aggie.

You want your body to go numb or you want to keep moving? I said.

I'm not sure, said Aggie.

I think that's normal, I said.

How would you know what's normal? she said.

That's a good question, smartass, I said, but I'm trying to make you feel better.

We lay side by side in bed. Aggie began to cry and I held her.

She finally fell asleep and my arm was trapped beneath her and I didn't want to wake her up so I let her lie on my arm all night long and in the morning when she woke up I told her that she wasn't going home again, that home had changed, that home, like thoughts, according to Marijke, were random patterns of atoms flying around and forever on the move. And I considered telling her that if thoughts and home were random patterns then actions were too, all actions, tender, desperate, lucid, treacherous ones and the promises we make and break, the secrets we share with dying Venezuelans, and the bruises and bleeding cuts on her back. All of them random patterns. And that they didn't mean a thing.

––––––

The rain that was forecast for today hasn't come.
Diego is obsessed with the sky and is worried that
if it doesn't rain soon his movie will be ruined.
He is wondering, out loud, about alternative
sources of rain. He's made a call to the *bomberos*,
the firefighters, to see how much water they hold
in their tanks and how far their hoses can spray it.

We're all at the table, eating toast and eggs
and fruit quickly, about to leave for our next
location. I'm not sure exactly where it is but I
think it's a hill, somewhere south of here. I'm
nervous about everything. Aggie can't go back
home and she can't go to school because if she
goes to school they'll make her go back home.
Marijke is talking to Aggie about astral projection
and while she talks she puts her hand gently
on Aggie's cheek. Elias is talking about the
constitution of the avocado which, when he bites
into it, makes him feel like he's eating a baby.
Alfredo isn't here yet but I think he'll meet us at
the hill. I only get bits and pieces of information.
I can hear Wilson telling Sebastian that his home
is where he can do his art and I can see him
listening and nodding respectfully. He doesn't
want Wilson to leave again so he's willing to
listen to his theories. Wilson smiled at me when I
handed him his plate of eggs and toast and he
whispered something but I couldn't understand it.
Miguel has already left the table and is hauling
equipment out to the trucks. Diego and José are

reading something, a piece of paper, and Diego
is pointing at it and talking very fast and rubbing
his arm vigorously. The rebel spirit of my
grandfather is directing this film! he said. José is
perfectly still, like a kid playing freeze tag, waiting
to be tapped. Neither one of them has spoken to
Marijke, or even looked at her. Aggie has a cut
lip and the red outline of a hand and all its fingers
on her left cheek and Marijke hasn't moved her
own hand from it yet. I think she's redirecting
energy but I'm not sure. I'm nervous. I need to
talk to Diego about getting paid and about
Aggie getting paid too, if she's also going to
help with the movie, but he seems so agitated
right now and is already worried about how much
everything is costing him so I'll wait until tonight
when hopefully he'll have gotten the shot that he
and the rebellious spirit of his grandfather are
looking for and his life will be worth living once
again. Now he looks a little sad. He's smiling at
me wistfully, I think, as though I remind him of
someone he once knew and liked.

We're at the hill and Alfredo still isn't here because
of some family situation and Diego is upset. Elias
has to listen to him while Diego explains that
when he is on a plane and thinks that it might
crash or when he's in a car and it's about to veer
off a cliff he doesn't think about his family. He
thinks about his film. How he has to finish his

film because it is his duty to finish his film. That's how he thinks. He picks up a stick and says it has as much meaning as his own unborn child and then throws it far into the scrubby bushes.

I hate meaning! he says. Why is everyone searching for meaning? Elias stands and listens to Diego. He looks at the sky and nods, as though God is telling him it's okay, Elias, my son, be patient, Diego won't be angry forever, just listen for a little longer.

Aggie and I have been hauling stuff up to the top of the hill. Fruit, juice, water, granola bars. We're wearing cowboy boots to protect us from the snakes. Marijke is sleeping in one of the trucks which are parked at the bottom of the hill and probably stuck in the mud. Her legs are protruding from the passenger side window. She doesn't have to be here today for this shot, she's not in it, but she didn't want to stay at the house all by herself because it makes her feel like she's dead. José the producer has gone back to Mexico City with some of the reels of film. Everyone is gaunt and exhausted. It's so hot out here and we're so high up and it feels like the sun is punishing us for trespassing.

This is another shot of a kiss. A woman is here from Cuauhtémoc to kiss Alfredo who finally showed up. She was supposed to be a Mennonite from Campo 6.5 but Diego couldn't find a local woman willing even to pretend to be Alfredo's lover so he's using this pale Mexican substitute. They've tied her hair back and put her in Mennonite clothes and moved her head over to the left for the shot so that it's more of Alfredo's face and less of hers that will be visible. They're about to be passionate on top of this hill.

Sebastian, the soundman, is giving Alfredo more lessons in kissing. I'm trying to learn too. I see that it might work to put my hand on the back of Jorge's neck and then move it slowly up towards his hair. Diego is telling Alfredo to infuse this scene with love and tenderness, to spread his passion over every inch of the shot softly and smoothly like mayonnaise. He is encouraging Alfredo to think of something romantic to say to the woman. Words are lubricants, Alfie, he's saying. Alfredo is squeezing his eyes shut and seems to be thinking hard of what that could be. Aha, he's got something good. He opens his eyes and points them, smouldering, at the woman and says, I'm not indifferent to you.

Diego is screaming. Not indifferent? he says. Not *indifferent?* He can't stand this life anymore and has wandered away to find a branch to hang himself from. From a distance we can see him still waving his arms around and pointing at the sky and grabbing his head and picking things up and throwing them but we can't hear him. It's like

he's playing charades and the thing he's been
given to act out is *apocalypse.*

Alfredo says good riddance. He calls him
Hitler and cracks open another vampiro. The
others are wandering around and looking into the
camera and up at the sky and getting things ready
for the shot. Sebastian has kissed the woman from
Cuauhtémoc at least seven times now, she's starting to giggle, and Alfredo is standing off to the
side with a strange smile on his face, watching and
nodding. Aggie and I are sitting on boxes off to
the side, braiding grass and talking. Oveja is lying
on the ground next to us, panting and farting in
the heat. We can hear Diego asking his actors
what they think is so fucking funny about kissing.

Alfredo has just pulled a gun on Oveja.
They're official enemies. Before the actual kiss
Alfredo is supposed to run, with ardour, to the
woman and grab her zealously. Oveja saw
Alfredo rehearsing this part and attacked him and
Alfredo took his gun out of his pants and
smashed Oveja on the head with it. Oveja backed
off a bit and stood snarling at Alfredo who was
yelling and ready to blow the dog to smithereens.
He fired a shot into the air. Diego is now yelling
also for Wilson to take the dog back down the
hill and put him in the truck with Marijke. He's
trying to explain to Alfredo that Oveja panicked
and was convinced that Alfredo's intention was
to kill the woman, not to kiss her, and how could

he know otherwise, he was a dog. Are you not more rational than a dog, Alfie? Diego was yelling. He can't understand your actions but you can understand his because you are a man. Now stop this and put your gun away. Alfredo is threatening to leave again for good and Diego is swearing one inch from Alfredo's face. I'm going to put away my notebook and walk down the hill with Wilson and Oveja.

Aggie, I said, stay here.

Why? she said.

I'm going to the bottom to talk to Marijke.

I'll come with.

No, stay here. I'll be right back.

I wanna come.

No, stay here. I'll be right back.

I'm coming with.

We caught up to Wilson and Oveja and I spoke to him quickly and softly in slangy Spanish that I'd learned from Jorge and that Aggie wouldn't quite understand. Wilson asked me if he could put his arm around me while we walked.

Why? I said. Are you okay? I knew immediately that that had been a stupid question but I didn't know what else to say. Aggie walked ahead of us with Oveja, and Wilson put his arm around my shoulders and told me I looked pretty. I told him I couldn't do any more naked things with him like lying in the field without clothes on. I told him that

I felt so guilty and so bad and that I was terrified of Jorge
finding out and killing me. Wilson said he could understand
that. But, I said, I wanted more than anything to be his
friend and to save his life. That came out wrong. He told me
I was funny, that I couldn't save his life, but that we could
be friends. It felt like we had come full circle, from one
obvious point to another one just like it. I felt like I should
have said other more important and unique things.

Wilson, I said.

Yes, Irma?

If you knew that this was your last day on earth what
kind of story would you write? I asked.

Given that I would actually use that time to write a story?

Yeah.

I don't know.

Oh.

But it's a very good question.

I was rejoicing silently in my heart. I had asked a good
question. And not only had I finally asked a good question,
I had asked a good question of someone I was trying to be
friends with as opposed to myself. A question that had
breath attached to it, that had left my own body. Jorge told
me not to ask questions, he hated them, he could always tell
when I was about to ask one and he'd put his hand up and
say no, please. Please. Was I betraying Jorge by asking a good
question of Wilson?

We got to the truck and Marijke saw us and pulled her
legs back inside through the window and smiled and said
she had missed us and what was up? She got out of the
truck and gave us all hugs. She looked tired. I wondered if

it was true that she had been fucking José. I told her that we had had to take Oveja away from Alfredo. We all decided to have some potassium-replacing bananas and water and a rest before we trekked back up the mountain. We heard more shots being fired and I explained to Marijke that Alfredo was angry again.

Oh my God, she said in German, is he killing people?

No, no, I said, he's firing his gun into the air. He doesn't know how to kiss properly.

And that's what's making him so mad? she said.

No, it's the dog, I said. Oveja attacked him.

Marijke laughed. Wilson was teaching Aggie how to walk on her hands but it was a logistical problem because of her dress.

Come here you pig, said Marijke. Oveja waddled over to her. He was bleeding from where Alfredo had bashed him on the head. Marijke stroked his nose and said loving things to him in German which I didn't bother translating for him.

Then we heard Diego's voice shouting from Wilson's radio. He needed Marijke after all, he had changed his mind, he was so close to his perfect shot, and we were supposed to run up the mountain to where they were shooting immediately.

What about the sky? said Wilson.

It's perfect, said Diego. Send the girls now and tell them to move fast.

Diego said that Elias was running down the mountain halfway to meet Wilson with a reel of film that Wilson was to put under the seat in the truck and lock the doors. And

Wilson was supposed to give Elias a certain lens that he'd bring back up the mountain and everything was supposed to happen now, immediately! We were all about to head up the mountain when we saw Elias tumbling towards us and screaming in pain and the reel rolled along beside him on the ground. When Elias came to a stop Wilson kneeled beside him and inspected his leg and said he had to get him to a clinic because he thought his ankle might be broken and he radioed Diego to tell him what had happened and that his shot might not happen right now after all and Diego went insane over the radio and said we were done shooting for the day and possibly forever. He said that even if he'd been the original Creator he couldn't have conceived of a more incompetent film crew than the one he had. Wilson switched his radio off. We carried Elias to the truck and he lay in the cab while Wilson drove and Marijke and Aggie and I sat in the back.

Do you think it's possible to rot without even feeling it? said Aggie.

Rot? said Marijke. Like, decompose?

Yeah, said Aggie.

Without knowing? said Marijke.

Yeah, said Aggie. Like until it's a bit too late.

This conversation was being shouted at top volume against the howling wind. I looked at Wilson through the back window of the cab, through the rear-view mirror. I saw him mouth some words to Elias. I could feel my stomach writhe inside of me.

I took my notebook out of my pocket and made a list of troubling things.

Aggie is now my responsibility.

Aggie has to go to school, at least in the fall. But where?

We have hardly any money.

Jorge might never come back.

Our father is going to sell the house.

I have to get a map.

We'll have no place to live.

We'll have to stand silently by the road like that Tara-humara family. Forever.

I miss my mom.

I'm a bad wife.

I tore the page out of my notebook and threw it away into the wind and watched it float up and over towards Belize or maybe Paraguay. I opened my notebook to the first page where I had traced my hand and wrote the words *we live only in your book of paintings here on the earth* along the length of my ring finger. But it was so bumpy that none of it was legible and the letters looked like little worms burrowing under skin.

When we got to the clinic we unloaded Elias from the truck and carried him in. He was still groaning but we had stopped worrying about him. Marijke had gone off to wander around in the cornfield next to the barn. We had to walk past three deformed dogs to get to the desk where the nurse was sitting. Is this a vet or a clinic? said Wilson. It's everything, I said. The nurse was my quasi cousin. She had white-blond hair like Aggie's. Our great-grandpa had had thirty-one kids with three different wives who kept dying and we had all lost track of who was really who. She might have come from a different campo, like maybe 4 or 2.5 or something. She asked me if I was a Voth and I said yeah, you? She said no, Nickel, but used to be a Voth. I thought so, I said. She didn't need to ask what was going on or who these guys were. She told us to carry Elias right into the doctor's room and lay him down on the stretcher thing and the doctor would be there soon.

We heard some screaming. Finally the doctor came and told us to leave so that he could examine Elias and we went and sat outside on a fence to wait. We heard more screams coming from the barn.

What is that? said Wilson.

A mother, I said. She's having a baby in that other room next to Elias's. We were all quiet, even Aggie, listening to the woman scream.

I would just say no way and take the doctor's gun and shoot myself in the head, said Aggie.

We listened to the woman some more. Except for those screams there was no sound at all.

That's her husband, I think, I said. I pointed to a guy sitting in a truck with a bunch of little kids.

Why doesn't he go in? said Wilson.

They don't do that, I said.

Elias finally came hobbling out of the barn with crutches that were too small so he was hunched over like a little old man. Wilson walked with him back to the truck and Aggie rounded up Oveja and I went into the corn to find Marijke so we could go. It took me a while and when I found her she was sitting in the dirt, crying. I crouched down next to her and asked her what was wrong and she told me that she kept opening and closing her eyes thinking that eventually, when she opened them, she would see her son standing there in front of her. She was afraid she was going nuts in this fucking desert. She wanted to go back to Germany but she was afraid that Diego would kill her.

I can't leave now, she said. Or his film will be ruined. And then he'll kill me. It's simple.

He won't kill you, I said. That would be stupid.

He keeps saying he'll kill Alfredo, said Marijke. So why wouldn't he kill me?

He doesn't mean it, I said. That's how he talks.

I feel like I'm disappearing, she said. Look at me. Do you see me?

Yes, I see you, I said.

I put my hand on her shoulder.

We should go to the truck now, I said. Elias is done.

Sometimes I feel like my life is an invention, she said.

Well, I said, sometimes the only way I know I'm alive is when I feel the pain in my chest, because there's no pain in heaven.

What makes you think you'll be in heaven if you're not alive? said Marijke.

I held my hand out to her and she took it and I pulled her up off the ground. I was just about to tell her that she was as light as air but remembered that that was the thing she was afraid of and I kept my mouth shut.

We drove home in silence, collectively worn out from

the sun and our own individually wrapped pain. The crew
had become smaller from being sick. Before it was hard to
squeeze more than four people into the cab of the truck
but now we could fit five. I asked Wilson to drop Aggie and
me off at the end of my driveway. We had to milk the cows
and then we'd come to the house to make some kind of
meal for everyone. We got out of the truck without saying
goodbye to anyone and found a box sitting in the middle
of the driveway.

It's more of your stuff from when you were little, said
Aggie. I was milking furiously while she took out the clothing from the box and held each little undershirt and dress
under the light bulb that hung down on a cord from the
roof of the barn.

Wow, this is hideous, she said.

You wore it too, I said. And it was Katie's before it was
mine probably. Put it back in the box and then put the
whole thing in the grain shed and come help me.

I wish Katie was here, said Aggie.

You do? I said. You never talk about her.

We're not allowed to, said Aggie.

Or it's just easier to forget, I said.

No, said Aggie. It's the hardest thing in the world to
forget.

Yeah, I said. You can talk about her with me if you
want to.

I don't want to.

You want her to be here, I said.

Yeah, said Aggie. But talking about her is useless.

No, it's not, I said. What do you remember about her?

Nothing, said Aggie.

Aggie, I said. That's not true. You do remember stuff. How can you want her to be here if you have no memory of her?

Well, you have memories of her, don't you? said Aggie.

Of course I do, I said.

And don't you want her to be here? said Aggie.

I said, I don't think your question makes sense.

How can you not know? said Aggie. Didn't you love her? It's not that, I said. Of course I loved her.

Dad said you love your imagination more than real life, said Aggie.

What? I said. That's not true!

I'm just saying that's what he said, said Aggie. Maybe it's true. So what?

We should hurry, I said.

Why should we hurry? said Aggie. Are you in love with Wilson?

Just put all that stuff back in the box, I said.

At dinner Diego delivered a motivational speech to the cast and crew. He apologized for losing his temper on the mountain. He lost his composure and put his hand over his eyes and said he was sorry for putting us at risk. He asked Elias how his ankle was. Morale was low. Every five minutes something was going wrong. Diego had bought a bottle of tequila and was pouring shots for everyone, even Aggie. The Mexican woman he had hired to kiss Alfredo on the hill was eating with us too, along with two of her kids. I asked her in

Spanish if she was having an okay time and she said she was waiting to get paid. Alfredo was lying on the couch with a pillow over his face. Diego acknowledged that the going was getting a little tough, that conditions were difficult and that time and money were running out, but he had faith that it would work out in the end and that seven months from now we'd all be wearing beautiful *vêtements* and drinking champagne on a party yacht at the Cannes film festival where the world had come to be blown away by our efforts.

The art of making a movie is an exploding bomb, he said, and while it destroys it also re-creates.

I attempted to translate this for Marijke but she didn't really understand what I was trying to tell her. I had made her a giant bowl of green salad for her anemia and I kept pointing to it like all those pieces of lettuce were shrapnel or something and somehow emblematic of the creative process. I thought about grabbing the bowl and tossing the salad high up into the air and then picking up the pieces and returning them to the bowl but that just seemed dumb and by then Diego had moved on to compare the art of making a movie to anal sex (absurd and painful at first) and to the resurrection of Christ.

We need more blankets, said Elias.

And water, said Sebastian.

Wilson walked me and Aggie and Oveja back to my house. I whispered to him that I thought Marijke was having a hard time, that she was worried about going crazy out here.

Even with all her theories and voodoo? said Wilson.

Well, I said, this is the desert. He nodded and said that made sense. He said it took him a year to recover from one of Diego's films. He'll take your soul, he said. And then you have to spend some time afterwards looking for it.

Marijke doesn't want to look around for her soul, I said.

For the sake of the mind, said Wilson, it's very important to be able to communicate loneliness.

Well, I said, Diego wants Marijke to run down the road.

Run down the road? said Wilson.

To clear her mind, I said.

What did she say about that? asked Wilson.

Nothing, I said. I didn't translate it for her.

Why not? said Wilson.

I don't know, I said. I just don't think it's a good idea.

Because she might not come back? said Wilson.

That was the end of our conversation. He briefly touched my shoulder and I nodded once, the way a man would. We said goodbye. Then the night started in for real.

Aggie had gone to bed and I was sitting in the dark at the kitchen table. I was thinking about my family. Mostly about my mother. I tried to cheer myself up by remembering something from long ago. We'd had a phone in Canada. It was brand new. It had never rung. I remember answering it when it rang for the first time and giving it to my mom. It was my aunt Hildie. Katie and I listened to our mom with some astonishment while she talked to Aunt Hildie on the phone. Yes, my mom had said to her, you told me that. Yes, she said, I won't forget. Yes, she said, I agree with you.

I have to go now. Yes, she said, I'll remember. Now Hildie, she said, you know I'd wish for you to die. Then she said goodbye and hung up the phone and went back into the kitchen like it was no big deal. Katie and I were laughing so hard and our mom stared at us and asked us in German what had gotten into us and we asked her the same question. She explained to us that Aunt Hildie had chosen that day to worry about what would happen to her if she fell into a coma and she didn't want to be artificially resuscitated and wanted our mom to remember that.

Is it possible to communicate loneliness if the only person you're sharing it with is yourself? I looked around my little house and thought: Oh! Is that a prayer? I got down on my knees and I bowed my head and folded my hands and whispered dear God, bring me love. Bring me love. Bring me true love. Bring me love. I opened my eyes and got back up and walked to the bedroom and got into bed next to Aggie and waited.

I waited and waited. Then there was a knock on the door. It was my father and he was there to inform me that he'd just sold my house to his something something, some kind of twice-removed whatever, and that I would have to get out and take Aggie, if she was there with me, but frankly he didn't care where she was, and find other lodgings. Maybe we could get work cleaning for Mexican capos. If we were lucky.

I slammed the door in his face and listened. Nothing. I thought he must be walking back to his house. Then I heard some Bible verses being quoted and realized that he was still there.

But I have prayed for thee, that thy faith fail not, he said. And then louder, a practised crescendo I'd heard a million times.

And he said unto him, Lord I am ready to go with thee, both into prison, and to death!

I wondered if I should make some coffee or go back to bed.

And he said, I tell thee, Peter, the cock shall not crow this day before that thou shalt thrice deny that thou knowest me!

I couldn't find my canister of coffee. I let a cupboard slam by accident and swore. I didn't want Aggie waking up.

Then he demanded that I let him into the house. I didn't say anything. He started yelling and Aggie eventually came out of the bedroom and together we stared at the door.

It's Julius Voth, I said.

Don't let him in, she said.

Then we heard another voice.

Who's that? said Aggie.

I think it's Diego, I said.

Our father asked him what he was doing there and Diego told him that he'd been outside staring at the sky, looking for signs of rain, and had heard yelling coming from my yard and then had started to wonder what was going on and if I was all right.

Well, now you can leave, said my father, and stay out of our business.

I will, said Diego, but why don't you go home also.

You will not tell me what to do on my own property, said my father.

Aggie and I sat silently at the table waiting for it all to end. It took a while. Arguments between two visionaries are lengthy, I learned. One of these men will be dead soon, I thought. While they argued Aggie made shapes on the table with flour. Tiny words, then bigger, like an eye chart. And hearts and clouds and cacti and planets. I went far away in my head, back to Canada, to snow, to forts, to ammunition that could melt, to red wrists from sleeves on parkas that were too short, to eyes frozen shut with ice.

SIX

MARIJKE HAS TO DIE TODAY. It's a little bit out of sequence but Diego is in a hurry to finish the shots that require the co-operation of the Mennonites. The other ones, the ones of nature or whatever, he can do elsewhere, somewhere down the road. My father has put a bounty on Diego's head, according to Diego. That if he doesn't take his filthy pornography-producing crew who live like pigs and rape his daughters and leave immediately he will end up with a bullet in his brain. Diego has also threatened my father with swift justice if he does anything to prevent him from finishing his movie. I don't know if I believe it.

I asked Diego when I'd be paid for my work and he said tomorrow. He said first he had to pay the cops to let Carlito go.

Carlito Wiebe? I said. Diego said yeah, Carlito Wiebe. Diego had hired him to play Alfredo's friend but Carlito was busted at Campo 4 for some kind of drug thing and was in jail at the moment. How much will it cost? I asked him.

Four thousand pesos, he said. Plus the cop wants a part in the movie.

Diego told me not to worry. He asked me if my father was insane and I said oh, do you mean Julius Voth? And he said yeah. Then he apologized for talking that way about my father. I told him Aggie and I had to get out of the house, that my father had sold it to somebody. Diego told me that Aggie and I can live in the house with the crew. He said Marijke would like it and the presence of females might keep her from wigging out.

On the way to the death scene location we stopped to quickly film a scene where Alfredo and Marijke talk in the car. Alfredo is supposed to tell Marijke that he just can't stop loving that other woman or whatever, and Marijke is supposed to ask him why he doesn't want to be with her,

Marijke, anymore. I leaned into the passenger side window of the car and told Marijke that this time she'd be looking right at the camera. She wasn't really talking to Alfredo but it was supposed to look like she was. Alfredo wasn't there. She was talking to a camera that was on top of Miguel's stomach. Miguel was lying down, sort of, driving the car with the camera on top of him. He could barely see over the dashboard. Elias and Sebastian and Diego sat in the back seat.

Tell her to look right into that spot just above the lens, said Diego. To count in her head to ten and then to talk to it as though it were the love of her life.

I told Marijke in German to count silently to ten and then to ask the spot just above the lens why he doesn't want to be with her anymore. Marijke nodded.

And then, I said, ask is it because my vagina is so big after having all these babies?

This time I had gone too far. Marijke smiled and said I must be joking. Diego wouldn't have written that. Was it for real? Okay, well, no, I said, but it's more interesting and don't you think it's kind of the truth?

We can't wreck his movie with things like that, said Marijke.

Nobody seeing the movie will understand, I said. So what difference does it make?

It's not true to my character, said Marijke. I mean her character.

What character? I said. She's a prop for Alfredo's dark night of the soul. For his excruciating existential dilemma. She's barely breathing.

Did Wilson say that to you? said Marijke.

Yeah, I said. Don't let Diego take your soul.

What are you talking about?

Oh, I don't know, I said.

Suddenly I was exhausted. Diego told us to hurry. He asked me if Marijke was sure of her line and I said yes.

Then let's roll, he said.

Miguel began to drive the car, haphazardly, down the road. It was obvious that he couldn't see where he was going. I stood and watched them leave. I counted silently to ten and then saw Marijke turn her head to the camera, her husband, to speak to him with a broken heart. I watched them disappear into dust. Then they came back and left again and came back and left again and kept doing that for a while until Diego had his shot. He and all the others huddled around the little viewing thing that showed them what they had on film and nodded in approval. Beautiful. Perfect. Wilson would take the rushes today and fly them to Mexico City before they could be destroyed by my father.

Are you coming back? I asked him.

Yes, he said.

We were tearing to the house so that Diego could talk to Alfredo again. The death scene was postponed because my father had told everyone in church that if they co-operated with Diego they might as well book themselves a window seat to hell and enjoy the ride. He told them that Diego was stealing their women and perverting the will of God. He'd also made his position clear in more tangible ways, according to Diego.

What does that mean? I asked him.

Nobody in the area will do business with the agents of Satan, he said. Alfredo had radioed Diego to tell him that he had gone into the store to buy cigarettes and had had to pay twice as much as he normally would. Same with his vampiros. And the Wayfarer's Inn wouldn't serve him at all. Alfredo told Diego he was done. He couldn't take the pressure anymore. This really was it for him. Diego told him to meet him at the house. He sent Sebastian off to the businesses with some more money and a heartfelt plea to allow him to make his art. He told Sebastian to tell as many people as he could that the premiere of the film would be held in Campo 6.5 and everyone would be welcome, young and old, and it would be beautiful and sacred and true to the gentle and forgiving character of the Mennonite people.

It sounds like a war, said Aggie.

That's exactly what it is, said Diego.

When we got to the house Alfredo was standing in the middle of the yard with his wife and my father. Diego jumped out of the truck and walked quickly over to them.

Let's go in the house, I said to Aggie.

No, I want to hear what they're saying, she said.

Aggie, I said. Let's go in the house.

No, I'm going to wait here. You go.

He might drag you back home, I said.

He can't, she said. Can he?

Of course he can, I said. Come into the house already. We'll have Oveja.

We walked past Diego and Alfredo and his wife and our father. Oveja barked at them and I told him to shut up.

Don't look at him, I said to Aggie. Don't act scared.

I'm not scared, she said.

Our father said something to us, something I couldn't understand. If it was a harsh word he said it with a catch in his throat, like he wasn't convinced. Or that may have been my imagination. Tenderness bleeding like sap through bark. Maybe not. Then he said something to Diego.

It's not your property, he said. It doesn't belong to you.

I'm renting this house, said Diego, and the land that it sits on. So leave now, please. We have work to do.

Whosoever shall seek to save his life shall lose it, said my father. And whosoever shall lose his life shall preserve it.

Pardon? said Diego.

I tell you, said my father, in that night there shall be two men in one bed. The one shall be taken and the other shall be left.

C'mon, Aggie, move your ass, I said. Let's go inside.

Two women shall be grinding together, said my father. The one shall be taken and the other left.

Irma, said Diego, what is he saying to me?

I mumbled a few words, nothing really, and pushed Aggie towards the house.

Two men shall be in the field, said my father, and the one shall be taken and the other left!

All right, said Diego, I think I understand now. But—

And they answered and said unto him, where, Lord? And he said unto them, wheresoever the body is, thither will the eagles be gathered together.

Okay, said Diego. Okay. His hands were up to say stop, please, stop.

Then Aggie and I were in the house and couldn't hear any more of what they were saying. We watched them from the kitchen window. Elias and Miguel had showed up and were standing out there too, looking up towards the sky and clearing their throats. Then Wilson came into the house and said that he had to go right then to the airport with the rushes. He was carrying them and a tiny stuffed backpack.

Can you take Aggie with you? I said.

What? he said. I don't think so. Why would I do that?

Why not? I said. She can help carry things.

Irma, I don't think that's a good idea, he said.

Why not? I said.

Well, he said, it just doesn't make any sense.

So? I said.

I had started to shake slightly, a bit of old-fashioned trembling, but I was trying not to let it show. Then Diego came into the house and told Wilson to bring back two or three more guys from Mexico City, and to explain to José, the producer, about the money. He spoke so quickly I couldn't understand exactly what he was saying.

Irma, said Diego, walk with Wilson to the truck and take Oveja. And then come back into the house.

No, I said. I don't want to leave Aggie in the house without Oveja, I said.

Just to get the rushes to the truck, said Diego, and then bring the dog back inside. Go now.

Oveja and Wilson and I went outside and walked to the truck, past my father and Alfredo and his wife and some of the other crew guys. Wilson put the reels of film and his backpack on the front seat and got into the truck and said he'd see me the next day or the day after and Oveja and I walked back, past all those people who were just looking at us and not talking, and into the house. Then Diego went back outside and said something to Elias who slowly walked away towards the other truck. Diego kept my father talking for a long time. Elias parked the other truck behind my father's truck so he couldn't drive away and then he came into the house to get a beer and take a deep breath.

What's going on? I said.

Diego doesn't want your father to go after Wilson and steal the film before he can get to the airport in Chihuahua. So I had to block his truck.

I looked out the window at my father standing in the middle of a circle of young filmmakers. Alfredo and his wife had gone to stand in the shade by the barn. His wife had a small, tough body and a huge smile with one dead tooth, and gold-green eyes. I imagined Diego saying cut and everyone going back to their real lives. I stared at my father from behind the windowpane. I knew he was getting tired, that his back was hurting him. He couldn't stand for very long because of the three-inch lift he had built onto the sole of one of his shoes after the doctor told him he had some kind of scoliosis that had twisted his spine into the shape of a snake. I didn't want him to hold his hands out that way, palms up, or to wipe the sweat off his forehead with the back of his hand and I didn't want to see him stammer for the Spanish or English words that would add to the sum of his rage.

He won't do that, I said.

What won't he do? said Elias.

He won't chase Wilson, I said. That's stupid.

You never know, said Elias. There's a black . . . there's a black storm . . . no?

Yeah, I said.

Moving like this in circles, he said. Inside. He can't control it.

Yeah, I said. Tornado.

Yes, said Elias. A tornado doesn't know what it's doing. He started to spin around the room intentionally bumping into chairs and walls and kitchen appliances.

I know, I said. You're a tornado.

We should play music, he said.

He put on some music that would drown out the voices from outside and Aggie and I watched our father and Diego argue to the beat of something called cumbia. Slowly everything became dreamlike and soft in the dying light. Aggie got bored and started making pictures on the wall with the green tape Diego used to indicate to the actors where they should stand. I heard Elias talking on his cellphone. He was excited that he finally had service here on the moon and he was walking around the house trying to make it last. Can you hear me now? I heard him say in Spanish. How about now? Is this better? He lost his connection. Then he swore. *Puta.* That was my girlfriend, he said. She just agreed to give her body parts away to a hospital or something like that.

That's pretty nice, I said.

She prefers to give her body to science than to me, said Elias.

Well, science is science, I said. I didn't know what we were talking about.

That's true, he said. It's precise and useful. How can I compete with science?

I didn't know if he was being serious or not. I told him she'd probably change her mind when she realized how much energy would be involved in donating body parts.

No, Irma, she'd be dead, he said, it would be afterwards.

I am living beneath sea level in a basement apartment in Vancouver, ostensibly taking courses in fine arts and Marxism, I said to myself. It was a line from a letter my cousin had sent to my older sister Katie way back one hundred thousand years ago in Canada. You should join me. You'll like it here! Sometimes I recite these ancient lines to myself when I don't know what to say because I always feel my eyes open up a bit afterwards, maybe even shine with something like excitement or guilt, or like pilot fish. Ostensibly taking courses in fine arts and Marxism, I say to myself. You should join me. You'll like it here.

Diego came into the house and told Elias to turn the music down. My father was alone in the yard, standing close to a shadow cast by the barn. He could have moved into the shade but he didn't. Alfredo and his wife were gone. Diego told me he wanted to speak to me privately in his bedroom and I followed him down the long hallway that used to belong to my cousins and through the door with the upside-down cross and into his room. He had bottles of what looked like urine lined up against one of the walls. He had piles of books and a very neatly made bed.

Please sit, Irma, he said. I sat on his bed and he sat next to me and put his hand on my shoulder. Aggie has to go back, he said. I promised your father I'd make her go back. If she doesn't go back he'll call the police and the newspapers in Mexico City and tell them I've kidnapped her.

She can't go back, I said. I promised her she wouldn't have to.

She has to go back, said Diego, or I won't be able to finish my film.

I know, I said, but she can't go back.

And when I'm finished making the film then I'll make sure that you and Aggie are safe.

How will you do that? I said.

Don't worry, he said, I'll find some way.

He's not really going to call the police and newspapers in Mexico City, I said.

How do you know? said Diego.

And who cares if he does? I said. You'll tell them you haven't kidnapped her and that'll be the end of it.

That's not really the point, said Diego. He wants her back in his house. And if she doesn't go home he'll fuck up the production.

No, I said. She can't go back.

Irma, said Diego, she has to go back. Please. I'm begging you now. Please tell her to go home.

I can't tell her anything, I said. She doesn't listen to me.

Then I'll tell her, said Diego.

No! I said. Please don't.

Diego and I stopped talking and stared at the line of books he had on the little shelf above his bed. We looked at those books beseechingly, as though they were UN peace workers sent to help us negotiate our impasse. I imagined them rearranging themselves on the shelf to spell out some cryptic answer, a solution, but they didn't move an inch.

Tell my father that Aggie is sleeping right now and will go home in the morning, I said.

She's in the kitchen playing cards with Elias, said Diego. Your father can see her through the window.

Tell him she's sick with parasites, I said.

Irma, said Diego, she's sitting in the kitchen and—

And that she can't infect our mother or she'll lose the baby. Worms will eat it from the in—

That's ridiculous, Irma, said Diego. You know it is.

Tell him it's like a quarantine.

He won't believe me, said Diego.

Then tell him Oveja has to go with her, I said.

No, said Diego. We need Oveja here and besides, your father will just shoot him if Aggie brings him home.

You said we could live here with you, I said.

I know, said Diego. That was before.

Well, then I'm quitting, I said. I can't work for you anymore. If you send Aggie home you'll lose me too.

You have no place to go, said Diego. He looked at me kindly, steadily, like a cop who's just busted a kid for a very minor offence, like it hurt him a little bit but the evidence was there and it was irrefutable.

I need to get paid, I said. I need to get my wages.

Yes, said Diego, that is correct. You're right. Wilson will bring your money back from Mexico City in one or two days. I promise. I radioed José about it.

I got up and left Diego's room and walked down the long hall and through the kitchen, past Aggie and Marijke and the others, and out into the yard to my father who was now standing by himself in the half-light, waiting. He was in the same spot. He could have moved over and leaned against the wall of the barn. He could have held his arms out as I approached him. He could have kept us all in Canada and shape-shifted with the times. He could have been a million things.

Let Aggie stay with me at my house tonight, I said. I need her to help me pack my things up and clean the stove and fridge and stuff before you change the locks. When we're finished I'll send her straight home. For good. And I won't bother you again.

My father looked so tired. Daughters, I imagined him saying to himself. Who are these people?

You can do those things alone, he said.

But I can't do them and the milking too and have it all done by the morning, I said.

I don't need you to do the milking anymore, he said. I've arranged for Klaus Kroeker to do it from now on.

Well, I said. I could hear a few soft strains of cumbia playing in the house. The stars mocked me, even the puny one all on its own in Texas, four hours to the north.

I thought: I've run out of words. I have nothing. I've failed. My father was quiet, waiting. He could stand and wait it out, wear me down. He could stand forever like the

Tarahumara family on the side of the road. I could learn about this. I touched my forehead, the space between my eyes, the source, according to Marijke, of my energy and my light.

Please? I said. That was all I had, apparently, nothing but a dim flicker. Just the one low-beam request for mercy. I looked down at the ground. I covered my face with my hands. My eyes burned and tears fell. I got down on one knee, then the other, and prayed quietly at my father's feet. When I was finished I opened my eyes and he was gone.

I need to use one of the trucks, I said.

Why? said Diego.

I'll bring it back in an hour, I said.

Where are you going? said Diego. It's very late.

To see a friend, I said.

Is Aggie going home? said Diego.

Yeah, I said. I'll drop her off on the way.

I want to start shooting early in the morning, said Diego. Like at five a.m. We have to do as much as we can before everything goes to shit. Alfredo is giving me three more days before he walks. He says.

I know, I said. I'll be back in time.

And Marijke is losing her mind, he said.

She's fine, I said. She thinks she's disappearing but that's all normal, I think.

———

Aggie and Oveja and I were in my house, standing beside the kitchen counter, and Aggie was trying to get the tap to run but it wouldn't.

Don't worry about it, I said. He's turned off the water. Go to the pump and fill up some buckets from the barn and put them in the back of the truck and then meet me in the grain shed.

Yeah, but what if—

Aggie, I said. I know it's against your religion to do anything I tell you to do but you're going to take a break from your religion, okay, and you're going to do everything I tell you to do starting right now.

Are we in trouble? said Aggie.

Well, you know, yeah, I said. A little bit. Which is why.

Why what? she said.

Why I have a plan, I said. And then later on, in a week or so, you'll be able to once again refuse to do some of the things I ask you to do.

All things? said Aggie.

Just a few, I said. Just to keep your soul from disintegrating. Okay? Please?

Aggie sighed heavily and Oveja stared mournfully at her, his eyes a well of deep concern. He was also a rebel, a fighter, and understood the significance of what I had asked her to do.

Let's quickly eat something, I said.

There was some leftover shepherd's pie in the fridge that wasn't working anymore since the generator died and Aggie ate the meaty stuff at the bottom and I ate the top layer of potatoes.

Then we both went outside and Aggie went to the pump to get some water and I went to the barn and let out all the cows. I punched their rear ends and shouted at them and that got Oveja all worked up and he came running over and started growling and nipping and chasing the cows out into the yard and into the cornfields and onto the road. Aggie came back from the pump and put the pails of water in the back of the truck.

What the hell are you doing? she said.

Back the truck up to the grain shed, I said.

Why should—

Aggie! I said. Do it. Remember what I said?

I know but—

No, Aggie, you don't understand. Right now you have to shut up and do everything I say.

I know but—

Aggie! My God! Are you fucking insane?

Fine! she said.

I ran to the shed and stood on a bale and started hauling Jorge's boxes out of the rafters. Aggie backed the truck up to the shed and hit the corner of it with the bumper. I yelled at her to stop. She got out of the truck and came into the shed and I told her to start loading the boxes into the back.

What is this? she said.

Something for Carlito Wiebe, I said. Let's go.

Wait, she said, let's take Oveja.

No, I said. He's running around with the cows. We'll come back and get him after. And besides, Carlito has a dog too, and they'd just fight.

———

Carlito Wiebe was angry with us for waking him up in the middle of the night but then he saw what was going on and he became less angry. He took the boxes out of the back of the truck and brought them into his dingy little kitchen and piled them up on top of each other. He leaned on the boxes and said a bunch of things and I wanted him to hurry up and buy the stuff and give me the money so we could leave.

I don't have enough on me right now, he said.

Well, how much do you have? I said.

I don't know, he said, I'll have to take a look.

He went off into another room and Aggie and I stood there. She was yawning. Off in the other room Carlito put on some kind of cowboy music and we heard water running for a minute.

Irma? she said. Are you a narco?

No, I said. Shhh.

Jorge's gonna kill you, she said.

Nah, I said.

Carlito came back and said he could give me about thirty thousand pesos. I like that music, he said. Do you?

Yeah, said Aggie, it's pretty good.

It's a new band from Durango, said Carlito. The singer just got out of jail.

Jorge told me it was worth at least a million pesos, I told him.

He's wrong, said Carlito. He was just talking big. I'm going back to bed if you're not interested.

I'll give you thirty thousand pesos' worth, then, and take the rest back, I said.

No, Irma, said Carlito. I don't mean to be a hard-ass but you don't know what you're talking about. You don't even know how much thirty thousand is. Besides what are you going to do with it? Carry it around with you in the back of that truck?

Aggie cleared her throat and I looked into her translucent eyes for a second and felt weakness leave my body like blood.

Nah, forget it, I said. I'll find someone else. C'mon, Aggie, help me load this shit back into the truck. I yanked the back of her dress.

Hang on, said Carlito. Tell you what. I'll give you forty thousand pesos. That's a good deal.

Fuck off, Carlito, I said.

Fuck off, Carlito, said Aggie. We went into the yard and hopped back into the truck.

He's coming outside, said Aggie. What if he shoots us?

That would solve so many problems, I said. I rolled my window down and pointed my pen flashlight into his eyes. He put his arm up to cover them and I turned it off.

Sorry, I said. I had to make sure it was you.

Irma, he said. I don't mean to pry but what the heck are you doing?

I'm selling drugs! I said. Jesus Christ, man. What the hell do you think I'm doing?

Irma, said Aggie. You sound a tiny bit hysterical.

Does Jorge know you're doing this? said Carlito. Did he send you?

No, he didn't, okay? I said. Just, you know, whatever. Give me forty thousand then. I have to go.

Tell you what, said Carlito. I'll give you fifty. But promise me you won't tell anybody, especially Jorge, who you sold it to. And also, do you girls want a bag of oranges? We waited for Carlito to run into his house and out again with a big sack of oranges that he put into the back of the truck.

Danke schön, I said.

Bitte, he said. And may God be with you.

Thanks, Carlito, I said. And with you.

Count the money, I told Aggie.

No, she said. I'm afraid it won't be the right amount.

Oh, okay, I said, you're right. Never mind. I told Aggie what the next step was and she put her feet on the dash and said she'd like to make a comment if she could, something having to do with what she called the paucity of my business sense, but I said no. We flew back to our parents' house and went running in to tell our father that the cows were loose, that Klaus Kroeker, the guy he'd hired to do the milking, must not have known how to close the gate properly. My father grabbed his gun from the rack in the kitchen and put on his boots and told me and Aggie to help him round them up. His face was burnt bright red from stubbornly standing in the sun all that day. I told him that we'd take the truck and go over to the south side of the field, near the broken crop-duster, and stop them there. It didn't really make any sense but he didn't seem to notice and he left, swearing and bleary-eyed.

We went into our parents' bedroom looking for our mother and there she was with the top of her nightgown down and she was nursing a baby. We all stared at each other except for the baby who kept sucking and gurgling and then our mother said in a soft, quiet voice, girls, what are you doing here? What's going on? And Aggie said you've had your baby! Nobody told us! Shhhh, said our mother. She was smiling. Come sit here with me, she said. And then we both went and lay down on either side of our mother and her new baby for a while and we touched the baby very gently so we wouldn't disturb it from eating and I told my mother that we had some hard news.

My mother was quiet for a long time. I wanted her to say something. The baby fell asleep and my mother took her nipple out of its mouth and gently laid the baby down beside her so it was tucked in between her and Aggie and then she put the top of her nightgown back on. She asked me to move so that she could get out of bed and she asked Aggie to stay with the baby and I helped her walk to the kitchen because she was still sore from the birth and she asked me to sit down at the table. She sat down too and put her hands on my hands.

How are you, Irma? she said. She touched my cheek and my forehead. We were whispering.

I'm okay, I said. How are you?

She smiled and said she was okay except that I was holding on to her hand so tightly she thought it might break.

Does Jorge know? she said.

No, I said.

But he's your husband, she said.

I know, I said. She was quiet for a bit, staring at something invisible on the wall.

Are you cold? she said.

No, I said.

Are you hungry? she said.

No, I said.

Will you be brave? she said.

I'll try, I said.

I love you, Irma, she said.

I love you too.

I pressed my fingers hard to my eyes. I put my head in my mother's lap and she stroked my hair. My precious Irma, she said. Then she sang a little bit of this hymn we all knew called "Children of the Heavenly Father." When she was finished singing she was quiet for a minute. She kept stroking my hair.

Your braids need redoing, she said.

I know, I said.

But there isn't time now, she said.

That's true, I said. She tried to help me up. She whispered to me that I should kiss the boys goodbye, they wouldn't wake up, and she would talk for a bit with Aggie. I got up and went into the boys' bedroom and looked at them. Doft was buried under his blanket, his fuzzy little head just barely poking out, and Jacobo had thrown his covers onto the floor. I leaned over each of my sleeping brothers and kissed them. They smelled like hay and sweat. I wanted to give them something to remember me by but I didn't have anything. I kissed each of them again. Then I remembered the oranges and I went out to the truck and took two of them out of the bag and brought them back in and went and put one orange each beside my brothers' heads. I went back into the hallway and I heard Aggie and my mother talking in her room. I heard Aggie say hold me closer, Mom, squeeze hard. They were both crying. I walked back to the kitchen and waited.

When my mother came out of the room she told me she had a very big favour to ask of me. I told her I'd do anything for her.

Take her with you, she said, and don't tell me where you're going.

I am taking her with me, I said. That's why we're both here. To say goodbye.

I know, she said. I mean the baby. Take her too.

SEVEN

I WROTE A NOTE AND SLIPPED IT under the door for Diego to find when he woke up. I told him the truck would be at the airport in Chihuahua and the keys in the ashtray. I thanked him for everything and wished him well with his movie. I asked him to please forgive me for leaving the shoot early and for taking the truck and to give Marijke a hug from me and goodbye to all the others. And I signed it.

I drove fast, straight into the rising sun. Aggie held the baby and stared at her.

Does she have your eyes? I said.

It's hard to say, said Aggie. Just one is open. It's really dark blue.

Hmmm, I said.

I don't think she has any pupils, said Aggie.

Of course she has pupils, I said.

I don't know, said Aggie, I can't see it.

Well, that's just because her eye is dark blue, I said. She must have pupils.

What does a pupil do, anyway? said Aggie.

I don't know, I said. I was calculating the amount of time it would take us to drive to Cuauhtémoc and wondering if the *farmacia* would be open so that I could buy some baby formula and bottles.

You should know that by now, said Aggie.

Okay, I said, they react to the light. They dilate and contract.

So, said Aggie. If she doesn't have pupils will the sun just burn holes right through her eyes?

She has pupils, I said.

Maybe she's blind, said Aggie.

See if you can make her blink, I said. Or just move your hand around and see if her eye follows it.

Aggie moved her hand slowly through the air in front of the baby's one open eye and then the baby closed that one too.

Well, said Aggie, that didn't really work.

She'll be fine, I said.

You always say that, said Aggie. You're always saying everything is fine.

No, I'm not, I said. I'm not an idiot.

She has your fists, said Aggie.

What do you mean, fists? I said. Hands?

She's a fighter, said Aggie.

I'm not a fighter, I said. They just ball up like that on their own. Stretch them out.

Aggie took the baby's hands in her own and gently pried them open. The baby was trying to scratch her own cheek. Her hands were flailing around all over the place.

Don't let her do that, I said.

Do what? said Aggie.

Tuck her hands in under the blanket so she doesn't scratch herself, I said.

Isn't it strange, said Aggie, that Mom gave us all those baby clothes and now we have a baby but none of the clothes?

Yes and no, I said.

Are we going to look for Jorge? said Aggie.

I don't know, I said. I don't think so.

Wilson? said Aggie.

No, I said. I don't know where he is.

Well, you don't know where Jorge is either, said Aggie. That's why it's called looking.

I said, she's still kind of scratching herself. Tuck her hands in. Or hold them away from her face.

I didn't say goodbye to the boys, she said.

They were sleeping, I said. They're all right.

See, said Aggie, you're always saying everything is all right.

I didn't say everything is all right, I said. I said the boys are all right.

The motor on the truck was loud but we could still hear the mourning doves.

Dad will kill Oveja, said Aggie.

No, he won't, I said.

Yeah, he will, said Aggie. Stop saying stuff you don't know. I hate that. He'll kill him for sure.

Well, now you're saying something you don't know, I said. Maybe Oveja will kill him first.

What's he gonna do when he finds out the baby is gone? said Aggie.

Nothing, I said. He barely noticed her. Mom will tell him she had dengue and died and is gone.

That's it? said Aggie.

That's all, I said. You have to be buried quick with dengue. Mom will tell him she put her with that other one behind the feed barn.

What about a funeral? said Aggie.

Not worth it, I said. Dad will say a prayer at dinner and send her soul to heaven.

What does Mom call her? said Aggie.

Ximena, I said.

What? said Aggie. For real? That's a Mexican name.

Well, we're in Mexico, I said.

Let's give her a Mexican last name too, said Aggie.

Sure, I said. Molina?

Ximena Molina, said Aggie.

Or we could call her Miep, I said.

Ximena Molina Miep? said Aggie.

Sure, I said.

How will we feed her? said Aggie.

I'm thinking about that, I said.

It started to get a little cloudy and after about twenty minutes it started to rain hard. Finally Diego could shoot the scene he needed so desperately. Except that we had his truck. We were driving to the airport in Chihuahua city. I stopped at a *farmacia* on the main road going out of Cuauhtémoc and bought some baby formula and bottles and a bag of infant-sized diapers and a package of three sleepers and a blue box of moist baby wipes. I bought a beach towel with a herd of wild horses on it against a setting sun to use as an extra blanket for Ximena and a forbidden teen magazine and a Snickers bar for Aggie. When I got back to the truck Ximena was screaming and Aggie was trying to get her to stop.

You have to walk with her, I said.

It's raining outside, said Aggie.

Walk under that canopy for a bit while I make her a bottle, I said. I read the instructions on the formula tin and carefully measured out four level scoops of powder. I had taken care of babies all my life but until now my mother had always provided the milk. I added clean water and I shook the bottle and then I squeezed a drop of it onto the inside of my wrist to make sure the temperature was perfect. It was a little cool so I rubbed the bottle between my hands for a minute. I considered starting the engine and putting the bottle on it to warm up fast but I didn't want the plastic to melt.

Aggie came back to the truck with Ximena, she was still crying but not as hard and she'd stopped waving her arms around, and I took her and gave her the bottle and Aggie took her magazine and chocolate. Ximena spit the rubber nipple out several times and tried to scream but I kept putting it back into her mouth until she got the hang of it.

Aren't you supposed to boil those bottles before you use them? said Aggie.

Yeah, you are, I said. I shrugged. I wiped the bottle with a sterilized baby wipe.

When Ximena had finished her bottle I burped her and changed her diaper on the seat of the truck.

Look at that, said Aggie. Is that normal?

Yeah, I said, it's her umbilical cord. It'll fall off in a few days.

We should keep it, said Aggie.

Sure, I said. It'll eventually shrivel up, though.

How long will that take? said Aggie.

I don't know, I said. Marijke keeps her son's umbilical cord in a little pouch around her neck.

How far is it to the airport? said Aggie.

About an hour and a half, I said.

Where are we flying to?

I'm not exactly sure right now, I said.

How about Canada? said Aggie.

The world seemed spectacular and beautiful and calm, like the sacred heart of Jesus, as my mother would have said. The world we were leaving, that is. But I guess that's how the world works. How it sucks you in by being all beautiful just when you're ready to leave. Jorge used to get me to walk and

talk with him when I was sad. He'd hold my hand and sometimes we'd skip all the way to San Miguel, the tiny village
down the road, because skipping is stupid but exhilarating
and it made us laugh. Words and movement, he said, would
push all the bad stuff away. I tried it on myself. I was starting
to think hard about my mother, wondering if we'd ever see
her again, and I didn't want to cry in front of Aggie.

Are you thinking about Mom? I said.

Yeah, said Aggie.

Well, that was all we said. So much for words. And
driving wasn't the same as skipping. So the bad stuff stayed
in our minds and we both stared straight ahead through the
dirty windshield. Ximena made odd noises like she was
trying hard to fill the void but didn't yet know exactly how
to articulate loss or, like Wilson had said, how to communicate loneliness.

We had Ximena and her sunset beach towel and diapers
and bottles and stuff and the woman behind the counter
asked us where our bags were and I told her we didn't have
any. Well, we have a bag of oranges, said Aggie. The woman
looked at the bag of oranges and frowned and looked at
Ximena and frowned more. I told her I wanted to buy three
tickets to Vancouver, Canada, or two if my baby could sit
on my lap. She said we'd have to fly to Houston first, or Los
Angeles, and then to Vancouver. She asked us when we
wanted to fly.

Now, I said.

Do you have passports? she said.

———

We were sitting on the curb in front of the airport. I was nervous, worrying that my father would drive up any second. We had half an hour to kill before our flight to Acapulco. We didn't have passports. Aggie was eating an orange and leaning way over so the juice didn't dribble onto her dress. Some of it fell onto the asphalt and a bee spotted it just like that. And then a bunch of them. The baby was awake again and waving her arms around like a shipwreck survivor.

We've learned something today, haven't we? I said.

Is this my new school? said Aggie.

We'll go to the beach, I said.

We don't have bathing costumes, said Aggie.

Bathing costumes? I said. They're not called that.

That's what they're called at school, said Aggie.

Are those books from the eighteen hundreds? I said. They're called bathing suits now.

Bathing *suits*? said Aggie. That's worse.

Men call them trunks, I said.

Trunks? said Aggie. Why?

I guess you can figure that out yourself, I said.

We'll teach Ximena how to swim, said Aggie. Just throw her in like those hippies.

What hippies? I said.

I don't know, said Aggie. Hippies. They throw their babies into water right after they're born.

They don't throw them into oceans, I said. Here, hold her for a second so I can eat my orange.

A Mennonite family walked past us and we all stared at each other. The father nodded and the kids trailing behind him all dominoed into each other because they were staring so hard and that made us smile.

Aggie, I said, if anyone asks you if you're Aggie Voth, say no.

I told Aggie we should go inside and wait. I told her to hold Ximena while I went into the washroom to make her a bottle and she said she'd think about fake names for us while she waited. I looked at myself in the bathroom mirror. Sweat was pouring out of me. It was so sudden. My hands were shaking. I tried to make the bottle but formula was spilling everywhere and I was gasping for air. An older woman came out of a stall and stood next to me washing her hands. We smiled at each other. *Está enferma?* she said. *No, no, estoy,* I said. I washed my face with cold water and dried it with toilet paper that stuck to my skin in small chunks like porridge. I took deep breaths and tried again to make Ximena's bottle and this time I did it without spilling any. I remembered my father using the words *confronted by freedom* when he described the perverted temptations of the world and then I heard a loud voice reminding those of us flying to Acapulco that it was time to go.

I'm Fiorella, she's Button and you're Ham Hock, said Aggie. We were walking to our gate. We'd only be in Acapulco for two hours and forty-five minutes before we had to catch another flight to Mexico City, heaven and hell, according to Diego, but his world was defined by extremes. I was hoping we'd find some little street to live on that straddled eternities. If life was always going to be like this there was no way I'd be able to do it forever.

I'll skip all the flying stuff (because recounting it exhausts me almost as much as living it did) and keep this story about the things that happened to us on earth. Basically, it was a nightmare with Ximena Molina (Button) Miep. Vomit. Wailing. Flailing. Streams of shit. Screams of anguish. Aggie and I were both covered in puke and a little crazy with mortification. Eventually I gave up trying to comfort Ximena and focused on comforting myself with the knowledge that X., my newest baby sister, even with her unfinished features and ruinous needs, was a very honest person at least. So far. And that I had been given the task of keeping her that way. And so, if she needed to do these unholy things, then so be it. She was an ambassador-at-large, not appointed to any one country, but on a mission to represent babies, and I was her servant and facilitator.

We got off the plane in Acapulco and went outside and got into a taxicab and I asked the driver to take us to a beach. We smelled bad. We looked awful. Ximena had fallen asleep all wrapped up in the towel, soaked in sweat and with a sweet expression on her face that underneath it seemed to say fuck you all, I possess vital intangibles and when I learn to talk the world will know its shame. She was growing on me.

Aggie and I stared out the windows of the cab and tried as best we could to act like this was all just another typical day. The driver asked me if we had bags and I said no, not really, just this plastic *farmacia* bag with diapers and stuff in it, and he said okay, no bags, and shrugged. He smiled at us through the rear-view mirror the way Wilson used to when he was driving the truck and I was sitting in the back. He asked us in Spanish where we were from and I said Canada. He asked us if we were here in Acapulco for a holiday and I said yes.

Just the two of you? he said.

Three, I said. I pointed at Ximena.

No husband? he said.

Well, yes, I said. There is. But he's . . . I'm a widow.

The cab driver said he was sorry. He said he was raised by a single mother and it was always hard for her. She had cried secretly at night. It's not impossible, though, he said. He told me I'd be all right. It was a different world now, he said.

Which resort are you going to? he asked me.

Oh, I said. It doesn't matter. Just any one with a beach.

They're all on the beach, he said. Do you have the name of your hotel? Aggie cleared her throat and Ximena sighed in her sleep. Everybody started honking their horns at once, it seemed, and music was playing in every car and I was sure I smelled salt water, like we were all in some kind of parade.

Can I just tell you something? I said to the driver.

Of course, he said. You can tell me anything. He turned his music down and glanced at me through the rear-view mirror.

I don't know the name of the hotel, I said. We don't actually have a hotel. We're only here for two hours and forty-five minutes and then we have to go back to the airport to catch another plane. I promised my sister I'd take her to a beach. She's never been to one before.

The cab driver said he'd take us to a quiet beach that real people from Acapulco went to and we could eat fish tacos and drink mango juice and splash in the waves and lie in the sun to dry off and then he'd take us back to the airport, no charge. He was feeling generous, he said, and that he could use some time off because he'd been working for something like eighteen hours straight and he couldn't feel his ass.

Okay, I said. That sounds like a good idea. *Gracias.*

For real? said Aggie. I hadn't seen her smile like that in ages.

Les gusta este lugar? he said.

Sí, sí, I said.

Me llamo Gustavo, he said.

Do you trust him? Aggie asked me in Low German.

Why not? I said.

You don't even know him! she said. What if—

So what? I said. We'll scream if he tries anything.

Aggie reminded me in Low German that we didn't have any bathing suits. Ximena woke up and started kicking and punching. Soon she'd be into full-blown wailing but she was still just frowning and sputtering and quiet enough that the car horns and music everywhere drowned her out. She stared at me with one dark eye like a pirate and tried to claw my face. I held her to the window so she could focus her wrath on the outside world. I'm not sure she saw anything except for a blur of cars and buildings and sky.

Que bebé tan hermoso! said Gustavo.

Sí, gracias, I said. Babies weren't called beautiful in the campo. I put my ugly face next to Ximena's and together we looked at the city of Acapulco and I remembered the lyrics of a song I used to sing in church with my parents when I was a kid. *Beautiful words, wonderful words, wonderful words of life. Words of life and beauty teach me faith and duty. Beautiful words, wonderful words, wonderful words of life.*

Tell him we have to stop somewhere to buy bathing suits, said Aggie.

I told her that for some reason I was kind of embarrassed to ask Gustavo to stop and Aggie said it was more embarrassing to show up at a beach without bathing suits and she had a point. I liked her life theory of decision making—choose the least embarrassing option—and so I asked him if we could quickly stop at a shop along the way. Yeah, it was no problem, he said. He would hold the baby while we ran in and grabbed something. It was just a little beach hut along the side of the road that catered to tourists. Aggie bought a white bathing suit in two pieces. There was a gold chain around the waist of the bottom piece with a little fake combination lock and the words *RICH BITCH* in shiny gold letters across the top. Mine was yellow with a big blue anchor on it.

When we got back to the cab Gustavo was talking to Ximena about his childhood. I heard him tell her that she would have to be strong as the daughter of a single mother. My life is hard to lead, he said, but in the end there is happiness. That to truly know happiness is to know the fleeting nature of everything, joy, pain, safety and happiness itself.

Ximena was lying on the front seat glaring at him like a female prisoner with her hands all balled up into fists but at least she was quiet, entranced by his voice. Aggie and I got back into the cab and Gustavo told all of us a story about how he used to be a mailman in Mérida and one day he had just lifted the lid off a mailbox to put the letters in it and a bird flew out and it scared him so much that he screamed and fell over backwards and down the stone steps of the house. He lost consciousness and when he woke up he was in the hospital and couldn't remember anything. It took him six weeks to get his memory back and when he went back to work they told him that his job had been given to somebody else. He became angry and then depressed, too depressed to look for another job, and then his wife became frustrated with their poverty and left him for another man and took their son with her. He never saw them again but his son sometimes visits him in dreams and sometimes Gustavo hears him whispering into his ear while he drives his taxicab around Acapulco.

Just one little bird, said Gustavo. Ximena looked at him suspiciously. I picked her up off the front seat and we drove to the beach where the real people go.

Aggie jumped around in the waves and I sat in the shade with Ximena who lay naked on her sunset towel, churning and shadowboxing. She never stopped moving. I took a peek at my body. Not good, I thought. I was so pale and bony. I looked like a skeleton in the sand. Like something only an archaeologist would be thrilled to get his hands on.

Gustavo had brought us mango juice and fish tacos that he got from a man in a *palapa*. They were friends. When he handed me the juice and tacos he told me I looked sad.

No, I said.

No? he said.

Estoy un poco triste, I said.

Gustavo smiled and nodded. He turned for a second to watch Aggie in the water and he waved and she waved back. Then he pointed at my stomach.

Nice anchor, he said.

Thank you, I said.

Do you know something? he said.

No, I said.

My wife and I used to come here when she was big and pregnant with our son. I dug a hole in the sand for her belly so she could lie on her stomach. It made her so happy. Our little son was incubated in the cool sands of Patricio Beach. When she lay there like that with her stomach in the hole nobody knew she was pregnant.

Then Gustavo prepared what he called his beach station. It was an elaborate performance and there were many steps involved. He set up his beach chair, the long kind you can recline on, by adjusting the back of it so that it was at a perfect angle. He left for a few minutes and returned with a little plastic table that he stuck in the sand next to his beach chair. He spread his towel over the chair so there were no wrinkles and it hung evenly over both sides. Then he left again and came back with another mango juice and some fish tacos and a newspaper which he carefully arranged on the little table. He adjusted his sunglasses.

He re-straightened his towel. He kissed his fingers and pointed them at the sky. He lay down on his chair and then spent a long time wrestling his newspaper into submission against the wind. He was quiet for a few seconds, reading. Then he decided to reach for his mango juice and as he did that something snapped and his beach chair collapsed and he knocked the little table over and dropped his newspaper which went flying off towards the water in several sections, entertainment, sports and crime.

I hadn't laughed in so long. I couldn't stop. I tried to. Ximena stopped wriggling and stared at me. Gustavo swore and turned around to look at me. One of the lenses in his sunglasses had popped out.

You did that on purpose, I said.

I did not! he said. Now I have to start again!

He went through the same process again and managed to maintain his position on the chair for a bit longer before another disaster struck. This time seagulls surrounded him and one even landed on his stomach and he called for help. But I had seen him deliberately put little pieces of fish taco all around his chair to attract them.

Help me! he said. I'm being attacked!

I loved Gustavo. If I'd been his wife I wouldn't have left him just because he was feeling depressed and not making any money. If I was his little son I'd be in the streets looking for him right now.

Why are you laughing at me? he said. My God! Help me!

————

It was time to go back to the airport. After Gustavo's performance he had offered to watch Ximena while Aggie and I jumped in the waves together, holding hands like little kids and shouting at each other over the wind like we used to do in the back of pickup trucks. Gustavo gave Ximena a bottle while Aggie and I changed out of our bathing suits behind some trees near the *palapa*.

Look at this, said Aggie.

What? I said.

She held up her hand and there was blood on her fingers. She curled her fingers to make a claw and made a feral animal sound.

Oh, I said. You've started. That's okay.

I don't have anything, she said. We have to stop again.

I was counting the money that was at the bottom of the plastic bag we used for all of Ximena's stuff.

I guess that's it for me, said Aggie.

You'll get used to it, I said. It's just a pain in the ass.

Goodbye childhood, said Aggie.

Take this and put it in your panties, I said. I handed her one of Ximena's diapers.

No! said Aggie.

Fine, then bleed all over, I said. We had a little fight then. I was trying to count and kept having to start again. I turned my back to Aggie to give her the option of using the diaper after all without me noticing. I made a point of counting out loud, slowly, while she figured it out.

One minute you're jumping in the sparkly waves for the first time in your life and completely *unable* to stop laughing and the next you're shedding the useless lining of your uterus and smearing messages in blood in porcelain bowls and sandy beaches. Words of shame like I'm sorry about this mess and the smell and I don't know why the hell I'm crying on such a beautiful summer day.

At the airport Gustavo held each of us close to his warm body, his beating heart, and told us that if we were ever in some part of Mexico, I can't remember now which part, we had to go to the lake of echoes and that anything we said would be cannonballed right back at us clear as day. If you say, for instance, the name of the person you love, then the world will say it back to you as though it is confirming that it understands.

You can yell anything, said Gustavo, and the world will confirm it. You could yell *Vive mucho tiempo el muerto!* Or you could yell *Esto es una locura!*

We will, I said. If we can find it.

Or you could yell *Chivas!* he said. *El Rebaño Sagrado!* That's my team.

What team? said Aggie.

Soccer, I said.

The sacred herd, said Gustavo. You haven't told me your names.

I know, I said. I'm sorry.

I understand, he said. I'm a cab driver. Nothing surprises me.

That's good, I said.

No, said Gustavo, it's a tragedy.

We said goodbye to Gustavo. But then he said wait a

minute and he ran to his cab and took something out of his glove compartment and ran back to us and handed me a tiny photocopied picture of a boy.

Is this your son? I said.

Yes, said Gustavo, it's Raoul Elisandro Lopez Mundo. He's nine years old. If you see a boy who looks like this please tell him to contact me, Gustavo, at the address printed on the back. He turned the paper over and pointed at the telephone number and address in Acapulco.

Where did you last see him? said Aggie.

At home, said Gustavo, in Mérida.

That's so far away, said Aggie. What's the population of Mexico? Now that she had bid farewell to her childhood and all of its impossible dreams she had suddenly become ruthlessly pragmatic. Gustavo and I shrugged.

Millions and millions, I said.

How will we find him? she said. And hasn't he changed since this picture was taken?

I know, said Gustavo, that's true. That's all true.

It would be a miracle if we found him, said Aggie.

Yes, said Gustavo.

Aggie put the photo into our plastic bag of random stuff and we stood on the curb outside the airport and waved goodbye again. Aggie made Ximena wave too, by waggling her arm around like a rag doll.

We all fell asleep on the plane to Mexico City. I was trying to stay awake long enough to make a mental list of the things that we needed. They were all simple things: food, shelter, clothing, money, school for Aggie, a job for me and a babysitter for Ximena. I had wanted to get my notebook out of the plastic bag but I couldn't reach it without waking up my sisters. Aggie's head was on my shoulder and Ximena was curled up in my lap with her arms around an empty bottle. I imagined Jorge and Wilson on either side of me, stroking my hands and agreeing to get along. We were all smiling. We'll live together as an unusual family, said Jorge. We'll have an apartment with big windows, said Wilson. Or a lighthouse with round rooms, said Jorge. The last thing I heard was the voice of an older woman who was sitting behind me and talking to a young man. Where is the art made from intense personal necessity? she said in Spanish. He answered her quietly, whispering, and I couldn't make out what he said.

When we landed the three of us moved dreamlike through the artificial world of the airport and then out and into the real world of Mexico City and for the first time in a million years it occurred to me that my chest wasn't hurting and it was as though I were experiencing a strange, foreign feeling like bliss or something which meant that either I had died in my sleep on the plane or I don't know what.

Where would you like to go? said the taxi driver at the airport.

Aggie and Ximena and I all looked at each other for a couple of seconds and then I said well, I guess the Zócalo?

The Zócalo? said the taxi driver. No, you don't want to go to the Zócalo now. There are thousands of people there protesting. It's a zoo. Total chaos.

I know, I said. I didn't know what else to say. It was the only place in Mexico City that I could name and that was only because Diego had been talking about it on that day when we were stuck in the field waiting for the right kind of rain.

I won't be able to drop you off at the Zócalo, said the taxi driver. Or even close to it. All the side streets coming off it are jam-packed too. It's not a good idea to go there.

I know, I said. That's okay. Just as close as you can get will be fine.

He shook his head and peered at us through the rear-view mirror. I smiled at him. He looked worried. I imagined myself reaching over the seat and moving my finger gently over the ridge of his furrowed brow the way Marijke had done to me on the day we met.

We drove down wide avenues and narrow streets and past a park where men were hanging upside down from ribbons and spinning around a very tall pole, it must have been two hundred feet up in the air. The ribbons were wrapped around their feet so their arms were free to stretch out like wings or to hold on to tiny horns and drums which they blew and banged on periodically while they spun upside down way above the earth.

What's that? said Aggie.

A tradition, said the taxi driver.

We turned around and peered up at the men from the back seat window until we couldn't see them anymore.

It's not going to work, said the taxi driver.

What won't work? said Aggie. Her braids had come undone and her hair was wild and twisted around her head like a sun corona. She was beautiful in a deranged way and I was relatively calm after my nap on the plane and Ximena was still very much alive and we had seen men flying serenely through the air and . . . well, that was enough.

Obrador won't accomplish anything with his tent city, he said. Calderón is official and it's done.

Ximena started to cry, this was bad news for her, and I made a bottle for her in the back seat with the last of the milk formula and the clean water. Aggie stuck her filthy finger into Ximena's mouth so she'd have something (toxic) to suck on while I made the bottle. She gently caressed the tips of Ximena's ears because Oveja had loved it and so why shouldn't a baby.

Are you here to sell cheese? said the taxi driver.

No, I said. I mean yes. Aggie looked at me and rolled her eyes and muttered a word in Low German that meant something like emperor with no clothes.

Where is it? said the taxi driver.

The cheese? I said. It's with somebody else.

The cheesemonger, said Aggie.

Right, I said. I asked Aggie in Low German if that was another ancient word she'd learned from her stone tablet textbooks and she smiled and said nothing.

We're meeting the cheesemonger in the Zócalo, I said.

He's next to the cobbler, said Aggie. Across from the haberdasher.

Really? said the taxi driver.

Okay, I said. No. We're not selling cheese.

I just thought you might be selling cheese, he said, because of the way you're dressed. I thought you were *vendequesos*.

Not all Mennonites sell cheese, I said.

Well, I know that must be true, he said.

We walked for blocks towards the Zócalo, taking turns carrying Ximena. It was loud. There were people everywhere. It was getting dark. We stopped at a *farmacia* along the way and bought more baby formula, bottled water, pads, toothpaste, toothbrushes, diapers, notebooks, pens, a package of three boy's sleepers (part of her disguise) and a primitive stacking toy for Ximena that Aggie insisted on buying even though I told her she was too young to appreciate it. Then we stopped in a clothing store and bought jeans, T-shirts and hooded sweatshirts for warmth *and* style, according to the clerk. Even so, we still looked like idiots. We looked at each other and laughed our heads off. We left the store self-consciously, a little shy, like astronauts stepping out onto the moon. Somebody will rescue us, I thought. Somebody will notice we're missing and come and find us and bring us back home and be so happy that they found us unharmed and healthy. That might not happen, was my next thought. Then the third and final thought in this dumb trilogy was: Well. Okay. There was more sub-thought to that one but essentially I had made a decision. There was a sidewalk kiosk that sold knives and strollers so we bought one of each of those for protection *and* comfort, although Ximena was too small really for a stroller so we used it for our stuff and I tied her tightly to my chest with my old dress, and kept on walking towards the Zócalo with ridiculous grins on our faces in spite of being almost completely broke now and having no discernible future.

EIGHT

THE THREE OF US STOOD IN AWE at the edge of the
Zócalo. I didn't know what to compare it to. Maybe a very
large field of corn, every stalk a human being, or a desert
night sky packed with stars, or a page in a notebook where
every available space is filled with ink, words, letters and
parts of letters.

C'mon, I said.

Where to? said Aggie.

Just follow me, I said.

What are we doing? she said.

I don't know, I said. Protesting.

Protesting what? she said.

I don't really know, I said.

It seems like we're just walking, said Aggie.

We sat down finally so that I could make another bottle for Ximena who had woken up starving and livid and with contempt for all she saw.

She's clawing out her eyes again, said Aggie.

Don't let her, I said.

Next to us was a group of young men and women banging on pots and pans and dancing and laughing and poking playfully at each other while they attempted to unravel some kind of banner with blood-red lettering. We stared at them. One of them yelled something incomprehensible into a bullhorn and the rest of them continued to dance around. Ximena was going nuts and Aggie was jiggling her a bit trying to calm her down while I prepared the bottle. The young men and women next to us started talking about the meaning of some English words.

The words *plangent* and *trenchant*, said one of the guys, they mean different things.

I've never heard of either one of them, said one of the girls. I think you're full of shit.

No, no, said the guy. One means incisive and one means sad or maybe reverberating but I just use them to mean HA HA.

The girl laughed again and Aggie and I looked at each other, confused. I thought the boy was in love with the girl. She mocked him and kissed him and laughed at him and jumped on his back. We continued staring. She reminded me of Katie and I wanted to say that to Aggie. I wanted to describe to her the way Katie rebelled, with jokes and smiles and affection and with some kind of tragically naive understanding that it would all be fine and even fun and definitely, ultimately, forgivable. But how do you talk about that?

Power was stolen in this case, said one of the guys.

Power is always stolen, said the girl. Again a huge grin on her face and kisses for everyone.

Here, feed her, I said to Aggie. I had finished making the bottle. I wanted to observe these people and make notes in my notebook.

No, you do it, said Aggie. I don't want her to throw up on me.

Use my old dress as a shield, I said.

No! I'm not gonna sit here draped in that ugly thing, she said. I'm going to look at stuff.

She started to walk away and I told her not to wander too far and to come back in twenty minutes. She waggled her ass at me. She didn't look back. She looked like a normal girl in those jeans and sweatshirt. I watched her walk in the direction of the National Palace, the place the seven Mennonite men came to a long time ago with grim hopes of making a land deal. I imagined her going in and saying hey! El Presidente! Time for a new deal! I fed Ximena. We looked deeply into each other's eyes while she drank. I liked the heavy, warm weight of her in my arms. I kissed her forehead and the motion made her lose her grip on the nipple and she craned her head around to my breast, her mouth open and searching for the thing she'd lost.

The jokey girl came over and sat down beside me. The boys were kicking a tiny beanbag or something around in a circle trying to keep it from falling to the ground. The girl told me she had noticed the three of us and was wondering where we came from. I was going to say Canada, but I said Chihuahua, the truth. She asked me if we had come to Mexico City for the protest and I said no, not exactly.

Are you tourists? she said.

No, not really, I said.

Have you been to Mexico City before? she said.

No.

There's a ruined temple beneath us, she said.

There is? I said.

It was once used for Aztec worship and human sacrifice, she said. She stroked Ximena's cheek with the side of her finger and made the sound we use to ward off rattlesnakes in the desert. Ximena stopped sucking on the bottle and stared at her.

Spanish conquistadors used bricks from the temple to help build their own capital, she said.

I nodded and smiled. They were like that, she said. Can I hold her?

Of course! I said. I handed Ximena over to the girl. I pointed at the enormous Mexican flag in the centre of the Zócalo.

I've never seen a flag that big before, I said.

Me neither, said the girl. She sang a Spanish song to Ximena who was eerily quiet and a little dumbstruck. Her tiny mouth was wide open like she'd forgotten there wasn't a nipple still inside it and she seemed unable to blink.

What's your name? I asked the girl.

Noehmi, said the girl. What's yours?

Irma Voth, I said. She's Ximena. And my sister Aggie is here somewhere.

Cool, said the girl.

Noehmi is showing Ximena to her friends. They're all crowded around her. They're taking turns holding her. Aggie hasn't come back from looking at stuff yet. When I took out my notebook Noehmi asked me if I was a reporter and I didn't know what to say so I smiled. So, you are? she said. No, I said. I don't think so. But you're writing things down in a notebook, she said. Why? I told her I wasn't sure. I told her I was making lists of the things I needed to do. Then I put the notebook away into the pocket of my new hoodie because I was embarrassed. Then, when Noehmi started to show Ximena around to her friends, I took it out again. I love my new notebook. I love the sound my new pen makes on the paper and the thickness of the pages. It terrifies me. There's so much to write about but I don't know where to start. I miss my mother. I wish I had something nerve-shattering to say. If trenchant and plangent mean HA HA then what's the point of any word? Just begin, I think. I have to find Aggie now.

We'll watch her, said Noehmi.

Are you sure? I said. She's extremely violent.

Absolutely! said Noehmi. We'll be right here. We're not going anywhere until there's a recount and Obrador wins. This is a peaceful protest, so Ximena will learn passive resistance from us.

I made another bottle for Ximena and gave it to Noehmi, just in case.

Can I ask you a quick question before you go? said Noehmi.

Sure, I said.

What was that language you were speaking with your sister? said Noehmi.

It's called Plattdeutsch, I said. It's like German, I guess. And we sometimes speak English and sometimes Spanish.

It sounds medieval to me, said Noehmi.

Yeah, I guess, I said.

What's your favourite? said Noehmi.

I don't know, I said.

English? said Noehmi.

I like it but Aggie doesn't know it very well.

What language do you dream in? said Noehmi.

English and Spanish, I said. Never Plattdeutsch.

Maybe that's because English and Spanish were the languages you learned secretly when you weren't supposed to, said Noehmi.

Is that what dreams are? I said.

I don't know, said Noehmi. She laughed. Nobody knows. Have you heard of lucid dreaming?

No, I said.

I'm reading this book called . . . *And Other Problems in Waking Life*, she said.

Other problems besides what? I said.

Sadness, loneliness, anxiety, depression, fear, despair, numbness, alienation, anger, heartbreak, she said.

Are there more? I said.

Maybe, she said.

Oh no, I said. And then, for some reason, I began to ramble on about languages, this torrential speech that had maybe been gestating inside of me for an unnaturally long time. I think Spanish is my favourite, I said. I told her that I had been born in Canada and started off speaking Plattdeutsch and then I went to school and learned English and loved it and never spoke Plattdeutsch if I could help it except with my dad who insisted on it. I told her that after school, if my dad was out, I'd teach my mom English words like *hula hoop* and *keep on trucking*. I told her I had a sister, Katie, and that we had whispered together all night long in English like other kids sneak smokes. I told her that when I was thirteen we moved to Mexico, to Chihuahua, and I started to learn Spanish even though my father had disapproved of that too.

Why? said Noehmi.

Girls weren't supposed to, I said.

Why? said Noehmi.

I don't know, I said. The usual reasons.

And then I told her that I was married to a Mexican guy and she said you are not!

I am, I said. But he left me.

And that's why you came to Mexico City? she said.

Sort of, I said. Noehmi looked closely at Ximena.

She doesn't look very Mexican, she said. But I guess she took after you. Do you share custody with your husband?

No, I said.

He doesn't want to see his kid? she said.

Well . . . actually, I said, Ximena isn't his kid.

Ahhh, said Noehmi. She smiled. She nodded her head as the universe revealed itself.

No, it's not that, I said. She's not my kid, either. She's my sister.

Really? said Noehmi. Why do you have her?

I don't know, I said.

Did your parents die? said Noehmi.

No, I said. I was beginning to understand something I couldn't articulate. It was a jazzy feeling in my chest, a fluttering, a kind of buzzing in my brain. Warmth. Life. The circulation of blood. Sanguinity. I don't know. I understood the enormous risk of telling the truth, how the telling could result in every level of hell reigning down on you, your skin scorched to the bone and then bone to ash and then nothing but a lingering odour of shame and decomposition, but now I was also beginning to understand the new and alien feeling of taking the risk and having the person on the other end of the telling, the listener, say:

Bad shit at home? You guys are running away?

Yeah, I said.

I understand, said Noehmi.

———

I wandered around the Zócalo looking for Aggie. I was a little nervous and also a bit relieved about the three of us being separated for the first time since our exodus. My arms were sore from holding Ximena and carrying stuff and I tried to drop my shoulders and shake out my stiffness and appear somewhat confident. I scanned the crowd but no Aggie. I headed towards the National Palace. It took me quite a long time to get to it because I had to meander around clumps of people and food stands and dancers and noisemakers and kids playing and mothers nursing babies and teenagers smoking cigarettes and old men and dogs and laughing families and praying nuns and choirs and pigeons and tarps and giant banners and unicycles and gladiators and boxers and soccer players. I saw a guy who looked exactly like Jorge and I stopped dead in my tracks, as they say, and panicked a little. It wasn't him and I didn't know if that made me feel happy or sad. Eventually it started to rain, gently at first and then hard. It felt good. People took out pieces of cardboard and garbage bags to protect themselves. I finally made it to the National Palace and went inside and there was Aggie staring at a massive mural. She was crying. I walked over to her and put my arm around her shoulders.

What's wrong, Aggie? I whispered.

She shook her head.

Are you afraid? I said.

No, she said.

I didn't know what to say or how to make her stop crying. I hugged her. I had forgotten how skinny she was.

Look at that, said Aggie.

The picture? I said.

It's called *México a través de los siglos,* she said.

It's making you sad? I said.

No, she said. Her face was covered in snot and she spoke in the spaces between her sobs.

I didn't know that a grown-up could do that, she said. She pointed at the mural. I didn't know that a person could do that.

I stared at it with her. She was in some kind of trance. Finally she asked me where Ximena was and I told her about Noehmi and that we should probably get back to her. If I had known more about anything I might have pointed out how Diego Rivera was asking all Mexicans to look squarely at the history of their lives, at the beauty and the misery and the pain and the struggle and the wreckage created by that profligate Cortés. I could have added too that Diego Rivera was completing his mural around the time the seven Mennonite men came to the palace to ask for the land in Chihuahua, now the scabby homeland of Aggie, Ximena and Pancho Villa, and how Mennonites always choose to live in places nobody else wants to.

Can we come back? said Aggie.

Of course! I said. As often as you like.

We snaked our way through the crowd and found Noehmi huddled under a lean-to made of garbage bags and using a flashlight to read her book . . . *And Other Problems in Waking Life.* Ximena was fast asleep under Noehmi's baggy sweater. Noehmi rested her chin on Ximena's head while she read.

There were fireworks going off in the rain. People were banging on pots again and there was sporadic shouting coming from all over the square. We crawled under the lean-to and sat down next to Noehmi and Ximena.

How was she? I said.

Perfection, said Noehmi.

Did she cry a lot? I said.

No, said Noehmi, hardly at all. I sang Jonathan Richman songs to her.

Who's that? said Aggie.

My hero, said Noehmi. He's old, like sixty or something, and he still loves the world and when you listen to his music he makes you love it too.

A guy walked past and said something about a blow job to Noehmi.

Go fuck yourself with Hitler's dick, said Noehmi happily. Are you guys hungry?

Noehmi's friends weren't there at that moment but they had cooked up some kind of meat with onions and peppers on a small barbecue they'd brought with them to the square. There are tortillas in that basket over there, she said.

While Aggie and I ate, Noehmi sang Jonathan Richman songs to all of us. We chewed and smiled and Aggie clapped.

Where did your friends go? said Aggie.

To get a camera, said Noehmi. They want to make a documentary about the protest.

Where are they going to get a camera? I asked.

I don't know, said Noehmi. They'll probably get side-tracked along the way. Or they'll come back with paint instead, or beer, or some new idea for a circus or something. They're social anarchists.

Oh, I said. I looked away. I scratched my arm and racked my brain for a fluid response and then quickly prepared some food.

Aggie and Noehmi were sleeping with Ximena between them on the tarp beside me. I tore a strip of material off my old dress and tied one end of it to Ximena's tiny wrist and the other end to Aggie's. When I lie down, I thought, I'll tie another strip of the dress from my wrist to Ximena's other wrist. And maybe one to Noehmi. I hope I don't wake her up. For a few seconds I thought about my little brothers who loved connecting things with rope. I wondered if I'd ever see them again and a torpedo of sadness struck me and moved straight through my body. Steady on, I said to myself. Earlier, right after the blow job incident, a man offered to buy Ximena, and Aggie pulled a knife on him, the new one that we bought earlier in the day. Noehmi's friends were called Alexis, Guillen, Dupont and Ernie. They're wasted, Noehmi told me. They were very nice and would die for her if she asked them to.

What do you mean wasted? I asked her. She said they were on another plane. She read something out loud to me from her book: *Katherine compared the energy of trauma to a cobalt bomb with a radioactive half-life of one hundred years.* I asked her what that meant and she said she didn't know exactly but that she loved the way it sounded. She thought maybe it meant that every trauma presents a choice: paralysis or the psychic energy to move forward.

Hmmm, perhaps, said Aggie, stroking her chin. I told her in Low German not to make fun of people who were more enlightened than her. She told me she was bored with shitball trauma talk and wanted to see more pictures. I told her to go to sleep and dream some up and she told me those were only words. But she did go to sleep, finally, thank God. After that Noehmi told me about her life. She told me that one year ago she broke up with her boyfriend and life became a nightmare. Her boyfriend was heartbroken. He tried to prevent her from leaving the apartment they shared and he drank non-stop all day and night. When she finally left to go and stay with her sister he somehow hacked into her emails. He suspected that she was seeing someone else and he tried to kill himself with booze and pills. All that stuff, she said. That crazy stuff. But it was desperate behaviour, she said. He had lost something he loved. There's no dignity in that. How can there be? He was a wild animal, she said. She told me that she still loved him.

Where is he now? I asked her. She pointed at Guillen and said right there. He's not my boyfriend anymore, she said. Dupont is. But Guillen has a different girlfriend. She said they were all friends. It was madness. It was awful. But that's normal. And now it's better.

I'm not sure what Noehmi's friends came back with, no camera anyway, none that I'd seen, but they were outside the lean-to singing now and playing drums in a circle. Other protesters were dancing around to their music and the rain had stopped and the air smelled clean. My desert friends, the stars, were invisible above the bright lights of the city.

———

In the middle of the night I untied myself from Aggie and Ximena and got up to find a pay phone. My fists were clenched when I woke up, ready to milk cows or kill kidnappers. Aggie was moaning in her sleep again like she was haunted. Dupont was sleeping next to Noehmi with his arm around her waist and the other boys were gone. The drums were piled neatly in a corner underneath the tarp. I had never used a pay phone before and I only knew one person with a phone. I put my coin in the slot and it fell into a little tray at the bottom. I did this over and over, like an idiot. An old woman walking past noticed that I was having trouble and helped me out. I thanked her and she held my face in her hands and squeezed. I tried to smile and she kissed me on both cheeks. I dialed Jorge's number and a man answered but it wasn't Jorge so I hung up. I didn't know what I would say to him anyway. I checked to see if my coin would come back to me. No. Well, I thought, now I know how a pay phone works. I didn't want to let go of the phone right away. I held it to my ear and pretended to have a conversation. I wondered if I was going crazy.

A guy with tattoos all over his body came and stood beside me, staring at the ground, waiting. I told my imaginary husband that I loved him and said goodbye. The man waiting for the phone had the name Esther tattooed across his throat.

It's all yours, I said, and he said thanks, I didn't mean to rush you. I started to walk away and the man said excuse me, but are you Irma Voth? My heart leapt into my throat and I whirled around to face him. How could this dark stranger possibly know my name?

That didn't happen.

I started to walk away and the man said excuse me, you forgot your bag.

Thanks, I said. I took the tattered *farmacia* bag from him.

Are you here alone? he said.

Yes, I said. Well, no, not alone.

You are or you aren't? said the man.

I'm not, I said.

That's good, he said, because it's dangerous for a woman to be on her own in Mexico City. Especially a tourist like yourself.

I'm not a tourist, I said.

You're from here? he said.

North of here, I said. But in Mexico.

I once lived just north of the border, he said. In El Paso.

I nodded and told him I'd been to El Paso a bunch of times.

I lived there with this woman, he said. He pointed to his throat.

Esther, I said.

Yes, he said. Esther. She's in Houston now.

He told me that he and Esther had managed to cross the border into Texas by paying off a guard and that they had made their way to El Paso where they both got jobs in a restaurant working under the table. Esther started to like one of the cooks and eventually she ran off with him and married him and even had a kid with him. The tattooed guy parked his car in front of Esther's new house and spied on

her. He cried in his car and tried to get her to love him
again by leaving gifts outside her door. Finally the guy she
had married got fed up and called the immigration people
and told them that this guy, the tattooed guy, was in
America illegally and they kicked him out of the country,
back to Mexico.

Now you're stuck with the tattoo, I said.

Yeah, he said, at first I wanted to have it removed but
that costs a lot of money. I tried to turn it into a different
word but I couldn't think of one.

In English you could have it say Rest Here, I said.

It's okay, he said. Now I'm happy to see the name
Esther on my throat every day.

Because you have good memories? I said.

No, he said, because it reminds me of this treacherous
world. If I'm ever foolish enough again to trust a woman I'll
look at myself in the mirror and see her name and I won't
make another mistake.

But it'll be backwards when you look in the mirror,
I said.

It doesn't matter what it is, he said. I see the ink, I feel
the pain of the needle pricking my throat, I see tiny bubbles
of blood, and I'm reminded of the day I pledged my love
to her.

There you go, I said. I'm Irma Voth. Pleased to meet
you.

I'm Jeronimo Galvez Paz, he said. Likewise.

We shook hands and said goodbye.

———

When I got back to the tarp Aggie and Ximena were gone. I woke up Noehmi and Dupont and asked them if they knew where my sisters were and they said no, they hadn't noticed them leave. I stood next to Noehmi and Dupont, who were rubbing their eyes and clearing their throats, and looked in every direction for as far as I could see. It was dark so I saw very little.

We'll help you find them, said Noehmi. She told Dupont to get up and find his flashlight.

Do you have a flashlight? I asked him.

No, said Dupont. She always expects little miracles of me.

Let's go, man, said Noehmi. Why is this ribbon tied around my wrist?

But then she forgets about them, he said.

Noehmi and Dupont walked off in one direction, it might have been east, and I went north, or maybe south. The point is we split up and began our search. I could tell you all the things I was feeling but there is one picture that sums it up and that's the one of that skinny guy running across a bridge holding his face and being chased by a mushroom cloud. My sister Katie had that picture tacked to her bedroom wall and she liked to make word bubbles for the skinny man that had to do with reasons for his panic. One day she ripped it off her wall and stuffed it into her garbage can. She said it was ubiquitous.

It's really true that a person can become rigid with fear. I felt my limbs stiffen as I walked across the Zócalo calling out Aggie's name and imagining one horror after another, each scenario worse than the one before it. I prayed. I made a deal with God, wondering how I could have prevented all of this from happening, and hating myself. I punched myself in the side of my head. Think, Irma, I said. I stopped walking and stood still in the centre of the Zócalo and all of the protesters, sleeping and awake. I scanned the crowd, looking for one white-blond head that would pop out of the darkness like a piece of toast. Okay, I said to myself, how can this even be happening? How can I have lost all of my sisters? This is without a doubt the shittiest moment in the history of my life. Then the words *history of my life* started to carve some kind of repetitive groove in my brain. I touched the space between my eyes, the source of light, my internal . . . whatever. What had Marijke told me? The history of my life, I said. The source of my internal . . . light. This was stupid. And then I knew.

I ran towards the National Palace at the far end of the Zócalo and found Aggie leaning against the door, asleep, with Ximena in her arms. I woke her up and hugged them both. Aggie hugged me back. We stayed that way for a long time. And then I asked her when the doors opened and Aggie said she didn't know but if we waited there we'd be the first ones in when they did open.

I didn't know where you were, said Aggie. I woke up and you were gone. I freaked out.

I'm sorry, I said.

Where did you go? she said.

I went to find a phone, I said.

Why? said Aggie. Who would you call?

I didn't call anybody, I said.

Here, said Aggie, can you hold her? My arms are killing me.

I took Ximena and stuffed her inside my sweatshirt. I rubbed her back a bit and hoped she wouldn't wake up for a while. I needed to sleep.

A couple of hours later the doors to the National Palace opened up and Aggie went inside so that she could stare at her mural. I had managed to find Noehmi and Dupont in the meantime to tell them they could stop looking and we had agreed to have breakfast together on the tarp when Aggie was finished looking at art. I waited outside with Ximena and gave her a bottle. We sat in the sunshine and she looked at me while she drank and I scanned the crowds and looked at her every once in a while too and smiled and told her she was holding up well. Are you a little lamb? I asked her. I tried to shield her eyes from the sun. Are you a warrior? I said. I told her I'd find us a real home that day. Somewhere, you know, out there. In the city. This one. It feels good to make plans with a baby. They seem a little more flexible than the plans we make with people who remember making them.

We all ate a delicious breakfast of eggs and peppers and avocados together in the sunshine on the tarp. Another day of protest had arrived, we had survived the night, and it was time for the three of us to get organized.

Where do you want to go? said Noehmi.

I don't know exactly, I said.

What kind of job would you like to have?

I'm not sure, I said. Anything, I guess.

Do you have enough money for one month's rent? said Noehmi.

I'm not sure, I said. We ate our eggs and I silently critiqued my organizational skills. There were lists that I needed to make.

Do you have a job? I asked Noehmi.

We're students, said Noehmi. Most of us still live with our parents.

What are you students of? I said.

Art, said Noehmi. Politics. History. Cinematography. Dupont is studying madness in film.

Me and Irma work in the movie industry, said Aggie.

We do not *work* in the movie industry, I said. We helped out on one movie in Chihuahua.

What movie? said Dupont.

I think it's going to be called *Campo Siete*, I said.

Who's making it? said Dupont.

Diego Nolasco, I said.

Dupont stopped chewing and looked at me. Really? he said.

Yeah, I said. Do you know him?

Are you serious? said Dupont. You were working for Diego Nolasco?

Yeah, I said. Just as a translator.

I helped carry things, said Aggie.

After that Dupont talked for a long time about Diego's other movies and Aggie and I explained how it was that we had worked for him and Dupont found it all kind of hard to believe but I think we finally convinced him that it was true. Dupont said he sort of knew someone from his university who almost got a job working for Diego and I asked him if that person's name was Wilson and he said no, it was Roberto. He wanted to know if we were still in touch with Diego and I said no, it had ended a bit awkwardly. He's a genius, said Dupont. Yes, I said. Noehmi gave us the address of her sister's husband's brother who owns a bed and breakfast in Condesa, a different part of Mexico City with a huge park in the centre of it. You could ask him for a job, she said. She said she'd call him and ask him too. You'd be perfect because you can speak English to the tourists and you'd probably be able to carry Ximena around with you while you clean rooms or whatever.

We'll come and visit you, said Noehmi. She gave me another piece of paper with her phone number and address. She lived in a place called Tacubaya, not far from Condesa. She had drawn a picture next to her address for Aggie. It was of the National Palace with me, Ximena and herself standing in front of it. Where's Aggie? she had written in a word bubble coming from my mouth. In there! she had written in another word bubble coming from her mouth.

She said she wanted me to have her copy of . . . *And Other Problems in Waking Life*. But you haven't finished reading it yet, I said. She said I could read it in the meantime and she'd start reading another book called *The Outsider*, which was written by a Frenchman named Albert Camus. He died in a car crash, she said. And the novel he was working on went flying all over the road.

Do you know *Nausea*? she asked me.

Well, I said.

Jean-Paul Sartre? she said.

No, I said.

He was married to Simone de Beauvoir? she said. I'll bet you've heard of her.

No, I said.

Well, said Noehmi, she was this really intense woman. She had a passionate affair with an American writer named Nelson Algren. He's one of my favourite writers. He was mostly a recluse and then one day he decided he should smarten up and celebrate something and he decided to have a party at his place but just before the guests were due to arrive he fell down dead in his house.

Oh no, I said.

It's perfect, she said. But that was long after he had an affair with Simone de Beauvoir. She had fun fooling around with him in America but then she went back to Sartre who treated her like shit. And yet, she said, somehow she managed to inspire women to be free. I was nodding. Isn't that ironic? she said.

Yes, I said. It really is.

One of my favourite books from when I was a young teenager is by Antoine de Saint-Exupéry, said Noehmi. It's called *Wind, Sand and Stars*. I'll get it for you, Aggie. It changed my perception of the world. Aggie and I thanked her and Dupont a million times for their friendship and they said we would meet again, soon, maybe after exams, but that we should call any time if we needed anything.

NINE

DIOS CON NOSOTROS? said Aggie.

Yeah, I said.

So what? she said.

Just that, I said. I don't want to fight about it.

We were sitting on a bench in the park in the centre of Condesa. Ximena was lying naked in the sunshine airing out. I had just given her a bottle and she was making little squeaking sounds. Lots of dogs were running around and there were some guys trying to teach them new things. They wanted the dogs to stand still and not run until they'd been given a signal but the dogs just ran whenever they felt like it. Some of the guys yelled at their dogs and smacked them and some of the guys were very patient and sighed discreetly.

I miss Oveja, said Aggie. We were waiting for Noehmi's sister's husband's brother to return to work from his lunch break. His name was Hubertus. We were tired and hungry, the usual problems of waking life. I gave Aggie some money and sent her off to buy some tacos and juice from a stand nearby. Different types of people walked past me and I stared at them and tried to hear what they were saying to each other. I heard one woman gently tease her boyfriend about his pants. They were too short. But honey, she said, I understand. You can't worry about the mathematical permutations of the ringing of the church bells *and* the length of your pants at the same time. It's true, said the guy, something had to give. Then she laughed and they disappeared like dreams. An English-speaking couple walked past me and all I heard was: the quote artistic community close quotes . . . I watched them fade into the distance also. I took out my notebook to write some of these things down. I didn't know what these fragments meant. I wanted to talk like them. I wanted to talk like other people. And then Aggie came back with the tacos and we ate together sitting on the bench with Ximena lying between us. Aggie passed me a taco and some of the stuff fell onto Ximena's bare stomach and she pursed her lips like she wanted to kiss someone but her eyes were panicky and Aggie quickly licked it off her stomach before it could burn her.

Good hustle, I said.

What? she said.

That's what my old volleyball coach in Canada used to say after a good dig.

What? said Aggie.

That's what my old volleyball coach in Canada used to say after a good dig.

What are you—

I said that's what my old volleyball coach in Canada used to say after a good dig!

Yeah, but—

Just never mind, I said.

We waited. We watched people and didn't speak. Little bugs landed on Ximena and I blew them away. Then I asked Aggie what she was thinking about. She didn't answer. I asked her again and she folded her arms across her chest and stared at something way off in the distance. Home? I said. She didn't speak. I bet you're missing that kid, Isaac, that boy with the blood disease. Didn't you tell me that if he cut himself he'd bleed to death? Ximena wriggled in the sunshine and Aggie kept her mouth shut. That's why you had a crush on him, right? I said. Because every little thing he did was like risking his life? I got a diaper out of the *farmacia* bag and put it on Ximena before she peed all over the bench. Aggie's eyes were closed. Isn't that what you said about him? Aggie?

Didn't he let you wear his MedicAlert bracelet for a couple of days?

Nothing, she said.

What's nothing? I said.

You asked me what I was thinking about, she said. Stop talking to me. We waited some more. I thought about ways to cheer her up. Finally I saw Hubertus walking up the sidewalk and jingling a set of keys. He unlocked the front gate of the bed and breakfast. I told Aggie to watch Ximena and stay exactly where she was.

Seriously, Aggie, please, I said. I understand that your opinion of my words is that they are just words, and in so many ways but not in every way you are absolutely correct. I understand precisely how you would enjoy wielding your power in this situation by saying fuck that, fuck Irma and her bossiness, fuck this obedient little sister business, fuck all these cheesy little rules and regulations and getting up and wandering off and making me crazy with worry but I'm begging you now, like I have before, and like I will again, to stay put, to stay out of trouble and to not get lost. Your safety means everything to me, Aggie. Nothing is as important to me as your safety. Nothing. Please. I love you more than anything in this world, Aggie, and I can't bear to lose you. I just can't. The world would end. My world would end. Aggie, I'm begging you.

My words aren't only words. They're pictures and tears and imperfect offerings of love and self-inflicted shots to my brain. Please? Will you steadfastly remain on this very bench and not sell Ximena or in any way jeopardize your safety or hers? Will you promise to pull your knife on anyone wishing to mess with you or purchase your sister? Yes or no.

Tiny movements at the corners of Aggie's mouth. She was an Olympian in self-control.

Aggie, I said. This is so important. I'm going now to find myself a job. This job, which I will find, will ensure that you and I have food to eat and a roof to protect us from the rain and the sun and walls to keep away bugs and kidnappers. If I don't go right now I'll miss my chance and all our hopes will die in the street and the rain will wash them into the gutter and then down into the sewer and then out into the ocean miles and miles and miles beneath the surface where there is not enough oxygen to spend any time retrieving them. They will be gone for—

Will you just go already? said Aggie. You could have had a job by now and already been paid like twice.

Okay, but will you? I said.

Will I what? she said.

Stay right here and don't move?

Maybe, said Aggie.

Aggie! I said. For—

Yes! she said. Irma. God. Go already. You're like Tante Greita.

Tante Greita was the name we'd given to our slowest cow, the one we loved the most but that needed to be smacked on the ass a lot.

Okay, but will you tie her to your body? I said.

Ximena? said Aggie.

Just in case you fall asleep or something, I said.

Aggie didn't say anything. She got my old dress out of the *farmacia* bag and draped it around her shoulders. Then she picked up Ximena and held her to her chest with one hand and expertly wrapped the two ends of the dress around Ximena with her other hand. I smiled and thanked her and she nodded once, very dignified. Ximena's head was up high, close to Aggie's, and they were both looking off towards the park. I walked off towards the bed and breakfast and turned around to look at them. From a distance they looked like a two-headed monster. I waved, not expecting Aggie to notice, but she waved back. She was watching me too and my heart was overwhelmed with love.

Irma Voth, I said.

And you've just moved to Mexico City? said Hubertus. We had already established that it was because of Noehmi that I was there asking him for a job. We were sitting at a wrought iron table in a little courtyard belonging to the bed and breakfast. White curtains billowed out of open windows all around us and it felt like we were on a tall ship. There were bunches of flowers everywhere, white lilies that appeared to be opening as we spoke, and a few small trees and a thick green hose that snaked around and almost tripped me. My first instinct was to slice it in half with a machete. There was a narrow cement staircase that led up to a room with a red door and a balcony. I wanted to live there, in that room. A woman in high heels walked around sweeping up petals and two older men spoke German to each other in a corner. One of them told the other that to his knowledge there was no word for kindness in the German language and the other man laughed loudly and banged his hand on the table.

Yes, I said. My sister and I are here to study.

Study what? said Hubertus.

Art, I said.

Art, said Hubertus. He nodded slowly and smiled. I heard my father whispering in my ear. Art is a lie, he said. I smiled nervously back at Hubertus and braced myself. I felt my mother moving her hand in a slow circle around my back the way the earth orbits the sun. Love is not selfish, she said. When life is a shit storm your best umbrella is art, said Hubertus. He laughed. I heard that in a movie or something, he said. I'm sorry.

That's pretty funny, I said. I tried to laugh.

Have you seen any good movies lately? he said.

I've never seen a movie, I said. But I worked on one recently.

Well, he said. Whatever. So you're interested in working here in La Condesa. Where do you live?

We don't have a place yet, I said.

And your school?

After I've found a job and an apartment I'll start to look for schools, I said.

Would you like a cup of coffee? said Hubertus. That's a start. First things first. He laughed again and apologized. He asked the woman in high heels if she would mind bringing us two cups of coffee and when she came back she put her arms around his head and kissed the top of it and said not at all, *cachondo*, cream and sugar? And Hubertus closed his eyes and said *sí, baby, eres muy simpática*. The woman's name was Natalie.

This is Irma, said Hubertus. She and her sister are here in Mexico City to study art.

Ah, said Natalie. Lovely! You've come to the right place. Will you be focusing on a particular medium?

Yes, I said. Things began to happen to me, then, involuntarily. My foot began to tap the ground and my throat made a crude noise.

Yes? said Natalie. Do you mind me asking what it is?

I was silent, waiting for the world to end. I smiled and looked at her and she smiled back at me, kindly, with pity or patience or amusement or disbelief that this cave woman had managed to teleport herself into the future straight into her and Hubertus' courtyard.

Well, she said. It's not an easy thing to articulate, is it? I understand.

Thanks, I said.

But I'm fascinated with artists, she said. I love reading about their lives. You know how they say that so many artists are melancholic?

I nodded, clueless, and sipped my coffee.

Apparently, said Natalie, the part of the brain that can obsess over dark things like death and pain and nothingness, which is depression more or less, is the same part of the brain that allows a person to obsess over the infinite challenges of art which produces something like stamina. I don't know. Or focus. The focus required to complete one long query. Am I making sense?

Hubertus started laughing again and questioned her use of the word *query*, suggesting that *project* might be a better one, and I said yes. Natalie started laughing then too, and told me not to take things so seriously. If I'm not making sense, she said, then I'm not making sense. So what?

We drank our coffee and talked a little bit more about practical things. Natalie came over and asked me if I knew what the trees were called. I said no. She told me they were jacarandas. She said that one March two years ago she was feeling suicidal. She had planned to step in front of a bus. Then she looked at the jacaranda tree and changed her mind.

You decided to hang yourself from it instead? I said.

No! said Natalie. It was the exquisite patience of the tree. She described the way the jacaranda tree waited and waited and waited, barren, ignored, unexceptional, until a certain day in spring when it would erupt joyfully and comically into life. Purple flowers everywhere! she said. Small children are lost every spring, hidden in the purple flowers, cars crash into cars because they can't see anything but purple flowers, people plunge fully dressed into ponds because the water is carpeted with purple flowers and invisible! If the tree could wait all year for a relatively brief moment of beauty, said Natalie, and continue to stay alive for centuries, then so could I.

You'll stay alive for centuries? I said.

I'll stay alive, said Natalie. I'm a pupil of the jacaranda tree. It has taught me that it's okay to lay low most of the time, to nest in the shadows . . . and then . . . explode!

Hubertus laughed and laughed. Shit goes DOWN! he said. Natalie smacked him on the head and then she picked up the green garden hose and wrapped it around his neck while she kissed him and he pretended to die.

At the end of this encounter I had a job as a maid. I hadn't managed to work the existence of Ximena into the equation.

I didn't want to ruin my chance at employment by insisting that while on the job I carry a misanthropic infant around on my back. Maybe she could appear on the scene like a jacaranda tree, out of nowhere, and she would inspire Natalie to live.

I walked out onto the street and heard the whistles of the knife sharpeners and the cries of gas and water men. I wondered if in Mexico City it worked the other way around too so that I could walk up and down the streets shouting out the names of things I needed as opposed to the names of things I had for sale.

Aggie and Ximena weren't on the bench. At first I thought maybe I had gone to the wrong bench but I saw taco filling all over it and little bugs eating it so I knew it was the right one. I wondered why it happened so often in life that just as you secured one corner of the tent another one would flap loose in the wind. I stared at the little bugs and tried to think. A one-man trumpet, tambourine and drum band walked past me. I know, I thought, we have to do everything ourselves if we want it to get done. I told myself to inhabit the mind and body of Aggie. I'm Aggie, I said. I'm sitting on the bench bored to death, restless as hell and poised to bolt. Where do I go? I saw a large statue, a sculpture of a woman, and I walked towards it. It was a buxom nude holding two jugs of spouting water. I stood next to her and looked around for Aggie and Ximena. In Chihuahua I couldn't shake Aggie and in Mexico City I couldn't keep her from taking off. I kept walking. A guy sat on the ground with books spread all around him. I stopped and stared at them.

Hay algún libro de Simone de Beauvoir? I said.

No, no tenemos, he said.

Me puede recomendar algún libro? I said.

Sí, he said. *Te gusta . . . ?*

No sé, I said.

Que tipo de libros lees? he said.

No sé, I said.

Has leído Nuestra arma es nuestra palabra?

I had bought my first book. *Our Word is Our Weapon.* Selected writings of Subcomandante Insurgente Marcos. Actually I hadn't paid for it because Aggie had the *farmacia* bag with Ximena's stuff and all our money but the guy sitting on the ground told me I could have it for nothing if I came back and bought something another time.

Will you? he said.

Yes, I said.

I remembered a similar conversation I'd had with Wilson when he told me that he was going to Mexico City to deliver the film reels and keep them safe from my father. I wondered what he said when he got back to Chihuahua and Diego told him that I had left. Maybe: Drat. Or maybe he hadn't said a word. Maybe he'd written a little story about me in his notebook that he would read someday at the festival in Guadalajara. I'd be there, somehow, in a wonderful outfit, standing in the darkness of the crowd, and I'd hear him speaking through the microphone. I wouldn't be able to see him because of very tall people in front of me but I'd hear my name and

I'd follow his impassioned voice towards him, towards the light.

I smiled at the bookseller. I held up my book and said thanks again and he saluted me and called me comrade. I found Aggie dancing by a pond. She was in a class of people learning how to tango. Ximena was tied to her chest and Aggie had never danced in her life so her movements were a little awkward but she was concentrating hard on keeping up with the instructor. The other students had partners but Aggie's was imaginary. She flung her head back and thrust her chest with Ximena on it out towards the water and strutted across the grass. Her arm shot up and then she brought the back of her hand down and swept it across her eyes tragically as if to erase all the horror and misery she'd seen.

Excellent! Excellent! the instructor said.

The music stopped and Aggie looked around and grinned at a few of her fellow students. The class was over. I walked up to her and said hello and she said oh, sorry, you're done already? I was just on my way back to the bench. Did you get a job?

Yeah, I said. I'm a maid.

I'm a dancer, she said. She stuck her elbows out and snapped her fingers.

Well, I said. I get paid.

Well, she said. I get applause.

Well, I said. I get paid and with that money I rent an apartment and buy food. And a television.

Well, she said. I get applause and with that affirmation of my amazing talent I feel happy and confident and cool.

Well, I said. Enjoy your life as a dancer.

Well, she said. Enjoy your life as a maid.

Thanks, I will, I said.

Good, she said.

We walked in grim silence towards something else. Ximena was squirming and gurgling with joy. She loved a good fight. I didn't know where we were going. When Aggie asked me if I could hold Ximena for a while I asked her if she could stay on one fucking bench for a while.

That's very mature, she said. I walked ahead of her and didn't look back for ages but when I did she was still there, tagging along. I asked her to put my book into the *farmacia* bag and then I noticed that she didn't have it.

Aggie! I said. Where's the bag?

We ran back to the pond and looked around but it was gone. No big surprise. We gazed out at the water and stared at our murky reflections. What would Gustavo Mundo, the taxi driver from Acapulco, think about all this? That losing all our money and material belongings was worth learning how to dance the tango? I guess that made as much sense as anything.

Well, said Aggie. So we have a book now.

Yeah, I said. I held it up like a papery shield.

We're doomed, she said.

I'm sorry.

Sure, I said.

When do you start your job?

Tomorrow morning.

———

I'm really, really sorry.

I am.

I am!

Show me some of your moves, I said.

Aggie looked a little shy. She untied Ximena from her chest and laid her out in the grass. X. immediately sprang into mortal combat with invisible enemies.

I could teach you, said Aggie.

Aggie and I badly danced the tango in the dying light while Ximena punched away the ghosts.

That night we tried to sleep in the park, leaning up against a statue of a handsome man that we pretended was our father, but the police told us we couldn't do that. We had no food for Ximena. The only way we could stop Ximena from screaming with hunger was to walk around so that's what we did. All around avenidas Michoacán, México and Amsterdam. Avenida Amsterdam had originally been a racetrack that circled the park. We walked a million laps. We kept watch over each other while we peed in bushes. We activated some kind of alarm on a blue car when we leaned against its bumper. We ran. We were cold. Aggie cried a little bit and said again how sorry she was. I tried to comfort her. We made up rhymes in Low German and tried to remember jokes. When we passed under street lamps we read a little bit of Subcomandante Insurgente Marcos's selected writings. We accepted a few pesos from a happy drunk couple who called us curious and wondered if we were real or a mirage. Sometimes we'd sit down on the grass but then Ximena would start to scream and I was afraid the police would get mad. In the early morning, when the sun began to rise, we gave our pesos to a fruit vendor setting up his cart and he gave us some avocados and juice in a plastic Baggie. Aggie peeled the avocados with her knife and we dipped them in the juice and tried to get Ximena to suck on them. I asked the vendor if he had an old rag I could use as a fresh diaper for Ximena and he gave me a soft white cloth with a picture of the Empire State Building on it. We washed our faces in a public fountain. I knew I would have to ask Hubertus for an advance on my wages and that made me nervous.

At 7:30 a.m. or maybe 8:00 the three of us stood on the sidewalk in front of the bed and breakfast.

Pray now, I told Aggie.

For what? she said.

What do you think? I said. Everything.

I don't know where to begin, said Aggie.

And let me do the talking, I said.

The real talking? said Aggie.

Yeah, I said. You pray silently for mercy while I speak out loud to Hubertus.

How will we keep Ximena from screaming? she said.

That's part of the prayer for everything, I said.

We could wait in the park, said Aggie.

No, I said. We tried that and you went dancing. Just put some avocado on your finger and put it in her mouth.

We could just walk around the block while you're talking to what's his name, said Aggie.

Forget it, I said. Pray.

TEN

WE WERE ALL SITTING IN THE little courtyard drinking hot coffee and eating eggs and beans and oranges. Natalie had run out to buy formula and a plastic bottle and some diapers for Ximena from the little store across the street. Aggie tried to drink from the green garden hose and I whispered to her in Low German that she shouldn't. Hubertus pretended not to have noticed and quickly brought us a bottle of water and some pineapple juice.

Aggie thanked him in Spanish and told him she'd been dying of thirst. She poured some of the water out of the glass bottle into her hand and splashed it on her face.

Aggie, I whispered. It's just for drinking.

You are sisters and you are Mexicans? he said.

Yes, I said.

What language are you speaking?

Spanish, I said.

I know, he said, but to each other.

Low German, I said.

I've never heard of Low German, said Hubertus. Is it like regular German?

Yeah, sort of, I said. Natalie had returned with the baby stuff and was preparing the bottle in the little kitchen next to the courtyard.

Irma, he said, I don't want to make you uncomfortable but there are some questions I have to ask.

All three of us stared at him and he laughed.

Don't be afraid, he said. You should see your eyes. All six of them! You girls are funny.

Sorry, I said.

Sorry for what? said Hubertus. He laughed again. I could tell that he was a little spooked by Aggie's wolf eyes, or maybe he wasn't. But she could go for ages without blinking like she was challenging you to fill the empty whites of her eyes up with something better than what she was seeing right then. She could wait forever.

Okay, he said. I have to ask you. Why are your little sisters here with you? I'm so sorry if this is a difficult question to answer. Is it?

Yes, I said. I tried to put the pieces of my life together in my head before I blurted out a stupid answer. I wanted to tell the truth but the truth, in its plain dress, was so ugly. I didn't want to say those words in front of Aggie because I thought they'd make her feel lost and helpless all over again. If I were somebody else I could answer with a mural or a tango down by the pond in the park or a poem. If I were Wilson. Or a gun if I were my father.

I'm sorry, said Hubertus. But if your parents are looking for you, I need to know. Your sisters are only children, still.

Natalie came trotting out of the kitchen in her high heels holding the bottle up like a victory flag. Here! she said. Let me feed that poor baby. May I? I handed Ximena over to Natalie and whispered that I was sorry she was so filthy. Natalie waved that all away, nonsense she said, and held X. close to her chest while she fed her.

They're not, I said.

They're not children? said Hubertus.

They're not looking for us, I said.

The only sounds in the courtyard were birds and Ximena ferociously sucking. I thought she might devour the plastic bottle itself and live forever with its outline bulging in her stomach.

How can you be sure? said Hubertus. Are they dead? I'm sorry for asking.

No, I said. They're alive as far as I know. Hubertus smiled and nodded. Aggie took a sip of pineapple juice. I noticed a plane flying high in the sky and spelling out a word with its jet stream, but then it disappeared.

My father doesn't like us, I said. He doesn't like girls. He doesn't like it when we get older and . . . there's something about his daughters that makes him crazy and . . . that's all.

Natalie looked up from her job feeding Ximena, and Hubertus looked at her and then at Aggie who may or may not have blinked.

My God, said Natalie.

Natalie, he said.

What? she said. Am I not allowed to speak?

Does he know where you are? said Hubertus.

No, I said. Nobody does.

What about your mother? he said. Won't she want you to come back?

Not if he's there, I said.

Hubertus nodded and tried to look grim. He spread his fingers out and examined the backs of his hands. He made loud breathing sounds. Then he rubbed his thighs vigorously. He looked at Natalie who had gone back to feeding Ximena. She ignored him. The birds continued to sing, or to make noises anyway.

So, said Hubertus finally. And you lost all your money when Aggie here (he nodded at Aggie and smiled) decided to enrol in an impromptu tango class in the park?

Yes, I said. She put the bag down.

Well, said Aggie, you can't dance the tango with a *farmacia* bag.

But you can dance it with a baby? I said in Low German.

What was I supposed to do? she said.

You could've stayed on the bench and not danced at all, I said.

I wasn't going to—

You could have stayed out of trouble, I said in Spanish.

Well, said Hubertus, what's life without trouble?

Yeah, Irma, said Aggie. What's life without trouble?

Yeah, I know life isn't life without trouble, I said, that's pretty clear. I'm just saying that you don't have to be the one to cause it all the time. Why don't you give somebody else a chance every once in a while?

I'm not! said Aggie. You're the one who married a—

Aggie, I said. Shut up.

You're married? said Hubertus.

Yeah, I said, but I don't know where he is, my husband.

Does he know that you're here? said Hubertus.

No, I said.

Hubertus asked Natalie to join him in the office of the bed and breakfast where their computer and desk were. Are they fucking now? said Aggie when they were gone.

If you want to live in a big city, I said, you have to learn not to say the first thing that comes to your mind because there are actually people here who can hear it. There's a population here.

Yeah, but they're strange people, don't you think? she said.

When they came back they told us we could live in a little room that was a part of the bed and breakfast. It was upstairs and in the back, overlooking other rooftops. It had a big bed and a pullout couch and a bathroom and a sink and a little fridge and a microwave oven and some painted pictures of fruit and other things on the wall and a tiny balcony. I would make breakfast for the guests in the morning and clean rooms and run errands in the afternoon. Aggie would go to school. Ximena would hang around being taken care of by me or by Natalie or Hubertus. In the evening I'd teach Natalie English so that one day she could pursue her dream of reading the complete works of Charles Dickens in their original form. Or something like that. She and Hubertus were laughing their heads off when they said it.

I don't know how to thank you, I said. I'll never forget your kindness.

Let's go, said Natalie. I'll show you your room and you can get some sleep and when you wake up we'll have lunch.

I don't know how to thank you? said Aggie in Low German. That's a stupid thing to say. We were lying in the giant bed with Ximena clean and fresh-smelling and drunk with satisfaction between us. You say thank you, said Aggie. Like this. Thank you.

I wish I was as smart as you, Aggie, I said.

I know, me too, she said. I pray for that every night.

Thanks, I said.

I've almost given up, though, she said.

Yeah, I understand, but thanks anyway, I said. Not only are you exceptionally smart you're also kind-hearted and considerate.

She moved her shoulder over a few inches so that it touched mine and then she moved back.

Are you being affectionate? I asked her.

When we woke up, Ximena had soaked the bed, right through her diaper and sleeper, through the blanket and the top sheet and the mattress protector and the mattress.

Shit, this kid is a lot of work, said Aggie.

We rinsed all that stuff in the shower and hung it over the balcony railing to dry. It was getting dark again. We went downstairs to find Hubertus and Natalie but they weren't around. There was a note for us. It was written on the back of an envelope and taped to the door of the office. They would be back late and there was some cash in the envelope that we could use to buy some food and diapers and there was also a small key to the kitchen, where the washer and dryer were. I'd start work in the morning. We went into the kitchen and ate some tortillas and cheese and salad. Then we wandered off into the neighbourhood to find a place where we could get our hair cut. We would use some of the food money. We wanted what we referred to as pixie cuts. Jagged and short. It was the only style I could remember from when I lived in Canada. Katie got one before she left for Vancouver, before she *tried* to leave for Vancouver, and it was maybe the first step on the road to our father's madness. I remember her showing it to me in our room and her whispering to me that it was called a pixie cut and this'll make him blind with rage and me agreeing and experiencing intense pain in my chest and stomach while she pranced around admiring herself, smiling at her reflection, fearless.

While we were getting our hair cut in a small shop on Avenida Michoacán the power went out and we were in the dark. The hairdresser asked us to wait for a few minutes but the power didn't come back on and Ximena was getting restless in my lap and banging her head against my collarbone and I was pulling bits of my hair out of her mouth and off her face and so we decided to pay and leave. The hairdresser asked us to come back the next day so that she could finish cutting our hair. When we got outside we saw each other in the light of the street lamp and Aggie laughed so hard she said she thought she'd wet her pants and I told her to try not to because she only had one pair.

You look like Wilf! she said. Wilf was my younger cousin, the one who lived in the filmmakers' house before he and his family went back to Canada. Three men walked past us and called us ugly *gringas* and Aggie swore at them in the coarsest Spanish slang I had ever heard. Not even from Jorge. Or Diego. We went back to the bed and breakfast and went into the kitchen and found a pair of scissors and took them back to our room. We brought a chair onto the balcony and Aggie finished cutting my hair. I picked up the blond strands and felt their baby softness between my fingers and then I threw them into the garbage can. I put my feet up on the railing. I offered to finish cutting her hair too but she said she liked the asymmetry of it and I shouldn't bother. Then we stared off at the city of Mexico, the D.F., the borough of Cuauhtémoc, our new home. We stayed out on the balcony for a long time looking at the lights and listening to the traffic and all the sirens. Way off in the distance we saw a building on fire. We talked a little bit about the things we had left behind, but not much. We talked about the universe, about loneliness. We talked about how to fall, the right way and the wrong way, to prevent injury, and if we could see our shadows from the light of Venus. We got a little cold but neither one of us wanted to go inside to get our sweatshirts because Ximena was dormant on the bed and we didn't want the sound to activate her.

That night Ximena woke up every hour on the hour howling at the world for all its timid resignation and coy duplicity and also, I think, at me directly for having no hair that she could twist around her little fist and pull until it came out by its roots. She could still vomit on me, though, so she did that a couple of times and then to top it off she head-butted me in the nose which actually brought tears to my eyes and made me plop her on the bed next to Aggie more roughly than I should have. Aggie woke up and said no, get her away from me and I said no, you have to walk around with her for a while now. I have to sleep.

I don't know what happened after that because Aggie took over and I lost consciousness. When I woke up they were both lying on the pullout couch, their eyes closed, their mouths wide open like sleep had caught them by surprise. If they'd been my captors this would be the moment I'd choose to run. A vile odour emanated from Ximena's ass. I peered closely at her chest and saw it rise and fall and rise again and thought: you live.

I went into the tiny bathroom and looked at myself in the mirror. Short and jagged. Good. I stroked the naked nape of my neck. I lifted up one lock of hair near my ear and measured it. One, maybe one and a half inches. Good. I looked at myself some more. Did I look like Katie? I don't know. I wanted to show my mother my new haircut. She would have smiled and shaken her head and kissed me. She would have been afraid for me. She would have covered her eyes and then peeked through them. She would have admired my daring. She would have rejoiced quietly, silently, and stored this moment in some dark and hidden pocket of her soul. I stared at myself a bit longer and tried so hard to see Katie. I tried to see my mother and I even tried to see my father.

The stuff that happened next was almost calm and manageable so I won't go into much detail. Aggie started school in September. She has a navy blue and white uniform that she hates and a clarinet that she practises on the balcony and one or two friends that come around every once in a while. She is drawing murals on our walls, on large sheets of wrapping paper that Hubertus buys in bulk. She has a so-called boyfriend whose name is Israel and who is also, coincidentally, a hemophiliac, so they must be careful when they punch each other and play around or he'll bleed to death. That's her type. The kind of kid who understands a soft and wounded interior. Israel told her that even sharp words can injure him but that was just a joke. His latest plan is to become a chainsaw artist. I've seen Israel run up the side of a building and then do a backwards somersault and land on his feet. He says that's his calling card.

I'm working. Cleaning rooms, making meals. Ximena, my antagonist, sits in her baby chair and watches me. Aggie and I both have cellphones. I tried to phone Jorge again and the operator told me that number was no longer in service. Otherwise I have Aggie's number and Hubertus's and Natalie's numbers and also Noehmi's number. We go for beers sometimes when she's not too busy with university classes and anarchy. Sometimes I walk over to the park to spy on that bookseller. I think and wonder a lot about Jorge. I wonder if he ever thinks about me or if he misses me at all. I wish I had been a better wife. And sometimes I pretend that I see Wilson. In bed, before I get up to work, I lie in the dark and imagine conversations with him and I remember the way he moved his hand across my body.

Ximena has learned how to bite and sit and point and lure people with her good looks. The tourists here at the bed and breakfast love her at first and then she starts to fight with them, stiffening her body into a blunt weapon, grabbing their noses and cheeks and lips and ears and twisting, screaming like an injured bird, and they give her back to me. Natalie says that when Ximena learns to walk Mexico City will know destruction similar to the scale of the 1985 earthquake.

Aggie's murals are almost all of our family. But they're conceptual, she says. Katie is a ghost that hovers over every scene and sometimes takes the shape of a crow or a breeze and Aggie is a rabbit. Our little brothers appear, when they appear, as raindrops. Our mother is a barn and I'm a tractor and our father is a big bell or the wreckage of the broken crop-duster. Aggie paints murals with these figures in different positions and doing different things. Sometimes she has us saying things, even the barn, but not usually. Aggie doesn't talk much about her murals and I've learned not to ask too many questions. One thing I like to ask and she doesn't seem to mind answering is: where's Katie in this one? I don't know if the purpose of each of her murals is to create a picture in which Katie can appear, or if she feels more free talking about the thing that represents Katie because she doesn't remember much about her so she isn't hampered by reality. One day I asked her where God was in her murals and she said TBA. I asked her what that meant and she said she didn't know but I'm pretty sure she does.

The other day I went out to buy some avocados and I took a different route to the store. I noticed a building with a sign on it that said *Citlaltépetl Refuge House*. There was a white poster in the window at the front of the building and there were black words on it that said, *When I came to Mexico City, I was dead. And here I started to live again.* There was a small open archway at the front of the building that led into a quiet courtyard. I walked inside and stood next to a wall with photographs on it. A woman came out of a little office and asked me if she could help me with anything and I told her I had seen the white poster in the window and it had made me curious about the building.

What happens here? I asked her.

We are a refuge for exiled writers, she said. The words on the poster are a quote from the Kosovar poet Xhevdet Bajraj.

Oh, I said.

Where are you from? she asked me.

From here, I said. I'm Mexican. I live a few blocks from here.

We have a few apartments for writers who are forced to leave their own countries, she said. And a small bookstore and library and a little café, as you can see. We have readings here sometimes and different types of events. Music, drama. We've tried to create a comforting and stimulating environment. She pointed at the tables set up in the courtyard.

Why are they forced to leave their own countries? I said.

For various reasons, said the woman. She explained some of those reasons to me and I nodded.

How do they leave? I said.

In different ways, she said. But always with unfinished business and a broken heart. Freedom has its price.

Where is he now? I said.

Who? she said.

The poet.

He lives nearby, she said. Here in La Condesa.

Well, I said. I didn't know what else to say. Then I thought of something. I have to go buy avocados, I said.

The woman said she understood. She loved them too. She thanked me for visiting and told me to keep one eye open for future events.

Last night Aggie agreed to guard Ximena, as she puts it, and I went out for a beer with Noehmi at a place called Tinto's which is sort of a halfway mark between her neighbourhood of Tacubaya and my neighbourhood of La Condesa. We sat across from each other in a red booth and she told me about the play she's working on.

It's a one-man show, she said. It takes place in total darkness until the very end. The audience hears voices and sounds but they don't see anything. She explained to me that at first the audience will hear the voice of a man, obviously suffering in some way. Then we'll hear the voice of a woman talking to a different man, then other voices, of kids, older people, a teacher. Gradually we'll realize that this man, the first man, is stuck in an air duct in the attic of a pawnshop that he's trying to rob so that he can buy drugs. It's his friend's pawnshop. The woman is his girlfriend and she's in the shop asking his friend if he's seen her boyfriend. He's been missing for days. His friend says he hasn't and starts flirting a bit with the woman. The man in the duct can hear all of this and it's killing him. But he's dying anyway. He's been there for a couple of days and he's dying of thirst. We realize that the other voices are the voices of the people he's remembering, the people in his life, his parents and his brother and his high school teacher. They are the voices of the people he is leaving behind as he dies. At the end of the play the lights come on for the first time and we see a man in a glass duct on the stage. That's all. There's no sound. No more voices. His face is pressed against the glass and he is dead. People don't know if it's over. They don't know if they should leave. Then, eventually, everyone does leave. They figure out that the play is over.

What do you think? said Noehmi. Do you think it'll work?

Definitely, I said.

Dupont is making the duct right now at his mother's apartment.

I'd like to see it, I said.

Actually, said Noehmi, I was wondering if you would provide one of the voices. It would just be a recording. But obviously the voices are really important because there's nothing else. I have to get them right.

I'd be one of the man's memories? I said.

Yeah, said Noehmi. I think your voice would be good for his second grade teacher. When he remembers her telling him that he can accomplish anything in life if he works hard and wants it badly enough.

I don't speak Spanish very well, I said.

Yeah you do, said Noehmi. You have an interesting accent and that's why your voice will be cool in the play. It'll stand out a bit from the others so that when your voice is heard the audience will be able to differentiate it more easily from the other female voices. You know what I mean?

I guess, I said.

He really likes her sandals and wants to marry her, said Noehmi. They're white and red and have three straps on them that cross the foot and a wedge heel. He starts putting on a bolo tie when he goes to school and slicking his hair over to one side to impress her.

The teacher?

Yeah, said Noehmi. And once, in the hallway after recess, he asks her to dance and that makes her laugh.

Does she dance with him? I asked. I thought about Jorge trying to teach me that dance, how I had failed him so spectacularly.

Well, I'm not sure if that will be explained, said Noehmi.

I'd say no, she doesn't, so he dances alone in the hallway. But he doesn't mind because he knows that he's impressed her and made her laugh.

Ah, I said. I smiled. For some reason, I don't know which one, I remembered my missionary aunt explaining to me in great detail how the jungle tribes of Ecuador used hot rocks to shrink heads. The features of the shrunken face remained exactly the same as they had been normally, except they were much smaller.

So? said Noehmi. Will you do it?

Of course, I said.

The next day I went for a walk, late in the day, before dinner. I took X. with me because Aggie was busy being taught skateboard tricks by Israel and I didn't want to go through fathoms of grief asking her to babysit. I had an uneasy feeling in my gut. I was a little nervous. There's a word in Low German for the way I felt but translated it means on top of and below a runaway horse which . . . well, I don't really know how to describe what I was feeling. It was too complicated and I was too stupid to unravel it all.

I walked past the bookseller in the park. Then I walked past him again. And one more time until I worked up the nerve to stop and say hello. The bookseller asked me if we had met once before and I said yes and that he had given me a book which I hadn't paid for. I handed him some money and he said thank you and asked me if I wanted another book and I said yes, but now I had no more money.

Again! Credit, he said, to keep you coming back. He smiled at me and I looked at the trees. He asked me if Spanish was my mother tongue and I said no. He said then what is? English?

No, I said. German. He rummaged around in his pile of books and gave me a copy of a book called *Jakob von Gunten*. It was written by Robert Walser, in German, a long time ago, around the turn of the last century. The bookseller told me that he kept books in different languages for tourists who happened to wander past looking for something to read. Robert Walser liked to walk around a lot, he said. He lived in a mental asylum for twenty years and somebody asked him if he was there to write and he said no, I'm here to be mad, and then one day he went for a long walk and lay down under a tree and died, said the bookseller. That's all I know about him. I hope you like the book. I thanked him and said goodbye. Then he asked me what my name was and I said Irma Voth.

What's yours? And he said it was Pushkin. But that I could call him Asher.

I stared at my new book. I flipped it over and flipped it over. What's it about? he said. I think it's about a boy who goes to servant school, I said. And then at the end he and the principal walk off into the desert.

All right, said Asher. Is that your baby? he said. Yes and no, I said. She's my sister actually. Asher waved at Ximena who stared at him soulfully. Natalie had bought a stroller for her and sometimes when she was in it she became curiously reflective. Asher handed X. a cardboard baby book and she took it and put it in her mouth and gnawed at it with a terrible hunger. Then she flung it so that it barely missed Asher's head and it fell onto the ground. He picked it up and gave it back to her.

Ximena and I kept walking. I pushed the stroller down the sidewalk towards the house of refuge for exiled writers. There were posters on the windows advertising different types of classes available to the general public.

The Bubbling Phenomena and Non-Compactness.

The "Almost Nothing" Precariousness in Art Since the 60s.

Taming Complexity.

Did Homer Describe an Eclipse in the *Odyssey*?

I read these posters and said the words out loud to Ximena. What do you think? I asked her. Did he or didn't he? She craned her head around and up to glare at me while I read. She had black rings of dirt around her neck. She wanted to keep moving.

When we got back home Aggie was alone and lying on the bed on her back. She told me she had something to show me and then she lifted her sweatshirt and showed me her belly button. There was jewellery stuck to it. I had it pierced, she said. Israel paid for it with his allowance. There was a tiny blue heart on a silver ring.

Does it hurt? I asked her.

Of course! she said. But I've got stuff to keep it clean.

Ximena had fallen asleep in her stroller so I left her there and lay down on the bed next to Aggie and closed my eyes. She asked me what was wrong and I said I didn't know. I was tired. I told her that I had used expensive perfume to kill some ants in a guest's room instead of going to the supply bin in the cellar to get the real bug killer because I didn't feel like going all that way. Then I panicked because the room smelled like perfume and I was sure that the guest would tell Hubertus or Natalie that I had used some of it for myself. So I lit a match to get rid of the perfume smell and then the room smelled like sulphur. I tried to turn the overhead fan on but the guest had hung wet clothing on it to dry and it was so heavy that the fan didn't spin very well and then stopped altogether and started to smell a bit like smoke. So then I opened the window to get rid of the sulphur smell and the smoke smell and the perfume smell but the screen was missing so a zillion flies flew into the room. Then I had to spend the next twenty minutes killing them and cleaning their bodies off the various surfaces and the whole time I was sweating like a horse because I was so afraid that the guest would come back to her room.

Did she? said Aggie.

No, I said.

What kind of perfume was it? she said. Poison?

Is that a kind? I said.

Yeah, said Aggie. Christian Dior.

What do you mean? I said.

Christian Dior is the name of the designer who makes the perfume, said Aggie.

How do you know that? I said.

Me and Israel get samples for his mom, she said.

I told Aggie that all the noise and confusion on the streets was overwhelming me a little bit. I told her that I missed the stars in Chihuahua and the sound of the wind rustling the corn.

Me encanta este lugar, said Aggie.

I know, I said. She was speaking mostly Spanish these days. She had told me that she liked it here.

I asked Aggie to tell me about her day in Plattdeutsch.

Why? she said. It was boring.

No, I mean just talk to me about anything in Plattdeutsch, I said.

She told me that she had gone to the museum of anthropology that day with her class and that she had really wanted to steal a tiny little artifact, a charm or something, that had once belonged to an Aztec warrior.

But you didn't, did you? I said.

Of course not, she said, you can't. They're under glass.

Oh, I said. But you wouldn't have anyway, would you? I said.

I don't know, she said. I might have if I thought I wouldn't be caught.

You would? I said.

Maybe, she said.

Don't, I said.

Why not? said Aggie.

Because it's stupid, I said. And you know it.

Then we started talking about Katie because I had remembered the time she'd been arrested for assaulting a police officer. She'd been walking home late from a bush party and the cop had stopped to ask her what she was doing out so late and she was kind of drunk and she kicked his car and told him it was none of his business so he drove along beside her saying stupid things and she was getting madder and madder and she threw her lip gloss at his face and so then he made the decision that it was his business after all and he stopped the car and dragged her into the back seat. She kicked and screamed and swore and that resulted in more assault charges or maybe mischief or something or other and she had to spend the night in jail.

She spent the night in jail? said Aggie.

Yeah, I said.

That's so fucking cool! said Aggie. Nobody ever tells me anything about Katie. What kind of lip gloss was it?

I don't know, I said. Chocolate mint.

What happened after that? said Aggie.

You don't want to know, I said.

I do so! said Aggie. You can't stop the story there. You don't know what I want to know and what I don't want to know.

Don't you know? I said.

No, she said. How would I know?

Well, I said. How do you think someone like Dad would have felt about his daughter being arrested for assaulting a police officer when she was coming home drunk from a bush party and then spending the night in jail?

All she did was throw lip gloss at him! said Aggie.

Aggie, I said.

What? she said.

You know exactly what, I said. You don't have to use your imagination.

After that Aggie did fun things to try to cheer me up. Sometimes she'd grab me around the waist when I wasn't expecting it, yell surprise and throw me down on the bed. I tried to do it to her one time and she laughed but said that I had to be careful with her belly button. She made up a game she called Baby Detective. I'd be lying in bed reading my new book or sitting on the balcony tying my shoes to get ready for work and I'd feel something. I'd sense that somebody was watching me. And I'd turn to see Ximena's big, spooky eyes. Sometimes from low down, close to the floor, and sometimes from high up, near the ceiling. Aggie would stand behind the open door and hold Ximena in different places so that only her spying little baby face poked out.

Then one afternoon when I was finished cleaning I went into our room to have a short nap. Ximena was in a playpen in the courtyard and Natalie was keeping an eye on her while she fixed up the planters. It was a very bright day and I had opened all our curtains in the morning when I went to work so that the sun would wake Aggie up for school. But when I walked into our room the curtains were closed and it was completely dark. Much darker than usual. I couldn't see anything. And there was a strange noise. I whispered Aggie's name and waited. I stood perfectly still for a minute trying to understand what was going on. Slowly, as my eyes adjusted to the darkness, I began to see little dots of silver light. At first I saw only a few but as time passed the room was filled with them and soon I was surrounded by them. I smiled. I understood. Aggie had covered the windows with thick, dark material she had found somewhere, maybe it was painted cardboard from school, and had used a pin or something tiny to prick hundreds of holes into the blackness to create sunlit stars. I took a step into the darkness and bumped into something hard. It was a floor fan, a small one, that Aggie must have tied strips of newspaper to and the fan was blowing them to make a noise like wind. I backed up a bit and felt the wall. It was cool and smooth. I carefully sat down on the floor and leaned against the door. I sat in the dark. I stared at the stars and listened to the wind.

I was still sitting there when Aggie came home from school and barged through the door and knocked me over. She switched on the lights and then said oh, you're here! There was a gecko on the wall beside my head. Aggie put her face next to it and said hey there, little gecko boy, did you enjoy your trip to Chihuahua? I thanked her for her gift of wind and stars and she said yeah, no problem, it was easy and then she showed me a giant painting she'd done in art class. It was of Katie in jail, doing a karate kick in her cell, her braids flying straight out behind her, trying to kick out the walls.

It's called *Chocolate Mint Lip Gloss*, said Aggie.

Wow, I said.

We laid it out on the bed and looked at it.

Did you ever meet her boyfriend? said Aggie.

What boyfriend? I said.

The boyfriend who hit her with his car, said Aggie.

What are you talking about? I said. I thought you said nobody ever talked to you about Katie.

I'm talking about her boyfriend who hit her with his car after their big fight, said Aggie. Mom said he couldn't see her in the snow or whatever. What are *you* talking about?

I put my hands over my eyes for a second trying to see something that wasn't there. Then I clasped my hands together so that my fingers met and formed a tiny pocket that held nothing. I looked at the wall and the gecko was gone. We had sunlight and traffic noise and breath. We had art. We had each other. We had ourselves. We had memories and we had lies. Those were the difficult-to-insure contents of our room.

What's your problem? said Aggie. Where's X.?

In the courtyard with Natalie, I said. In her playpen. Katie didn't have a boyfriend.

Yeah, she did, said Aggie. Mom told me.

Well, I said, no, she didn't have a boyfriend.

Well, said Aggie, whatever.

So, it couldn't have been the boyfriend who accidentally hit her with his car in a blizzard after a big fight, I said.

Who hit her then? said Aggie. She got up and went into the bathroom. I could see her reflection in the mirror. She was cleaning her belly button with a Q-tip soaked in sterilizing solution, dabbing it gently over and over, thoroughly.

Dad hit her, I said.

She stopped dabbing at her belly button.

She told him she was moving to Vancouver and he said she couldn't go and she said yeah I'm going, or something, and then she took off and was running down that road behind the second barn. I guess she was trying to get to the highway to hitchhike to the city and he took off after her in the truck and hit her.

She shouldn't have told him she was going, said Aggie.

I looked at her reflection. She had started dabbing at her belly button again, that little portal that connected her to her past. She kept dabbing while I talked so that eventually she had the cleanest belly button in all of Mexico.

Well, actually she didn't tell him that she was going, I said.

You just said she did, said Aggie.

I mean she did tell him that she was going, I said, but only after I told him.

You told Dad she was going to Vancouver? said Aggie. Why would you do that?

Because I didn't want her to go, I said.

You shouldn't have told him, said Aggie.

She was really excited about going, I said. I mean she was sad to be leaving but she was also really happy.

Uh-huh, said Aggie.

And it made me so mad, I said. That she was so happy about leaving. And she made me promise not to tell Dad.

So you promised you wouldn't? said Aggie.

Yeah, I said.

But then you did, said Aggie.

I know, I said. Yeah.

And then Dad went after her in his truck which is what you wanted him to do, said Aggie.

Yeah, I said, but to bring her home.

You shouldn't have told him, said Aggie.

And then he came home and told Mom he couldn't find her, I said. He put the truck in the garage and just waited around for a day or two for it to snow hard and then he told the cops that she had been upset about a fight with her boyfriend and had run off onto the road into the blizzard and still hadn't come home. So they went looking for her and found her body in the ditch. They said she had been hit by a car or a truck.

Dad said well, it must have been the boyfriend who hit her, and the cops said okay, who's her boyfriend and Dad said he had never met him and didn't know his name. He told the cops that Katie had been upset before she left and he had asked her what was wrong and she had said she and her boyfriend had had a fight. So then the cops said oh, okay, we'll ask around in the community. We'll talk to some of her friends to see if we can get some information and Dad said yes, thank you, that would be good. The cop asked Dad if he had a photograph of Katie and he said no. The cop said no photographs? And Dad said no again. He said our families don't have photographs.

A couple of days later the cops came back to our house and said that nobody in the community knew who her boyfriend was. Maybe it was a boy from the city, said Dad. And the cops said maybe. Then they said maybe it wasn't her boyfriend who hit her. And Dad said maybe not. He said maybe it was a trucker or a farmer in the area who had thought that he had hit a deer or a dog and had just kept going. Dad said the snow had been blinding that night and it would have been impossible for anyone to have seen her especially in the dark. The cops asked Mom and Dad some questions. They asked them why they thought Katie was running in the dark in a snowstorm wearing a light jean jacket and runners. Dad said she was upset about the fight with her boyfriend, he had already told them that. They said yes, but the fight must have happened earlier that day or even before that and why had she waited until so long after the fact to run off into the night. That didn't fit with their knowledge of human psychology and impulsive behaviour. Dad said well, he had thought that she had been talking to him over the phone that evening so the fight may have occurred over the phone immediately before she took off. The cops said well, they had contacted the Manitoba telephone system and there was no record of any phone activity that evening at all. None. Well, said Dad, the fight may have occurred earlier but Katie may have taken some time to work herself into a frenzy and then made the rash decision to run off into the night. Maybe, said the cop. Then he said that the autopsy had indicated that Katie's body had been in the ditch for longer than just that evening. Maybe two or even three days. Dad said that didn't make any sense at all and questioned the reliability of science. The cops asked Dad if maybe he had got the day wrong. They wondered if Katie had gone missing two or three days earlier, when the weather had been exceptionally clear and sunny and anybody driving down the road would have been able to have seen a running girl on the shoulder. Dad said no, he would have noticed if she'd been gone all that time, obviously. Then the cops were quiet for a second and asked Mom and Dad if they could talk to me alone.

Mom and Dad went outside into the yard and the cop asked me what kind of a girl Katie was. I said she was a fun girl. He asked me if she had had a boyfriend. I said yes. I was lying. The cop asked me if I knew who the boyfriend was. I said no, I had never met him. The cop said but she talked about him? I said yes, she did sometimes, not often. Then the cop made me tell him what she had said about her boyfriend and I said all she said was that he was funny and easygoing and made her laugh and liked her a lot. I didn't know what else to say. I didn't know anything about what boyfriends might be like. The cop asked me where he was from and I said I didn't know. Maybe the city. The cop asked me how Katie would have met a boy from the city when we were living so far away from it and she didn't have a driver's licence. I told the cop I didn't know. Then I thought of something and I told the cop that Katie had told me that her boyfriend had a really bad temper. That sometimes she'd say something or do something, anything, like tap the dashboard of his car with her foot, and he'd fly off the handle. He was really violent.

The cop said well, first he was funny and easygoing and now he's violent? I told the cop that he was both of those things, according to Katie. The cop asked me if she had ever called him by his name or had always spoken of him as her boyfriend this and her boyfriend that. I said yes, that she had never called him by his name. The cop said okay, can you tell me if there was any fighting between your dad and Katie? I said no, never. They asked me if any of the things she did ever made him angry and I said no, not at all. They asked me if I was sure about that. They said it was normal for fathers to sometimes become exasperated with their teenage daughters, to yell at them, or to forbid them from doing certain things. I didn't say anything. They asked me again if Katie had ever made Dad mad and I said no, never. Then the cops left and Mom and Dad came back into the kitchen. Mom went to take care of you and the boys, you were in the other room, and Dad asked me what

I had said to the cops. I told him and he said that was fine. Then the next day we were on our way to Mexico.

Aggie came out of the bathroom and took off her shirt. She put on a different one. Yeah, she said. That's when Mom told me about the boyfriend. When she came into the room where me and the boys were playing. She lied to me too. Then Aggie took that shirt off and put the other one back on. She took *Chocolate Mint Lip Gloss* and taped it to the wall beside the door. Then she walked out.

I found a blue emergency candle in the washroom cupboard and lit it and stuck it into an empty jar and brought it to the bed and set it there under Aggie's art. For the next hour or two I watched over Katie as she kicked out the walls around her. Finally around midnight or one in the morning Aggie came back and squeezed into bed next to me and Ximena and fell asleep in her clothes. In the morning I got up before she did. I got ready for work and then I woke her up for school.

After that Aggie painted a giant mural on brown paper and hung it over our bed. It was our family praying and holding hands around the table in our old kitchen in Canada. Katie's body was lying in the centre of the table and there were other regular dishes of food with spoons in them and steam coming up. All our eyes were closed except for our father's and he was staring straight at me. She painted a mural of a police lineup with three girls, herself, me and

Ximena, looking out at the camera, dirty and dishevelled and lost.

I asked Aggie if we could take those murals off the walls and put them in the closet. Why? she said. You don't want to be reminded of the fact that you're the daughter of a killer? I told her I was sorry for telling her the truth and she told me never to lie to her again.

ELEVEN

NOEHMI AND I WERE WORKING on the play. Well, all I really did was read my lines into a digital tape recorder over and over in different ways until she was happy with the way they sounded. I'll play yourself to you, she said. I listened to myself. I'm the memory of a doomed man, I thought. I couldn't save him. We sat in the darkness of the courtyard late at night after Aggie and Ximena and Natalie and Hubertus were asleep.

One more time, said Noehmi. Can you say it in a softer voice? Almost a whisper. Remember, your voice is being heard by a man dying of thirst and shame.

If you work hard, I whispered. If you want something badly enough. If you believe in yourself and never give up . . .

That's good, said Noehmi. But just try it with a bit more of a pause in between the sentences.

Okay, I said. If you work hard. If you want something badly enough. If you believe in yourself and never give up . . . I asked Noehmi if she thought it was true, what I was saying.

I don't know, she said. Do you?

I don't know, I said.

But it's the kind of thing a grade school teacher tells a kid, right? said Noehmi. It's a cliché and it's meant to be ironic in this context. Like, look where he is, right?

But he remembers it, I said.

Yeah, said Noehmi. For some reason it's one of the things he remembers.

Because he had a crush on her?

Yeah, said Noehmi. Sort of, that's a part of it. I don't know. She was just that person in his life who felt he had something to offer to the world.

When we were finished it was too late for Noehmi to go home so I got her a rollaway cot out of the shed and we hauled that upstairs to our room and she slept over and in the morning Natalie and Hubertus were so happy to see her that they made breakfast for all of us and I got to postpone going to work for a while. Dupont came to pick Noehmi up and I tried not to stare at them while they kissed. I tried not to notice how their lips met and opened and how they held each other close and casually in a loving embrace. They left and then Natalie asked me if I had noticed that Aggie seemed to be in a really bad mood.

Yeah, I said. She'll get over it. It's her age, I think.

Yeah, said Natalie. All those hormones.

Yeah, I said. And everything changing.

Yeah, said Natalie. Or not.

Yeah, I said.

Later that evening, when Aggie finally came home from school, which I think she was skipping with Israel these days mostly to hang out in Parque México with a pack of dogs, she told me that she was going to call the cops to tell them that our father was a murderer.

Aggie, I said. You are not.

Yeah, I am, she said. That's what normal people do.

What cops are you gonna call? I said. Cops in Chihuahua? In Canada?

Cops right here in D.F., she said.

They won't care, I said. They'll just laugh at you and tell you to stop bugging them.

Then in Chihuahua, said Aggie.

Same thing, I said. They won't believe you. Or even if they do they won't give a shit.

Fine, then in Canada, said Aggie.

Don't you think they already know? I said. Why would we have left for Mexico right after they came to talk to us if Dad didn't have something to hide?

So, she said. Now they can come and find him. We'll tell them where he is.

Aggie, I said, it doesn't work that way.

And then Mom and the boys can come and live with us in Mexico City and we can get a real house to live in instead of a hotel room.

It's not that simple, I said. The cops in Chihuahua would have to want to co-operate with the cops in Canada and they won't. They won't care and besides Dad has his own story.

You don't care about justice? said Aggie. You don't care about the truth? Don't you care about Katie? How do you know Dad isn't gonna kill someone else?

Well, I said. That's why we're fucking here! I didn't tell you the truth to make you all mad and do stupid things. I told you the truth because you had done up the room with the stars and the wind and I wanted to give you something in return. I told you the truth because I wanted you to stop hoping that Katie would somehow come back home and now I wish I hadn't.

I knew Katie wasn't going to come back home, said Aggie. Do you think I'm an idiot? Do you think I thought she could find us in the fucking desert?

Yeah, but that's not because we were lost, it's because she's dead! I said.

I know! said Aggie. I just thought maybe she wasn't. I thought maybe she was still in Vancouver.

Not *still* in Vancouver, I said. She never made it to fucking Vancouver!

Fine! said Aggie. Then just still alive, okay?

I know! I said. And that's why I wanted you to know the truth!

So okay, fine! said Aggie. Now I know the truth and I have to call the cops because that's what people do when they find out that someone has been murdered. Were you aware of that?

Do you know what would happen if you called the cops? I said. Then they'd know where you are and they'd be on Dad's side because he'd give them some money and they'd call you a mischief-making runaway and they'd take you and Ximena back home and that would be the end of it except for Dad beating the shit out of you and probably out of Mom for lying to him about Ximena being dead and I would never see you again and it wouldn't bring Katie back to life and you'd be dead inside forever! So, go ahead and make the call. Here, use my cell.

I threw my cellphone at her and missed. It hit the wall and a piece of it flew off and then the battery fell out of it. Ximena woke up and started laughing at us and jumping hard in her crib so that it rolled on its little wheels from one end of the room to the other. The people in the room below us banged on their ceiling. Aggie picked up the pieces of my phone and reassembled it and gave it back to me. I held it in my hand like an injured bird, tenderly. Aggie went and lifted Ximena out of her crib and changed her soaking diaper. I put my phone down on the bed and went into the bathroom to wash my face. I stood on the toilet and looked through the tiny barred window out at Mexico City. I couldn't see the end of it, the horizon where the sky met the earth, but I could remember clearly where it was. I could remember my father sobbing in the barn three days after we moved to Chihuahua. My mother had asked me to find him and tell him that supper was ready and I stood in the doorway of the barn and watched him cry, he was sitting on a bale and he had taken off his hat and he hadn't seen me in the darkness and then I cleared my throat and told him we were eating and he looked up at me and he said Irma, why did you tell me she was leaving? Why did you do that?

The next morning I was cleaning the big room on the second floor, the one that looked into the courtyard and not out towards the city, and I noticed an open newspaper lying on the floor beside the bed. There was a photograph of Diego Nolasco and the article was about the Mexico City premiere of his new movie *Campo Siete*. I looked at his picture and smiled hello, how are you? Then I ran upstairs to my room and got my notebook and ran back down and copied all the information. I folded the paper and put it on top of the little table by the window. It had never occurred to me that one day Diego's movie would be finished and available for the world to see. It hadn't occurred to me that all that energy, all that running around, all that waiting and all that anguish could result in one coherent song. I don't know why I thought of Diego's movie as a song. I had nothing else to compare it to, I guess, besides the Bible. The story hadn't made any sense to me, not really. It was all so chaotic and haphazard, like a dream with missing pieces, and rushed and then delayed and then right and then wrong and then broke and then euphoric and the skies weren't perfect and then they were and the real tears were fake and the fake tears were real and everyone was fighting and angry and having sex with each other and getting arrested and making threats and freezing at night and burning in the day and starving and stoned and exhausted and confused and sick and lonely and terrified. I wanted to see it. The idea alone of seeing *Campo Siete* obsessed and exhausted me.

I decided to see the movie by myself. I had thought about taking Aggie with me but I didn't want her to see Alfredo, her friend's dad, making pretend love to Marijke. I didn't want her to sit beside me moaning in agony or pretending to vomit. I also didn't know how the movie ended and I was afraid that maybe Oveja would be shot, or disappear somehow, and that Aggie would be devastated all over again. Then I thought about how angry she'd be with me if I didn't take her so I changed my mind and decided we'd go together and that the disturbing picture of a naked Alfredo or a wounded pit bull would be one that she would have to deal with on her own. I guess, at thirteen, there is almost nothing harder to bear than images of dead dogs and naked middle-aged men, but that's life.

I don't know how to describe the feeling of going to a movie. We went. Natalie and Hubertus agreed to babysit Ximena and even gave us extra money for popcorn. Aggie put on eyeliner. We took a bus to the theatre and paid for tickets and went inside and sat down in soft chairs and fought a little bit for the armrest in the middle (Aggie won) and waited in the dark. There were a lot of people. There was a lot of noise. And then it got very quiet and even darker and the curtain opened and the movie started. It was more exciting than anything I could remember happening, ever.

I still don't know what the movie is really about. I'm not smart enough. Or I don't want to know. I don't know. I cried all through the movie. I saw the skies and the cornfields and the faces of people I recognized. Even when Marijke said the lines that I had given her, the wrong ones, lines that were supposed to be funny, I cried. Diego had been right. It didn't really matter what words they used because all of their thoughts and feelings were being expressed in other more magical ways. Souls communicating with souls. It was amazing. I wish I could explain it. I wish I knew. There were dark circles under Marijke's eyes that I hadn't noticed before. She looked a little haunted. There was something about her I could see now, in her movie character, that I hadn't noticed in real life. For a second she stared directly into the camera and I thought no, no, Marijke, not directly into the camera. What did I tell you? Everything seemed to be out of place, the faces, the words, time. All the pictures strung together and people in them, walking, talking, kissing, dying. I felt so happy. Or maybe it wasn't happiness. There was something that I was beginning to understand but I didn't know what it was. It was like watching my own life. It was a pathway into myself. It was like the man dying in the duct in Noehmi's play as he hears the voices from his past. Maybe seeing a movie is like dying, but in a beautiful way. There are words that I want to say but they aren't strong enough to describe how I felt. Or they're too strong. And suffocating. Somewhere in the middle of those words is a word like, I don't know, peace or something. Harmony? That might be right, but probably not exactly.

So there we were. I cried quietly for everything that I had lost and for a few things that I had found and for reasons I couldn't explain and Aggie was I think trying hard not to giggle. We saw Oveja and she grabbed my arm and said he's alive! Which I thought was interesting in its way. In the way that it might not actually be true but that it seemed true in that very moment. I saw myself lying under a tree with my back to the camera. Diego had used me as a body double for Marijke who had refused to do that scene because of the snakes. It was amazing. I had never seen a photo of myself, let alone a moving picture. I saw Marijke's giant face fill every inch of the screen. I almost screamed. When we saw the kids from our campo Aggie said ha! Look! It's Aughte! And somebody behind us told her to be quiet. The fields and the skies were so empty and lonely and alluring. I asked Aggie in a whisper if it made her want to go home and she said no in a loud voice and was told again to shut up. The movie ended and we stretched our legs out and got ready to leave but then the lights came on and a woman with a microphone walked up to the front of the theatre and onto the stage and said that tonight was a very special night because Diego Nolasco was with us and would now be answering questions from the audience.

I didn't know what to do. I didn't want Diego to see us and tell someone, anyone, the police, our father, where we were. But the lights were on and if we stood up now and tried to leave we'd be completely conspicuous and I imagined

Diego calling out hello Irma and Aggie, *cómo están?* So I
hunkered down a bit in my seat and told Aggie we'd stay for
the questions and then leave.

Can I ask one? said Aggie.

No! I said.

The woman behind us had clearly been tested. My
God, she said, have you no respect?

I'm sorry, I said. We do, we do. I'm sorry.

Aggie turned around to say something to the woman
and I dug my fingers into her leg and whispered in Low
German that she should just shut up and stay calm and then
the woman started to say something about how Aggie was
a kid, a punk, and shouldn't be there and I thought about
agreeing with her but then Diego's voice was everywhere
and he was up there on the stage in nice clothes and talking
into the microphone and smiling and there was applause, a
lot of it, that drowned us all out and Aggie settled back into
her chair and the woman did too and we all more or less
listened to what he had to say.

> Audience member: How did the Mennonites feel
> about a movie being made about them?
> Diego: There was some interference, certainly.
> There was some resistance initially. But
> eventually they realized that we were there
> to make a respectful film which I think
> you would agree with, having seen it now.
> Alfredo, who plays the husband, was very
> co-operative and helped smooth things out
> for everyone. For the most part the

Mennonites were happy to have us there and were very generous with their time and their land and homes, locations where we shot.

Audience member: Had you considered opening the film in Chihuahua, where the Mennonites might have seen it?

Diego: I had, yes, and I still want to bring it to the community so that they can see it, but the logistics of that, now, are still . . . complicated.

Audience member: The film is stunning. It's awe-inspiring. Thank you for making it. My question is, what was the shoot like? What were some of the difficulties you encountered?

Diego: Thanks. Um, thanks a lot. Well, we had to wait for the right weather, often. It was the rainy season when we were shooting, it was supposed to be, but the rain didn't come when it was supposed to so we had to use artificial rain. That was problematic but it worked eventually. There also, it was often very hot, and in fact we lost . . . or one of our lead actors went missing for several days because . . . she had heatstroke and went missing in the desert. She walked away from the shoot and got lost. We had warned her not to walk but . . . Originally I had a girl from the community that I had hired as a translator and sort of companion but she was . . . she wasn't able to stay so . . . But . . . anyway . . . the actress was okay in the end. She had to be

hospitalized for exhaustion or . . . for several
days so during that time we shot other scenes.

Audience member: Hello Diego. I want to first of
all congratulate you. In my opinion *Campo
Siete* is a masterpiece. You are an extraordinary
artist. You've transformed a place of austerity
and poverty into a place of strange beauty. I
don't know how you do it but I think I can
say for everyone here tonight that we are all
so grateful that you *do* do it. Congratulations.
Bravo.

Diego: Oh, well, thanks very much.

Audience member: Why did you choose to make
a movie about Mennonites?

Diego: I don't care about the Mennonites as
a group. Not at all. I'm interested in the
fact that nobody would understand their
language and that they were uniform. There's
no distinction, one from the other, and so
they are props, essentially, for pure emotion.
Even their setting, you don't know what era
it is or where, blonds in Mexico, it doesn't
matter, ultimately, when all you want is to
communicate an emotional truth.

Audience member: I read something in one of
the papers here months ago that there had
been a violent incident at the campo where
you were making the film. Can you speak
of that?

Diego: Yes, there was a shooting.

Audience member: Did it involve your crew or any people involved in the making of the film?

Diego: No. No, no, it was . . . there was a shooting at the farm down the road.

Audience member: In the paper it said that the shooting was drug related. I found that so surprising, that the Mennonites would be involved in that type of thing.

Diego: Yes, well . . . it is, I guess. I don't know the details. I believe it was a debt of some kind.

Audience member: A drug debt?

Diego: Yeah . . . I think so. The guy who lived there was just . . . he just stored the drugs for . . . I don't know who. It's a very remote area so it's a good place for that. The people are very poor. There were . . . there aren't many opportunities. And apparently the person came to get the . . . to get it . . . and it wasn't there and he became very angry and killed the . . . guy.

Audience member: In the paper it mentioned, I think, that the victim was related to a member of your crew.

Diego: Member of my crew? No, no, I don't think . . . oh, yeah, well . . . the person I was talking about before, the girl I had hired as a translator for Marijke . . . that person . . . the victim . . . or . . . he was her relative.

Audience member: He was her father?

Diego: He was her husband.

Audience member: I understand you used natural lighting in the making of your film. I'm curious about how that worked for interior shots.

Diego: I'm sorry?

Audience member: I understand you used natural lighting in the making of your film. How did you manage to get enough light for the interior shots?

Diego: If there's not a lot of natural light coming in from windows or with one or two lamps, then that's how it is. The shot is dark. *(He turns to the woman who introduced him, indicating that he'd like the question-and-answer period to be over.)*

Woman: We only have time for one or two more questions. Yes?

Audience member: Are you in the process of working on something new? Are you writing another script?

Diego: Yes, of course. I'm always working on something new.

Audience member: Can you tell us what it's about?

Diego: It's not about Mennonites, that much I'll say. *(The audience laughs and Diego smiles and waves goodbye.)*

Audience member: Is it—

Woman: I'm sorry, we'll have to stop there. Thank you, Diego, for— *(The audience bursts into applause and drowns out the woman and Diego waves again and leaves the stage.)*

———

Aggie and I left the theatre and walked into a park across the street. It was very dark for Mexico City. We sat down on a small wooden bench and Aggie whispered things to me, the consolation of a thirteen-year-old. He came back! she said, beautiful words and sweet promises and hugs, while I wept. Aggie didn't loosen her grip, though. Then later, at home, after she had fallen asleep with streaks of eyeliner on her face and Ximena had polished off her bottle and flung it at the wall, I took my notebook out and wrote a list of the sins I had committed. It's good to have an itinerary even if it only leads to hell.

> I broke a promise and told my father the truth, that Katie was planning to go to Vancouver, because I didn't want her to leave and because of that she ended up dead.
> I lied to the police about everything because I didn't want my dad to go to jail and because of that we had to move to Mexico where the life gradually drained out of my mother.
> By lying to the police I killed my soul and stopped believing in an afterlife because life after death seemed almost exactly the same as life before it.
> I selfishly took a job as a translator which resulted in Aggie being curious about filmmaking and late nights and boys which resulted in her being beaten by our father.

I stole Jorge's drugs to sell for money to run away
   from home and buy plane tickets with my little
   sisters so we wouldn't end up being killed by
   my father. (I also took Diego's truck for a
   while, which constituted more stealing.)
By stealing Jorge's drugs to sell to Carlito Wiebe
   to save myself Jorge ended up dead.
I killed my sister.
I killed my mother.
I killed my husband.
I killed my soul.

I read over my sins. I hit myself on the side of my head.
I pressed my hands into my face. I tried to push back. I walked
into the bathroom and looked at myself in the mirror. I saw
the red outlines of ten fingers on my face. I picked up the
bottle that Ximena had thrown away and put it in the sink.
I walked back into the bedroom and looked at my sleeping
sisters. I remembered Jorge's foaming shoes. How he
waited on that corner. His shame. My shame. I didn't know
what to do. I wondered if this was how it always was when
you realize big things, for instance, that you're a serial murderer, that all you can do is go into different rooms and
look at things and people and not understand. Marijke had
been wrong. What's terrible is not easy to endure and what's
good is not easy to get. Why had she looked so haunted in
the movie? I don't know. I touched the spot between my
eyes, the source of my internal light and cosmic energy.
I waited for something to happen but nothing did. I knelt
beside the bed and covered my face again with my hands

and prayed for forgiveness. Please God, I said. Help me to live. When I opened my eyes nothing had changed. I closed them again and again. I remembered Marijke telling me that she had done that too, in the desert, hoping that the next time she opened her eyes she'd see her son. And then I remembered that she had never told me why she'd stopped aging at fourteen. I closed my eyes and tried to see Jorge. I opened them again and went back into the bathroom and sat on the edge of the tub and washed my feet thoroughly and then dried them very carefully, between each toe, all over. I went to bed. I dreamed that I was standing in the front yard of my house in Canada and waving goodbye to everyone I loved. I had to go away, I didn't know where, and the sun was shining beautifully and my grandma and my parents and my brothers and sisters and Jorge and all my friends from school were standing on the front steps and smiling and waving and telling me they loved me. Maybe they were crying a little bit but they were also trying to look happy and positive. And in that moment it was too much, I felt all the love, more than I had ever felt before in my life, a universal love, and I didn't want to go after all. But in my dream I had to go. I didn't know why.

After that day I developed a headache that wouldn't go away. I saw lightning flashes in the corners of my eyes like two storms coming in slowly from both the east and the west. Aggie bought me a giant bottle of Tylenol and I popped them all day long while I tried to get my work done. Natalie said that it might be because of the changing season, it was spring and the jacarandas were exploding, or it might be allergies or it might be stress. Or it might be a brain tumour, said Aggie, pressing down on my optical nerve. It's just storms, I'd say. I don't know.

Do you hear thunder? said Aggie. Do you feel the wind picking up in your brain? She threw the giant bottle of Tylenol at me and I shook them straight out of the bottle into my mouth without using water to wash them down. Hubertus got me a bunch of vitamins and minerals and cod liver oil too, but none of that stuff worked at all. He told me not to work for a few days and lie in the dark with a cold cloth on my forehead so I tried doing that but lying around all day just made me restless and nervous. Aggie stayed home from school to take care of Ximena so I could rest but that wasn't really working either because X. liked to crawl all over me and suck on the wet washcloth and Aggie was getting bored and pissed off. She wanted to go to school and she wanted to see Israel and get on with her regular life.

I'm trying to work something out, I told her.

What are you trying to work out?

I don't know, I said.

That's why the storms?

Do you study English in school? I asked her.

Israel's mom thinks you should talk to a priest.

I'm not Catholic, I said.

She said it doesn't matter, said Aggie. You get to hear him say my daughter.

Say my daughter?

He has to call you my daughter, she said. It's just how they talk.

You went? I said.

Yeah, I go sometimes with Israel. His mom makes him.
Really? I said.

So the next day I asked Natalie if she could watch X. for
an hour or so while I went to church and she said sure
and I found a church and walked into a confession booth.
I waited for the priest to call me his daughter but he didn't.
He waited for me to speak, to confess something, and
I wanted to tell him all about the lies and the stealing and
the murders but I couldn't speak. I didn't want to tell him
anything because I was still afraid that if I did, something
bad would happen to my father. I was silent. The priest
asked me if I was going to talk to him and I said no. Then
after a little while he told me that he had quite a lot of
people to talk to that day. I didn't say anything. He said so
if I wanted to come back another time that would be okay
with him but that he should probably make himself available for other people now. He said it kindly. He apologized for his awkwardness. I waited for him to say my
daughter. I didn't say anything. He asked me again if
I would prefer to come back another time and I still didn't
say anything and then he said please, my daughter, I honestly don't know what to tell you.

I was back in my bed with lightning raining down on my
cerebral cortex and Ximena's screams drifting up from the
courtyard. I was still trying to form a picture of Jorge in my
mind. I saw Katie getting ready to leave, stuffing clothes

into a backpack and begging me to promise not to tell. I saw my father as a little boy on a road in Russia. I was trying to get to the bottom of things. I was trying to formulate a thought. Or a cure. Even a cure that had only one part would be enough for now. Aggie was walking around with Ximena trying to get her to calm down after she bit into a live electrical cord. She was singing to her, a silly little Low German song about ducks swimming in the sea. It was a new kind of scream for Ximena. She was in real pain. She had suffered a serious shock. I was familiar with her entire repertoire of screams and what they meant but this was something much different. She was surprised and hurt. She was fragile after all, a helpless baby. I listened to her screams and then I put the pillow over my head but I could still hear them. And then, because my little sister had bit into an electrical cord and would not be consoled, or something, I'm not sure why, really, the gathering storms in my head disappeared and I had figured out the solution to my own problem. I understood what it was to want someone to stay. And I knew what to do next. And I knew the answer to my own question: if this was the last day of your life what kind of a story would you write?

YOU MUST BE PREPARED TO DIE!

I read over the original heading in my notebook, the one that Diego had given me a long time ago to record my thoughts and observations. I pondered his dark advice. I scratched out the word DIE and wrote LIVE. Then that seemed cheesy and too uncooly emphatic so I added the words SORT OF. AT LEAST TRY. Even that seemed bossy so I added, in parentheses, a joke: OR DIE TRYING. Then I told myself that it wasn't funny and crossed it all, every word of it, out and started again.

I'm on a plane to Chihuahua city. I have a photograph for my mother that she will have to hide and only look at while my father's in the field. It's of the three of us, her Mexico City girls. Aggie has a pierced eyebrow now and the craziest smile and most beautiful eyes and Ximena is struggling to get out of my arms so that she can assault the photographer (Noehmi). I'm holding on to her and saying something. My mouth is half open and my eyebrows are furrowed, like always.

Natalie and Hubertus gave me the money for a ticket and said all they wanted in return was for me to promise to come back. Aggie didn't want to come with me which is good because I didn't want her to either. She's young enough that my father could force her to stay at home and I didn't want to go through that again. Aggie wants to go see thousands of naked people in the Zócalo having their picture taken. Noehmi is on her spring break from university so she's going to take care of Ximena (whom she has started calling Cricket) so that Aggie can still go to school while I'm gone and Natalie's friend Fernande is going to do my job for me for the few days that I'm away because she needs extra money to pay her divorce lawyer. Ximena can't come, obviously, because she's not even supposed to be alive. This time, if my father asks me where my sister is, I'll ask him the same question.

———

I'm on the plane. I don't know what to write.
Should I write down my dreams?

The time is 11:02 a.m. My name is Irma Voth. I'm
on a plane. I'm not a good person. I'm not a
smart person. I might be a free person. If this is
how it feels.

I scratched that out because there were only parts of it I
thought were true and closed my notebook and looked out
the window at air. I opened my notebook again thinking
that I had all sorts of ideas and things to write about but
now I'm not sure. I heard my mother's voice. Irma, she
said, just begin.

I want to be forgiven. I want to be forgiven for causing
the deaths of so many people I've loved. I feel like that
might never happen. I don't know how it will happen or if
it will happen. I don't think it will but I want it to. I don't
feel forgiven by God. I want to be forgiven by the people I
love. Wilson told me that art is redemptive. My father told
me that art is a lie. I can't forgive myself but I can forgive
my father. And my hope is that we'll both be brought back
to life.

I rented a small red car at the airport in Chihuahua city
and drove the twisty desert mountain road to Cuauhtémoc
and then I drove the flat, hot highway home to Campo 6.5.

I drove past Carlito's rundown house and Alfredo's well-kept farm with plastic flowers in the planters and past the crashed crop-duster where I'd asked Jorge to meet me for the first time. I saw a cow with his hoof stuck in the runner bars that were there to prevent him from escaping. I knew from experience not to try to help him because he'd be violent and enraged. I drove past the filmmakers' old house which had been my cousins' old house. I felt the tender touch of Wilson's dying hand on my body, on every part of it, and heard him call me beautiful. Are you still alive? I said.

The house that Jorge and I had lived in was missing. There was black grass where it had been. That's all. No sheds either. Nothing. Jorge, I said. I'm so sorry. I pictured us in a lighthouse in the Yucatán, slow dancing in a round room, looking out towards the Caribbean Sea.

I kept driving. I saw my little brothers playing with a dead snake or something on the driveway and my mother leaning against the fence like she'd been out there for a long time, weeks, maybe months, just waiting for me to show up. I got out of the car and waved to her and started walking towards her and then she began to run. She was running and laughing. She was running and laughing! And then we were hugging each other so hard, my God, she was strong. She wouldn't let me go. My brothers joined us in this wild, joyful embrace and then I saw my father coming out of the house, using his hand to shade the sun from his eyes, and he also came towards us, not running and laughing but walking firmly and steadily. And I remembered a few sentences from *Jakob von Gunten*, which the bookseller in the park had given me:

And one day I would be a beggar and the sun would be shining and I would be so happy, and I wouldn't ever want to know why. And then Mamma would come and hug me—what nice imaginings these are!

And then I parked the car and walked towards my old house. The curtains were closed and it was late in the day, stars were everywhere, and I could hear the incomprehensible noises of different animals attempting to communicate with each other in the dark and the voices of my brothers and my parents singing some old ancient song in Low German and I stood outside the door for a while and listened before I went inside to say hello, how are you?

ACKNOWLEDGEMENTS

For their tremendous efforts in the making of this book I'd like to thank Sarah Chalfant, Michael Schellenberg, Hannah Griffiths, Louise Dennys, Marion Garner, Kelly Hill, Deirdre Molina, José Molina and Nicola Makoway.

On page 175 I quoted from a beautifully written obituary sent to me in a letter from a friend. I know that it ran in the *Globe and Mail* newspaper but regret that I have no idea when and do not know who was being so well celebrated.

Many thanks to Neal Rempel for kindly giving me permission to use some of the details of his play *The Last Words of Duct Schultz* for my own purposes in the book, beginning on page 214.

MIRIAM TOEWS is the author of four previous novels: *Summer of My Amazing Luck*; *A Boy of Good Breeding*; *A Complicated Kindness* (winner of the 2004 Governor General's Literary Award for Fiction) and *The Flying Troutmans* (winner of the Rogers Writers' Trust Fiction Prize), and one work of non-fiction, *Swing Low: A Life*. She lives in Toronto.

A NOTE ABOUT THE TYPE

The body of *Irma Voth* has been set in Monotype Garamond, a modern font family based on roman types cut by Jean Jannon in 1615. Jannon followed the designs of Claude Garamond, cut a century earlier. Garamond's types were in turn based on the work of Francesco Griffo in the late 15th century. Monotype Garamond's italics are derived from types designed in France circa 1557 by Robert Granjon.